International Standard Book Number: 0-914222-09-0

Library of Congress Catalog Card Number: 80-66312

The German Colonies
in
South Russia

Volume II

by

Rev. Conrad Keller

Translated from the German Edition

by Anthony Becker

Second Edition

American Historical Society of Germans from Russia
Lincoln, Nebraska

Die deutschen Kolonien

in

Südrußland.

II. Band.

Die Beresaner Kolonien: Landau, Speier, Sulz,
Karlsruhe, Katharinental, Rastadt und München
historisch, geographisch und statistisch beschrieben und
als deutsches Kulturbild aus den südrussischen
Steppen dargestellt

von

P. Konrad Keller,

freiresigniertem Pfarrer wirklichem Mitglied der bibliographischen
Gesellschaft an der Kaiserlichen-Neurussischen Universität und
Ehrenmitglied des Klemensvereins in der Diözese Tiraspol.

Eine von der Beresaner Jubiläumskommission gekrönte
Preisschrift mit vielen Porträts und Illustrationen.

Herausgeber Jakob Zentner, Sohn von Konrad.

Odessa, 1914.

Kommissionsverlag des Klemensvereins, Deribasstraße Nr. 13.

*This is a reproduction of the original title page of Die Deutschen
Kolonien by P. Conrad Keller, published in Odessa in 1914.*

Translation of Original Title Page:

The German Colonies
in

South Russia

Volume II

Historical, geographical and statistical description of the Beresan Colonies: Landau, Speier, Sulz, Karlsruhe, Katharinental, Rastadt and München, with a portrayal of their German cultural life

by

Father Conrad Keller,

a retired parish priest, member of the Bibliographic Society of the Imperial New Russian University and honorary member of the Klemens Society of the Diocese of Tiraspol.

* * *

Selected as prize publication by the Beresan Jubilee Committee, it contains many portraits and illustrations.

* * *

Publisher: Jakob Zentner, son of Konrad.

Odessa, 1914

Translator's Acknowledgements

I wish to thank, particularly, Professor J.S. Height for his kind help in proof-reading the translation, and my wife, Catherine, who patiently typed and re-typed the manuscript, also my daughter Barbara who helped in proof reading.

I also wish to thank Msgr. G. P. Aberle of Hague, North Dakota, U.S.A., for the loan of the copy of Rev. P. C. Keller's second volume of "Die Deutschen Kolonien in Sudrussland."

A.B.

CONTENTS

Foreword To The Second Edition

Dr. Becker's translation of the second volume of Keller has now been out of print for some months. Because of its great value to hundreds of American and Canadian families in their genealogical research, there is a continuing demand for it. The American Historical Society of Germans from Russia, with the kind permission of Dr. Becker, therefore undertook the publication of this second edition.

Advantage was taken of the new printing to correct typographical and other errors that were found in the first edition.

The many Beresaner descendants on this continent owe a debt of gratitude to Dr. Becker for providing them with this translation of such a valuable work about their forefathers.

Adam Giesinger
Editor
AHSGR Journal

Foreword To The First Edition

It was, above all, through the dedicated scholarship of Father Conrad Keller, a native of the colony of Sulz, that the histories of the Catholic mother-colonies in the district of Liebental and the Beresan were preserved in the two volumes which he published in Odessa in 1905/14. The fact that these have become extremely rare and scarcely available anywhere makes it all the more noteworthy and praiseworthy that Dr. A. Becker has undertaken the formidable task of translating Keller's major works into English and making them available to the present day and future descendants of the former colonists.

After having published the first volume dealing with the history of the Liebental colonies in 1968, Dr. Becker is now presenting the companion volume which comprises the history of the seven mother-colonies in the Beresan district. Apart from the historical and cultural material that encompasses a century of development, the book also contains the census records of 1840 for all the inhabitants — a most valuable source of information for the genealogical researcher.

This standard work will be warmly welcomed not only by scholars but also by the numerous descendants whose forefathers came from the Beresan colonies. Certainly, all who are interested in the field of Russian-German history owe Dr. Becker a debt of gratitude for his dedicated zeal and industry in producing Keller's important work in an English-language edition, and thereby preserving it as a precious heirloom for generations to come. In doing so, Dr. Becker has brought to fulfilment the wish of the original author, who acknowledged that he had written the book with the intention of informing future generations about the life and achievements of their ancestors.

Jos. S. Height
Professor of German
Franklin College,
Franklin, Indiana

AUTHOR'S PREFACE

The book presented here does not wish to be called *"The History of the Beresan Colonies,"* but makes only the modest claim to be a description with historical, geographical and statistical aspects. If I call the work a cultural portrait, this is not to be taken in the strict sense, for a cultural portrait composed by an expert on the German Rhine would, in every respect, appear more attractive and colorful than my own composition originating in the steppes of South Russia.

In the present volume I shall present only a general outline of a cultural portrait and brief biographies of the bearers of that culture, with the reservation that I intend to describe the periods and phases of the cultural development more precisely in subsequent volumes which, with God's help, I propose to write. In this book my principal aim has been to provide an accurate report of the origin, ancestral homeland and genealogy of the individual families. Only in rare instances have I succeeded in this endeavour, after long and indescribable difficulties, by comparing and collating the various family records, which were quite often written in Old Russian and sometimes highly inaccurate.

Through these accounts, it has become possible to re-establish the cultural relationship of the Beresan people with the ancient homeland on the Rhine from which their ancestors emigrated to the desolate, uncultivated steppes a hundred years ago. On the basis of these accounts, every Beresan countryman can locate his surviving kinsmen on the Rhine and relate to them the fateful story of his grandparents, and indeed, his own experiences.

A word about the sources used in this book; with the exception of a few articles published in periodicals and calendars, no printed works on the Beresan Colonies have hitherto appeared. Consequently, only materials found in Archives could be utilized in this book.

The principal source for the history of the colonisation of South Russia was the archives of the former Welfare Committee in Odessa, whose records of 1849 were intensively used. In addition, the archives of the Beresan District, although kept in poor order, proved to be a rewarding source of statistical information, particularly for the years 1811 to 1818. Also the archives in Landau provided rich material for several parts of the book, but this cannot be said of the other parish archives. Very little material could be used from the community archives of the various colonies since they were in disorder and fragmentary.

From foreign sources I was able to use the manuscripts found in the archives of the Society of Jesus in Cracow and in the clerical Collegium Germanicum in Rome. The statistical data concerning the present condition of the individual colonies was submitted incompletely by some and not at all by others. This is much to be regretted in the interest of the book's completeness and reveals the indifference of some people about the history of their homeland.

Of the various people who contributed to this volume by sending in special reports from the past, I can name only a few. The brothers, Joseph and Thomas Zentner of München and the schoolmaster, Edward Butsch of Katharinental, graciously collected folklore and reports of the good old days and sent them to me to be included in the book. To these gentlemen I hereby express my deepest thanks.

In conclusin, I appeal to everyone, from the Beresan or elsewhere, who has more or better information about any subject I have treated in my book, to communicate with me orally or in writing.

And now, out you go, dear little book, into the wide world and greet all the Beresan people, near and far, and tell them about their grandparents and forefathers. And if anyone should ask questions you cannot answer, tell him or her, "Be patient, my friend, soon there will be two little sisters, dressed in blue, who will be more knowledgeable and capable of providing a more precise account of the things you wish to know."

The Author

Historical Review

Today's southern Russia corresponds in its location and its area almost completely to old Scythia, as Herodotus described it for us two thousand years ago. According to his description, Scythia then embraced all lands on the northern shores of the Black Sea, from the mouth of the Danube northeastward to the Don, the area which now is southern Bessarabia, the provinces of Kherson and Ekaterinoslav, the northern part of the province of Tauria and most of the region of the Don Cossacks. Only the mountainous part of the Crimea, then called the Tauric Chersones, was excluded from Scythia.

The Greek and Latin writers described these areas in frightening terms. Pliny described the northern portion of Scythia as 'damned by nature with the whole region buried in thick fog'. The horrors of the Black Sea region which the old writers described were believed by the Greeks and Romans for a long time, but the adventurous Greeks crossed the unfriendly sea in their frail vessels and landed on its shore. In spite of the raw climate and nomad robbers, they were not disheartened. They pushed bravely forward into this region and endeavoured to carry on trade with the robber people. Surrounded by cruel nomads and warlike horsemen, they built settlements on the Pontus Euxinus (Black Sea). Their settlements, which had a small beginning, gradually grew. From here they pushed fearlessly northward where, according to legend, everything was covered with ice and fog. In this manner, a whole series of Greek trading colonies arose. Of these, the most important were: Chersones, near today's Sevastopol; Tyras, today called Ackermann; Ordessos at the mouth of the Tiligul on the Black Sea, and Olbia near the colony, Illinsky, on the Bug, where the Beresan people bought the land from Mussin-Puschkin.

The Olbia people carried on a brisk trade with the Scythians living in the region, and became intermarried with them. One such intermarried tribe, called Kallipids, lived near the Beresan in Herodotus time, when it was called Rodos and also Sagarius. The Kallipids, who were horse breeders, had large herds of excellent horses which they sold to the Greeks.

North of the Kallipids, perhaps on the Tchitchekleya, lived the Alazon, whose origin was most likely Slavic. They sowed corn, onions, leeks, lentils and millet for their own use. Above the Alazon, near Vosnesensk, lived the Agricultural Scythians. They grew corn, not so much for their own use as for trade. They carried on a vigorous corn trade with the Greeks and learned their customs and language. The Greek trading colonies were located on the Black Sea. Later, these were under the jurisdiction of the Romans until the time of the great migrations during the fourth to the ninth century after Christ. All races who participated in the great migrations from the east to the west and south moved through Russia. Some of these people settled in this region until they were driven out by other strong tribes and thus pushed further west. In later years there were Mongolians, Tartars, Italians and Turks in this region.

In the eighteenth century, these steppes on the shore of the Black Sea were apparently under no jurisdiction, and for a long time were a bone of contention between the Poles, Russians, Turks and Tartars. Eventually, after a long war, Russia gained sole control over this fruitful land. Through the 'Treaty of Jassy', signed on the 29 December 1791 between Russia and Turkey, the land between the Bug and the Dniester Rivers became Russian territory.

Prince Potjomkin immediately started a project for settlement of the newly formed province of Otchakov, as it was then called. He formed more settlements such as Kherson, Nikolayev, and Grigoriopol. Even though Potjomkin died almost immediately, his project for the new provinces did materialize.

The Saporogian Cossacks were Potjomkin's favourites because, through their gallantry in the previously mentioned Turkish War, they brought great glory to him.

They also brought him great sorrow since they fell into disfavour with Czarina Catherine II. They stubbornly rejected the advice of the good Potjomkin who wanted them to settle down as peaceful farmers. He did, however, have permission from the Empress to settle the Saporogians in the new province of Otchakov in the Beresan. There were already 40 Cossack colonies settled there under Colonel Sutyka.

After Potjomkin passed away, this decree was rescinded and the Saporogians were ordered to settle in the Kuban. Not all of the

Saporogians moved to Kuban, many stayed in the province, preferring to work as serfs or as crown peasants. Many carried on robbery which could be done without much dexterity in the disorganized conditions of the new province.

In my youth, the old people of the Beresan often told the following story. Twelve of these daring Saporogian rascals formed a band and swore on their souls' happiness to rob and steal everything and, if necessary, to kill. All stolen goods were to be divided evenly among themselves. If one or more should be caught, the remainder were obligated to free them at the risk of their own blood and life. The booty was hidden in a secure place and no one was allowed to remove the treasure or to disclose the secret location. Only the last survivor was permitted, before his death, to relate to a relative the secret of the hidden treasure or to permit its removal.

These robber bands and many others were a destructive force to the prosperity of the Beresan Colonists. Yearly, for almost fifty years, horses were stolen, not five or ten, but hundreds of them. Eventually, these bands were dispersed; some were sent to Siberia, others were hanged. Only one robber lived to the year 1876 when, at 120 years of age, he came to Sebastianfeld (Malach) with his nephew in order to dig up some of the buried treasure. The old fellow had a plan of the cave where the treasure was supposed to be buried. They dug for several days, but one night the old man disappeared with his nephew and the other workers. Whether or not they found the treasure I could not learn. North of the colony of Sulz, near the Keller settlement, this band was supposed to have buried some treasure under a slab of stone on which was carved the figure of a duck.

The Beginning and Spread of Christianity in the Beresan Region

The church historians, Hippolytus and Eusebius, report that besides the apostles Philipp and Mathias, the apostle St. Andrew particularly preached the gospel in this region. According to these writers, Andrew brought the Gospel through Asia Minor to the big city of Sebastopolis (now Suchum-Kale). From there he proceeded to Chersones in Taurida and according to Nikitin Paphl, went up the Dnieper as far as the area of Kiev. In so doing, he must have passed the populous Olbia which was located at the estuary of the Dnieper. Thus we must assume that the Apostle preached the Good News of the Kingdom of God in Olbia, where there were so many people and so many sinners.

One can imagine what it might have been like if St. Andrew had gone some 35 kilometers west into the Beresan to preach the word of God to the Kallipids, who were also very sinful people. We would thus have had his footsteps in our homeland, and the ground of Beresan would have become holy as a result of it. Perhaps where our churches now stand, St. Andrew also stood and preached the Gospel of Salvation as our priests are doing today.

St. Andrew encountered difficulties, as did St. Clemens Romanus, the patron of the Tiraspol Diocese. Church history tells us that St. Clemens, along with many other Christians, was banished to the Crimean Peninsula by Emperor Trajan. There this holy man met many Christians who were condemned to hard work in the marble quarries. While at this heavy work they suffered from scarcity of water. As a result of the prayers of St. Clemens, a large spring appeared in this arid land, which proved a great comfort for these workers. Through this miracle and his fiery preaching, the holy man converted many of the people living there. According to the legend, the holy man conducted missions in the area around the Crimea and converted many of the idolaters to Christianity. To the region of Chersones, one can also add the populous cities of Olbia and Ordessos on the Tiligul. Consequently, it is most likely that he preached the holy Gospel in the above-named cities which carried on active trade with Chersones as well as in the neighbouring villages of the Beresan, where the Kallipids lived.

After the martyr death of St. Clemens in the waves of the Black Sea, the reports of Christianity from this district are scarce. Towards the end of the second century after Christ, the Ostrogoths settled between the Don and the Dnieper and also in the Beresan, while the Visigoths remained between the Dnieper and the Theiss. From the third century on, these Goths carried on a bitter war with the Roman Emperors and made devastating raids in the Roman provinces, as well as in Asia Minor and Greece. From there they brought back captured priests who preached the holy gospel to their victors.

The Gothic bishop Theophilus, was already present at the Council of Nicea, but his Episcopal See is not indicated. As early as 347 A.D., Bishop Cyrillus of Jerusalem states that there were bishops and priests, indeed even monks and nuns, among the Goths. Later, the Gothic Bishop Ulfilas translated a portion of the Bible into the Gothic language, and thereby created the oldest existing literary document in a Germanic language.

In the year three hundred and eighty one (381), St. Aetherius, bishop of Chersones, while on his way home from Constantinople to the Crimea, was attached and killed by pirates near the Island of Beresan. The Christians living there buried his body on the Island of Beresan, which was then called 'Aas'. They also placed a very nice tombstone on his grave. Since that time the area has been called the Island of Holy Aetherius. Professor Stern has already worked for several years on Beresan Island, hoping to find some artifacts that would shed light on this burial place. Perhaps he will soon find the grave of St. Aetherius and the Beresan people would then have an ancient, venerable shrine near them.

In the eleventh century there were Catholic Missionaries with the Petchenegs (Patzinaks) who were living to the north of the Black Sea, and consequently also on the Beresan River.

It was the saintly Bishop Bruno, also called Bonifatius, and his 18 companions, who traveled through Russia and Poland preaching the gospel. When they heard of the wild and gruesome Petchenegs, they decided that they must also bring the word of God to these people. The Russian Prince advised them to stay away from these heathens as they would receive only torture and death. But the conscientious missionaries did not let themselves be deterred, but rather, went to these people without fear. At the beginning they converted 30 people through their preaching, but could accomplish no more. These wild Petchenegs ganged together, attacked the saintly missionaries with devilish cruelty and killed them with their hatchets (1008 A.D.). The Russians ransomed the remainder at a high price and built a monastery in honor of St. Bruno, who became famous for his great miracles.

In the middle ages, after the capture of Constantinople by the Crusaders, the Italians, Genoese and Venetians established a commercial republic on the shores of the Black Sea. Their metropolis was Kaffa, the present day Theodosia in the Crimea. From that time on, many Catholic missionaries, especially Dominicans and Franciscans, came to this region and preached the gospel to the local inhabitants, who were schismatic Christians, Mohammedans and heathens. The closest Franciscan monastery to the Beresan was located on Aleschka Island, near the city of Kherson. After the conquest of the city of Kaffa, in the Crimea, by the Turks in 1475, nearly all of the diocese and monasteries disappeared. A few Catholics remaining in this district were without priests; only occasionally Catholic missionaries, who were mostly captives as a result of the Turkish War, ventured among these poor abandoned people, secretly bringing the comfort of the Holy Religion.

Geographical Review

The wide illimitable steppe extending between the Bug in the east, the Dniester in the west, the Black Sea in the south, and the forests of Podolia in the north, formerly called the province of Ochakov, is a treeless, flat, undulating plain crossed by rivers running from the north to the south. Most of the rivers form a large estuary with sandbars, before emptying into the sea. Only the estuary of the Beresan has no sandbars, and is thus in direct communication with the sea.

In its lower portion, the Beresan is fed by springs which never dry up; whereas, the upper portion is dry during the whole summer. The Beresan, called the Rodos, and also the Sagarius in antiquity, gets its origin near the German colony of Waterloo, 80 versts north of the city of Otchakov. It runs in a southerly direction through the centre of the colonies of Speier, Landau and Sulz. At Sulz, it is joined on the left by the Fox River. As it flows on, it is joined on both sides by other small rivers, unitl it empties into the estuary at the village of Kasandrowka. About 4 versts along the estuary, the river Antshikak joins it, then turns south-west and is joined by the small river, Kiltshen. At the colony of Koburtschy, it is joined by the Salik and its small estuary, then flows west from the city of Otchakov into the Black Sea. The valley of the Beresan is very fruitful, the fertile black soil is 1/2 to 1 arshin thick. This is why the Beresan valley is heavily populated. Nearly all nationalities inside Russia find some of their people in the Beresan. Most of all, one finds the German colonists, whom I will now describe in considerable detail.

The German Colonists
of the Beresan District

*"What can be dearer to us on earth, than the soil
from which we were created, on which we have grown,
united with it in every thought."*

Wimpheling.

The ukase of the Russian Czar, Alexander 1, issued on the 20
February 1804, had many delayed reverberations in Germany. Every
spring, large numbers of migrants assembled in the cities, where the
Russian Commissars had their offices, and there enrolled as Russian
colonists. Large migrations occurred in the years 1808 and 1809.
These migrations usually went by land over Bohemia, Silesia,
Moravia and Galicia, to the Russian border town of Radzivillov,
where they would sometimes rest for one or two months. In Radzivillov, there was also a Russian Commissar, who gave the immigrants Russian citizenship, as well as their first allowance of
money. Here also, the migrants received their first instructions as
to what they were to take and were given a guide to accompany them
to their destination. In Radzivillov, many young people became married, as all young families had the privilege of obtaining land (60
dessiatines) in the proposed newly founded colony. At these weddings
there was music, dancing, and naturally drinking. The musicians
were usually gypsies, some of whom would accompany the colonists
as far as their destination, stay there and eventually marry with the
colonists.

From Radzivillov the road turned south towards Odessa, the
rallying point for all migrants. One night it happened that one group
camped near a grain field. Through carelessness while cooking, a
woman got some burning straw too close to the grain field and in

an instant the entire field was ablaze. There followed a great deal of screaming and commotion; the colonists wished to extinguish the fire but they had no water. What was to be done? They all hitched up their wagons and fled. But horsemen soon collected them, and on the next stop they were brought into court. The guides explained that the people had not set the fire intentionally and that the settlers were under the special protection of the Czar. Without further ado the colonists were released.

The first of these groups arrived in Odessa in the summer of 1809. Many of these colonists soon moved to the Beresan, where they built themselves huts with clay and reeds. Under these circumstances, they spent a very unfavourable winter.

The second trek came to Odessa late in the fall when the weather was already cold. Some spent the winter in Odessa, quartered with the German colonists of Liebental and Kutschurgan. Next spring, as soon as the snow was melted, the so-called "new colonists" gathered together and under the guidance of Franz Brittner, the mayor of Liebental, moved out along the road to Vosnesensk, which at that time was called Sokolo. From here they went on to Anovka, where those who were going to the Beresan turned right, while those who were going to Rastadt and München, turned left. The colonies of Speier, Landau, and Sulz were settled in the Beresan valley. The colony of Karlsruhe was founded in the Fox Valley, a side valley of the Beresan.

The colonies of Rastadt and München were founded in the Tchitchekleya Valley. The two Evangelical colonies of Rohrbach and Worms were settled at the same time in a valley adjacent to the Tiligul, slightly west of the Beresan. The colony of Katharinental was founded in the Fox Valley in 1818, while the colony of Waterloo was founded at the source of the Beresan, and the colony of Johannestal on the Sasik.

Since 1813, all the afore-mentioned colonies formed the Beresan district. The land area of these colonies comprised 55,597 dessiatines, granted to them by the crown; each married couple receiving 60 dessiatines. In the first years, the Beresan colonies belonged to the Liebental District, but in 1813, the Beresan District was formed with headquarters in Landau.

The district was under the jurisdiction of a mayor, two councillors, and a secretary. The secretary did not have a vote in legal decisions, but usually dominated the mayor and the councillors.

The Chief Mayors of the Beresan District

Theobald Brucker, Karlsruhe
1813-1818

Theobald Brucker was born in Offenbach, Rheinpfalz (Rhinepalatinate) in 1779. His education must have been fairly good as the orders which he wrote showed good thought and common sense, and his spelling was quite accurate. He married Apollonia Garrecht in his homeland, and with their three children, moved to Russia in 1809, settling as an immigrant in Karlsruhe. Because he was intelligent, energetic and a good mechanic, he was soon noticed by the supervisors of the colonies, and in due course he was assigned various duties relative to the settlers.

At first the Beresan colonists were placed under the jurisdiction of the Liebental district, but the great distance of 120 versts, made inspection difficult for the chief mayor. Consequently, Theobald Brucker and Peter Jäger from Landau, were temporarily appointed as magistrates to supervise the work of the settlement and settle legal matters, until the Beresan district office was formed by Inspector Friedrich Strohmeyer. In 1814, Brucker was appointed chief mayor of the Beresan district by the district supervisors. He became very active in his new sphere of influence. He liked order and consequently, he was very strict and severe in dispensing justice. He was correct to the minutest detail.

It happened one time that he gave an order about the tidiness of the homes, and threatened to flog those who disobeyed. His own wife violated the rule. Brucker had her arrested, and as mayor, sentenced her to be caned. The inspector and the councillors, however, prohibited the execution of this sentence.

Naturally such an energetic, upright man could not last long in office where the officials of the department were addicted to corruption and bribery, and where of late, disorderly colonists were creating problems everywhere for the energetic chief mayor. He finally saw intrigue towards himself from all sides, and was convinced that under the circumstances he could no longer work for the well being of his fellow Germans. Therefore, he asked to be relieved from his office; he sold his homestead in Karlsruhe and moved to Nikolayev. His services there as a mechanic were much in demand, building Dutch windmills. Later, he moved to the estate of nobleman Koslov, for whom he worked several years. After this, he moved to Sulz, where he set up a business and built a grist mill of stone. In 1843, Rumania, at that time called Wallachia, invited German colonists as farmers. Brucker moved there with his sons, but he had no luck there either, and soon died a poor man. His sons Joseph and Georg-Jakob, also died there, but one son, Johannes, moved back to Russia with his family, where he lived for many years as a miller.

Michael Fischer, Landau
1818-1825

Michael Fischer, son of Anton, was born in 1777 in the colony of Aschbach in the Rheinpfalz (Rhinepalatinate), married Margaretha Paul, from Kapsweyer, and moved to Russia in 1809, where he settled as an immigrant in the colony of Landau. During his administration, the colonies of Katharinental, Waterloo, Johannestal and the neighbouring colonies of Stuttgart, Friedrichstal and Julienfeld were settled. Mayor Fischer executed the duties of his office with great prudence and energy. But still he was soon in conflict with the Beresan commissioner, Krüger, who tyrannized all his subordinates, and over-ruled Mayor Fischer's office. Mayor Fischer became poor; he died in a stonequarry where he worked, crushed by some falling rocks.

Michael Fischer was the ancestor of most of the Landau Baptists, who left the faith of their fathers during the years 1869 to 1872. It is noteworthy that a brother of Michael Fischer, who settled in Baden, became mayor of Kutschurgan.

Johannes Imel, Landau
1825-1834

Johannes Imel, son of Michael, was born in 1781, in the village of Erlenbach, in the Rheinpfalz, and married Magdalena Helbling. In 1809, he moved to Russia, and settled as a colonist in Landau. During his term in office, considerable misfortune befell the Beresan colonies. Various illnesses, cattle disease, grasshoppers, and the unforgettable famine of 1833 brought the young colonies great distress. Mayor Imel was an intelligent, energetic man, but sometimes too strict. He showed great prudence in expending the loans advanced by the government, and in distributing the gifts from many private people of Odessa and surrounding towns. In 1833, he sent his son, Nikolaus, and Johannes Mosbrucker, to Poland to buy grain cheaply. The grain was brought to Landau and put in a large storage granary.

In 1830, Mayor Imel received 75 rubles from the Fürsorge Committee, as a gift for his services. Johannes Imel lived to quite an old age; near the end he suffered considerably from rheumatism and gout.

Georg Strasser — Rohrbach
1834-1836

Georg Strasser was born in Germany in 1787, and went to Russia in 1809, settling as a colonist in Rohrbach. He was councillor for several years when Imel was the chief mayor. He distinguished himself through his knowledge of the laws of the colonies. As mayor, he was praised for his honesty and zeal.

Peter Brilz — Landau
1837-1841

Peter Brilz, son of Franz, was born in the village of Ingenheim, in the Rheinpfalz. In 1809, he moved to Russia with his parents, where his father built a new home in Landau. He married Elizabeth Stolz in Landau. He was praised for his affability and good judicial qualities. During his term in office, the second church was built in Landau.

Matthias Fleck — Landau
1841-1864

Matthias Fleck, son of Johann, was born in 1802, in the village of Wingen, in Alsace (France). He came to Russia with his widowed mother (whose maiden name was Schlick) in 1809, where they settled as colonists in Landau. In 1824, he married Elisabeth Böspflug. During the 23 years of his term of office, many important events occurred in the Beresan, and in the German colonies in south Russia. The Crimean War of 1854-1856, was such an event, in which the German colonists distinguished themselves by giving all possible help.

The attention of the authorities was focused on Mayor Fleck because of his untiring work, his versatile talents as an organiser and his tactful behaviour. He was asked to undertake various confidential assignments outside the Beresan district; these he always carried out to the satisfaction of his supervisors. During the war hardly a day passed when he was not sent somewhere to keep things in order. For this he received several decorations from the authorities. To the Beresan people he emphasized the importance of strict self-discipline. He enforced the curfew, prohibited costly weddings and baptisms, and particularly dancing on Sundays and religious holidays. He restored Christian order in the community, as well as strict discipline in the families.

In order to lend authority to his injunctions, he often drove to neighbouring colonies in the evening with his renowned adjutant, a Cossack known as Michael Durlacher. Woe to anyone they would catch in the dance hall, who had not time to hide! They would make the acquaintance of Michael Durlacher's whip, and often would carry the blue marks for weeks as a memento of the mayor's visit.

Mayor Fleck also did a great deal towards the building of the new parish church. He was always ready to help the poor and needy; but he was strict with rascals and lazy individuals. Shortly before he died, he was in Koslov to promote recruiting. There he got a chill, became ill, and died on the 29 December 1864, mourned by all the good people. He was the first person for whom funeral services were held in the new church.

Joseph Fichter — Landau
1864-1866

Joseph Fichter was born in 1812 in Landau, son of Joseph Fichter from Riedselz, in Alsace, and Annamaria Jerg. He was the first mayor born in Russia. He was a quiet, but energetic man, who always stood up for the rights of the colonists, and also kept good order. But he did not please President Lysander of the Fürsorge Committee at that time, because he did not promote the plan to move the Orphans' fund to Prischib in the Molotschna. Along with the secretary, Anton Riedinger, he was removed from office and the candidate, Christian Imel, was made mayor.

Christian Imel — Landau
1866-1869

Christian Imel was born in 1817 in Landau, son of the previously noted mayor, Johann Imel, and Magdalena Helbling. As mayor, he always maintained good order, promoted community well-being of the individual colonies, and conscientiously fulfilled his obligations.

Franz Marsal — Speier
1868-1871

Franz Marsal came to Landau from Speier as a poor man. He married the widow, Matresa Schanz, whose maiden name was Schaf; he became a colonist in Speier. As mayor, he was orderly and strict.

At this time the Baptists were proselytizing in Speier. Marsal took strict measures; he forbade gatherings in private homes, and had those caned who violated the order.

Peter Gerhardt — Speier
1871-1872

Peter Gerhardt was born in Speier in 1829. He posssessed no special educational background, but was very capable and industrious. Through his own studies, he learned Russian, and also acquired much knowledge about agriculture. As mayor, he was strict and tried to maintain good order everywhere. He directed his attention particularly to the decaying morals in the Beresan colonies. The curfew was strictly enforced, and he urged the communities to pass a resolution to get rid of the numerous taverns in the villages, and to keep the youth out of these dens of vice. Gerhardt was the first mayor after the new order, and was hence-forth called the "District Chief." He was deputized for the territorial office in Cherson, and on one occasion, made a brilliant speech there, defending the German colonists against propagated slander.

Gerhardt was a German colonist through and through; he made every possible effort to ease the burden of the colonists and to protect their rights. For this, he was respected and esteemed by all. Still his salutary activities on behalf of the people of the Beresan, were soon interrupted. He died after a short illness, on October 19, 1873, at the age of 42; a truly religious Christian. All of the Beresan clergy attended the funeral, as well as a very large crowd of people from the surrounding district. Father Tchernyachowitz gave the funeral sermon as a result of which, everyone broke into tears. Not one of the priests was able to finish the ceremony, because they were all crying.

Peter Gerhardt was a wealthy man and was one of the first persons of the Beresan colonists to own a large estate. With Colonist Jakob Schmalz from Speier, he bought (1862) the estate of Admiral Besuarow, for 18 rubles a dessiatine, including livestock, buildings, and equipment. After his death, all of the movable property was sold at auction for the sum of 20,000 rubles.

Andreas Delzer — Johannestal
1872-1873

Andreas Delzer was a pupil of district secretary, Anton Riedinger, and was the community secretary in Johannestal for one year. As mayor, he was very industrious, prudent and just.

Jakob Schmalz — Speier
1873-1876

Jakob Schmalz, son of Johannes, was a wealthy innkeeper, and a very capable man. As mayor, he was praised for his desire to maintain order, his affability in his associations, and his desire for justice.

Matthias Brilz — Landau
1876-1886

Matthias Brilz was a pupil of Anton Riedinger, and was municipal secretary in Landau for several years. Brilz was a very industrious, prudent, and upright mayor, who understood the regulations well. He tried very hard to get the Beresan people to pay the balance owing on their land, and with much effort, he succeeded. After a considerable time, he was able to straighten out the Orphan's Fund, and to start a savings bank. During the last Turkish Russian War, he was decorated with the Silver Medal and the badge of the Red Cross for diligent service.

Karl Janzer — Katharinental
1886-1895

Karl Janzer was previously the secretary at Katharinental. He understood Russian well and fulfilled the duties of the office of mayor conscientiously and wisely. Sometimes he was too strict, but he was just. He made no discrimination between friend and foe, but did only what was right. He died in his home a few years ago, a good Christian.

Martin Kary — Landau
1895-1911

Martin Kary was a sergeant in the army, and spoke Russian well. During his administration, the Beresan Central School was moved from Neufreudental to the imposing school building recently constructed in Landau. Also during his tenure in office, the 100 year jubilee for the Beresan colonists was celebrated.

Valentin Schardt — Karlsruhe
1911-

Valentin Schardt was born in the Karlsruhe colony on the 16 October 1852, son of colonist Michael Schardt and Elizabeth Berger. He received his early education in the parish school, finishing in 1864. Then he attended private school in order to improve his education. He was a church elder for 6 years, fulfilling the duties of this office so diligently, faithfully and carefully, that Father Stankewitz called him a "son of the church." He was cashier for several years at Landau, while a candidate for mayor. Since 1911, he has been mayor of the Landau district, which office up to now, he has administered to everyone's satisfaction. During his short term in office, he has already accomplished many good things. At his urging, the needy Beresan settlers in the Turgai district received 6000 rubles as charity. The border regulation of the Beresan crown land, the construction of the telegraph station in Landau, and the founding of the mutual credit association in Karlsruhe are largely due to his initiative. He is also the owner of much land and raised pure-bred livestock on his estate at Kratovka.

Order of Succession of
Beresan District Secretaries

Adolf Peterson — (1814-1818)

Adolf Peterson was born in Dorpat in 1776. He was deputy commissar in Kurland; when the Beresan district was settled, he came here in the service of Inspector Strohmeyer. When the Beresan district office was created, he became the first secretary.

Friedrich Stelzer (1818-1821)

Nothing is known about this person.

N. Spiry (1821-1823)

Spiry came from Germany in 1819 with the emigrants from Württemburg. He was first village secretary and later district secretary.

N. Heilmann (1823-1826)

Nothing is known about his life.

N. Wallenmeyer (1826-1831)

Nothing is known about his life.

N. Wilmersdorf (1831-1833)

Nothing is known about his life.

Nikolaus Imel (1833-1838)

Nikolaus Imel was born in Landau in 1814, son of Johann Imel and Magdalena Helbling. While his father was mayor, he studied in the district office, where he proved to be very efficient, and was soon able to take over the position of district secretary. Later he taught school in Landau and Speier, where, if I am not mistaken, he died.

Paul Veitenheimer (1838-1841)

Paul Veitenheimer, son of Gottfried, was born in 1792, in Wallstadt, Baden. He came to Russia in 1818, where he settled as a colonist in the newly formed colony of Katharinental. He apparently had benefited from a good education at home, for his spelling was perfect, and his hand writing was excellent. At first he was a teacher in Katharinental, then he took the position as secretary in Landau. Later, for many years, he was the village secretary for both Katharinental and Karlsruhe at the same time. Those following him were all capable people.

Anton Riedinger (1841-1866)

Anton Riedinger was born on the 17 January 1817 in Landau, son of Nikolaus Riedinger from Langkandel, Rheinpfalz, and Theresa Rink. Because he was a quiet intelligent boy, his father had him well instructed and sent him to the Fürsorge-Komitee to further his education. He made good progress and in 1837, was sent as an interpreter to the Beresan district office. In 1841, even though he wa still very young, he was made district secretary by the Beresan Inspector. He administered this heavy duty diligently, conscientiously and to everyone's satisfaction for a period of 25 years. He also had many pupils who learned the duties of Secretary from him; some of these were; Johann Hirsch from Rastadt; Friedrich Hörner, from Speier; Johannes Renner, and Philipp Steckel from Karlsruhe; Erasmus Tremel, from Sulz; Andreas Delzer from Johannestal; Heinrich Reich and N. Süss from Rohrbach; Friedrich Steiner, from Katharinental; Michael Fleck, Matthias Brilz, and Franz Böhm from Landau, and several Russians from the surrounding district. Also Father Rudolf Reichert took Russian instruction from Riedinger before he entered the Seminary. Riedinger was a very kind man in his associations with both the rich and poor. He was always ready to give good advice to anyone who might ask. For writing a letter of reference, he usually accepted whatever the recipient wished to give; he was always ready to defend the poor and down-trodden in court. In 1866, he was removed from office through the intrigue of some spiteful people. He lived in quiet seclusion in Landau for several years, and if I am not mistaken, died in 1871, a good Christian.

Franz Böhm (1866-1871)

Franz Böhm, son of Philipp, was born in 1844, in Speier. He attended the clerical Seminary in Saratov, and after completing the preparatory courses, returned home, and worked as a helper to the District Secretary Riedinger. In 1866, he was made district secretary. During his administration, the new regulations for the German colonies were brought in by which the German colonists lost some of their rights and privileges and in civil matters were subject to the same laws as Russian crown peasants. In 1871, he was chosen as deputy for the colonists and was sent to Cherson, where he lived a long time. Later he was the Community Secretary in Speier; lastly, he was administrator for Joseph Tremel in Parutino, where he also died. Böhm had a good knowledge of the colonial laws and was an accomplished orator.

Johann Stein (1871-1886)

Johann Stein was born on the 4 January 1853, in the colony of Landau, the son of Peter Stein and Margaretha Wanner. He received his early education in the parish school, which he attended for

11 years. In 1866, he started as a student secretary in the Landau district office. In 1868, he moved over to the Beresan office of Inspector Philippow. He received a good recommendation from the Fürsorge-Komitee because of his good behaviour, and because he spoke Russian well. In 1870, he was sent as an assistant to the district secretary in Landau.

He supervised this office for 15 years to the complete satisfaction of everyone, as indicated by the following distinctions which he received from the authorities. On the 28 October 1877, he received 25 rubles from the Minister of Finance as a gift for dedicated service. On the 8 November 1878, he received a certificate of merit from the Minister of the Interior. For exemplary administration of his office during the years 1881 to 1885, he received three letters of commendation from the magistrates of the District of Odessa. He received his greatest honour on the 23 April 1886 when the Czar presented him with the Silver Medal on the Stanislaus sash.

During his time in office, the people of Beresan received titles to the crown land upon which they had originally settled. Through his efforts, the 'Orphan Bank' was properly organized and the Savings Bank was started. In 1883, he was chosen as a county representative for the Odessa district, where he remained until 1898. He was also a member of the Odessa 'Regional Tax Authority' for business and trade, and also a member of the Regional office for conscription.

In 1910, Johann Stein once more became the district secretary in Landau where he is still busy promoting the welfare of the Beresan Colonists.

Michael Stein (1886-1892)

Michael Stein was born in Landau 1 May 1860. After finishing his education in the parish school, he studied privately for the examinations for elementary school teacher, which he passed in Kherson in 1881. He received his first appointment as a teacher in the community school in Katharinental, where he taught until 1883, when he moved to Landau to teach. After one year, he received his first appointment as a teacher in the community school in Katharinental, where he taught until 1883, when he moved to Landau to teach. After one year, he received the appointment as village secretary, and in 1886, he was placed in charge of the office of the district secretary. He remained in this position until 1892 when he moved to Odessa where, along with his brothers, Johann and Christian, he build a brick factory. During the yers 1903 to 1905, he farmed on rented land. In 1905, he was made the administrator of the estate of Daniel Sattler, near Otschakow, where he stayed until 1912. Since 1912, he has been the administrator for the estate of B.A. Natschejev, in the province of Jekaterinoslav.

Christian Wanner (1892-1895)

Christian Wanner was born in Landau in 1853. After completing the parish school, he entered the Seminary at Saratov, completed some courses there, then taught in Blumenfeld, and subsequently became the village secretary in Karlsruhe. In 1892, he was district secretary in Landau where he worked until 1895, dying shortly thereafter.

Adam Gratz (1896-1900 and 1907-1910)

Adam Gratz, son of Peter, was born in Landau on the 12 July 1850. On completing the parish school, he left home and entered the junior Seminary in Saratov, completing his courses in 1868. His first appointment as teacher and sexton was in Sulz, where he later also took the position as district Secretary. From 1878 until 1880, he was district Secretary in Rastadt. In 1881, he moved to Odessa as a tutor in the Orphan School, and later became the choir director in the Catholic church there. In 1883, he passed the examinations as a private tutor, and founded a two class school in Radtadt, where he remained until 1894. From 1894 until 1896, he was the secretary in Schönfeld, also tutor and teacher. From 1896 to 1900, he was the district secretary in Landau. In 1901, he passed the examinations in civil law, which he practised until 1906. From 1906 to 1907, he was administrator for Joseph Tremel. In 1908, he again became district secretary in Landau, where he remained until he death on the 12 August 1910. Adam Gratz was capable and conscientious, as well as a good singer.

Lorenz Reichert (1902-1907)

Lorenz Reichert, son of Georg, was born in 1867 in Landau. He received his education in the Senior High School in Odessa. He received his first appointment as a teacher in 1889, in the elementary school in Katharinental, where he worked diligently for 2 years. From 1892 to 1897, he was the village secretary in Karlsruhe. In 1897, he moved to Odessa where he took over the position as teacher in the church school and administrator of the church orphanage. In 1898, because of illness, he returned to the country, and took the position of community secretary in Speier.

In 1902, he got the position as district secretary in Landau, where he remained until 1907. In the fall of 1907, he was selected by the people as their deputy in the Odessa district, and in the regular meeting of this district in December 1907, he was elected to the board of the Odessa district Land Office, which position he still holds. After this, he was reappointed every three years.

In addition, he has been active in the Kherson Land Bank, where he was a member of the Auditing Commission during the years 1910, 1911, and 1912. In the meeting in December 1912, he was elected as Inspector of the Kherson Land Bank, and as senior candidate, was re-appointed for another three years.

L. Reichert was a good legal councillor and a skillful speaker. He fulfilled his office with tact and prudence, to everyone's satisfaction, for the benefit of his compatriots, the German Colonists in Russia.

The Colony of Landau

The colony of Landau lies in the Province of Kherson, 110 versts from the city of Kherson, and 115 versts from the capital city of Odessa. The colony is located on both sides of the Beresan in a north-south direction. It is 3 versts long, and has several side streets. The main street on the left side of the river is interruped by 3 ponds extending into it from the east; in the upper colony, it is interrupted by the Sheep Valley and Sheephill, in the central portion below the church, by the Valley of the Wells and in the lower section by the Lochbaum Valley. In the central portion of the colony on the right side of the river, opposite the church, is the Russian valley, and in the lower colony, the Brilz Valley and plateau (Kurgan), extend into the Beresan. In the north on the right side of the river, is Hill Street, whose people are called "Bergler." South of this, is the Alley of Jonas, and still further south opposite the lower colony, the "Stehleritzsky." Behind the main street, towards the east, is Peter Street; further east behind the church is Sock Hill, with several houses. In the south, beside the Valley of the Wells, is the beautiful Potter Street (also called Musicians' Street) with two rows of houses extending from the east to the west. East of the lots in the central portion of the colony is Dog Alley, and south of this, the tenants. The lower colony from Seifert to the end is called "Muns."

The best buildings are in the central portion of the village. First is the lovely parish church, placed in a prominent position on Sock Hill. To the left and in front of the church, is the rectory; opposite the church, where the lower row of houses are, is the fine two story school for girls. South of the rectory, is the parish school and town hall. Across the dell in which the wells are located, and adjacent to the two story district office is the boarding school of Father Reichert.

21

Opposite the district office, is the luxuriously built Beresan Central School, which was called the Beresan University in a Russian paper. Further south, there are many fine private homes, the pharmacy, the Co-operative Society Building, Post Office, Hospital, and the warehouse. Northward, above Potter Street, is the Russian Orthodox Church and School.

The homes were mostly built along one plan; they were usually 8 faden long, 4 faden wide, and each one story, 1 1/2 faden high.* There were usually 2 rooms, a kitchen and an antechamber, with the front of the house facing the street. The roof was made mostly with reeds, but of late, roof tiles and sheet metal are being used. The barn and farm buildings were usually behind the house, sometimes under the same roof. Behind the buildings was the place for threshing. The entire yard was fenced with a stone wall, 2 archin high. In the early years, there was usually a fruit garden behind the threshing place, but now they have nearly all disappeared; instead, they plant only potatoes and other vegetables in these gardens. The Beresan Valley, through which the river winds, is approximately 100 faden wide. The ground is good black earth and very rich. The main occupation of the people of Landau is, agriculture and cattle raising. The climate is quite agreeable, as is evident from the healthy inhabitants.

The people are of medium height, usually with long trunks and short legs, but there are some who are quite tall.

The language in Landau, is closer to that of Alsace than the Rhinepalatinate. The people of Landau say, "zwie Gäul and zwu Küh," i.e. two horses and two cows; also "ich geh ä mit," (I'll go along too). There are approximately 10 people above the age of 80. The people are quite industrious, but in no great hurry. The name 'Landau' was given to the settlement by Franz Kaiser, as there were many people from the Palatinate living there at that time. Before the settlers arrived, the place was called "Twelve Wells." There is an abundant supply of good water in Landau. Of the original twelve wells, there are only two in use today.

Stones of good quality abound on all sides of the colony. When the first colonists came, the whole flat valley of the Beresan was filled with shrubs and reeds, as tall as the people, as well as various types of grass. There were consequently, many wild animals, particularly wolves, which attacked the cattle herds in packs, even in broad daylight. The senior citizens also state that the Beresan River used to be much higher and full of fish, which may or may not be true. I noticed in the deeds of 1811, that there was a scarcity of water for the cattle, suggesting that the Beresan River was already dry at that time. In the Russian Valley, there is a Russian yard in which

* 1 faden = 6 feet.

part of a foundation can still be seen. It was an earth hut built near another, surrounded by a stone wall. In these huts lived a Russian family, perhaps Saporogians; they had large herds of sheep. A sheep hut stood there for many years. One of these inhabitants, Michael Hobhaut, a big, strong fellow, with sticky fingers, worked for old Jakob Wanner until he died. He received the name 'Hobhaut' in the following manner. The hide of a sheep had disappeared. While it was being searched for, but with no success, Michael came to the office to say that "Ich habe die Haut." (I have the hide). Since he could not speak German very well he said "hobhaut." Subsequently, he became known as Michael Hobhaut. In the Russian yard, there were also two women of very heavy stature. They worked for the physician. Anoton Dukart. The others of the Russian yard moved away when the Germans settled there.

*List of the Settlers in
the Colony of Landau and the names
of their original homes
1839-1840*

"It is challenging indeed, to trace ones family history, since the family tree is for the individual, what the history of the Fatherland is for the Nation."

ELIAS TEGNER

1. **Leo Kary** 33, from Elchesheim, Baden; son of Jacob.
WIFE: Marianna Gress 27, from Reimersweiler, Elsass; daughter of Anton.
CHILDREN: Anton 11, Michael 4, Katharina 1.
2. **Jakob Schreiber** 34, from Wingen, Elsass; son of Michael.
WIFE: Marianna Fröhlich 31, daughter of Philipp, from Hirschtal, Rheinpfalz.
CHILDREN: Christina 13, Elizabeth 10, Margaretha 6, Anton 2.
MOTHER: Teresa Fröhlich 66, née Heilig, daughter of Ignaz.
(a) Ludwig Kühlwein 58, son of Heinrich, fromLimbach, Rheinpfalz.
WIFE: Christina Fröhlich 46, daughter of Philipp from Hirschtal, Rheinpfalz.
3. **Adam Gab** 63, from Rohrbach, Rheinpfalz; son of Georg.
WIFE: Elizabeth Marquart 58, daughter of Konrad.
CHILDREN: Martin 32, Anton 25, Marianna 36, Margaretha 20.
(a) Martin Gab 32, son of Adam.
WIFE: Elizabeth Pfaff 31, daughter of Jakob, from Elchesheim, Baden.

CHILDREN: Franz 8, Anton 5, Peter 3,Mariana 6, Magdalena 1.
(b) Anton Gab 25, son of Adam
WIFE: Annamaria Böhm 21, daughter of Michael.
SON: Rudolf, age 1.
    4. **Joseph Glaser** 32, from Schönau, Rheinpfalz, son of Franz.
WIFE: Marianna Gab 36, daughter of Adam, from Rohrbach, Rheinpfalz.
CHILDREN: Joseph 9, Rudolf 5, Katharina 11, Genovefa 2.
    5. **Philipp Glaser** 32, from Schönau, Rheinpfalz, son of Franz.
WIFE: Katharina Schwartz 21, from Reimersweiler, Elsass; daughter of Karl.
CHILDREN: Adam 2, Marianna 1.
MOTHER: Magdalena Gress 65, daughter of Matthäus.
    6. **Anton Gratz** 66, son of Martin, from Lembach, Elsass.
WIFE: Salomea Müller 58, daughter of Simon
CHILDREN: Martin 34, Peter, Ludwig 22.
(a) Martin Gratz 34, from Lembach, Elsass.
WIFE: Marianna Wock 35, daughter of Adam, from Steinfeld, Rheinpfalz.
CHILDREN: Barbara 10, Franziska 6, Simon 3.
(b) Peter Gratz, son of Anton.
WIFE: Margaretha Reichert 26, daughter of Joseph.
SON: Nikolaus, age 1.
(c) Ludwig Gratz 22, son of Anton.
WIFE: Magdalena Hilfer 19, daughter of Georg.
    7. **Rudolf Schulz** 53, from Rohrbach, Rheinpfalz, son of Leonhard.
WIFE: Magdalena Burghard 30, daughter of Joseph.
CHILDREN: Jakob 1, Katharina 6.
STEP-DAUGHTER: Marianna Burghard 6.
    8. **Matthias Huck** 47, from Herxheim, Rheinpfalz, son of Franz.
WIFE: Barbara Helbling 47, daughter of Johann, from Wingen, Elsass.
CHILDREN: Maria Eva 20, Marianna 18, Elisabeth 13, Joseph 8.
(a) Johann Freidig 22, from Schönenburg, Elsass, son of Peter.
WIFE: Maria Eva Huck 20, daughter of Matthias.
CHILDREN: Katharina 1.
(b) Jakob Fäth 22, from Herxheim, Rheinpfalz, son of Sebastian.
WIFE: Marianna Huck 18, daughter of Matthias.
CHILDREN: Elisabeth 1.
    9. **Jakob Matz** 40, from Kapswever, Rheinpfalz, son of Anton.
WIFE: Margaretha Walter 38, daughter of Christian, from Wingen, Elsas.
CHILDREN: Joseph 12, Anselm 10, Georg 8, Felix 6, Marzellius 4,

Marianna 5, Katharina 1.
MOTHER: Magdalena Schmidt 71.
(a) Johann Walter 43, from Wingen, Elsass, son of Christian.
WIFE: Eva Vollmer 38, daughter of Georg, from Freckenfeld, Rheinpfalz.
CHILDREN: Joseph 16, Vinzenz 3, Margaretha 11, Annamaria 9, Franziska 5.
(b) Georg Gress 23, son of Anton.
WIFE: Katharina Walter 19, daughter of Johann.
10. **Adam Hirschspiegel** 56, son of Karl, from Lembach, Elsass.
WIFE: Annamaria Himmelspach 40, from Herxheim, Rheinpfalz, daughter of Georg.
CHILDREN: Johann 7, Katharina 14, Marianna 9, Thekla 4.
(a) Johann Barth 27, son of Joseph.
WIFE: Margaretha Hirschspiegel 24, daughter of Adam.
CHILDREN: Benedikt 1.
11. **Joseph Reichert** 55, from Herxheim, Rheinpfalz, son of Johann.
WIFE: Marianna Hilfer 55, from Mörlheim, Rheinpfalz, daughter of Michael.
CHILDREN: Georg 21, Michael 19, Marianna 17.
(a) Nikolaus Reichert 31, son of Joseph.
WIFE: Marianna Krenitzky 24, from Poland, daughter of Martin.
CHILDREN: Kunibaldus 5, Georg 3, Apolonia 1.
12. **Ludwig Dihlmann** 27, from Schönau, Rheinpfalz, son of Peter.
WIFE: Eva Ott 21, daughter of Johann.
SISTER: Christina Dihlmann 22.
13. **Georg Fleck** 38, from Wingen, Elsass, son of Johann.
WIFE: Franziska Heidt 38, from Leimersheim, Rheinpfalz, daughter of Jakob.
CHILDREN: Georg 16, Johann 10, Elisabeth 13, Philippina 9, Magdalena 7, Franziska 3, Eva 1.
(a) Karl Schireck 52, from Lembach, Elsass, son of Thomas.
WIFE: Annamaria Strohmeier 52, daughter of Georg.
14. **Joseph Stolz** 33, from Hassel, Rheinpfalz, son of Andreas.
WIFE: Elisabeth Senn 30, daughter of Michael, from the colony of Speier.
CHILDREN: Christian 8, Margaretha 13, Wilana 4, Marianna 2.
FATHER: Andreas Stolz 64.
15. **Johann Ott** 53, from Steinfeld, Rheinpfalz, son of Kaspar.
WIFE: Katharina Vollmer 53, from Freckenfeld, Rheinpfalz, daughter of Peter.
CHILDREN: Annamaria 16.

(a) Franz Ott 23, son of Johann.
WIFE: Margaretha Stark 19, daughter of Anton.
(b) Peter Ott 24, son of Johann.
WIFE: Maria-Anna Dillmann 24, daughter of Peter.

16. **Joseph Dukart** 34, from Hayna, Rheinpfalz, son of Anton.
WIFE: Marianna Zimmermann 31, daughter of Martin from Kapsweyer, Rheinpfalz.
CHILDREN: Joseph 8, Johann 2, Katharina 13, Franziska 10, Margaretha 4.
(a) Anton Dukart 25, son of Anton.
WIFE: Marianna Nollet 23, daughter of Georg.
CHILDREN: Franz 1, Georg Breitenbach 11, an orphan.

17. **Sebastian Hemerling** 51, from Schulenberg, Preussen.
WIFE: Christina Schützle 40, daughter of Christian.
CHILDREN: Johann 20, Eramus 10, Jakob 7, Elisabeth 8.
STEP-CHILDREN: Johann Roll 8, Marianna Roll 11.
(a) Jakob Himmelspach 30, son of Georg.
WIFE: Barbara Hemerling 24, daughter of Sebastian.

18. **Joseph Wanner** 22, from Schweighofen, Rheinpfalz, son of Jakob.
WIFE: Annamaria Schnell 23, from Hördt, Rheinpfalz, daughter of Joseph.
CHILDREN: Matthias 1.
MOTHER: Magdalena Wanner 63, daughter of Johann. She had a daughter named Magdalena, aged 15.

19. **Valentin Paul** 42, son of Philipp, from Kapsweyer, Rheinpfalz.
WIFE: Elisabeth 40.
CHILDREN: Katharina 17, Marianna 10, Elisabeth 1.
(a) Michael Müller 75, from Herxheim, Rheinpfalz, son of Martin.
WIFE: Marianna Sitter 65, from Kapsweyer, Rheinpfalz.

20. **Balthasar Jonas** 40, son of Georg, form Steinfeld, Rheinpfalz.
WIFE: Margaretha Morell 26, daughter of Johann, from Rheinzabern, Rheinpfalz.
CHILDREN: Thomas 17, Adam 1, Annamaria 10, Elisabeth 4.
(a) Franz Jonas 34, son of Georg (as above).
WIFE: Martha Wolf 20, daughter of Michael.
CHILDREN: Matthias 6, Paul 3, Jakob 1, Katharina 4.

21. **Martin Kiefer** 39, from Schweighofen, Rheinpfalz, son of Friedrich.
WIFE: Elizabeth Hoffmann, from Offenbach, Rheinpfalz, daughter of Johann.
CHILDREN: Magdalena 14, Margaretha 12, Marianna 10, Katharina 2, Elisabeth 1, Christian 8.

(a) Leonhard Weber 67, from Altstadt, Rheinpfalz, son of Joseph.
22. **Johann Imel** 58, from Erlenbach, Rheinpfalz.
WIFE: Magdalena Helbling 56, from Wingen, Elsass, daughter of Johann.
CHILDREN: Joseph 17, Elizabeth 13.
(a) Christian Imel 23, son of Johann.
WIFE: Annamaria Heckel 20, daughter of Jakob.
(b) Kaspar Imel 20, son of Johann.
WIFE: Julianna Kaiser 18, daughter of Franz.
23. **Nikolaus Riedinger** 52, from Kandel, Rheinpfalz, son of Franz.
WIFE: Theresa Ring 53, (from same place) daughter of Kaspar.
CHILDREN: Anton 21, Margaretha 16, Marianna 12,, Jakobina 9.
(a) Leonard Riedinger 23, son of Nikolaus.
WIFE: Katharina Himmelspach 20, daughter of Joseph.
CHILDREN: Anton 1.
24.   **Joseph Schnell** 63, from Leitenheim, Elsass, son of Joseph.
WIFE: Marianna Ily 40, from Malsch, Baden, daughter of Joseph.
(b) Martin Schnell 20, son of Joseph.
WIFE: Maria-Eva Wanner 20, daughter of Jakob.
CHILDREN: Markolin 1.
MAID: Regina Krenitzsky.
(b) Georg Schnell 26, son of Joseph.
WIFE: Magdalena Reichert 23, daughter of Joseph.
CHILDREN: Julianna 2, Marianna 1.
25. **Georg Thomas** 34, from Herxheim, Rheinpfalz, son of Anton.
WIFE: Klara Zander 24, daughter of Georg.
CHILDREN: Elisabeth 1.
FATHER: Anton Thomas 60, son of Anton; had a daughter, Christina 17.
26. **Franz Riedinger** 33, fromKandel Rheinpfalz, son of Franz.
WIFE: Annamaria Schäfel 20, from Trimbach, Elsass; daughter of Franz.
CHILDREN: Helena 9, Franziska 3, Margaretha 1.
(a) Nikolaus Riedinger 27, son of Franz.
WIFE: Elisabeth Fries 24, daughter of Anton.
CHILDREN: Anna 1.
BROTHER: Jakob Riedinger 20.
(b) Widow, Genovefa Noth, daughter of Georg Himmelspach.
27. **Franz Schäfel** 68, from Trimbach, Elsass; son of Johann.
WIFE: Margaretha Hüttel 58, daughter of Johann.
CHILDREN: Adam 34, Johann 27, Franz 18.
(a) Johann Schäfel son of Franz.

WIFE: Eva Fäth 27, daughter of Sebastian.
CHILDREN: Michael 4, Dominik 3, Magdalena 7, Elisabeth 6, Margaretha 1.
(b) Adam Schäfel 34, son of Franz.
WIFE: Magdalena Gratz 32, daughter of Anton.
CHILDREN: Martin 11, Franz 9, Barbara 5, Margaretha 3, Marianna 1.

28. **Michael Hoff** 25, from Kapsweyer, Rheinpfalz, son of Johann.
WIFE: Maria-Eva Bullinger 22, daughter of Peter, from Herxheim, Rheinpfalz.
CHILDREN: Michael 1.
SISTER: Cäzilia (Cecilia) Hoff 22.

28(a) **Franz Fries** 33, from Braunsberg, Preussen, son of Joseph.
WIFE: Barbara Hoff 30, daughter of Johann.
CHILDREN: Adam 13, Kajetan 10, Michael 4, Katharina 6.

29. **Anton Fries** 48, from Braunsberg, Preussen, son of Joseph.
WIFE: Christina Stolph 47, daughter of Christian.
CHILDREN: Peter 18, Anton 16, Franz 12, Georg 10, Joseph 7.
(a) Johann Fries 36, son of Joseph.
WIFE: Josepha Imel 25, daughter of Joseph, from Waldhambach, Rheinpfalz.
CHILDREN: Franz 16, Michael 9, Jakob 5, Barbara 14, Margaretha 10.

30. **Peter Stein** 46, from Klimbach, Elsass; son of Jakob.
WIFE: Katharina Paul 38, daughter of Philipp, from Kapsweyer, Rheinpfalz.
CHILDREN: Michael 17, Georg 13, Joseph 4, Jakob 1, Elisabeth 15, Eva 11, Margaretha 8, Katharina 1.
(a) Peter Stein 24, son of Peter.
WIFE: Margaretha Wanner 19, daughter of Jakob.
CHILDREN: Magdalena 1.

31. **Anton Gress** 55, from Reimersweiler, Elsass; son of Matthias.
WIFE: Elisabeth Schmidt 57, daughter of Johann, from Surburg, Elsass.
CHILDREN: Kaspar 16, Christina 14.

32. **Michael Berger** 35, from Klimbach, Elsass; son of Peter.
WIFE: Barbara Kunz 33, daughter of Christopher, from Berg, Rheinpfalz.
CHILDREN: Peter, Johann 6, Elisabeth 13, Rosalia 11, Apollonia 2.
(a) Peter Berger 27, son of Peter.
WIFE: Franziska Bösherz 22, daughter of Daniel, from Schleithal, Elsass.
CHILDREN: Annamaria 2.

33. **Andreas Stehly** 66, from Schönenburg, Elsass; son of Jacob.

WIFE: Katharina Deutsch 56, daughter of Michael, from Herxheim, Rheinpfalz.

(a) Jakob Stehly 36, son of Andreas.

WIFE: Margaretha Pfoh 28, daughter of Georg, from the colony of Rastadt.

CHILDREN: Elisabeth 3.

(b) Joseph Stehly 39, son of Andreas.

WIFE: Katharina Schloss 30, daughter of Joseph, from the colony of Sulz.

CHILDREN: Johann 8, Michael 4, Franz 2, Annamaria 1.

34. **Thomas Jäger** 29, from Bergzabern, Rheinpfalz; son of Peter.

WIFE: Friederika Sander 32, daughter of Georg, from Ilshofen, Würtemburg.

CHILDREN: Balthasser 9, Katharina 5, Martina 3, Barbara 1.

(a) Christian Jäger 24, from Bergzabern, Rheinpfalz; son of Kaspar.

WIFE: Margaretha Wock 20, daughter of Anton, from Kapsweyer, Rheinpfalz.

CHILDREN: Peter 1.

(b) Michael Gress 24, from Reimersweiler, Elsass.

WIFE: Margaretha Jäger, daughter of Kaspar.

CHILDREN: Franz 1, Margaretha 1.

35. **Adam Wock** 60, from Kapsweyer, Rheinpfalz, son of Martin.

WIFE: Magdalena Waxel 52, daughter of Jakob, from Jockgrim, Rheinpfalz.

CHILDREN: Sebastian 9, Apolonia 16.

(a) Adam Wock 23, son of Adam.

WIFE: Annamaria Stehly, 20, daughter of Andreas.

CHILDREN: Kolumba 3, Marianna 1, Apolonia 1.

(b) George Wock 27, son of Adam.

WIFE: Annamaria Kroll 25, daughter of Christian, from the colony of Rastadt.

CHILDREN: Sophie 4, Marianna 2.

36. **Joseph Moser** 40, son of Christian, from Reimersweiler, Elsass.

WIFE: Christina Vollmer 36, daughter of Georg, from Freckenfeld, Rheinpfalz.

CHILDREN: Anton 15, Christian 13, Joseph 8, Marianna 10, Magdalena 4, Katharina 2, Christina 1.

37. **Johann Wilhelm** 66, son of Nikolaus, from Schweighofen, Rheinpfalz.

WIFE: Elisabeth Stolph 59, daughter of Franz, from Niederlauterbach, Elsass.

(a) Johann Wilhelm 26, son of Johann.

WIFE: Anastasia Kunz 30, daughter of Martin, from Bietingen,

Baden.

CHILDREN: Christian 3, Franz 1, Annamaria 5.

(b) Franz Eilhelm 22.

WIFE: Annamaria Ferkner 20, daughter of Johann.

38. **Christian Ekrod** 36, son of Adam, from Wallenheim, Rheinpfalz.

WIFE: Maria-Eva Dörr 30, daughter of Daniel, from Herxheim, Rheinpfalz.

CHILDREN: Elisabeth 11, Magdalena 8, Margaretha 6, Joseph 1.

39. **Michael Böspflug** 26, son of Valentin, from Herxheim, Rheinpfalz.

WIFE: Margaretha Marsal 22, daughter of Christian, from Wingen, Elsass.

CHILDREN: Matthias 4, Johann 2, Jakob 1, Margaretha 1.

(a) Widow of Valentin Böspflug, née Juliana Wingerter 56, daughter of Anton.

CHILDREN: Daniel 16, Bernhard 14.

40. **Johann Zimmermann** 37, from Kapsweyer, Rheinpfalz, son of Martin.

WIFE: Apolonia Müller 37, daughter of Michael, from Herxheim, Rheinpfalz.

CHILDREN: Michael 15, Johann 13, Martin 4, Rosalia 11, Annamaria 9, Katharina 2.

41. **Peter Brilz** 42, son of Franz, from Ingenheim, Rheinpfalz.

WIFE: Elisabeth Stolz 38, daughter of Andreas, from Hassel, Rheinpfalz.

CHILDREN: Michael 16, Christian 13, Peter 8, Matthias 4, Elisabeth 15.

(a) Martin Zimmermann 66, son of Johann, from Kapsweyer, Rheinpfalz.

WIFE: Magdalena Hamann 56, daughter of Ignaz, from Lembach, Elsass.

(b) Franz Gress 21.

WIFE: Katharina Breitenbach 20, daughter of Georg.

42. **Stephan Brilz** 38, son of Franz, from Ingenheim, Rheinpfalz.

WIFE: Frau Eva Diebig 38, daughter of Peter, from Leimersheim, Rheinpfalz.

CHILDREN: Franz 16, Georg 14, Lorenz 8, Adam 2, Magdalena 9, Barbara 4.

(a) Widow Brilz, née Barbara Glaser 37, daughter of Franz.

CHILDREN: Jakob 14, Franz 12, Joseph 11.

43. **Nikolaus Imel** 25, son of Johann, from Erlenbach, Elsass.

WIFE: Elisabeth Renner 24, daughter of Franz, from Steinweiler, Rheinpfalz.

CHILDREN: Joseph 5, Georg 3, Xaver 2, Philipp 1.
(a) Felix Hartmann 27, son of Johann, from Baden.
WIFE: Margaretha Imel 22, daughter of Johann.
CHILDREN: Johann 5, Magdalena 1.
    44. **Martin Makelke** 33, son of Christoph, from Preussen.
WIFE: Elisabeth Ganz 27, daughter of Martin, from Bietingen, Baden.
CHILDREN: August 10, Michael 5, Ferdinand 3, Franziska 12, Katharina 1.
ORPHANS: Johann Makelke 15, Theresia Makelke 24.
    45. **Johann Martin** 70, son of Michael, from Kandel, Rheinpfalz.
WIFE: Elisabeth Hessler 64, daughter of Peter, from Hambach, Rheinpfalz.
(a) Widow Fichter, daughter of Johann Martin.
CHILDREN: Michael 9, Stephan 7, Emelda 5, Katharina 2.
(b) Franz Michel 28, son of Peter, from Hayna, Rheinpfalz.
WIFE: Franziska Martin 27, daughter of Johann.
CHILDREN: Martin 7, Christian 3, Marianna 1.
    46. **Michael Aman** 40, son of Ludwig, from Lingenfeld, Rheinpfalz.
WIFE: Katharina Geis 38, daughter of Peter, from Wanzenau, Elsass.
CHILDREN: Konrad 10, Jakob 8, Adam 1, Annamaria 15, Karolina 13.
(a) Peter Gress 27, son of Anton, from Reimersweiler, Elsass.
WIFE: Franziska Aman 23, daughter of Ludwig.
CHILDREN: Michael 2, Marianna 4.
(b) Jakob Aman 34, son of Ludwig.
WIFE: Annamaria Philipps 28, daugher of Johann.
CHILDREN: Johann 9, Ferdinand 2, Philipp 1.
(c) Widow of Joseph Phillips, née Dorothea Bockenmeier 66, daughter of Michael.
CHILDREN: Philipp 21, Martin 20, Adam 19.
    47. **Johann Weisgerber** 25, son of Jakob, from Altstadt, Rheinpfalz.
WIFE: Marianna Lefrank 18, daughter of Joseph, from the colony of Sulz.
CHILDREN: Anton 1, Barbara 4, Margaretha 2. (The two girls were children from his first wife, Maria-Eva Daum).
(a) Father Jakob Weisgerber 63, son of Jakob, from Altstadt, Rheinpfalz.
CHILDREN: Philipp 22, Martin 20, Georg 18.
(b) Widow Elisabeth Kunz 25, daughter of Jakob Weisgerber.
CHILDREN: Georg, Elisabeth 8, Emilia 3.
    48. **Anton Erhard** 58, son of Karl, from Neuhäusel, Elsass.

WIFE: Elisabeth Frenzel, daughter of Peter.
CHILDREN: Christian 20, Konrad 12, Katharina Wingerter 18, Regina Erhard 17, M. Katharina 14.
ORPHANS: Philipp Holfinger, Elisabeth Krenitzsky.
(a) Anton Erhard 23, son of Anton.
WIFE: Marianna Schropp 20, daughter of Sebastian.
(b) Peter Erhard 26, son of Anton.
WIFE: Franziska Bockenmeler 24, daughter of Adam.
CHILDREN: Theodor 3, Regina 1.
49. **Bernhard Peter** 59, son of Matthias, from Schleital, Elsass.
WIFE: Barbara Thomas 64, daughter of Jakob.
(a) Kaspar Peter, son of Bernhard.
WIFE: Helena Kautzmann 24, daughter of Joseph, Kirchhardt, Baden.
CHILDREN: Alvarius 2, Maria-Eva 1.
(b) Philipp Peter 23, son of Bernhard.
WIFE: Maria-Eva Gab 18, daughter of Adam.
CHILDREN: Adam 1.
50. **Adam Hirsch** 37, son of Nikolaus, from Herxheim, Rheinpfalz.
WIFE: Franziska Schöner 32, daughter of Franz, from Lingenfeld, Rheinpfalz.
CHILDREN: Konrad 8, Peter 9, Vinzenz 4, Georg Michael 1, Katharina 13, Margaretha 11, Barbara 2.
51. **Georg Leingang** 48, son of Johann, from Rülzheim, Rheinpfalz.
WIFE: Barbara Klaus 46, daughter of Michael, from Oberrödern, Elsass.
CHILDREN: Jakob 21, Philipp 9, Peter 4, Elisabeth 18, Marianna 12.
(a) Anton Leingang 24, son of Georg.
WIFE: Marianna Gratz 20, daughter of Anton.
CHILDREN: Lukas 1.
52. **Jakob Jahner** 38, son of Adam, from Jockgrim, Rheinpfalz.
WIFE: Franziska Eichenlaub 33, daughter of Franz, from Herxheim, Rheinpfalz.
CHILDREN: Peter 8, Gottlieb 2, Marianna 15, Cecilia 10, Magdalena 5.
(a) Father Franz Eichenlaub, 73.
SON: Georg 37, was a dwarf.
53. **Martin Klang** 60, son of Johann, from Herxheim, Rheinpfalz.
WIFE: Barbara Mühl 65, daughter of Joseph.
(a) Christoph Deckert 36, son of Georg, from Hennbrüken, Bayern.
WIFE: Margaretha Klang 32, daughter of Martin.
CHILDREN: Johann 5, Daniel 1, Katharina 8, Margaretha 2.

(b) Wendel Heidt 28, son of Philipp, from Leimersheim, Rheinpfalz.
WIFE: Barbara Klang 28, daughter of Martin.
CHILDREN: Christian 5, Matthias 1.
54. **Michael Fischer** 63, son of Anton, from Aschbach, Rheinpfalz.
WIFE: Margaretha Paul 48, daughter of Philipp, from Kapsweyer, Rheinpfalz.
CHILDREN: Michael 20, Stanislaus 9, Julianna 17, Marianna 5.
55. **Philipp Weiss** 35, son of Jakob, from Waldhambach, Rheinpfalz.
WIFE: Elisabeth Fichter 30, daughter of Joseph, from Schönau, Rheinpfalz.
CHILDREN: Apolonia 4.
56. **Peter Lochbaum** 39, son of Andreas, from Lingenfeld, Rheinpfalz.
WIFE: Katharina Weisgerber 35, daughter of Jakob, from Altenstadt, Elsass.
CHILDREN: Michael 8, Adam 5, rochus 1, Elisabeth 14, Cäzilia 2, Franziska 1.
(a) Adam Lochbaum 34, son of Andreas.
WIFE: Maria-Eva Weibel 26, daughter of Franz, from Weilstadt, Baden.
CHILDREN: Michael 4, Katharina 1.
(b) Konrad Lochbaum 25, son of Andreas.
WIFE: Katharina Schuh 21, daughter of Bernhard. (Lutheran).
CHILDREN: Margaretha 2, Juliana 1.
57. **Konrad Reis** 45, son of Georg, from Wollmesheim, Rheinpfalz.
WIFE: Katharina Eichenlaub 39, daughter of Franz.
CHILDREN: Daniel 18, Peter 16, Jokob 2, Margaretha 13, Katharina 10, Barbara 5.
58. **Michael Bösherz** 32, son of Kaspar, from Schleital, Elsass.
WIFE: Josepha Reichert 20, daughter of Franz.
CHILDREN: Antonia 1.
BROTHER: Daniel Bösherz 19.
(a) Joseph Schnell 29, son of Joseph, from Leitenheim, Elsass.
WIFE: Barbara Bösherz 24, daughter of Kaspar.
CHILDREN: Martin 3, Anton 1, Katharina 1. Katharina Bösherz 13, sister of wife.
59. **Jakob Gerber** 32, son of Christian, from Salmbach, Elsass.
WIFE: Maria-Eva Scheibel 27, daughter of Michael, from Klimbach, Elsass.
CHILDREN: Anton 10, Elisabeth 7, Annamaria 3.
FATHER: Michael Scheibel 78, son of Michael.

60. **Anton Koffler** 44, son of Matthias, from Durmersheim, Baden.

WIFE: Regina Gerber 38, daughter of Christian, from Salmbach, Elsass.

CHILDREN: Peter 13, Johann 11, Theresia 15.

STEP-CHILDREN: Jakob Brinster 12, Georg Brinster 8, Klara Brinster 10, all children of Kaspar Brinster.

(a) Heinrich Schuh, Lutheran.

WIFE: Marianna Brinster 19, daughter of Kaspar.

61. **Johann Stark,** 48, son of Johann, from Lingenfeld, Rheinpfalz.

WIFE: Barbara Bufler 39, daughter of Georg, from Reimersweiler, Elsass.

CHILDREN: Ludwig 21, Peter 15, Heinrich 10, Joseph 5, Stephan 2, Katharina 22, Mariana 11.

ADOPTED CHILDREN: Kaspar 15, Georg 10, Magdalena 12, children of Kaspar Kost.

62. **Jakob Zimmermann** 35, son of Martin, from Kapsweyer, Rheinpfalz.

WIFE: Elisabeth Fäth 35, daughter of Sebastian, from Pfortz, Rheinpfalz.

CHILDREN: Johann 10, Jakob 8, Georg 3, Regina 4.

63. **Michael Matz** 40, son of Anton, from Kapsweyer, Rheinpfalz.

WIFE: Elisabeth Mochilewskaja 38, daughter of Johann, from Poland.

CHILDREN: Adam 19, Peter 15, Annamaria 12.

(a) Christian Michel 21, son of Peter.

WIFE: Marianna Matz 21, daughter of Michael.

CHILDREN: Martin 1.

64. **Heinrich Gress** 42, son of Matthias, from Reimersweiler, Elsass.

WIFE: Katharina Stein 38, daughter of Jakob, from Klimbach, Elsass.

(a) Sebastian Wingerter 21, son of Georg.

WIFE: Marianna Gress 18, daughter of Johann.

CHILDREN: Katharina 1.

65. **Philipp Weiss** 63, son of Bernhard, from Schleital, Elsass.

WIFE: Franziska Gerlinger 64, daughter of Balthassar.

(a) Jakob Weisgerber 26, son of Jakob from Altenstadt, Elsass.

WIFE: Margaretha Fäth 30, daughter of Sebastian.

CHILDREN: Franz 16, Michael 14, Jakob 12, Heinrich 9, Konstantin 4, Lorenz, Eva 10. (The first named may be step-children).

66. **Nikolaus Daum** 50, son of Adam, from Herxheim, Rheinpfalz.

WIFE: Katharina Philipps 44, daughter of Joseph, from Rohrbach,

Rheinpfalz.
CHILDREN: Johann 12, Lorenz 10, Theresia 6, Franziska 1.

67. **Bernhard Müller** 61, son of Bernhard, from Herxheim, Rheinpfalz.
WIFE: Maria-Eva Ring 61, daughter of Franz.
(a) Christoph Müller 27, son of Bernhard.
WIFE: Elisabeth Gotting 21, daughter of Philipp, from Albersweiler, Rheinpfalz.
CHILDREN: Andreas 1.
(b) Johann Fischer 20, son of Michael.
WIFE: Apolonia Müller 21, daughter of Bernhard.
CHILDREN: Michael 1.

68. **Andreas Kary** 37, from Elchesheim, Baden.
WIFE: Annamaria Stolz 34, daughter of Andreas, from Hassel, Rheinpfalz.
CHILDREN: Peter 13, Philipp 1, Marianna 11, Elisabeth 5, Katharina 3.

69. **Joseph Himmelspach** 43, son of Georg, from Herxheim, Rheinpfalz.
WIFE: Magdalena Schmidt 44, daughter of Johann, from Klimbach, Elsass.
CHILDREN: Johann 22, Jakob 19, Anton 11, Joseph 8, Marianna 12, Magdalena 5.
(a) Johann Himmelspach 37, son of Georg.
WIFE: Annamaria Wilhelm 30, daughter of Johann, from Schweighofen, Rheinpfalz.
CHILDREN: Marianna 10, Magdalena 9, Katharina 2, Elisabeth 1.

70. **Georg Stolz** 53, son of Karl, from Berg, Rheinpfalz.
WIFE: Magdalena Frenzel (or Brendel?) daughter of Peter.
CHILDREN: Martin 20, Regina 12.
(a) Benedikt Bast 22, son of Joseph.
WIFE: Barbara Stolz 19, daughter of Georg.

71. **Franz Kaiser** 66, son of Franz, from Hatzenbühl, Rheinpfalz.
WIFE: Apolonia Butscher 56, daughter of Heinrich, from Kandel, Rheinpfalz.
(a) Franz Müller 30, son of Bernhard, from Herxheim, Rheinpfalz.
WIFE: Magdalena Kaiser 27, daughter of Franz.
CHILDREN: Ladislaus 4, Marianna 1.
(b) Andreas Stolz 28, son of Andreas, from Hassel, Rheinpfalz.
WIFE: Elisabeth Kaiser 21, daughter of Franz.
CHILDREN: Andreas 2, Michael 1.

72. **Helena Zimmermann** widow, age 37, daughter of Anton Thomas.
SECOND HUSBAND: Leonhard Hartmann, 36, son of Johann.

CHILDREN: Felix 7, Jordan 4, Christian 2, Daniel 1.
CHILDREN OF FIRST HUSBAND, GEORG ZIMMERMAN: Joseph 14, Barbara 12.
(a) Martin Zimmerman 25, son of Michael, from Kapsweyer, Rheinpfalz.
WIFE: Magdalena Stark 23, daughter of Johann, from Lingenfeld, Rheinpfalz.
CHILDREN: Johann 4, Elisabeth 2.
WIDOW: Margaretha Zimmermann 63, daughter of Peter.
73. **Peter Kunz** 30, son of Christopher, from Berg, Rheinpfalz.
WIFE: Maria Müller 28, daughter of Michael, from Herxheim, Rheinpfalz.
CHILDREN: Valentin 8, Joseph 6, Katharina 4, Maria-Eva 2.
SISTER: Katharina Müller 47.
74. **Georg Stein** 47, son of Jakob, from Klimbach, Elsass.
WIFE: Margaretha Häckel 44, daughter of Joseph, from Riedselz, Elsass.
CHILDREN: Peter 17, Georg 12, Franz 9, Matthias 2, Barbara 19, Magdalena 4.
75. **Rudolf Gab** 27, son of Adam, from Rohrbach, Rheinpfalz.
WIFE: Apolonia Kunz 22, daughter of Martin, from Berg, Rheinpfalz.
CHILDREN: Anton 4, Joseph 1.
WIDOW: Magdalena Kunz 57, daughter of Joseph.
CHILDREN: Joseph 18, Anton 15.
(a) Franz Kunz 31, son of Martin.
WIFE: Katharina Nollet 31, daughter of Michael, from Altenstadt, Elsass.
CHILDREN: Bonaventura 4, Jakob 2, Katharina 5.
76. **Georg Wingerter** 43, son of Anton, from Herxheim, Rheinpfalz.
WIFE: Elizabeth Stein 43, daughter of Jakob, from Klimbach, Elsass.
CHILDREN: Vinzenz 3, Maria-Elisabeth 15, Katharina 12, Margaretha 6.
77. **Jakob Wolf** 34, son of Michael, from Schweighofen, Rheinpfalz.
WIFE: Elisabeth Brendel 33, daughter of August, from Arzheim, Rheinpfalz.
CHILDREN: Kaspar 5, Blasius 2, Joseph 1.
(a) Georg Kiefer 41, son of Andreas, from Schweighofen, Rheinpfalz.
WIFE: Magdalena Wolf 36, daughter of Michael.
CHILDREN: Georg 8, Jakob 6, Alexander 1, Katharina 5.
78. **Martin Frank** 75, son of Peter, from Kapsweyer, Rheinpfalz.
WIFE: Maria-Eva Hoffmann 53, daughter of Michael, from Offenbach, Rheinpfalz.

(a) Nikolaus Frank 33, son of Martin.
WIFE: Katharina Michel 32, daughter of Peter, from Hayna, Rheinpfalz.
CHILDREN: Peter 11, Joseph 2, Eva 5, Katharina 4, Barbara 1.
(b) Kaspar Frank 40, son of Martin.
WIFE: Marianna Zimmermann 26, daughter of Michael.
CHILDREN: Stephan 16, Anton 14, Georg 12, Johann 9, Matthias 3, Nikolaus 2.
79. **Jakob Häckel** 41, son of Johann, from Riedselz, Elsass.
WIFE: Annamaria Riedinger 37, from Kandel, Rheinpfalz.
CHILDREN: Franz 16, Georg 12, Franz-Jakob 9, Adam 4, Jakob 2, Elisabeth 14, Franziska 10, Margaretha 1.
Michael Riedinger 21, brother of Annamaria.
80. **Nikolaus Roth** 55, son of Georg, from Hayna, Rheinpfalz.
WIFE: Margaretha Wingerter 48, daughter of Georg.
CHILDREN: Michael 23, Katharina 16.
(a) Franz Hilfer 26, son of Georg.
WIFE: Marianna Roth 21, daughter of Nikolaus.
CHILDREN: Dionysius 1
(b) Konstantin Kautzmann 24.
WIFE: Katharina Roth 18.
81. **Anton Schmidt** 37, son of Johann, from Klimbach, Elsass.
WIFE: Margaretha Metz, daughter of Georg, from Hayna, Rheinpfalz.
CHILDREN: Jakob 7, Magdalena 8, Katharina 3, Marianna 5.
(a) Johannes Mosbruker 23, son of Johann.
WIFE: Elisabeth Heck 18, daughter of Johann.
82. **Franz Häckel** 37, son of Joseph, from Riedselz, Elsass.
WIFE: Josepha Dekele 24, daughter of Kasimir.
CHILDREN: Jakob 14, Franz 12, Berhard 3, Margaretha 9, Barbara 6, Klara 1.
(a) Heinrich Ede, Lutheran.
WIFE: Magdalena Scherer 28, daughter of Michael.
CHILDREN: Christina 9, Thekla 1.
(b) Matthias Gress 50, son of Matthias, from Reimersweiler, Elsass.
WIFE: Klara Baumstark 40, daughter of Johann, from Reihen, Baden.
CHILDREN: Anton 24, Ferdinand 22, Michael 12, Barbara 16, Katharina 9, Annamaria 6, Maria-Eva 4, Thekla 3.
83. **Georg Vollmer** 67, son of Peter from Horst, Rheinpfalz.
WIFE: Katharina Huber 66, daugher of Heinrich.
(a) Michael Vollmer 24, son of Georg.
WIFE: Katharina Stöbner 23, daughter of Peter, from the colony of Sulz.

CHILDREN: Luzia 2, Katharina 1.
(b) Phillipp Rössle 30, son of Joseph, from Baden.
WIFE: Annamaria Vollmer 26, daughter of Georg.
CHILDREN: Michael 8, Adam 1, Maria-Eva 6, Magdalena 1.
84. **Johann Koch** 35, son of Johann, from Lembach, Elsass.
WIFE: Margaretha Marsal 33, daughter of Christian.
CHILDREN: Georg 14, Johann 10, Jakob 8, Barbara 7, Margaretha 5, Maria-Eva 2.
(a) Georg J. Badinger 32, son of Georg, from Albersweiler, Rheinpfalz.
WIFE: Katharina Koch 27, daughter of Johann, from Lembach, Elsass.
CHILDREN: Michael 8, Georg 9, Markus 1, Elisabeth 2.
85. **Johannes Mosbrucker** 47, son of Peter, from Bundental, Rheinpfalz.
WIFE: Elisabeth Heidt 47, daughter of Jakob, from Leimersheim, Rheinpfalz.
CHILDREN: Christian 17, Peter 1, Katharina 14, Margaretha 11.
Joseph Mosbrucker 49, brother.
86. **Kaspar Marsal** 23, son of Christian from Wingen, Elsass.
WIFE: Maria-Eva Schaf 24, daughter of Lorenz, from Leimersheim, Rheinpfalz.
CHILDREN: Christian 3, Matthias 1, Marianna 6.
MOTHER: Margaretha Marsal 45, daughter of Georg Dörr.
CHILDREN: Johannes 12.
87. **Matthias Schöner** 30, son of Franz, from Lingenfeld, Rheinpfalz.
WIFE: Katharina Gab 34, daughter of Adam, from Rohrbach, Rheinpfalz.
CHILDREN: Anton 6, Margaretha 8, Brigitta 4, Elisabeth 1.
(a) Anton Schöner 36, son of Franz.
WIFE: Katharina Walter 34, daughter of Christian, from Wingen, Elsass.
CHILDREN: Joseph 12, Matthias 1, Franziska 16, Katharina 13, Salomea 8, Maria-Eva 8, Elisabeth 3.
88. **Peter Michel** 61, son of Anton, from Hayna, Rheinpfalz.
WIFE: Katharina Völkeler 57, daughter of Georg, from Herxheimweyer, Rheinpfalz.
CHILDREN: Xaver 20, Georg 19, Elisabeth 10.
(a) Peter Roth 49, son of Georg, from Rheinzabern, Rheinpfalz.
WIFE: Susanna Hoffmann 29, daughter of Jakob, from Offenbach, Rheinpfalz.
89. **Christian Fleck** 43, son of Johann, from Wingen, Elsass.
WIFE: Elisabeth Heidt 43, daugther of Jakob, from Leimersheim, Rheinpfalz.

CHILDREN: Matthias 19, Christian 16, Joseph 13, Kasimir 10, Magdalena 15, Marianna 7, Monika 1.

90. **Johann Jonas** 25, son of Georg, from Kapsweyer, Rheinpfalz.
WIFE: Margaretha Fleck 20, daughter of Christian, from Wingen, Elsass.
CHILDREN: Matthias 1.

91. **Kaspar Jäger** 47, son of Peter, from Bergzabern, Rheinpfalz.
WIFE: Katharina Wanner 37, daughter of Jakob.
CHILDREN: Johann 11, Anton 9, Joseph 4, Kaspar 2, Barbara 17, Elisabeth 15.

92. **Anton Engel** 51, son of Lorenz, from Herxheim, Rheinpfalz. ⚓
WIFE: Barbara Zimmermann 39, daughter of Martin, from Kapsweyer, Rheinpfalz.
CHILDREN: Franz 16, Joseph 15, Christian 14, Johann 6, Anna 13, Isabella 10, Elisabeth 8.
MOTHER-IN-LAW: Annamaria 69, daughter of Anselm Walter, from Wingen, Elsass.
(a) Jakob Stein 23, son of Georg.
WIFE: Margaretha Marsal 19, daughter of Johann.

93. **Jakob Wanner** 41, son of Jakob, from Schweighofen, Rheinpfalz.
WIFE: Elisabeth Helbling 38, daughter of Johann, from Wingen, Elsass.
CHILDREN: Jakob 16, Thimothäus 14, Johann 6, Margaretha 18, Katharina 10, Marianna 8, Elisabeth 3, Magdalena 1.

94. **Paul Veitenheimer** 48, son of Gottfried, from Weilstadt, Baden.
WIFE: Magadalena Mildenberger 29, daughter of Joseph, from Kirchardt, Baden.
CHILDREN: Christina 14, Annamaria 12, Philippina 11, Susanna 7, Elisabeth 2, Anton 16, Johann 9, Nikolaus 4.
(a) Anton Riedinger 21, son of Nikolaus.
WIFE: Elisabeth Wingerter 19, daughter of Georg.

95. **Matthias Fleck** 34, son of Johann, from Wingen, Elsass.
WIFE: Elisabeth Böspflug 34, daughter of Valentin, from Herxheim, Rheinpfalz.
CHILDREN: Georg 14, Michael 9, Joseph 8, Jakob 3, Peter 1, Elisabeth 5.
MOTHER: Margaretha Fleck 61, daughter of Adam Schlick from Wingen, Elsass.
(a) Lorenz Engel 45, son of Lorenz, from Ramberg, Rheinpfalz.
WIFE: Margaretha Fleck 40, daughter of Johann.
CHILDREN: Georg 10, Johann 1.

96. **Barbara Ehrmantraut** 48, widow, daughter of Peter Flick,

from Jockgrim, Rheinpfalz.
CHILDREN: Ludwig 16, Karl 12, Karolina 14, Marianna 9, Annamaria 8, Elisabeth 4.
(a) Peter Ehrmantraut 20, son of Georg.
WIFE: Elisabeth Gab 18.
(b) Rudolf Ehrmantraut 22, son of Georg.
WIFE: Barbara Nikolaus 20, daughter of Georg.
CHILDREN: Joseph 1.
97. **Marianna Schmalz** 43, widow, daughter of Christian Marsal, from Wingen, Elsass.
CHILDREN: Michael 14, Valentin 10, Marianna 16, Maria-Eva 2.
(a) Gottlieb Fischer 24, son of Michael.
WIFE: Margaretha Schmalz 19, daughter of Georg.
CHILDREN: Michael 1.
98. **Georg Hilfer** 50, son of Michael, from Mörlheim, Rheinpfalz.
WIFE: Margaretha Rühl 50, daughter of Martin, from Herxheim, Rheinpfalz.
(a) Dionysius Kautzmann 24, son of Joseph, from Kirchhausen, Württemberg.
WIFE: Maria-Eva Hilfer 22, daughter of Georg.
CHILDREN: Plazidus 3.
(b) Joseph Hilfer 22, son of Georg.
WIFE: Regina Krinitzsky 18.
CHILDREN: Hyazint (son).
99. **Joseph Burghard** 49, son of Theobald, from Wingen, Elsass.
WIFE: Elisabeth Walter 48, daughter of Christian.
CHILDREN: Georg 19, Katharina 16, Maria-Eva 14.
(a) Michael Schaf 24, son of Philipp.
WIFE: Salomea Burghard 24, daughter of Joseph.
CHILDREN: Vinzenz 1.
100. **Georg Dauenhauer** 39, son of Valentin, from Dahn, Rheinpfalz.
WIFE: Margaretha Fröhlich 38, daughter of Philipp, from Hirschtal, Rheinpfalz.
CHILDREN: Markus 16, Georg 13, Ludwig 11, Jakob 9, Christian 6, Joseph 2.
101. **Michael Böhm** 60, widower, son of Adam, from Herxheim, Rheinpfalz.
CHILDREN: Marianna 9.
(a) Rudolf Böhm 24, son of Michael
WIFE: Franziska Gab 23, daughter of Adam.
CHILDREN: Dominika 3, Marianna 1.
(b) Michael Böhm 26, son of Michael.
WIFE: Magdalena Stolz 24, daughter of Georg.

CHILDREN: Rudolf 4, Franz 2, Marianna 1.

102. **Valentin Dauenhauer** 72, son of Joseph, from Dahn, Rheinpfalz.
WIFE: Apolonia Walter 65, daughter of Philipp, from Wingen, Elsass.
(a) Christian Dauenhauer 26, son of Valentin.
WIFE: Annamaria Stumpf 20, daughter of Jakob.
CHILDREN: Klara 2, Marianna 1.

103. **Johann Huck** 46, son of Karl, from Herxheim, Rheinpfalz.
WIFE: Marianna Fichter 42, daughter of Joseph, from Schönau, Rheinpfalz.
CHILDREN: Georg 5, Kornelius 2, Katharina 15, Margaretha 8.
STEP-CHILDREN: Ferdinand 13, Karl 6, Helena 4, Sophia 2.
These last four were children of Matthias Endres.
(a) Adam Schaf 23, son of Philipp.
WIFE: Marianna Huck 20, daughter of Johann.
CHILDREN: Joseph 1.
(b) Joseph Fichter 27, son of Joseph, from Riedselz, Elsass.
WIFE: Marianna Müller 25, daughter of Bernhard.
CHILDREN: Marianna 4, Elisabeth 1.
MOTHER: Annamaria Fichter 60, daughter of Georg Jerg.

104. **Xaver Fröhlich** 38, son of Philipp, from Hirschtal, Rheinpfalz.
WIFE: Margaretha Schmidt 34, daughter of Joseph, from Queichhambach, Rheinpfalz.
CHILDREN: Franz 14, Johann 13, Philipp 2, Raimund 1, Marianna 9, Elisabeth 7, Margaretha 5.

105. **Georg Zander** 62, son of Georg, from Vollstein, Prussia.
WIFE: Dorothea Stolz 54, daughter of Christian.
(a) Augustin Zander 29, son of Georg.
WIFE: Margaretha Scheibel 29, daughter of Michael.
CHILDREN: Ludwig 5, Maria-Eva 3, Magdalena 1.
(b) Rudolf Riedinger 24, son of Franz.
WIFE: Katharina Zander 20, daughter of Georg.
CHILDREN: Elisabeth 1.

106. **Klara Philipp** 50, widow, daughter of Joseph Marz, from Rohrbach, Rheinpfalz.
(a) Joseph Jungmann 29, son of Adam.
WIFE: Marianna Philipp 19, daughter of Georg.
CHILDREN: Agnes 2.
(b) Johannes Nollet 22, son of Michael.
WIFE: Franziska Philipp 18, daughter of Georg.
CHILDREN: Katharina 1.

107. **Barbara Roll** 43, widow, daughter of Johann Kühn, from Leimersheim, Rheinpfalz.

CHILDREN: Johann 12, Wendelin (?), Rosina 9, Katharina Wixel 18.

108. **Georg Sock** 50, son of Joseph from Kirchardt, Baden.
WIFE: Katharina Wetzstein 32, daughter of Michael from Katzenbühl, Rheinpfalz.
CHILDREN: Katharina 2.
(a) Adam Bockenmeier 50.
WIFE: Margaretha Müller 34, daughter of Heinrich.
CHILDREN: Kaspar 12, Joseph 7, Georg 1, Katharina 5, Marianna 3.
(b) Katharina Philipp 33, daughter of Heinrich Müller.
CHILDREN: Joseph 5.

109. **Anton Huck** 52, son of Matthias from Obschester, Bohemia.
WIFE: Eva Breidenbach 47, daughter of Martin from Mühlhausen, Baden.
CHILDREN: Michael 17.
(a) Nikolaus Huck 20, son of Anton.
WIFE: Barbara Stark, daughter of Anton, from the colony of Rastadt.
CHILDREN: Michael 1.

110. **Peter Gab** 29, son of Adam.
WIFE: Annamaria Paul 28, daughter of Philipp.
CHILDREN: Christian 3, Edward 1, Margaretha 7, Marianna 5, Elisabeth 2.

111. **Johann Philipp** 29, son of Georg.
WIFE: Margaretha Ehrmantraut 28, daughter of Georg.
CHILDREN: Kasimir 1, Johann 1, Maria 8, Magdalena 5.

112. **Georg Koch** 31, son of Johann, from Lembach, Elsass.
WIFE: Barbara Fischer 26, daughter of Michael.
CHILDREN: Gottlieb 4, Magdalena 7, Katharina 1.

113. **Sebastian Berger** 37, son of Peter.
WIFE: Katharina Ott 27, daughter of Johann.
CHILDREN: Nikolaus 4, Jakob 2, Annamaria 9.

114. **Georg Heidt** 40, son of Jakob from Leimersheim, Rheinpfalz.
WIFE: Barbara Fischer 36, daughter of Johann from Herd, Baden.
CHILDREN: Nikolaus 7, Margaretha 5, Elisabeth 2, Theodor Maurer 2, an orphan.

115. **Georg Himmelspach** 47, son of Georg, from Herxheim, Rheinpfalz.
WIFE: Magdalena Urlacher 55, daughter of Georg, from Klimbach, Elsass.
(a) Kaspar Bösherz 23, son of Daniel.
WIFE: Marianna Himmelspach 22, daughter of Georg.

116. **Martin Müller** 28, son of Bernhard.
WIFE: Theresia Doll 29, daughter of Johann.
CHILDREN: Franz 6, Johann 4, Anna 5, Margaretha 2, Elisabeth 1.

117. **Joseph Paul** 36, son of Philipp from Kapsweyer, Rheinpfalz.
WIFE: Katharina Steckler 30, daughter of Franz.
CHILDREN: Johann 10, Anton 4, Katharina 12, Magdalena 1.
118. **Johann Ehrmantraut** 24, son of Georg.
WIFE: Margaretha Glaser 21, daughter of Franz.
CHILDREN: Franz 2.
MOTHER: Annamaria 55, daughter of Joseph Forst, from Salmbach, Elsass.
119. **Michael Nollet** 49, son of Matthäus, from Altenstadt, Elsass.
WIFE: Margaretha Vollmer 57, daughter of Georg, from Freckenfeld, Rheinpfalz.
CHILDREN: Peter 16.
(a) Michael Nollet 24, son of Michael.
WIFE: Margaretha Kaiser 23, daughter of Georg.
CHILDREN: Michael 3, Marianna 1.
120. **Johann Bär** 50, son of Jakob, from Schukrawetz.
WIFE: Katharina Zimmermann 35, daughter of Michael, from Kapsweyer, Rheinpfalz.
CHILDREN: Michael 10, Peter 4, Marianna 13, Helena 7, Katharina 2.
121. **Jakob Becker** 45, son of Joseph, from Kapsweyer, Rheinpfalz.
WIFE: Christina Riedinger 35, daughter of Franz, from Minfeld, Rheinpfalz.
CHILDREN: Michael 13, Katharina 15, Christina 10, Elisabeth 8.
(a) Sebastian Stark 23, son of Adam.
WIFE: Margaretha Becker 19, daughter of Jakob.
CHILDREN: Katharina 1.
122. **Michael Dukart** 40, from Hayna, Rheinpfalz.
WIFE: Marianna Paul 45, daughter of Philipp, from Kapsweyer, Rheinpfalz.
CHILDREN: Johann 9, Joseph 3, Alexander 1, Margaretha 16, Magdalena 14, Elisabeth 1.
123. **Johann Wanner** 34, son of Jakob, from Schweighofen, Rheinpfalz.
WIFE: Josepha Kunle 32, daughter of Johann, from Steinegg, Baden.
CHILDREN: Joseph 9, Peter 6, Johann 4, Kaspar 2, Jakob 1, Margaretha 8.
24. **Martin Ohlhäuser** 49, son of Martin, from Spechbach, Baden.
WIFE: Katharina Bochard 46, daughter of Johann.
CHILDREN: Michael 8, Georg 6, Katharina 14, Franziska 3.
(a) Peter Ohlhäuser 23.
WIFE: Magdalena Dilmann 20.
125. **Daniel Bösherz** 51, son of Jakob, from Schleital, Elsass.
WIFE: Maria-Eva Reiss 50, daughter of Georg, from Wollmesheim, Rheinpfalz.

CHILDREN: Katharina 12, Klara 10.

126. **Michael Engler** 38, son of Georg from Kuhardt, Rheinpfalz.
WIFE: Margaretha Jud 36, daughter of Matthias from Freckenfeld, Rheinpfalz.
CHILDREN: Paul 11, Franziska 5, Christina 2, Elisabeth 1.

127. **Lorenz Friedrich** 48, son of Michael, from Neukostheim, Elsass.
WIFE: Barbara Hirsch 39, daughter of Jakob, from Herxheim, Rheinpfalz.
CHILDREN: Katharina 18, Margaretha 12, Franziska 11, Agatha 3, Barbara 2, Apolonia 1.
(a) Michael Hirsch 25, son of Jakob.
WIFE: Magdalena Ehrmantraut 23, daughter of Georg.
CHILDREN: Albin 2, Ambrosius 1.
MOTHER: Apolonia 91, daughter of Questian.

128. **Joseph Kautzmann** 58, son of Joseph, from Kirchheim, Württemberg.
WIFE: Walburga Remüller 48, daughter of Gottfried, from Sondheim.
CHILDREN: Gabriel 21, Nikolaus 6, Sabina 19, Magdalena 14, Annamaria 10.

129. **Nikolaus Bacharonowsky** 40, son of Basilius, from Russia.
WIFE: Eudokia Stachowska 33, daughter of Demetrius.
CHILDREN: Anselm 10.
(a) Anton Schwartz 35, son of Karl, from Wanzenau, Elsass.
WIFE: Magdalena Wilhelm 25, daughter of Johann.
CHILDREN: Gundivaldus 2, Katharina 5, Barbara 1.

The Founding of the Colony of Landau

The colony of Landau was founded during the years of 1809 and 1810. When the first migrants arrived in the late summer of 1809 there was nothing but a desolate, empty steppe. Of the promised dwellings, there were none to be seen. They stopped on the meadow near the site where the Central School is now located. Mayor Brittner announced that the new colony was to be settled here and ordered them to unload their wagons. They all looked around and, seeing nothing but the wide steppe, there followed much crying and wailing. Many voices were heard to enquire, "How can this wilderness be our new home?" Since there was no alternative, they soon consoled each other in the hope of a better future. With the help of God, who had already escorted them here, they would succeed.

They all got to work, searching for a suitable place to prepare accommodations for the coming winter. The best place for this purpose was believed to be the small 'valley of the wells.' On the north side of this valley, the father of each family dug a cave, covered the roof and front with reeds, placed their meager belongings therein, and thus completed their home. These were cold and damp during the winter. Under these circumstances, various illnesses soon appeared. By spring 60 people had died, mostly small children. It was a most trying time for these poor settlers. By early January 1911 most of the Crown houses were finished, with the statistics as follows:

There were 108 families, consisting of 234 males and 236 females, all Catholics. The property of the colonists consisted of 91 horses, 404 horned cattle, 106 wagons, 1085 loads of hay, 118.5 tschewert wheat, 70.5 tschetwert oats and 0.5 tschetwert corn. There were no potatoes.

WAINWRIGHT: Johann Ott.
LINEN MANUFACTURERS: Peter Schaf, Franz Glaser, and Georg Hilfer.
CARPENTERS: Nikolaus Kaspary, Franz Schöner, and Martin Klang.
WEAVERS: Jakob Stritzinger, Joseph Reichert.
CABINET-MAKER: Matthias Wind*
BUTCHERS: Philipp Paul and Michael Schmidt.
SHOEMAKERS: Johann Schmidt, Rudolf Schulz and Peter Morschhäuser.
MASON: Anton Matz.
TAILORS: Anton Thomas, Andreas Stehly.
NAILMAKER: Peter Jäger.
SCHOOLMASTER: Georg Ehrmantraut.
SURGEON: Anton Dukart.

On the 6 October 1811 the Beresan inspector read the following order: "Each farmer must plant 2 tschetwert of winter wheat and in the spring of 1812, 1 tschetwert of wheat and 1 tschetwert of oats." For the Landau colony this amounted to planting 432 tschetwert.

After a period of 6 years (1817-1818), the statistics for Landau were: Ninety-seven families, 245 males and 223 females, altogether 468 souls.

The property owned by the colonists was:
339 horses, 642 horned cattle, 55 sheep, 473 pigs, 71 ploughs, 63 harrows, 97 wagons, 66 distaffs and 7 weaver looms.

Tradesmen were as follows:
Carpenters 2, cabinet-maker 1, millers 2, tailors 3, weavers 4, shoemakers 1, blacksmith 1, and 4 masons. The amount seeded was as follows:

---

*Moved to Odessa.

	tschetwert	tschetwerik
Winter wheat and rye	109	3.0
Summer wheat	187	3.0
Barley	70	6.0
Oats	158	7.0
Potatoes	147	3.0
Corn	3.0	0.5
Millet	6.0	7.5
Peas	6.0	1.0
Lentils	1.0	1.5
Beans	5.0	0.25
Hemp	1.0	7.5
Flax	2.0	7.25
Totals:	695	47.50

(1 tschetwert = 8 tschetwerik = 10.0 pud = 6 bushels).

The Landau Community Land

The Landau community contained 9228 dessiatines of which 120 dessiatines was church land. The land formed an irregular quadrangle, located on both sides of the Beresan. On the south, the boundary is formed by the Sulź community land and the so called Keller Steppe; on the west by the Johannestal community land; on the north by the Speier community land, and on the east by the property of Karlsruhe and Katharinental. The surface of the land is mostly level. Only the Beresan and its adjoining valleys cut into it. The ground is largely composed of black earth covering a layer of loam and, to some extent, gravel. In the early days, when the weather was suitable, the ground was very fruitful. But through continuous yearly exploitation and poor cultivation, the land was gradually depleted of its nutrition, and only with extraordinary favourable weather conditions does it produce a passable harvest.

For several years the people of Landau leased some land located on the border of Sulz to the Bulgarians who produced some very nice cabbage and vegetable gardens thereon. These gardens, which were watered from a spring, provided vegetables for the whole Beresan district and returned good profits to the tenants. The forest and the district plantation garden, started in 1842, have perished.

The Parish of Landau

The colony of Landau now has 245 lots with 2457 inhabitants, all Catholics. Of the other denominations there were several officals, craftsmen and domestics, mostly Russian Orthodox, who remained only temporarily. A Russian Orthodox Church was build in Landau several years ago. Since 1811, the parish of Landau belongs to the deanery of Nikolayev in the diocese of Tiraspol. The Schönfeld mission also belongs to the parish of Landau and is largely occupied by migrants from Landau. There is a post office and a telegraph station in Landau.

The Story of the Parish

In the early days of the Beresan settlement, the colonists approached the governor-general, Duke de Richelieu, with the request that he obtain a priest through the proper channels. Richelieu, who was a staunch Catholic himself, promised the colonists to fulfill their request as soon as possible. He forwarded the request to Prince Alexander Galitzin asking that a priest, who spoke German well be sent immediately to the German colonies near Odessa. For a while they were under the supervision of one of the parishes previously foimed. The closest parish to the Beresan was Nikolayev. However, the priest here could not speak German. Consequently, the Beresan colonists were included with the parish of Severinowka for awhile. On the 26 May 1810 the bailiff rang the bell in every colony, announcing that anyone who had children to be baptised was to bring them to Landau. After all the people concerned with the children's baptism had gathered, the expedition, with the help of a guide, moved to the west. The journey over the wastelands, mostly uninhabited Steppe, crossed many hills and valleys for nearly 100 versts, as far as the small market town of Severinowka which belonged to the estate of Count Severin Pototzsky. A Catholic church had been in existence there since 1800. The priest in Severinowka at that time was Father Paulus Krutschkowsky. He received the colonists with great kindness. On the 29 May 1810 he baptized 10 children from Landau, 7 from Speier, 5 from Sulz, 3 from Karlsruhe, 8 from Rastadt and 1 from München. On the 5 June 1811 the last group of children from the Beresan were baptised in Severinowka.

On the 11 June 1811 the Beresan inspector, Friederich Strohmeyer, wrote to the office of the mayor in Landau: "The Crown is constantly concerned for the well-being of the people who are fortunate enough to be Russian subjects. In a short while the rectory in Landau will be build. We will soon have a priest to lay the cornerstone for the church. The building must be constructed rapidly. It is not possible to get stone cutters; therefore, I order you to send 13 wagons from Landau to Rohrbach, to bring back pre-cut stones and unload them near the rectory."

In May 1811 the following priests of the Society of Jesus came to Odessa from Polotsk: Father Andreas Pierling for Selz, Father Anton Jann for Landau, Father Hubertus Reimers for Rastadt and Father Oswald Rausch for Josephstal. The priests assigned to Odessa were already there by 1811.

Father Anton Jann came to Landau as the first priest on 10 September 1811. The rectory was not yet finished and he therefore had to make private arrangements for a while. The newly founded parish of Landau at that time encompassed Landau, Speier, Sulz and Karlsruhe.

The Pastors in Landau

FATHER ANTON JANN, S.J. — 1811-1813

Father Anton Jann was born in Burgau, Schwaben on the 30 April 1784. He received his secondary education with the Jesuits in Augsburg. Here he learned that the order of the Society of Jesus was still in existence in White Russia. He also found out that a novitiate of this society was still open in Dvina. This devout youth was moved with the desire to join this much slandered Society of Jesus. He made the journey by foot and arrived at Dvina on the 15 August 1803 on the Feast of the Ascenion of Mary. His request to enter the society was granted. After completing his novitate he was sent to Petersburg for 3 years to teach German. At the completion of his theology and philosophy studies he was ordained a priest and sent to the mission near Odessa. The newly founded parish of Landau in Beresan was his first assignment. He arrived there on the 10 September 1811. Since the rectory was not yet completed he found private quarters with the widow Brilz (nee Stoll). On his arrival Father Jann found neither a rectory, church, nor chapel. He celebrated mass in the crown houses until the rectory and an attached hall were completed. Mass was then held in the hall.

Father Jann did everything possible to have a parish church built as soon as possible but, since the Beresan people could not agree among themselves about the church, his efforts were in vain. He worked very hard at his duties as priest. There were many people ill at this time and, since he also looked after the parish of Rastadt, there were many days when he could not get away from the ambulance. In 1813 he moved to the parish of Josephstal, near Odessa, where he worked for 7 years as a pious, exemplary, conscientious priest, saving souls.

When the Jesuits were expelled from Russia in 1820, Father Jann first went to Tarnopol where he taught classical languages for 4 years. Later he went to Bukovina for 6 years as a missionary.

From 1836 until 1848 he was a parish priest in Gratz. In 1848 he was the father confessor for Bishop Zingler of Linz and the Prefect for the Jesuit College at Linz. When the Jesuits were driven out of Linz by the revolutionaries, Father Jann went to the colony of Sachku as an assistant curate. Here he soon became seriously ill. He received the last sacraments and thanked God for having had the privilege to work in this order, to live and die in it. He died on the 7 April 1851 and was buried in the church yard at Sachku.

I wish to recall one instant of his life. When the priests wished to depart from Linz and had already gathered in the refectory for the evening meal, Father Jann requested permission from the Rector to publicly declare his faults since he was the oldest, least important, and least deserving. The Rector granted his permission. The old priest then knelt and prayed, telling of his shortcomings, among many tears and sobs. Moved by the specatacle, they all knelt and prayed the "mea culpa" for all their faults.

This was the first priest for Landau. In Beresan his memory itself is blessed.

ANDREAS PIERLING, S.J. — 1813-1814

Father Andreas Pierling S.J. was born in Petersburg on the 7 March 1782 where his father was a rich merchant and innkeeper. Pierling was a devout Catholic and in his inn the Jesuits were frequent visitors. Through them, young Andreas and his brother Jakob became acquainted with the priests and their order. Andreas did his first studies in Strassburg and later in Salzburg. The Jesuits had been granted permission to open a novitiate in Dvina which Andreas entered on the 30 August 1804. Here he completed his studies of philosophy and theology and laid the foundations of Christian perfection and the priesthood. On completing his studies he was ordained and, in 1811, was sent to the Odessa mission. His first position as a priest was in the newly founded parish of Selz, in Kutschurgan, where he worked for 2 years as a zealous shepherd of souls and a loving father. His first undertaking was to build a church and rectory. In 1813 he was moved to Landau, where he diligently pursued the duties of a good priest. He wished to build a church here but the discord and stubbornness of the Beresan people thwarted this pious undertaking.

In 1814 he was sent to Odessa as the French preacher. Later he returned to Landau. In 1816 he was appointed Superior of the Odessa Mission and once again moved to Odessa. In 1819-1820 he was the parish priest at Kherson. Here he was expelled from Russia along with the other priests of the Society and he found a new home in Galicia where he held positions as pastor and also as director of the novitiate. Then, as Superior, he was appointed to the College at Innsbruck. Through his punctuality and obedience to his superiors and his affable manners towards his subordinates, he gained their affection and respect. Father Andreas had a particular reverence for the Holy Sacrament. With deep regret and fervent devotion, he said Mass daily and visited the Saviour in the tabernacle as often as he could. He tried to instill these praiseworthy virtues in his subordinates so that they would always walk faithfully in the eyes of the Lord and become perfect in Christian virtue.

In his last illness he showed great forebearance and submitted to the will of God. All present were moved to tears. Even though he was extremely weak, he prayed the breviary until the day he died. After receiving the last sacraments he started to recite the "Benedictus Dominus" in a weak voice even though he had already lost the fight for life.

Then a small bell was rung calling all the priests and brothers to the room where he was dying. A priest began the prayers for the dead; the sick man repeated these quietly. At 3 o'clock on the 12 November 1841, at the age of 59, after 37 years in his Order, Father Andreas Pierling quietly and blissfully died. His body was buried at Innsbruck attended by an enormous crowd of both priests and lay people.

FATHER FRANZ HOFFMAN, S.J. — 1814-1815

Father Franz Hoffmann S.J. was born on the 6 September 1788. There is nothing in the records of his birth place. He entered the order of the Society of Jesus on the 28 September 1810. After completing his studies in 1814, he was ordained to the priesthood and was immediately sent to Landau. Since he was in Landau for only one year, his accomplishments were limited. In 1815 he was moved to the newly founded parish at Mannheim where he worked very diligently at his church duties. In 1818 he was moved to Orscha as the rector of the boarding school and professor of French. In 1819 and 1820 he was in the College in Vitebsk. In 1820 he resigned from the Society of Jesus and nothing further is known about him.

FATHER FRANZ SCHERER, S.J. — 1816-1820

Father Franz Scherer S.J. was born in Bavaria (the locality is not given) on the 23 February 1788. He did his first studies at the college in Augsburg which at that time was under the direction of ex-Jesuits. Through the virtues and knowledge of these distinguished people, the good youth learned about the Society of Jesus which was suppressed in Germany but still functioning in Russia. Unable to fulfill his desire to enroll in this Society after completing his sixth year, he travelled by foot to distant Russia and was accepted by the Society in the novitiate at Dvina.

After completing the novitiate and usual studies of the Society and after he was ordained, he took the vows of "Coadjutor Spiritualis." In view of his outstanding work in the pastorate he was permitted to profess the three vows of the order. After one year as Rector at the boarding school for boys at Polotzk, he was assigned to the large Catholic mission at Odessa. In 1816 he was sent to Landau in the Beresan as the pastor. His assignment in this colony, which was settled by people from various parts of Germany, was not an easy one. Above all, he had to contend with ignorance, rudeness, insubordination, immorality and violation of Sunday. This called for diligent, courageous, kind and loving leadership. He preached diligently and often heard confession. Whenever he visited a colony he conducted some catechectical instruction. He set a good example for his parishioners in every way and requested that they earnestly try to improve their lives and to make their repentance more sincere.

He was very opposed to dancing and to the expensive weddings which sometimes lasted for several days, frequently accompanied by immorality, drinking and fighting. His sternness did not please many of the Beresan people. A section of the community of Karlsruhe and Sulz accused the priest of having boxed the ears of one of the youths during a Catechism class and of having forbidden them to live according to their popular traditions.

Father Scherer was not intimidated by these accusations, particularly since the colonial magistrate supported him in his efforts against the prevailing vices. Commissar Krüger issued a circular to all offices of the mayors with strict orders that they must conscientiously obey the Father's directives or they would receive lashes or neck irons, after which his requests were obeyed. He failed only in one thing, namely, his desire to build the parish church at Landau before he was moved. Only in Sulz was he able to build the first house of prayer in 1819.

In 1820 he had to leave his difficult but much loved work in the Beresan (like his colleagues) and go to Galicia. His first appointment here was as professor at the Gymnasium (Secondary School) at Tarnopol. In 1838 he was sent to Graz as Professor of Rhetoric and Spiritual Advisor in the College. In 1843 he went to Linz as preacher and in 1845 to Innsbruck as minister in the Theresianum. After one year he was moved to Graz for the third time, to take over the office of the procurator.

In the revolutionary year of 1848, when the Society of Jesus was expelled from Graz, the energetic action and cool-headedness of Father Scherer was destined to play no small role. He courageously went to the front door of the house and prevented the on-storming bands of robbers from looting the house. After the other priests had left the college and town, the courageous Father Scherer remained behind and provided a temporary lodging for the library and all other objects which had escapted the hands of the plunderers.

Later he was assistant priest in the parish of Heilbrunn and house chaplain at Graz. In 1858 he ws appointed administrator of the Kapornak estate which the priests had bought in Hungary. He was then 70 years old, but still the restless, busy priest. He proceeded with prudence and tireless energy and succeeded in rebuilding the system from the ruins left after the attack by the thieves. The limit of his unshakable courage was unbelievable.

As he grew older, he also grew weaker. Finally, in 1866, he had to relinquish his position as administrator. He was sent to St. Andrew as spiritual advisor where he spent his last years in prayer and contemplation. He was respected by all his colleagues because of his faithful obedience to the rules of the order and he was admired for his fresh spirit which persisted to his last days. He gave to all the example of a life dedicated to the common good.

He received the Last Sacraments on May 21, 1869 at St. Andrew at the age of 81. He died the death of the righteous, having served 63 years in the ministry.

ALBIN MARZINKEWICZ — 1820-1828

Father Albin Marzinkewicz, Carmelite (white friar), came from Volhynia and was born in 1785. He joined the Carmelite order in his youth where he received his education. He was ordained a priest in 1811. When the Jesuits were expelled from Russia they were replaced by other orders. Archbishop Sestrinzewicz searched in every monastery for priests who understood and spoke the German language to minister to the German Catholic colonies. Father Albin Marzinkewicz volunteered as a candidate for the German colonies even though he spoke German poorly. He was sent as priest to Landau, where he arrived on the 30 September 1820.

But what a difference between the Jesuit and the Carmelite! The Jesuit lived all year in a simple house with an attached chapel where he held prayers. The Carmelite immediately asked for a large new rectory and magnificent church.* The Jesuit supported himself on the salary of 300 rubles and did not worry about his portion of Crown designated parish land. The Carmelite immediately demanded 500 rubles, and made every effort to obtain for himself the 120 dessiatines so designated in the general survey of 1812. The Jesuit liked the sheep, the Carmelite was more fond of the wool! For days on end the Jesuits were kept busy visiting the sick. The Carmelite let the sick die, while he took joy rides to Ignatowicz or Maleschwicz. Although there was no priest in Rastadt, the Carmelite sent back the carriages that came to fetch him for the sick so that many died without the Holy Sacraments. Because of this he was reported.**

In Landau he built a fine rectory and a church that was neither magnificent nor well built. After 12 years the church became dilapidated and had to be torn down. Because of neglect of his duties, he was frequently reported and eventually he was moved to Selz. Here, also, after a short while he was reported. He was then removed from the colonies by the authorities and sent to the Carmelite monastery in Lutsk. He must be given credit for the care and attention he gave to the parish registers.

FATHER KAJETAN MAZIEWSKY — 1828-1832

Father Kajetan Maziewsky, a Dominican, was born in 1754. He was already fairly old when he entered the Dominican Monastery at Stolpy, in the province of Kiev, where he received his education. He was ordained in 1798 after he completed his studies. Archbishop Sestrinzewicz was searching for priests to replace the Jesuits who had been expelled. Father Provincial of the Dominican order recommended Father Maziewsky as he understood German fairly well. Shortly thereafter, he was sent to Selz in the Kutschurgan as the parish priest. He remained there for seven years, diligently performing his duties to everyone's satisfaction.

In Selz he was reprimanded for taking a Pole with a false passport into his house. The investigation took a long time, the end results being that the priest had to pay a fine of 10 rubles.

In 1828 he was sent to Landau as the parish priest where he worked very diligently for four years at his religious duties. Even when he was sick and weak, he still conducted the Christian teaching himself. He visited the school and often gave sermons. He loved to celebrate the children's First Communion with great solemnity. In later years he was frequently ill and was confined to bed the last month before he died. At the request of Mayor Imel, Father A. Sobolowsky from Odessa was sent to help him. Father Maziewsky

---

*The colonists at this time were very poor and, consequently, the church could not be built.
**See archives of Odessa Church, 8 February 1824.

received the last Holy Sacrament and died December 31, 1832 and was buried by Father Sobolowsky on January 3, 1833. His grave is located in the present church, between the altar of the Virgin Mary and the pulpit. Father Maziewsky cultivated the parish land himself and consequently carried on a sizable operation. His horses, oxen and farm implements were sold at a sale on January 10, 1833 for 934 rubles and 90 kopecks.

Father Sobolowsky remained in Landau for 1 month, then Father Kaspar Borowsky came as vice-curate. He remained until October 1833 at which time he was sent to Josephstal.

FATHER ERASMUS BOROWSKY — 1833-1848

Father E. Borowsky came from White Russia to Landau in 1833, the year of the great famine. The circumstances in Landau at this time were very depressing. The need was great everywhere. There was no bread, no seed, no feed. The people suffered from various diseases and a pestilence had struck the cattle. Everywhere one looked there was only grief and misfortune, and none of the essentials of life. The people were despondent and depressed and believed that they had been forsaken by God and man.

To comfort the poor and unfortunate in these circumstances required a man of great faith and paternal love. Such a man was Father E. Borowsky who, through God's will, was sent to Landau at this time. By words and deeds, he showed his new parishioners the way to God. 'Everything that God does is for our own good, and when He sends us grief and sorrow, He has His reasons, even though we may not understand them. We must therefore trust in God and with forebearance give ourselves over to His Holy wishes. God can wound, but He can also heal. Trust in God, He will surely help!' And truly God did help.

To start with, the Crown granted the people advance loans. Father Borowsky knew many farmers in Poland, so he sent Nikolaus Imel and Johannes Mosbrucker there, where they were able to buy large quantities of wheat cheaply with the Crown money. Sometimes there was a whole caravan of wagons bringing wheat from Poland to Landau. The wheat was placed in a special bin where it was stored for the benefit of all the Beresan colonists. As a result of the example set by Father Borowsky, the surrounding noblemen and towns arranged to collect money and other necessities, to be distributed to the poor colonists through the priests.

Above all, Father Borowsky spared no efforts to raise the low level of religious life in Beresan and to inspire the people to Christian virtues. In the pulpit, in the confessional, in his Christian teachings, and in the schools, he instructed his parishioners about their religion and about their civic duties so that they might all become faithful, staunch and good citizens. His first love was for the poor whom he was always comforting and aiding, so that in all truth he could be called the "priest of the poor."

Through his life he set a good example for he performed his duties carefully and conscientiously. He built the second parish church in Landau which stood until 1863. His many tiring activities soon undermined his health so that later he was often sick. In spite of this he continued his duties. In the latter part of 1848 he became seriously ill and was given the Last Sacraments. The evening before Christmas he died. The Lord called his faithful friend to Himself to celebrate the holy Feast in Heaven. His grave is beside that of Father Maziewsky in the present parish church.

FATHER FRANZ WOITKEWICZ — 1849-1850

Father Franz Woitkewicz was born in 1805 and ordained in 1834. He was vicar in Roschanistock in the Province of Grodno. He came to Landau on Whit Sunday. He was a giant, both in size and strength, and became known as "big Frank." He was so strong that he could raise a 5 to 6 pud sack of wheat with one hand. He brought three helpers with him from Poland, two boys and a girl who was later married to Daum in Landau. Father Woitkewicz worked the parish land himself. He also had many cattle and therefore needed many hired men and maids.

He received little praise for the administration of his parish. He spoke German poorly and read his sermons. He neglected confessions, Christian teaching and school visitations. He frequently attended weddings and baptisms. Worst of all, he always collected money in advance and even charged more than the regular fees. This displeased the community generally. A complaint was forwarded to the authorities and subsequently Father Woitkewicz was moved from Landau. Nothing further is known about him.

FATHER CHRISTOPHER PIETKEWICZ — 1850-1854
(See transl. Vol. I, 181).

FATHER DIDAK SAMBOR — 1854-1852

Father Didak Sambor was a Bernardine monk born in Lithuania in 1798 and ordained in 1828. Father Sambor was a cavalry officer in Austria and from there he entered the monastery. (See transl. Vol. I, 144).

FATHER ADALBERT MITROWSKY — 1862-1865

Father Adalbert, also known as Donatus Mitrowsky (or Medrowsky), was born in 1803 and ordained in 1827. He completed building the present church. (See transl. Vol. I, 189).

FATHER ALEXANDER SCHATURSKY — 1865-1866

Father Alexander Schatursky (or Schadursky) was born in 1804 and ordained in 1818. He died in Belzy on 5 September 1871. (See transl. Vol. I, 189).

FATHER ZENO KALINOWSKY — 1866-1867

Father Zeno Kalinowsky was born in 1809 and ordained in 1833. He died in Petersburg (?). (See transl. Vol I, 144.)

FATHER GEORGE LEIBHAM — 1867-1869

Father George Leibham was born in Franzfeld in 1843 and ordained on 11 June 1867. He died at Paninskoje on December 31, 1910. (See transl. Vol. I, 226).

FATHER BALTASSAR KRAFT — 1869-1873

Father Kraft was born at Blumental on the Molotschna. After completing his studies in the Parish School in his home, he entered the Seminary in Saratov in 1861. He was a diligent and capable student and completed his studies very successfully in 1865. He was ordained by Bishop Vinzenz Lipsky on the 26 March 1866 and sent as administrator to Paninskoje on the Volga. He performed his duties diligently. In 1869 he was moved to Landau, while Father Leibham was moved to Paninskoje. The situation in Landau at this time was somewhat difficult as the Baptists were causing problems. There was also an altercation about the school master in Sulz, and the religious life of the Beresan people was atrocious. This required the young priest to be wise and gentle, but firm. In the beginning he succeeded in recalling many who had gone astray and also to settle the dispute about the school master. But a great misfortune befell him. While making a sick call to Blumenfeld during a heavy frost, he caught a severe cold and almost lost the use of his voice. As a result, he was frequently not able to preach or sing. Because of this misfortune, he found his duties much too heavy and asked to be moved to the parish at Rohleder. Here he worked as hard as he was able and as an enduring memorial he built there a beautiful parish church.

In 1880 he was sent to Rownoje, Seelmann, as priest and dean, where he carried on his duties for 15 years. In his last years he was denounced for sheltering and supporting several proscribed Polish priests. For this he received a severe reprimand which so greatly grieved him that he became seriously ill shortly thereafter and died on April 5, 1895.

FATHER JOHANNES BURGARDT
Administrator and Dean 1873-1877

Father Johannes Burgardt was born in the colony of Pfeifer, Gnilushka, in 1846. On the 12 September 1861 he entered the seminary at Saratov, completing his course in 1869. He was ordained in Saratov on the 31 August 1869 by bishop Lipsky and was appointed vicar at the Cathedral. On February 4 (1870) he was sent to Neukolonie as administrator, where he worked zealously for 3 years. On the 29 April 1873 he was sent as administrator and dean to the newly formed deanery in Landau. The Baptist proselytizing at this time had reached its peak and Bishop Zottmann believed he had the right man in Father Burghardt to quell this evil. But that was a mistake. Father Burghardt was not wise enough, nor did he have enough love in his heart to bring back the misguided people to the faith of their fathers. One does not convert people by thundering and scolding. He was powerless in preventing the spread of the Baptist sect. Recognizing this, he asked for a transfer. On 11 February 1877 he was sent to Tonkoschurowka as administrator and on 27 January 1878, as Inspector and Professor to the Seminary at Saratov. Here he seemed more out of place than in Landau. As Inspector he was too gruff and strict, had little insight and love for the pupils and lacked educational methods. As a professor he knew little and was too conceited, demanding unquestioned recognition of his authority as professor. Other circumstances, upon which I will not dwell here, resulted in his request for a country parish. On the 27 September 1880 he was moved to Pfeifer where he was born. Here he was active in the ministry until 1894. On 14 May 1894 he was moved to Göbel as parish priest, and on 28 April 1903 to Husaren in the same capacity. In 1910, at his own request, he was permitted to retire. He lived in seclusion in Pfeifer where he died on 10 June 1912.

FATHER VALENTIN SCHAMOTULSKY — 1877-1879

Father Valentin Schamotulsky was born in 1838. While studying in Kiev University, he transferred to the seminary in Saratov. He completed his studies in 1863 at which time he was ordained. He was the military Chaplain in Kutais in the Caucasus from 1868 until 1875. In 1875 he was sent to Bachmut and in 1877, to Landau. His work in Landau was not very fruitful as he spoke German very poorly. He was not familiar with the customs or traditions of the German colonists and therefore could influence them little. In 1879 he became the military chaplain at Bieliklutsch and soon thereafter was moved to Manglis where he died in 1890.

FATHER JAKOB DOBROWOLSKY — 1879-1899

Father J. Dobrowolsky was born August 8, 1854 in the colony of Mariental, near Odessa. He was ordained to the priesthood September 4, 1877. He built the new rectory in Landau in 1892 and bought a new organ from the firm of Sauer. He also built a very nice church in Schönfeld which at that time was supervised from Landau. (See transl. Vol. I, 154).

FATHER VALENTIN GREINER — 1899 until now

Father Greiner was born in 1861 in Josephstal on the Baraboi. On the 9 December 1884 he was ordained. (See transl. Vol. I, 186).

Parish Property

The parish was endowed with 120 dessiatines of land of which the first priests of the Society of Jesus made no use. The parish land was divided from the community land for the first time in 1821. It was on the boundary of Johannestal where the colony of Julienfeld was formerly located. In the forties it was incorporated into the Karlsruhe boundary. In former times the priests cultivated the land themselves but presently it is being leased at 14 rubles per dessiatine. The salary of the parish priest is 300 rubles.

The surplice fees are as follows: weddings 2 rubles, baptisms 1 ruble, to publish banns 1 ruble, mass for the dead 1 ruble, low mass 1 ruble, high mass 1 ruble, 50 kopecks.

The Parish Church

In 1811 when the first priest, Father Anton Jann, came to Landau, a church was to built. Some of the materials were already at hand, but those communities incorporated into the Landau parish could not agree on the amount of money to be spent on the church. The Landau colonists wanted all colonies of the parish to share equally in the cost. The rest of course, did not agree as they all wished to build a church or prayer house for themselves. Since the people of Landau had the priest, they reasoned that they should build the church themselves. As a result, the church was not built.

In 1812 they built a large hall on one side of the rectory where services were held until 1821. In this same year Father Marzinkewicz built the first church, just in front of the gate of the present church wall. The foundation and steeple can still be seen. The first church was so poorly built that it was ready to collapse after 12 years and had to be closed. After this, Sunday and Holy Day services were held in Speier. The church was torn down in 1833 but, because of the severe depression, the construction of the new church was postponed. The new church was built in 1837 by Father Erasmus Borowsky. The altar was on the north; the church extended from the small gate of the small street to the steps of the former church. It was approximately 78 feet long and 42 feet wide. The steeple was built separately and stood where the present parish garden is located.

The New Parish Church

The present attractive church was built in 1863. Every property owner had to bring in 2 loads of good field stones and every colonist had to provide labour. Besides these services, the cost of the rough structure of the church came to 26,000 rubles. The church was built of field stone in Romanesque style. It was consecrated by Bishop Anton Zerr on the 13 October 1896.

The church is 120 yards east of the main street, on the Sockberg. It is 126 feet long, 60 feet wide and the walls are 24 feet high. The steeple is incorporated into the church and is 96 feet high. Above the roof of the church, the steeple contains three stories. The bell tower and sound louvres are in the top story. In the vaulted belfry there are three well harmonised bells which were used to summon the faithful to the services. Above the bell tower is the pointed roof of the steeple, 24 feet high. It is topped by a golden cupola and a cross.

The church has 2 portals and seven windows on either side. The two windows in the sanctuary are stained glass and cost 280 rubles. The roof is covered with sheet metal. The church is enclosed by an attractive stone wall and trees have been planted in the yard. The front steps, eight in number, lead through the main entrance into the church. The inside of the church has a single nave, with the semicircular choir loft supported on massive Romanesque arches. On both sides of the church there are rows of pews. Just to the right of the entrance, beneath the choir loft, there is a large picture of the crucifixion.

Adjacent to the third window, in front of the choir loft, the pictures of the stations of the cross begin. On a pedestal between the third and fourth windows there is a statue of St. Aloysius. The confessional, in beautiful Gothic style, is located beneath the fourth window. Adjacent to the fifth window is the lovely 'Heart of Jesus' altar made of artistically carved wood. It rests on a platform three steps above the floor. The altar measures 6 feet long, 56 inches wide and 18 feet high. The (table) top of the altar is 28 inches high.

The front panel of the altar is made of beautifully carved wood, depicting the Holy Sepulcher with the figure of the sleeping Saviour in the grave. On top of the altar is the tabernacle with a lovely golden Sacrament chamber. Just to the right of the tabernacle there is a picture of Christ praying in the garden of Gethsemane, the Angel with the cup of sorrow, the sleeping disciples, and the mob of soldiers with the traitor Judas in the forefront.

Above these pictures there are three niches. The center niche contains a statue of the Sacred Heart of Jesus. In the right niche there is a statue of Holy St. Francis and in the one on the left there is a statue of St. Anthony of Padua. Above the statue of Jesus, in a small vault, is the most 'Sacred Heart of Jesus' with a small cross.

If we go into the sanctuary once more, one sees above the communion rail the statue of St. Philomena and two pictures of the stations of the cross. The main altar is made of carved wood and was obtained from the Stuflesser Art Firm along with the statues of St. Clemens and St. Philomena; it cost 2500 rubles. The altar is on a platform 3 steps high and is 12 feet long, 56 inches wide and 18 feet high. The height of the altar table is 42 inches. In the center of the front panel, there is a lovely carving of the 'Last Supper' according to Rafael. On the right is the sacrifice of Melchisedech, on the left the sacrifice of Abraham.

Above the altar table is the tabernacle with the sacrament chamber, both covered with gold. On either side of the tabernacle there is the figure of an angel kneeling in prayer. On the right of the angels is the Presentation of Jesus in the temple, and on the left the boy Jesus in the temple. Among these pictures are the symbols of the seven holy sacraments. Above the tabernacle is the picture of the Holy Family. On the right of this is the statue of St. Gabriel and on the left is the statue of St. Raphael, the patron of the church. Above the picture of the Holy Family hovers the figure of God the Father. Above all of these, there is a small cross.

Turning around, one looks across the communion rail and sees the lovely statue of St. Clemens Romanus, and two steps further on one is in front of the altar of the Virgin Mary. This is on a platform 3 steps up, is 6 feet long, 56 inches wide and 18 feet high. The altar top is 42 inches high and above it there is a nicely carved receptacle with the crib and the Christ child, the Virgin Mary, Saint Joseph, many angels, and the shepherds from Bethlehem.

Above and to the right of the crib is the statue of the 'Visitation of Mary' and on the left, the Annunciation. Above the tabernacle is the statue of the Blessed Virgin, on the right the statue of St. Elizabeth and on the left the statue of St. Catharine. Above the statue of the Mother of God is a heart with a small cross.

Immediately adjacent to this altar is the plain pulpit. Underneath it is the marble baptismal font. Between the third and fourth windows the statue of St. Agnes stands on a pedestal. In the center of the church are two chandeliers. In the choir loft there is an organ which cost 4000 rubles. The floor of the church is wood and painted red.

The Graveyard and Chapel

The first graveyard was located where the house of Kaspar Frank now stands. Later the dead were buried beside the church where the present parish garden is located. The graveyard was located in its present site in 1821 but, through necessity, required gradual enlargement. The graveyard chapel, built in 1887, is in need of repair.

Rectories

The first parish house in Landau was built in 1822 by Father Marzenkewicz and was remodelled several times. The present rectory was built in 1893 by Father Dobrowolsky. It contains 7 rooms, with a kitchen and the necesssary barns and sheds. In front of the rectory there is a small flower garden and in the back of the yard is a small vegetable garden.

School Affairs

For a long time Landau did not have a school house and school was conducted in the community warehouse. In 1827 the first school house was built where the post office is now located. It contained two rooms. In one room the teacher lived, while classes were conducted in the other. The instruction was from 8 to 11 in the mornings and from 1 to 4 in the afternoon. The subjects were: reading, writing, arithmetic, and singing. The books were ABC books, large and small catechisms, the Schwarz Catechism, the Spiess Catechism and Bible History. Some had brought small reading books used in the Bavarian elementary schools in Germany from which some school masters prescribed lessons. The punishments for the students were kneeling, strapping, getting locked up with or without dinner, kneeling on wood, or blows with rods on the unmentionable. The following custom was also practised; when school boys or girls distinguished themselves for some reason, they received a ticket from the school master on which was written 'Pacem' (Peace), good for 3 or 4 times. In the event that the student was to receive punishment, he could present his ticket and the teacher would tear off a portion instead of punishing the child. Another custom to make the students apply themselves more diligently was the so-called 'contest days' which were usually held one or twice a week. On the designated day all of the students in the same class would be thoroughly examined on their assignment in Biblical History. He who made the least mistakes would go to the head of the class. Bitter tears were sometimes shed by those who fell from the head of the class to the bottom.

The present school house in the upper village was built in 1852. It had 3 class rooms and 2 small rooms for village offices. The school in the lower village was built in 1879 on the back street and had 2 rooms. At the present time there are 5 teachers in Landau, each receiving 360 rubles. There are 339 school children.

The school masters in Landau since its founding were; Georg Ehrmantraut, Kaspar Jäger, Nikolaus Imel, Anton Jäger, Ludwig Gratz, Georg Fleck, Peter Fleck, Christian Fleck, Joseph Jäger, Martin Zimmermann, Franz Wanner, Philipp Weber, Christian Kunz, Jacob Kunz, Sigmund Böhm, Johann Dukart, and several others.

The Central School of Beresan

The Central Schools in South Russia owe their existence to the colonists' very good friend, Privy Councillor Eugen Von Hahn, as I have already mentioned elsewhere.* The purpose of this school was to train young German colonists as teachers and clerks (secretaries). The program in the Central schools was similar to a three-year intermediate school. At some of these schools one year of teacher training was added.

After the Central school was opened in Grossliebental in 1869 for the Liebental district, the Fürsorge Committee proposed that the Beresan district also build a Central school in Landau or one of its other villages in the district. however, since the particular colony was to build the school at its own cost, the old Beresan colonists declined the honor. Only one new colony, which temporarily belonged to the Landau district, offered to construct the new school. That colony was Neufreudental and the Central school was opened there in a private home in 1873. There was either insufficient money, incompetent leadership or poor teaching. In any case the school had a miserable existence during its first years and had to close in 1881 (?).

In 1885 Pastor H. Hänschke was appointed to Neufreudental. He was most interested in education and, together with the district supervisor, did everything possible to again open the school. Actually, they were successful. In the fall of 1886 the classes were reopened. In the beginning, things went well. There were 30 students and the examination results at the end of the year were very favourable. However, the happy beginning did not last long. The Russian teacher, who was also the principal, started to drink and the school got a bad reputation causing most of the pupils to leave. As a result of his intemperance, he became ill and there would be weeks and months in which there was no instruction and the degradation of the school was inevitable. The parents threatened to withdraw their children if things did not improve. Pastor Hänschke sent a complaint to the director of the community schools and asked that the useless teacher be removed. The director sent an official to Neufreudental to investigate. However, the school director was posted elsewhere and conditions in Neufreudental remained unchanged. The teacher, who was nearly always drunk, remained at the school. He appeared very

*See transl. of Vol. I, p. 80.

seldom and, because of his crude behaviour and bad administration, the school once more came close to dissolution. In the winter time the children had to sit and study in the room that had only 8 degrees of warmth. Naturally, they had to wear their coats and galoshes. Sometimes their hands would be so cold that they could not hold the pen.

The death of the unfortunate teacher of the school in 1897 put an end to the lamentable conditions. The next teacher who came was also Russian, but a sober man who brought new life to this totally neglected school. The enrollment increased sharply and the school soon gained a good reputation. The Beresan Catholics, who until now had kept their children from the school, began sending their sons to Neufreudental after a religious instructor was appointed there. Under these circumstances, there were approximately 60 students until the year 1907.

In 1906, as new schools were being founded everywhere, the Beresan Catholics realized that they too could have had a Central School in their midst if they had not been so indifferent. The matter was discussed as to whether or not this omission could not be corrected be moving the Central school from Neufreudental to Landau. Fortunately there were men available who were able to have this idea approved by the competent authority and permission was granted to move the school to Landau. Now it ws necessary to build a new school as it was only on this stipulation that permission for the move was granted.

At several meetings enthusiastic addresses were given with the result that in one month, through voluntary contributions, they were able to collect sufficient money to build a very fine school. The building was completed in the fall of 1907 and was blessed on October 5, 1907. It was two stories high, built of cut field stone with a metal roof, and cost 25,000 rubles. The school yard was enclosed with a stone wall and planted with various trees.

At present the following teachers are at the Central School:

1. Principal—B. Alexejew. He receives 1000 rubles, also living quarters and fuel.
2. Peter Heim—teaches German, and receives 1000 rubles.
3. Rostrowsky—teaches Russian, and receives 1000 rubles.
4. J. Schindler—teaches music and singing, receives 200 rubles.
5. Teacher of Handicrafts—receives 200 rubles.
6. Father E. Reichert—teacher of religion, receives 300 rubles.

Adjacent to the school there is board and room available at very reasonable rates for students from distant areas.

The Girls Junior High School in Landau

A school for advanced education for German Catholic girls in the Tiraspol diocese had been needed for some time. The need for such a school was felt by all faithful Catholics but no one wished to make the first move to bring the idea to fruition.

The project of building a continuation school for Catholic girls in Landau was proposed by Father H. P. Greiner. He went to Odessa with the intention of opening a third elementary school at Landau, if he could receive the necessary permit from the school authorities. As a result, he had a meeting with some people in Odessa who advised him not to establish an elementary school but recommended instead, the opening of a girls' school in Landau.

A. Scheniewsky, Inspector of elementary schools, had also recommended this project. On his return, Father Greiner had a meeting with the more intelligent citizens of Landau who were all in agreement that a three class-room girls' school with an elementary school should be opened in Landau. The building was completed in two years and the girls' school was a reality. Immediately, an organization for educational welfare was formed which took over the operation of the girl's school. The school was blessed on the 13 October 1907 and officially opened on the 20 August 1908 at which time Father Hilfer gave a very worthy address on the education of girls.

Every new beginning has its problems and the Landau Girls's School was no exception. It was difficult to get suitable teachers for the new school. There were no secondary or highschools in either Russia or Poland where young Catholic girls were trained. Still, the founder of the school did everything possible to obtain suitable lady teachers, but was not always successful.

In spite of this difficulty, the Catholic parents in South Russia gradually developed trust in the school and brought their children to the school from all areas.

The enrollment in the school increased visibly and one nursed the hope that it would grow still more so that a fourth class would have to be added. But fate would have it otherwise. In the year 1909 the Organization of Educational Welfare was dissolved by the authorities and the girls' school lost its juridical founder and hence its right of existence. However, after a search, a man was found who took the school over in his name and directed it. Only the school boarding house temporarily remained under the jurisdiction of the local pastor.

At the present time there are six teachers at the school with the number of students at approximately 90.

The Native Priests of the Landau Parish

FATHER RUDOLF REICHERT *Honorary Canon*

Father Rudolf Reichert, son of Nikolaus, was born in the Landau colony in 1843. After completing his parish school under the old teacher, Kaspar Jäger, he received private instruction from the district secretary, Anton Riedinger. Thus, being well prepared, he entered the seminary in Saratov in 1861. He was an industrious, capable student, and completed the whole course of the clerical seminary in 1866. He was ordained by Bishop V. Lipsky on the 4 September 1866 and was posted to the seminary as manager and religious instructor. In 1867 he was posted to Odessa as religious instructor in the secondary school and soon thereafter as a German missionary.

While in Odessa he became acquainted with many educated people and, realizing that his seminary training was rather inadequate, he promised himself to correct his omission by continuing his studies privately. For this reason he withdrew from society in order to obtain time to continue his private studies. He also attended lectures as an auditor at the New Russian University, especially the lectures in History and Geography by Professor Philipp Bruns. He was well liked by most of the professors and they were always pleased to see him.

In 1871 a group of professors undertook an expedition to Vienna to the World Exposition. They chose Father Reichert to be their business manager and paid his expenses for the whole trip.

When Prelate G. Rasutowicz was granted his resignation on the 15 November 1876, Father Reichert was appointed parish priest in Odessa and dean of the Odessa Deanery. At first, most of the parishioners wished to have a Polish parish priest. Also, conditions during the last years of administration of the aged prelate Rasutowicz had become intolerable. The various quarrels and friction between the priest and the trustees about the building of houses and the many rumors revolving about the prelate undermined the reputation of the pastor and the clergy in Odessa. On top of all this there was the mixture of many nationalities, each with its individual peculiarities, wishing their own priest. Father Reichert was very courageous, knowledgeable, and had practical common sense. He tried to correct all of these problems to everyone's satisfaction. Through his numerous activities for the benefit of the parish and his kindness in his relations with the parishioners, he soon won their hearts and respect and stayed 22 years with his trusted flock. He supervised matters like a prudent commander-in-chief and wherever he found a failing, he would give it special attention. Above all, he brought the financial problems of the parish into an exemplary state and endeavoured to post honest people everywhere. If he saw that someone was abusing his position or conducting it badly, there would be severe reprimands or perhaps worse. On the outside, his situation always appeared exemplary and through his sensible behaviour, his affable nature and energy, he gained the high regard and esteem of the government officials in Odessa. In his time he was one of the most respected and outstanding personalities in Odessa and was often referred to as "Little Bismark."

He paid particular attention to the school. He built an attractive school in Odessa with large class rooms and also prevailed upon the Deanery in Odessa to build more schools. He wrote several textbooks according to the new method to be used in the parish schools and he translated the Deharbe Catechism into Russian to be used in the secondary schools. In order to propagate the new course of instruction, he conducted conferences for the teachers in the years 1882-1885.

In 1888 he built an Alms House to accommodate 50 people, both male and female, at a cost of 26,000 rubles. In 1892, for the first time, he published the almanac entitled "Hausfreund," the first Catholic literary product in the Tiraspol Diocese.

He founded the first Catholic Benevolent Society in Odessa. He also obtained two Catholic cemeteries and had trees planted therein. He started a vacation camp for orphan children located in a nice forested region.

In 1894 he founded a trade school in the villa, owned by the parish, for the orphans and colonists' children so that they might learn different trades. Near this school there was also a house and a chapel for invalid priests. A priest who followed Father Reichert, for some unknown reason, had the school destroyed and as a result the priests' house and chapel became useless.

Father Reichert was instrumental in building the church and rectory in Jelisawetgrad. He also played a large part in introducing the strict Gregorian chant in the parish church of Odessa.

In the last while there was a group of parishioners who tried to hinder his activities and to give him a bad reputation among the higher authorities. Since he had always been a peace-loving man, he could no longer carry on his work under these circumstances. Hence he had himself transferred to Mariupol. But, his spirit broken, he soon became ill and went to Odessa for a rest in a nursing home. He died on the 14 March 1905 after having received the Last Sacraments. He was buried in the churchyard in Odessa. He gave most of his belongings and his voluminous library to the seminary in Saratov.

FATHER JOSEPH WANNER

Father Wanner was born in the colony of Landau in 1845 and ordained on the 15 April 1867. He died on the 8 January 1898 in Preuss. (See transl. of Vol. I, 181).

FATHER JOHANN SCHNELL

Father Johann Schnell was born in Landau in 1847. After completing the course in the Landau parish school, he entered the boys' seminary in Saratov. After completing his studies there, he entered the clerical seminary. He was ordained by Bishop V. Lipsky on the 28 March 1871 and sent as administrator to Marienburg on the Kirghiz Steppes. Soon thereafter, he was sent to Krasna in Bessarabia as administrator where he worked for 11 years as a good faithful shepherd of his entrusted flock.

Even though he had only mediocre talents and read his sermons, his words were profound, providing a wholesome inspiration for penance. He was just as inspiring in the confessional and his Christian teachings. In the schools he tried to provide good instruction to the children about the sacred truths and lead them in the right direction.

In the beginning Father Schnell had many obstacles to overcome. Gradually, as people realised that his motives were only love of duty, they willingly followed his instructions.

In 1882 Father Schnell was made dean of the Bessarabian Deanery. He was a very religious man and even made pilgrimages to Chenstochov in Poland. He died an edifying death in Krasna in 1884 and was buried there.

FATHER RAPHAEL FLECK *(Canon)*

Father Raphael Fleck, born in 1854 in the colony of Landau, was the son of the renowned singer, Joseph Fleck. After completing his studies in the parish school, he went to the colony of Karlsruhe where he received musical instruction from the choir master. In 1868 he entered the seminary in Saratov. After completing his studies there, he was ordained by the late Bishop Franz Zottmann on the 27 February 1877 and was immediately appointed as the Bishops' Chaplain.

When Father Eduard Glas was moved from Saratov, Bishop Zottmann placed young Father Raphael Fleck in charge of the Cathedral and also made him dean of the Saratov Deanery. Shortly thereafter he was made a domestic prelate, assistant judge in the esslesiastical court, religious instructor in the secondary schools in Saratov, and professor of liturgy and singing in the seminary. This was too much for any one man, particularly one of medium talents. Later he also lectured on moral and pastoral theology and, for a time, also taught

Latin in the minor seminary. In 1893 he was appointed rector of the seminary in Saratov where he lectured in hermeneutics, exegetics, moral and pastoral theology. Despite his diligence and strenuous efforts to do justice to all these duties and offices, his intellectual energies floundered. He became mentally ill and was relieved of his duties. During his later years he lived with his sister in Landau.

FATHER KASPAR JAGER

Father Kaspar Jäger was born in Landau on the 18 April 1857 and was ordained on the 27 April 1880. He was pastor in Kleinliebental for 23 years. In 1907 he resigned and on his retirement, returned to Landau. In 1909 he took charge of the small parish of Klosterdorf but, because of his illness, he soon had to give it up. Later he lived in Kleinliebental. In an effort to regain his health he had gone to Wörishofen, Germany on three different occasions. However, the results of his cure were only temporary.

FATHER VALENTIN HARTMANN *Honorary Canon*

Father Valentin Hartmann was born in November 1858 in the colony of Landau. After completing the studies at the parish school there, he entered the boys' seminary in Saratov. After completing the courses there he entered the clerical seminary. On completing his studies, he was ordained on the 10 January 1882 by the late Bishop Franz Zottmann. His first duties as administrator were at Jamburg, near Jekaterinoslav, where he was sent in 1891. Jamburg at this time was one of the biggest parishes in the Tiraspol diocese and it was a heavy assignment for this young, inexperienced priest. Still he had the will and good health to perform all his functions and remained calm throughout these unpleasant circumstances. In 1896 he was sent as the parish priest to Mariupol where he administered both aforementioned deaneries. In 1897 he was made pastor of Odessa and dean of this Deanery. Here he encountered many problems for, after the departure of Father Reichert, the Poles wished to have a Polish priest.

In Odessa he created a lasting memorial when he built the beautiful St. Clemens Church on the Moldowanka. In 1904 he was sent as pastor to Jekaterinoslav and appointed dean of the two deaneries of Jekaterinoslav and Berdjansk. In 1907 he received a golden pectoral cross.

In 1910 he became the rector of the clerical seminary at Saratov and assistant judge of the consistory and domestic prelate at the Cathedral. In 1911 he resigned from all these offices and became the parish priest for the quiet country church of Josephstal, near Odessa, where he carries on his duties until the present time.

FATHER MARKUS MARSAL

Father Markus Marsal was born in Landau in 1848. He was ordained by Bishop Anton Zerr on the 8 December 1885. Father Marsal was quite old when he entered the ministry. First he was a farmer, then a chamberlain for Father Burgardt, and only later did he become a student in the seminary at Saratov. At one time during his course at the seminary he was made the business manager and was praised for his thrift. He was a zealous parish priest in Christina, Rothamel, Sulz, Wolkow, and at the present time is in the parish of Neukolonie.

FATHER FLORIAN SCHULZ

Father Florian Schulz was born in Landau on the 26 May 1873, the son of Jakob Schulz and his wife Katharina, (née Fichter). Until he received first communion, he attended the local parish school and later received additional instruction. He entered the seminary in Saratov in 1888, completed his studies in 1896, and was ordained by His Grace Bishop Anton Zerr on the 8 June 1896. He received his first appointment as Administrator of the parish of Kandel in the Odessa diocese. In 1897 he was sent to Blumenfeld in the parish of Sulz, where he remained until 1 July 1899. From Blumenfeld he was moved to the large parish of Hildman, in the deanery of Kamenka, as Administrator. As a result of overexertion he became fatigued and ill. At the present time he is building a church in the mission of Ilawla.

FATHER MARKUS ZIMMERMANN

Father Markus Zimmermann was born in Landau in 1878 and was ordained in 1902. He was sent to Heidelberg as vicar. He became ill and died on the 27 May 1903.

FATHER ANTON FLECK, DR. PHIL.

Father Anton Fleck was born in Landau in 1874, entered the seminary in Saratov and after completing his assignment, he continued his studies abroad. After receiving his Doctor of Philosophy, he returned to his home and was appointed the Italian Preacher in Odessa. Shortly thereafter he was called to the seminary at Saratov. In 1913 he was made a Prelate. (There is no further information available).

FATHER MICHAEL HILFER, M. PHIL.

Father Michael Hilfer was born on the 4 August 1882 in Felsenburg, the son of Dionysius Hilfer and Maria-Eva (née Haaf). His father died when he was one-and-a-half years old. His mother married Wihelm Böhm, from Katharinental, who also died after four years of marriage.

Young Michael went to live with his Uncle Georg Haaf who took the place of his father. Georg Haaf belonged to those dwindling German colonists who took pride in maintaining order, discipline and modesty in their homes. Young Michael had to abide by these salutary regulations and even now, as a priest, he recalls with gratitude and reverence the happy days he spent in his uncle's home.

When he was six years old he attended the Katharinental parish school at which time there were two capable teachers, Lorenz Reichert and Johannes Schmidt. Father Johannes Schneider, who often visited the school, explained the Christian truths to the beginners in a most popular way.

After completing his studies in the parish school in Katharinental he moved to Landau. Here he found his second step-father Franz Hof, a dear, solicitous father who did everything possible for the boy to further his education. After all difficulties were overcome, he entered the seminary in Saratov in 1894 where he put in six years of interrupted studies. Due to overwork he became ill and had to discontinue his studies for two years while convalescing. He eventually completed his studies at the seminary in 1905 and was ordained on the 26 May 1905 by Bishop Kessler.

In the fall of 1905 he entered the religious Academy in Petersburg, completing his studies in 1909 and receiving the degree of Magister S. Theologiae Primi Ordinis (Master of Theology, first order). In his thesis for his Master's degree he answered the burning question, "What benefit did the Catholic Church obtain from the theological movement represented by the German theologians, Herman Schell, Albert Erhard, Father X. Kraus and others?" While still at the Academy, Father Hilfer had decided that his most important function would be to improve the conditions in the German colonies. For this purpose he had written several articles in the "Klemens" under the pseudonym Franz Waldau. These articles all dealt with vital questions concerning the German Catholics in Russia. As a result, he was unanimously elected editor of the Deutsche Rundschau by the Klemens Society in May 1909. He took over this office on 1 October 1909 and even today this is the only Catholic paper in Russia. Since 1909 he has also been the editor of the reliable Volks-Kalender. He is a member of the board of directors for the Klemens Society and the Catholic Auxiliary Society.

FATHER MARKUS GLASER, DR. THEOL. AND PHIL.

Father M. Glaser was born in Landau on the 25 April 1880, the son of Joseph Glaser and Anna-Maria (née Kunz). He attended the parish school in Landau from 1887 to 1892 where he made good progress under the guidance of teacher, Christian Kunz. Following this he received two years of private instruction from the above-named teacher, preparing himself to enter the seminary in Saratov. After passing the second year examinations for the seminary for boys, he studied very hard and successfully completed his studies in June 1897. In the fall of the same year, he entered the Clerical Seminary. With diligence and perseverance he pursued his studies in Theology and Philosophy for three years. In 1900 he left Russia to continue his studies elsewhere* and in June 1903 he received his Doctor of Philosophy. He was ordained on the 24 June 1905, in Minsk, by Archbishop Count Georg Schembek. He returned to his home in Landau to celebrate his first mass on the 30 June 1905. In the fall of 1907 he left once more to continue his studies.

On the 21 June 1907 he received the degree of Dr. of Theology. He returned home and on the 21 July 1907 he was made Professor of Dogma in the seminary at Saratov. On the 17 August 1907 he became instructor in Apologetics and Latin in the boys' seminary. He was made a domestic prelate on the 18 August 1907 and on the 10 September 1907 he became Inspector of the Tiraspol Seminary. On 12 August 1908 he was made a Canon. From 28 August 1906 until 1 October 1910 he was Vice-Rector at the Seminary. Besides being an Inspector, Professor of Dogmatics and Liturgy, teacher of Latin and French, he was also a member of the "Consilium a Vigilantia." Father Glaser was praised as a capable professor, devoted priest, and a pleasant, affable person.

FATHER RAPHAEL ERHARDT

Father R. Erhardt was born in Felsenburg in 1881. His father had moved from Landau. He entered the seminary in Saratov and, after completing his studies there, was ordained in 1904. He was active in the ministry for several years when he became ill and returned to his home where he still is.

SUBDEACON ROCHUS STEIN

Rochus Stein was born in Landau in 1880. He entered the seminary in Saratov and completed his studies in 1911. He then entered the Catholic Academy in St. Petersburg.

*Lay Persons who were either born in
Landau or worked there*

ANTON DUKART *Physician*

Anton Dukart was born in Hayna, Rheinpfalz in 1767. He studied medicine in his homeland and in 1809, after completing his training, he moved with his family to Russia and settled in Landau as a colonist. He was quite competent and provided unlimited free service

*He studied at the Collegium Germanicum in Rome.

to the poor, sick colonists. As a result he was made physician of the colonies in Landau, Speier, Karlsruhe and Sulz, by the officials. He had a large practise throughout the Beresan as well as among the neighbouring noblemen. Sometimes he would spend the whole day on his pony (making calls). As he did not understand Russian well, he always took Matthias Judt with him as interpreter. On one occasion, while they were in Tatorowka near Sulz, they were set upon and robbed by thieves. Fortunately, the thieves were caught, and Dukart and his interpreter were able to recover their horses and other things. Anton Dukart was a respected, honest man. He died in Landau in 1827. He left behind a widow, who was later married to Joseph Braxmeier of Sulz, and several children whose descendants are still living.

MICHAEL DUKART *Physician*

Michael Dukart was born in Hayna, Rheinpfalz about 1795. I am not able to determine whether he was related to Anton Dukart. If I am not mistaken, Michael Dukart came to Landau as a trained physician in 1821. He apparently received his certificate in Surgery in 1814. He seems to have liked Landau for, on the 6 February 1823, he married Marianna Paul from Landau and settled as a colonist. He did not have any official recognition, but as a renowned physician and surgeon, he covered the entire district and was particularly well known to the noblemen. He received an attestation from Princess Maria Feodorowna Baratinskaja in Anatolowka for having healed various illnesses. In 1830 he received a thank you note from Ternowka for healing cancer. In 1832 he also received a certificate from the administrator of landowner Kirijakow on the Bug, attesting to his skill. After much hard work, grief and charity, which he provided for suffering mankind through his ability, he died in Landau in 1845 (?), the death of the righteous.

JOHANN DUKART *Pharmacist and Army Surgeon*

Johann Dukart, son of the physician Michael Dukart and Marianna (née Paul), was born in Landau on the 14 May 1829. He attended the parish school in Landau and was one of the most capable and industrious students of the famous teacher, Kaspar Jäger Sr., from whom he received a certificate of merit on completion of his schooling.

On the instruction of the Fürsorge Committee, when he was old enough, he was sent as an apprentice to the chemist shop of Assistant Chemist Krull in Kherson. Here he wrote his examinations as Druggist's Assistant in 1847. He received a certificate of merit and was sent to the hospital in Odessa to start his training as an Army Surgeon. While in the hospital, he was assigned to various departments. He proved himself skillful, diligent, capable and faithful. After he had gained sufficient theoretical and practical knowledge, he returned to his home in Landau where he worked as a "doctor" for many years, tending to the needs of his sick countrymen in the Beresan. During the war he was very busy with the military which was stationed in the Beresan for a long time. He received considerable recognition from the authorities for this service. He also received various other commendations and tokens of distinction.

Because of his perseverance in the distribution of smallpox vaccination, he was honored with the silver medal on the 4 September 1856. On the 5 November 1879 he was awarded the insignia of the Red Cross. He also did a great deal for the German colonists of the Beresan. Whenever a Russian official arrived and made some illegal request from the district office, he was referred to the "doctor" who understood Russian well and spoke it fluently. He would persuade the gentlemen that the colonists were not obliged to carry out their request.

Johann Dukart was also an exemplary Christian father, strict in his daily routine and with the education of his children. In addition to his practice of medicine, he also farmed and raised cattle through which he became very wealthy. He was one of the first in the Beresan to buy an estate, on which his sons are still settled.

He died serving the suffering of mankind and left behind numerous descendants.

JOHANNES DUKART *Physician M.D.*

Johannes Dukart was born in the Beresan on his father's estate (Jakob Dukart) on the 28 November 1883. He spent his childhood with his parents and also received his first schooling at this time. In his twelfth year, he was placed in a boarding school in Nikolayev, by his parents, in preparation to attend secondary school. In 1896 he entered the secondary school in Nikolayev and completed it successfully in 1904, receiving his graduation certificate. After due consideration, he resolved to faithfully follow in the tradition of his family and study pharmaceutics. For this purpose he left Russia for the lovely Munich where his request for permission to enter the university was granted and he matriculated in the faculty of Medicine.

In 1909, after five years of diligent study, he wrote his inaugural thesis for his Doctorate in General medicine and presented it to the Faculty of medicine of the Royal Bavarian Ludwig-Maximilian University in Munich.

In 1910, after having had his treatise accepted and having passed the oral examinations, he received his Doctorate in Internal Medicine, Surgery, Obstetrics and Gynecology. After all these examinations, the much troubled young man had to write the Russian State Examinations for which he had to prepare himself. Since he had a good command of the Russian language and was quite intelligent, he was able to obtain the Russian Certificate in three months through the University at Charkov.

After this examination he again left Russia in an effort to perfect his training. He also became greatly interested in the modern, widely known methods of nature cures.

For this purpose he visited many such sanatoria and stayed for a long time in Worishofen, near Munich, where he studied and practiced the method of Father Kneipp's* hydrotherapy.

Since 1912 he has been active in Nikolayev as a naturopath and Kneipp therapist. May Dr. Dukart continue to heal the sick and relieve pain, just as his ancestors have done in the Beresan for a century.

GEORG EHRMANTRAUT *School Teacher*

Georg Ehrmantraut (formerly Trautmann), was born in the village of Winzenbach, Alsace to Lutheran parents whose family name was Trautmann. After completing his studies in a teachers' Seminary, he was appointed to his native village as teacher and sexton. Since Winzenbach was a community of both Lutherans and Catholics, with a communal church, Trautmann was the sexton for both churches.

It happened that on the occasion of an important feast day the Catholic community invited a famous singer by the name of Barbara Flick from Jockgrim in the Palatinate. The young sexton became acquainted with this lovely singer, fell in love with her and proposed marriage. After she had accepted the proposal, Georg Trautmann asked for his father's consent. The elder Trautmann turned a deaf ear and threatened to disinherit his son if he did not leave this "little flop-headed"** girl. It was the time when the emigration to Russia was under way. Since all requests to the old man were of no avail, the young Trautmann decided to migrate. He went to his father and said, "Good, if you wish to disinherit me, I shall no longer bear your name. I will change my name, become a Catholic, and after marrying the girl, I will migrate to Russia." This is what he did. He reported to a Russian agent, enrolled under the name of "Ehrmantraut," became a Catholic, and married Barbara Flick. He moved to Russia with other immigrants, settled as a colonist in Landau, and was their first school teacher.

---

*Sebastian Kneipp (1821-1897) parish priest in Worishofen was one of the pioneers of cold water therapy (Kneipp-Kuren).

**"Kreuzköpfin"—(flop-head) a nickname used by Lutherans to disparage Catholics.

Later, he was alternately community secretary and school teacher in Landau where he died in the thirties (1830-39). He left a widow with several children. One branch of the family later moved to the colony of Rastadt. Later, his Lutheran brothers (Trautmann) also came to Russia and settled in the colony of Worms.

KASPAR JÄGER SR. *School Teacher*

Kaspar Jäger was born in Bergzabern in the Palatinate, son of Peter-Joseph Jäger, a nail-smith, and his wife Margaretha, whose maiden name was Hoffmann. The ancestors of the Jäger family came from the village of Barbelrot, which was about a two hours drive from Bergzabern. The Jäger family is still settled there today.

After completing his studies there, he received his teacher's diploma. At this time the migration to Russia was at its peak. Peter Jäger and his family decided to migrate to the promised land of Russia.

They made the journey to Russia in 1805, arriving at the Russian border city of Radzivilov in the late fall. They stayed there for the winter, and in the spring of 1806 they arrived at Odessa where they stayed with some German colonists not far from this city. The young teacher, Kaspar Jäger, instructed the children of the colonists living there, until 1809, when the Beresan colonies were settled. He then moved to the newly formed colony of Landau along with his parents. From 1811 to 1813 Kaspar Jäger was the village secretary. Later he became teacher and sexton, which position he held for many years.

The school teachers appointed in the other colonies were mostly uneducated. Consequently, since they had no professional education, Teacher Jäger had to go to the other colonies with the priest to help instruct those receiving first communion. It was at this time that the Jesuits were expelled from the colonies and, as a result, instruction in the schools and catechism classes were neglected. Jäger always had good order and discipline in the school. He also worked hard in teaching the children to sing will so that they could sing along in church during Mass.

The feast of Thomas Aquinas was particularly solemn as he was the patron of the young school children. On this particular day all of the children gathered in the school, dressed in their Sunday clothes, the girls mostly in white. Here the teacher would address the children, telling them of the virtues of St. Thomas and asking his dear children to try to imitate him. Then they would all get in line, the teacher would start to sing a hymn and the procession would proceed on to the church. When they arrived there they would be met by the priest who gave them a warm address. This would be followed by solemn high Mass in which only the teacher and the school children were permitted to sing.

In 1827 the load of the two offices of teacher and sexton became too heavy. Therefore Christian Fleck, who was formerly a pupil of Jägers, was appointed sexton for the Landau community with the consent of the priest. Teacher Jäger worked as a diligent, indefatigable servant for his master in the school and aided in moulding two generations of worthy citizens and good Christians.

In 1842, because of the intrigue stirred up by malevolent people, he resigned his position as teacher in Landau and moved to Nikolayev. Here he was employed as teacher and sexton in the Catholic parish school for 5 years. He was very industrious in the school and endeavoured to keep good order in every assignment and to prepare good church singing.

The people of Landau soon realized that without the elder Jäger nothing seemed to prosper. Consequently, they sent a deputation to Nikolayev in an effort to bring their "dear old school-master" back home. Since the old man did not like the Polish environment, and was often homesick, the deputies found the assignment relatively easy.

Now he worked in the old home in the same manner but lacking the force and energy. Also, the people were not the same as they had been previously. The good old German customs were gradually disappearing from family and community. The youth was rude and impudent. There was discord in the families and in the community.

This period started after the death of the god-fearing priest Father Erasmus Borowsky in 1848. He was followed by the avaricious Father Woitkewicz and the thoughtless Father Pietkewicz who set a poor example and thereby did much harm. Teacher Jäger realized that changes were occurring in his homeland which did not please him. In 1857 he turned his position over to his son, Anton, and took over the position of teacher and community secretary in the colony of Karlsruhe. He carried on his duties diligently and faithfully for three years. This was his last assignment.

He died on the 3 March 1860, the death of the righteous. On the 4 of March his body was taken from Karlsruhe to Landau in a large procession. An immense crowd of people attended his funeral on the 6 March when he was laid to rest in the Landau church yard. A large marble cross, appropriately inscribed, marks his grave.

Kaspar Jäger Sr. was one of the most prominent citizens during the early development of the Beresan district and the best qualified to spread culture in the German colonies in South Russia. During the years 1810 to 1860 he influenced the youth, not only in Landau but also in the other colonies, as he educated many of their capable teachers. Many of the noblemen in the surrounding areas also brought their children to him for instruction.

He received many attestations from various priests for his services to the common welfare. Even the higher government officials recognized his service and paid their respect. In July 1853 he received a certificate of Honorable Commendation from the Minister of Imperial Domains "for forty-five years of untiring zeal in the service of the community schools." Kaspar Jäger was survived by six sons and six daughters.

KASPAR JÄGER JR. *Teacher and Organist*

Kaspar Jäger was born in Landau on the 27 October 1837, the son of Kaspar Jäger, the teacher, and his wife Katharina, née Wanner. He received his first instructions in his home, later in the parish school under the guidance of his father.

He was a quiet, modest boy, and even in his youth he cherished the hope to become a school teacher in the colony. His wish was granted when his father moved to Karlsruhe as a teacher and secretary in 1857. Here the opportunity presented itself to learn the duties and tasks of a teacher and also practice them.

When his father died in 1860 he had to step in and take over the situation. He fulfilled the requirements with diligence and punctuality to everyone's satisfaction. After he had worked in Karlsruhe for three years, he moved to Katharinental as teacher and organist. He worked here successfully for eleven years. At his urging, a twelve-piece band was organized in which Jäger played the cello. In 1874 he moved to Steinberg where he worked for nine years as teacher, sexton and secretary, showing the same energy, prudence and diligence as previously. In 1882 he was called to Nikolayev as teacher and organist where he has been continually for fifteen years.

In Nikolayev he was town councillor and a member of the Society for the Prevention of Cruelty to Animals. In 1894 he went abroad to visit the home of his father in Bergzabern where he found many third and fourth cousins still living. In 1897 he moved to the small colony of Antonowka where he continued the art of teaching the young for ten years. After having worked efficiently and indefatigably for 50 years, he retired in 1907. Ten of his students became priests and many others became important personages. Kaspar Jäger also wrote the hymn book "Alleluja" and the score to it. Presently, he lives in Nikolayev where he bought himself a house.

ANTON JÄGER *School Teacher and Sexton*

Anton Jäger was born in Landau in 1832, the son of the teacher, Kaspar Jäger, and Katharina Wanner. He received his education from his father and was very capable and industrious. In 1852, when still a young man, he was able to accept the appointment of School Teacher in Sulz. He was a hard working teacher and a very amiable person so that, even today, his former pupils remember him with love and respect.

In 1857 he left Sulz to accept the appointment of teacher in Landau, the position previously held by his father. He worked for several years and died, if I am not mistaken, in 1862 in Landau, the place of his birth.

JOSEPH JÄGER *School Teacher*

Joseph Jäger was born in Landau in 1835, the son of the teacher, Kaspar Jäger, and Katharina Wanner. He received his education from his parents and from the Landau parish school. After the death of his brother, Anton Jäger, he took over the position of school teacher in Landau and administered it prudently and zealously.

In 1899 many of the people of the Beresan district bought land near Voronezh. He also moved there and acquired an estate of 624 dessiatines. He lived there for several years in peaceful seclusion and died a few years ago.

MARKUS JÄGER *Teacher and Secretary*

Markus Jäger was born in Sulz in 1856. He was the son of Anton Jäger who was teaching school at that time. He prepared himself well at home and was able to enter the seminary in Saratov. After completing five years in the seminary he left to take a teaching position in Göttland where he remained for many years.

JOHANNES JÄGER *Teacher*

Johannes Jäger was born in Göttland in 1889, the son of the teacher, Markus Jäger, and Elisabeth Gromut. He spent part of his youth in Göttland and part in Landau. He received his training as a teacher from his father. In 1908 he wrote the examinations for Community Teacher in the Teacher's Seminary in Kherson. Since 1 March (1908) he has been the teacher, sexton and secretary in Sebastianfeld.

There were several other brothers who were also school teachers, but no information is available on them.

CHRISTIAN FLECK *Sexton*

Christian Fleck was born in the village of Wingen, in Alsace, the son of Johannes Fleck and Margaretha Schlick. In 1809 he came to Russia with his mother. She was a widow and also a renowned singer. The whole family settled in Landau.

He had a fair education and was a good singer. With this background he gained permission from the priests in 1827 to be the sexton for all of the Beresan colonies under the Landau jurisdiction.

It was his duty to accompany the priests when they held services in the other colonies or if there were other priestly functions to attend to. Christian Fleck was a good, Christian man. He died of old age while living with his son, Kasimir.

CHRISTIAN FLECK *Teacher and Secretary*

Christian Fleck, the son of Christian Fleck and Maria-Elisabeth Heidt, was born on the 22 December 1822. He received his education from old Kaspar Jäger and Anton Riedinger in the district chancellery office.

At the beginning he was a teacher's helper, then the community secretary in Landau which office he fulfilled for many years to the satisfaction of the whole community. He was a capable fellow, he knew the law well and was an excellent singer. After turning the office of secretary over to someone else, he opened a business in Landau through which he became very wealthy. He died an old man in his home in Landau.

MATTHIAS FLECK *School Teacher and Sexton*

Matthias Fleck was born in Landau on the 26 April 1822. He was the son of Christian Fleck and Maria-Elisabeth Heidt. He was a student of the senior Jäger who trained him to be a capable teacher. While still single, he took over the position of school teacher in the colony of Speier. He married Marianna Geiger in 1840 and settled as a colonist in Speier. He performed his duty well and punctually for many years and died at an old age in Speier. He was a quiet, good, Christian man and an excellent singer.

JOSEPH FLECK *a Famous Singer*

Joseph Fleck, the son of Christian Fleck and Maria-Elisabeth Heidt, was born on the 13 March 1827. He received his training in the parish school. He learned quickly and after completing his studies there, he apprenticed with a master smith. After completing his training, already married, he opened his own business which he operated for many years and through which he became quite wealthy. He was one of the first people in the Beresan to own his own land. He was capable, amiable fellow and a wonderful singer with truly the voice of an angel.

KASIMIR-PETER FLECK *Sexton*

Kasimir-Peter Fleck, the son of Christian Fleck and Maria-Elisabeth Heidt, was born in Landau in 1830. He attended the parish school in his home colony and received instruction in singing from his father. When his father became too old and feeble to continue in the office of sexton, the young Kasimir was entrusted with the position. He carried on in this position for many years, to the satisfaction of the whole community and also the priests of Landau. He was a capable fellow, was well read, could speak standard German well, and knew how to tell a story. He played the clarinet well and often played at weddings with the Zimmermann brothers. The favourite German folk songs would then be sung accompanied by music. He had a fine, full baritone voice which harmonized very well with the voices of his brothers, Christian, Joseph and Matthias. These four brothers were renowned singers throughout the district. Anyone in Landau who listened to the Christmas matins and hymns, or to the Passion during Holy Week, or the funeral hymns, would remember them for the rest of his life.

JOHANN FLECK *Teacher*

Johann Fleck was born in Landau in 1835(?). He attended the parish school and, on finishing his studies there, went to Karlsruhe to study music. From there he went to the Catholic seminary in Saratov. After completing his preliminary courses, he left the Seminary and accepted a teaching position. Later he lived in Schönfeld, near Nilolayev, where he operated a farm. From Schönfeld he came to America and died soon after.

MICHAEL RIEDINGER *Organist*

Michael Riedinger, son of Anton, was born in Landau in 1848. He was a good student and finished his training in the parish school. Because he seemed to be a promising student, his father sent him to the ecclesiastical seminary in Saratov. In the seminary he proved himself capable in music and singing. He received special instruction in this department and soon became so advanced as to give his own concerts. These concerts drew large crowds and all were astonished at the virtuosity of this young artist. He left the seminary in 1871 to settle in Landau as a music teacher and later moved to Nikolayev. He became the choir director in the Catholic Church there and had a strong influence on the Catholic music of that time. Unfortunately, the young artist was stricken by a malignant disease and died soon thereafter. He died in Odessa in 1883(?).

He composed some very excellent masses. He married a Russian girl and they had one son. His son, Woldemar, is the station-master at Snamenka. His brother, Sebastian Riedinger, also spent some years in the seminary after which he became a soldier and married a rich Polish girl. Now he is said to be a rich land owner.

JOSEPH ZIMMERMANN *Sexton*

Joseph Zimmermann, the son of Peter Zimmermann and Agatha Frölich, was born in Landau on the 28 January 1878. He completed his studies at the parish school with a very good record and then went to study in Karlsruhe with the famous organist, Edmund

Schmidt. Later he spent some time with the musicians, Johann Stein-gass, Johann Pultmann and Sebastian Seelinger, in Rastadt.

In 1899 he had to enlist in the Army. In 1900 he moved to China with the Fusilier Battalion, Number 15, Fourth Brigade as there was a revolution there at that time. For this expedition he received a silver medal. In 1901 he enrolled as a flute player in the orchestra of the above-named battalion. In the autumn of 1903 he played dinner music in the presence of the Czar and his family while they were staying at Livadia in the Crimea. He was discharged from the Army in 1903 and took on the position of sexton in Blumenfeld. In 1904 he went to Japan with the Territorial Reserve and enrolled in the band of the Second Reserve Battalion. Because of his zealous service he was made a non-commissioned officer in 1905 and allowed to go on furlough. In 1906 he was a private tutor on the estate of Tscheweniewka. From 1906 to 1911 he was organist in Speier, and from 1911 to 1912 he was organist in München. Since 1913 he has been private tutor in the boarding school of Father Z. Reichert in Landau.

ROCHUS BÖHM *Organist and Teacher*

Rochus Böhm, the son of Franz Böhm and Elisabeth Weisgerber, was born on the 3 September 1869 in New-Landau. He went to Sulz in 1882 to study music under the guidance of Erasmus Tremmel. In 1884 he went to Speier to continue his studies under Sebastian See-linger and the next year returned for the same purpose. From 1886 to 1887 he visited classical teacher, Derewitzsky, in his private school in Landau. From 1890 to 1893 he was in the army. From 1894 to 1897 he was the organist in Sulz. On several occasions he and his choir were invited elsewhere. From 1897 to 1900 he was the organist in Landau. In 1900 Father Rudolf Reichert invited him to Mariupol as organist. In the fall of 1901 he took the position of organist and religious instructor in Strassburg. From 1902 to 1908 he was first the German teacher, then organist and religious instructor in Mann-heim. From 1908 to 1913 he was organist and teacher in Baden and Kleinliebental, and now is the organist and teacher in Schönfeld.

RAPHAEL STEIN *Organist and Teacher*

Raphael Stein was born on the 18 May 1886, in Felsenburg, in the parish of Christina where his parents, Franz Stein and Rosa Fleck, had emigrated from Landau. On the recommendation of Father N. Kraft, the boy was sent to the clerical seminary in Saratov by his parents, where he studied music and singing in addition to his other subjects. The organist at the Cathedral at that time, W. Sur-zinsky, was also the singing teacher in the seminary and he soon detected the musical talent of the young boy. He took him under his guidance and advised him to apply himself to music. Unfortunately, he soon became ill and had to leave the seminary. He returned home where he prepared himself for the elementary teacher's examinations which he successfully passed in 1905. He was posted as teacher to Halbstadt by the district school inspector where he also fulfilled the duties of sexton and secretary. In a year he moved to Baden as organist and teacher and there he married Rosa Tremmel, daughter of Erasmus from Sulz. After two years, he moved to Mannheim as teacher and organist where he remained for one year. From Mannheim, he was invited to the classical secondary school in Karlsruhe to singing and music. In order to learn more about music he went abroad. In Freiburg, Switzerland he attended the Gregorian Academy and Conservatory and took private instruction from Dr. Peter Wagner, the director of Vatican chorale, harmonics and counterpoint.

After the final examinations he received two certificates, one from the academy regarding church music, and one from the conservatory for playing the organ. After returning home he stayed one year in the secondary classical school in Karlsruhe. After this he went to Sulz as teacher and organist where he still is today. In Sulz he organized a choir which was famous throughout the entire neighbourhood for its religious songs. He produced 30 compositions, most of them pertaining to church music. Among his more notable works are two compositions for Mass: 1) St. Michael's Mass — 4 voices in harmony, and 2) Mass in honor of St. Raphael, the Archangel — 4 voices with organ accompaniment. There were also the four Marian closing hymns, "Ave Regina Coelorum," and "Salve Regina," with four voices in harmony. The remaining were small pieces such as marches, "to celebrate the 19th February as the deliverance from serfdom in Russia on the 50 year jubliee celebration," and also a waltz, "Memory Waltz."

JAKOB DAUENHAUER *Benefactor*

Jakob Dauenhaurer, son of Georg Dauenhauer and Margaretha Frölich, was born in Landau in 1830. He was a good scholar and finished his studies in the local parish school after which he spent his youth in quiet seclusion. He married Marianna Böhm from Katharinental. Since it was becoming too crowded in Landau, and in fact, the whole of the Beresan, many young colonists and their families moved to rented land. Jakob Dauenhauer moved from Landau to an area behind Nikolayev where, along with some other people from the Beresan, he rented some land cheaply. Through hard work and thrift he was able to save money and was soon able to buy his own land. He became quite rich, owning approximately 9000 dessiatines of land. Riches and good luck did not change him. He remained plain, good, honest, and generous.

Near Heikowka, where his land was located, there were many Catholics living on rented land and some on their own estates, but the closest priest was quite some distance. Consequently, they could not always receive the Last Sacraments in times of illness. For this reason, Jakob Dauenhauer built a church at his own expense and obtained a priest for it. The church and rectory cost 30,000 rubles. He also gave the church a gift of 200 dessiatines and paid for the publication of the hymnal. The church was built in 1898 and was consecrated by His Grace Bishop Joseph Kessler on the 3 May 1907.

Father Ignatius Dowblis was appointed the first priest on the 30 January 1901. The generous, devout man saw his work successfully crowned. The good Lord will repay him.

MICHAEL STOLZ *Organist and Pharmacist*

Michael Stolz was born in Landau in 1873. He entered the clerical seminary in Saratov on the 26 August 1886 and completed the minor seminary in 1891. Because of illness, he left the seminary and devoted himself to music during his convalescence. From 1893 to 1897 he was organist in Landau and from 1897 to 1900 he was a teacher, secretary and organist in Steinberg. In 1900 he took the position as organist and religious instructor in Landau, where he remained for 6 years. Then, for 6 months, he was the bookkeeper for the Landau Cooperative Society. Meanwhile, he bought the drugstore in Landau and in 1911 he obtained his diploma as a dispenser apprentice. Eventually he obtained his pharmacist's diploma and, in addition, was the bookkeeper for the agricultural warehouse of the Odessa district.

VALENTIN WALTER *Pharmacist*

Valentin Walter, son of Stephan, was born in Landau in 1877. He entered the seminary in Saratov where he completed the course of instruction in the minor seminary and also three courses in the clerical seminary. Following this he entered a drug store in Petrowsk in the Caucasus. After serving his apprenticeship, he went to the University of Jurjew (Dorpat) where, after some diligent studying, he obtained his diploma as a druggist's assistant and obtained a position in a drug store in Moscow.

JOSEPH SCHNELL *Engineer*

Joseph Schnell was born in Landau in 1869, the son of Christian Schnell and Marianna Fischer. After completing his studies in the local school he attended a technical school in Kherson. After successfully completing his studies there, he entered a Polytechnical School in Braunschweig, Germany and graduated as a chemical engineer. Now he is director of a sugar refinery in Switzerland.

VALENTIN KARY *Officer*

Valentin Kary was born in Landau on the 13 January 1863. After completing his studies at the local parish school, he received some private instruction in order to prepare himself for entry into the military academy. He passed the examinations and was posted to the Odessa Officer Training School, completing his training in 1885 as a Cadet. As a non-commissioned officer, he went to Kiev where he received free tuition in the university. In 1887, because of a suspicion that he belonged to a secret society, he was discharged. He then went to Nikolayev where he spent several years studying languages.

Subsequently, he became married, and after his father-in-law vouched for him, he was again able to enlist. Presently he holds a very important position in the commissariat in the military district of Kiev.

JOHANNES WEISSGERBER *Officer*

Johannes Weissgerber was born in Nikolayev on the 13 January 1858. He was the son of Philipp Weissgerber, a colonist of Landau. He received private instructions after which he entered the Officer's Training School in Odessa. After completing his studies, he was posted to the Reserve Battalion with the rank of Cadet. In 1880 he was made a Lieutenant and in 1883 he became a member of the Provost Battalion. There is nothing more known about him.

PETER HEIM *Teacher*

Peter Heim, son of Peter, was born in the colony of Preuss (Krasnopolje) in the province of Samara on the 16 October 1868. He received his training in the seminary at Saratov. He completed the two courses of the clerical seminary and took over the teaching position in the community of Rosenweit in the province of Jekaterinoslav. After one-and-a-half years, he was offered a much more important appointment in the colony of Alexanderheim in the parish of Kostheim, where he remained for 5 years as a teacher, sexton and secretary. in 1894 he applied for and obtained the position of teacher in Leitershausen, where he remained for 13 years and 5 months. In 1907 he left the Molotschna and settled in the Beresan as German teacher in the Central School in Landau and also in the four-class girls' school.

Peter Heim was an excellent teacher and held diplomas both as a private tutor and elementary school teacher. He received the Silver Medal on the Waldimir Sash from the school authorities for his zeal in promoting elementary education in the district. He also received the small Bronze Medal with ribbon in national colors for his contribution to the census of 1897.

Peter Heim was an industrious, capable teacher and a pleasant, kind man.

JOSEPH SCHINDLER *Teacher*

Joseph Schindler was born in the Heidelberg colony on the Molotschna on the 18 August 1883. After completing his studies in the local elementary school he entered the Prischib Central School, completing his studies there in four years. After writing his examinations as a public school teacher, he accepted a position in Leitershausen where he remained until 1906. From 1906 to 1908 he was the German teacher in the secondary school of Father Scherr in Karlsruhe on the Beresan. Since 1908 he has been the teacher of German and also singing in the girls' school in Landau. J. Schindler was a diligent, industrious teacher and a quiet, devout man.

I wish to name the following, who did not submit any particulars about themselves:

Christian Kunz, teacher; Raphael Koch, teacher; Michael Deck, teacher, Sigismund Böhm, teacher, Johann Böhm, organist; Johann Stolz, organist; Sebastian Gratz, secretary; Anton Gratz, secretary; Michael Reichert, secretary, Alfons Stein, book-keeper, son of Johann; Markus Jäger, teacher, son of Markus; Kaspar Jäger, teacher, son of Markus; Anton Jäger, son of Markus.

The Celebration of
the One Hundredth Anniversary
of the Beresan Colonies
in the colony of Landau
30 September 1910

The 30 September 1910 was a glorious, memorable day for the colonists of the Beresan and it is therefore not possible to overlook this occasion when writing about these colonies. On this day all of the clergy of the Beresan district united in an effort to have their parishioners return to the Mother Colony of Landau, to celebrate a solemn public worship, to thank God for his mercy and favours bestowed upon their fore-fathers, and also themselves, through His infinite kindness and compassion, during the past one hundred years.

The Beresan colonists immediately perceived this as a day to declare their gratitude and loyalty to the Imperial Ruler and to the Russian fatherland, and to express their devotion in the presence of the distinguished representatives of the government.

The following were invited to the jubilee festivities: Bantysch, the Governor of Kherson; N. F. Suchomlinow, titled marshal and court official of the province of Kherson; M. A. Reno, the district Grand marshal; L. G. Lutz, member of the Duma; Bely, director of public schools; Schenwesky, inspector of public schools; Prelate Tschernjachowitsch, chief Mayor of Liebental and the Kütschurgan districts, any many other important personages. The priests present were:

Father Strömel of Rastadt; Father Hein of München; Father Pauer of Katharinental; Father Beilmann of Karlsruhe; Father Scherr of Karlsruhe; Father Eberle of Schönfeld; Father Desch of Christina; Father Butsch of Elisabethgrad; Father Schneider of Blumenfeld; Father Hatzenböller of Sulz; Father M. Fix of Franzfeld; Father Frank Loran of Kleinleibental; Father Böchler of Strassburg; Father Johann Zimmerman, Father K. Keller, and the two pastors (Lutheran) from Worms and Rohrbach.

On the morning of the great celebration all the Beresan people were dressed in their best clothes, the streets were clean and the homes were decorated with the national flag. Across the streets were triumphal arches and the school children stood in their holiday clothes with gaily coloured little flags in their hands to greet the above-named distinguished visitors. The Governor was delayed for some unknown reason, delaying the start of the divine service until eleven-thirty. The High Mass was celebrated by Father Strömel, while Fathers Butsch and Desch acted as the Levites. The festive sermon was preached by Father Hilfer.

The singing and music during the Mass was excellent. Especially inspiring was the rendition of "Holy Lord, We Praise Thy Name," which was sung by all the people and accompanied by the orchestra at the close of the Mass.

After Mass, all of the Beresan people and their guests went to the Central School where the banquet had been prepared. The table in the large school hall had been set for over 400 people. Across from the entrance, the beautiful portraits of the Czar and the Czarina appeared in full splendor, embellished by the inscription, "God bless the Czar!"

After the guests had taken their places and eaten a cold lunch, the member of the Imperial Duma (parliament), L. G. Lutz, got up and with considerable pathos, made a long patriotic speech which received much applause. It closed with the enthusiastic singing of the National Anthem. After the National Anthem had been sung a second time, Mr. Lutz composed a most humble telegram to be sent to His Majesty, the most serene Lord and Emperor. The telegram was sent in Russian, of which the following is a literal translation:

"To the Minister of the Interior;

I humbly request your Excellency to lay before the throne of His Majesty, this message of loyalty and faithfulness of his subjects.

"Your Imperial Majesty;

We Germans in South Russia have gathered to celebrate the One Hundred Years Anniversary of having settled here. Filled with profound devotion to our Russian fatherland, we pray that Almighty God may preserve your Majesty's health for many years to come. Your most humble subjects pray that our Lord and Emperor may graciously believe that we are prepared always and everywhere to protect your throne with our lives, and regard it as a sacred duty to be grateful to our dearly beloved Emperor and our great Fatherland."

L. G. LUTZ, Member of the Duma, on behalf of the assembled people.

In October 1910 the Minister informed the Magistrate of the city of Odessa that His Majesty was pleased with the telegram on which he had appended, "I read your telegram with pleasure. I express my thanks."

After the telegram was composed, court official, N. F. Suchomlinow, gave a short but moving speech in which he said, "I know the German people in South Russia, and after having them for neighbours for many years, I can say that they have always done their duty as loyal subjects. I do not believe that they could be unfaithful to the Fatherland or to the Czar." An enthusiastic "Hurrah" and the singing of the national anthem was the response to the warm address of the distinguished gentleman.

After this speech the banquet began and, with the first glass of champagne, Mr. Suchomlinow again arose and proposed the first toast to His Majesty, the Czar, and the whole Czar household. As a reply to the toast the entire gathering once more sang the national anthem.

Following this, Mr. L. Reichert gave a substantial historical talk in Russian. Prelate and Dean Tschernjachowitsch spoke in Russian on the achievements of the Beresan clergy in the field of public education.

Then Pastor Adt from Worms delivered a brilliant address in which he expressed feelings of warm commendation and brotherly spirit on behalf of the Protestant communities in the Beresan. The festivities were closed by a long, impressive speech given in German by Father J. Scherr. He told the story of the first migrants to come to the Beresan district and reviewed the many graces and favours which the good Lord had bestowed upon them in the course of one hundred years. In popular and convincing fashion, he described the care and concern of the Russian Government to enable the small, helpless group of German farmers and tradesmen to become the bearers of civilization to the vast and mightly land of Russia.

After the festivities, telegrams bearing good wishes were read from: Governor Bantysch (who came after the banquet); from his Grace J. Kessler, Bishop of Tiraspol; from I. Anischewski, district representative; from Fathers M. Glaser and A. Fleck, professors at the seminary at Saratov; from J. Gerhardt, captain of the Odessa command.

There were also telegrams from the Catholic parishes of Germany from whence the colonists came, namely; the parishes of Landau in the Rhinepalatinate; Speier (Rhinepalatinate), München (Bavaria); Rastadt (Baden); Karlsruhe (Baden). These were read by Father Hilfer, and all expressed congratulations to the people of the Beresan district.

At the celebration the decision was made to donate 6,175 rubles, contributed by the three German districts of Liebental, Kutschurgan and Beresan, towards the construction of the Romanov Memorial at Kostroma.

On the completion of the Jubilee celebration, a committee determined that the money left over from the celebration would be awarded as a prize for the writing of the history of the German Colonists in the Beresan. The judges elected were Father Scherr, Father Hilfer and L. Reichert, who bestowed the price on the author of this book. The Beresan Jubilee Celebration will remain a delightful, unforgettable memorial to all who had taken part.

The material Wealth and General Conditions of the Landau Colony

The colony of Landau is situated on both sides of the Beresan in a north-south direction. There is a main street and several parallel and cross streets. Since its settlement, it has been the main village of the Beresan colonies. At the present time there are 245 homes and 2457 people, 1 Catholic church, 1 Russian church, 2 Catholic parish schools, 1 Russian church school, 1 central school, 1 girls' Junior High School, 1 hospital, 1 Old Folks Home, 1 drugstore, 1 orphan's bank, 2 doctors, 1 veterinarian, 1 postoffice and telegraph station, 1 superintendent, 1 justice of the peace and 1 lawyer.

The community land of the Landau colony contains 9228 dessiatines; privately owned both near and far from the colony there are about 65,000 dessiatines. The community land is divided as follows: in the house-yards there are 200 dessiatines, vegetable garden 51 dessiatines, vineyards — amount not known, ponds made by dams 10 dessiatines, stone-quarries 3 dessiatines, clay pits 2 dessiatines, cultivated land 6131 dessiatines, roads 30 dessiatines.

Good land for cultivation rented at 12 to 20 rubles per dessiatine, hay fields at 10 to 15 rubles. For pasture land, each proprietor paid as follows: for cattle over 1 year of age, 1 ruble 75 kopecks per head; for cattle under 1 year there were no charges. The horse herder received 1 ruble per animal, the cow herder received 18 kopecks and the calf herder received 30 kopecks. There were 12 community bulls. The number of cattle in the community was not recorded.

In Landau there were 3 families who owned more than 120 dessiatines and 9 families who owned 60 dessiatines each. Sixteen families owned more than 30 dessiatines each, 77 families owned 30 dessiatines, and 32 families owned 20 dessiatines, 40 families owned somewhat more than 8 dessiatines, 11 owned 7 dessiatines, 12 families had less than 7 dessiatines. There were 292 land owners; 60 farmers owned only a house-and-yard lot. There were 238 people completely without land.

Besides these, there were approximately 800 families who had left Landau and moved elsewhere.

There were approximately 100 Russian hired men and women in the colony, about 10 Jewish families and one gypsy kinship whose ancestor was Gypsy Wanka.

In Landau there were 2 steam-driven flour mills, 3 blacksmiths, 3 carpenters, 1 baker, 3 potters, 3 tailors (Jews), 1 shoemaker (Gypsy), 1 butcher, 1 horse dealer, 1 bake shop, 1 co-operative store, 1 wine cellar, 6 booths, 1 tavern, 1 warehouse for farm equipment and 1 inn.

There were 2 markets in Landau from which the community received 835 rubles revenue annually.

The freight charges to Nikolayev, where the colonists sent their products, were 8 to 12 kopecks per pud.

The community paid the following taxes; Crown taxes 676 rubles, 72 kopecks; land purchase payments 1943 rubles, 48 kopecks; land estate taxes 2880 rubles, 93 kopecks; community taxes 9542 rubles, 92 kopecks.

The Colony of Speier

The colony of Speier is located in the province of Kherson. 106 versts from the capital of Odessa and 4 versts from the border of the Landau district. The colony is located on both sides of the Beresan River, approximately 8 versts from its origin. To the north of the colony there are two valleys, one the Forest Valley, and the other, the Stuttgart Valley of the Beresan district; this is apparently where the river originates.

The main street of the colony is on the left side of the river and runs in a north-south direction, approximately 3 versts long. In the upper end of the colony, on the right side of the river, there is an estate named Worovka. Hill Street starts here; it is 1 1/2 verst long, ending at the racing hollow. Steleritszky Street, starting at the racing hollow, has mostly small houses inhabited by landless cotters. In the lower colony, and just to the left, there are two ponds that intercept Main Street.

The main buildings in the colony are the rectory, the church, the very fine new school, the council office and several very attractive private homes. The homes are similar to those in Landau, but there are many homes here with very high foundations and three windows on the front of the house. This is seldom seen in the other colonies.

The yards are all surrounded by stone walls. Along the length of the street there is an alley of acacia trees, giving the colony a picturesque appearance.

Good drinking water is plentiful in the colony; the tea well at the north end of the colony receives praise for its tasty water. There are also stone quarries all around where the poor people are able to earn their daily bread during the winter.

When the first settlers came here the place was bleak and dreary with grass as tall as a man and overgrown with reeds and creepers. One could get through this only with great difficulty.

A Moldavian lived where the colony is now located, but later he moved away. It must have been most discouraging for these poor colonists, who had previously lived in the beautiful Rhine region, to move to these wild steppes where only wolves, foxes and other wild animals made their home. But one comfort remained, their trust in the help of Almighty God. This trust saw them through their dreary situation.

On Main Street, south of the church, between the lots of Kaspar Wanner and Matthias Dietrich, was the spot where the first settlers stopped. They had come from Odessa in the fall of 1809 under the guidance of Franz Brittner, mayor of Liebental. At that very spot the wagons were unloaded; the poor tired migrants had arrived at their distination. They could now rest a bit after their long, difficult journey which had taken them eighteen weeks.

They could not remain idle for very long as it was already harvest time. Winter was just around the corner and there were no homes to live in. Every family received some money with which to buy wood and other materials to build a hut. It was already too late to build a house. The head of every family dug a square hole in his own lot, covered it with a roof of reeds and wood and their winter home was finished. This accommodation during the winter was cold and damp; consequently many became ill and died during the winter.

The rest of the group, who had spent the winter with the Liebental colonists, arrived in the spring of 1810. The land was surveyed for the crown houses and the colony of Speier was born.

The name "Speier" was given to the colony by the settler, Johannes Schanz. He had previously lived in the Palatinate not far from the city of Speier. The main occupation of the colonists was agriculture and ranching. Constitutionally, the colonists were strong and healthy and mostly big of stature. Their language was more Alsatian than Palatinate; the Speier people say, "Ich geh ä mit," (I will go with you.)

Settlers in the Colony of Speier
in the Beresan District
1839-1840

1. **Thomas Dietrich** age 42, son of Peter, from Blankenborn, Rhinepalatinate.
WIFE: Katharina Kunz 35, daughter of Michael, from Bietigheim, Baden.

CHILDREN: Joh Philipp, age 7, Matthias 1, Maria-Eva 14, Gertrud 11, Katharina 9, Barbara 2, Franziska 1.

2. **Joseph Helbling** age 41, from Wingen, Alsace.
WIFE: Marianna Scholl, age 36, daughter of Michael from Walldorf, Baden.
CHILDREN: Joseph 10, Margaretha 16.

3. **Jakob Dinius** age 39, son of Adam, from Hatzenbühl, Rhinepalatinate.
WIFE: Annamaria Buscholl, age 36, from Lanquedoc, France.
CHILDREN: Adam 17, Jakob 15, Ludwig 11, Peter 9, Klara 13, Susanna 1.

4. **Philipp Kuhn** age 39, son of Johann, from Leimersheim, Rhinepalatinate.
WIFE: Katharina Schäfer, 34, daughter of Michael from Bietigheim, Baden.
CHILDREN: Philipp 12, Michael 10, Pius 4, Ludwig 1, Franziska 16, Katharina 14, Elisabeth 7.

5. **Michael Geis** 39, son of Peter, from Wanzenau, Alsace.
WIFE: Marianna Schardt, 38, daughter of Georg, from Leimersheim, Rhinepalatinate.
CHILDREN: Jakob 16, Michael 11, Kaspar 6, Johann 4, Annamaria 13.

6. **Kaspar Wanner** 28, son of Jakob, from the colony of Landau.
WIFE: Klara Dinius, 32, daughter of Adam, from Hatzenbühl, Rhinepalatinate.
CHILDREN: Michael 6, Kaspar 4, Jakob 1.
STEPDAUGHTER: Maria-Eva Helbling, 12, daughter of Ludwig.

7. **Johann-Jakob Schwab** 53, son of Michael, from Leimersheim, Rhinepalatinate.
WIFE: Margaretha Schmalz, 41, daughter of Peter, from Salmbach, Alsace.
CHILDREN: Theodor 21, Joseph 19, Johann 17, Michael 8, Andreas 6, Magdalena 12, Elisabeth 10.

8. **Johannes Marthaler** 24, son of Johann.
WIFE: Katharina, 20.

9. **Georg Adam Schaf** 32, son of Lorenz, from Leimersheim, Rhinepalatinate.
WIFE: Marianna Schäfer 32, daughter of Michael from Bietigheim, Baden.
CHILDREN: Wendelin 5, Kaspar 1, Katharina 9, Maria-Eva 3.
MOTHER: Eva-Katharina Weszler, 58, daughter of Johann.

10. **Joseph Buscholl** 67, son of Simon, from Lanquedoc, France.
WIFE: Magdalena Bernard, daughter of Peter, from Hagenbach, Rhinepalatinate.

CHILDREN: Susanna 14.
(a) Nikolaus Buscholl 22, son of Joseph.
WIFE: Katharina Wetzstein, 21, daughter of Michael.
CHILDREN: Klara 1.
(b) Johannes Buscholl 20, son of Joseph.
WIFE: Barbara Würtz, 19, daughter of Joseph Würtz.
CHILDREN: Michael 1, Marianna 2.

11. **Joseph Gleiszenberger** 73, son of Joseph, from Gablons, Bohemia.
WIFE: Katharina Stentz 74, daughter of Philipp, from Edenkoben, Rhinepalatinate.
(a) Philipp Kratz 25, son of Anton, from the colony of Landau.
WIFE: Marianna, daughter of Christian, 36, from Salmbach, Alsace.
CHILDREN: Anton 2, Friedrich 1, Margaretha 13, Marianna 9, Katharina 5.

12. **Peter Schütz** 42, son of Jakob, from Lindenberg, Rhinepalatinate.
WIFE: Friderika Gerhard 33, daughter of Jakob.
CHILDREN: Christian 3, Katharina 1.

13. **Peter Barth** 37, son of Georg, from Rheinzabern, Rhinepalatinate.
WIFE: Maria-Eva Kuhn, 36, daughter of Johann from Leimersheim, Rhinepalatinate.
CHILDREN: Franz-Peter 16, Johann 8, Philipp 5, Michael 2, Elisabeth 14, Barbara 10.
(a) Michael Barth 36, son of Georg (as above).
WIFE: Margaretha Schaf, 28, daughter of Lorenz.
CHILDREN: Magdalena 7, Katharina 3, Elisabeth 1.

14. **Martin Barth** 45, son of George (as above).
WIFE: Katharina Frank, 26, daughter of Nikolaus.
CHILDREN: Peter 16, Michael 14, Johann-Adam 13, Nikolaus 4, Georg 2, Maria-Eva 10, Angela 1.

15. **Joseph Zent** 45, son of Michael, from Wingen, Alsace.
WIFE: Franziska Samtmann, 27, daughter of Christian.
CHILDREN: Martin 16, Michael 14, Johann 6, Peter 1, Magdalena 11, Franziska 3, Katharina 1.
(a) Augustin Hertz 25, son of Anton from Bietigheim, Baden.
WIFE: Katharina Zent, 22, daughter of Joseph.

16. **Philipp Schaf** 48, son of Adam, from Leimersheim, Rhinepalatinate.
WIFE: Franziska Ehret, 38, daughter of Georg, from Salmbach, Alsace.

17. **Michael Heinrich** 26, son of Adam, from Schleital, Alsace.
WIFE: Katharina Bast, 26, daughter of Johannes.

CHILDREN: Joseph 2, Adam 1.

(a) Katharina Würtz, 54, widow of Adam Heinrich, and daughter of Adam Würtz.

CHILDREN: Michael 4, Barbara 13.

(b) Christian Walter 30.

WIFE: Katharina Heinrich 28, daughter of Adam.

CHILDREN: Joseph 2, Barbara 7.

(c) Matthias Heinrich 21.

WIFE: Katharina Steif, 20, daughter of Rudolf.

18. **Ludwig Judt** 32, son of Matthias, from Freckenfeld, Rhinepalatinate.

WIFE: Elisabeth Schäfer, 20, daughter of Michael.

CHILDREN: Peter 7, Matthias 5, Franziska 9, Margaretha 1.

19. **Joseph Deutsch** 29, son of Adam, from Jockgrim, Rhinepalatinate.

WIFE: Elisabeth Schwartz, 27, daughter of Karl, from Eberbach, Alsace.

CHILDREN: Matthias 5, Franz 3, Johann 1.

20. **Martin Dietrich** 33, son of Peter, from Blankenborn, Rhinepalatinate.

WIFE: Annamaria, 26, daughter of Jakob.

CHILDREN: Elisabeth 1.

(a) Joseph Dietrich 35, son of Peter (as above).

WIFE: Kreszentia Heck, 30, daughter of Lorenz, from Elisheim, Baden.

CHILDREN: Georg 6, Jakob 2, Rosina 9, Margaretha 1.

(b) Katharina Schwindhammer, 26, widow, daughter of Lorenz Heck.

CHILDREN: Joseph 3, Jakob 1.

21. **Johannes Schmalz** 36, son of Peter, from Salmbach, Alsace.

WIFE: Elisabeth Völker, 34, daughter of Dominik, from Germersheim, Rhinepalatinate.

CHILDREN: Jakob 13, Johann 11, Albert 2, Georg-Adam 1.

22. **Marianna Würtz** 43, widow, daughter of Michael Kunz, from Bietigheim, Baden.

CHILDREN: Melchior 20, Adam 18, Joseph 16, Thomas 12, Katharina 10.

23. **Christian Samtmann** 56, son of Georg, from Wingen, Alsace.

WIFE: Katharina Gerhardt, 42, daughter of Jakob, from Obersimten, Rhinepalatinate.

CHILDREN: Margaretha 9.

(a) Michael Marthaler, 23, son of Johann.

WIFE: Marianna Samtmann, 18, daughter of Christian.

CHILDREN: Annamaria 1.

24. **Anton Metz** 40, son of Jakob, from Hayna, Rhinepalatinate.

WIFE: Katharina Amann, 42, daughter of Ludwig, from Lingenfeld, Rhinepalatinate.
CHILDREN: Anton 18, Adam 16, Karl 14, Barbara 12, Agnes 10, Katharina 5, Pelagia 2.
STEP-CHILDREN: Joseph Müller 13, Johannes 12, Peter 5, (children of Jakob Müller).
(a) Joseph Heid 73, son of Kaspar, from Kuhardt, Rhinepalatinate.
WIFE: Margaretha Martin, 75, daughter of Johann.
(b) Georg Schardt, son of Michael.
WIFE: Maria-Eva, daughter of Johann Berger.
CHILDREN: Matthias 3, Franz 1, Katharina 2.
   25. **Johannes Schröder** 33, son of Michael, from Bietigheim, Baden.
WIFE: Annamaria, 20, daughter of Nikolaus Aspenleiter.
CHILDREN: Philipp 11, Johann 3, Georg 1, Franziska 7.
(a) Johannes Bär, 69, son of Jakob.
WIFE: Maria-Eva Hamburger 71, daughter of Valentin.
   26. **Johannes Berger** 47, son of Matthias, from Jockgrim, Rhinepalatinate.
WIFE: Katharina Senn, 40, daughter of Michael, from Oberseebach, Alsace.
CHILDREN: Martin 16, Franz 10, Katharina 13, Elisabeth 11, Magdalena 7, Theresia 6, Franziska 4, Annamaria 2.
(a) Matthias Aspenleiter 27, son of Nikolaus.
WIFE: Margaretha Berger, 21, daughter of Johann.
CHILDREN: Johann 1, Margaretha 2.
   27. **Johann Krank** 31, son of Joseph, from Mörlheim, Rhinepalatinate.
WIFE: Margaretha Senn, 28, daughter of Michael, from Oberseebach, Alsace.
CHILDREN: Valentin 6, Johann 5, Philipp 2, Franziska 3.
   28. **Adam Meyer** 46, from Albersweiler, Rhinepalatinate.
WIFE: Katharina Burgard, 62, daughter of Johann, from Steinfeld, Rhinepalatinate.
STEP-SON: Philipp Acker, 14, son of Michael.
(a) Rudolf Zander 20, son of Georg.
WIFE: Marianna Meyer, 19.
CHILDREN: Elisabeth 1.
(b) Philipp Bast 30, son of Johann, from Kuhardt, Rhinepalatinate.
WIFE: Katharina Acker, 28, daughter of Michael.
CHILDREN: Johann 1, Agnes 4.
   29. **Georg Hecker** Son of Georg, from Rülzheim, Rhinepalatinate.
WIFE: Margaretha Bast, 37, daughter of Johann, from Steinfeld, Rhinepalatinate.

CHILDREN: Martin 18, Georg 10, Annamaria 16, Katharina 14, Barbara 12, Margaretha 5, Kunigunde 3, Angelina 1.
Joseph Holzschuh, 69, son of Jakob.

30. **Joseph Bast** 33, son of Johann, from Steinfeld, Rhinepalatinate.
WIFE: Annamaria Philipp, 27, daughter of George, from the colony of Landau.
CHILDREN: Margaretha 10, Agnes 5, Katharina 4, Marianna 2, Barbara 1.
(a) Martin Bullinger 27, son of Peter, from Herxheim, Rhinepalatinate.
WIFE: Katharina Bast, 26, daughter of Johann.
CHILDREN: Maria-Eva 5, Martina 2, Annamaria 1.

31. **Markus Dauenhauer** 36, son of Valentin, from Dahn, Rhinepalatinate.
WIFE: Angelina Kary, 27, daughter of Jakob.
CHILDREN: Georg 13, Franz 9, Magdalena 5, Margaretha 2, Katharina 1.
(a) Jakob Kary 74, son of Franz, from Elchesheim, Baden.
WIFE: Anastasia Heck, 73.

32. **Jakob Hechler** 34, son of Matthias, from Pfortz, Rhinepalatinate.
WIFE: Katharina Herz, 28, daughter of Anton, from Bietigheim, Baden.
CHILDREN: Philipp 7, Joseph 5, Matthias 2, Johann 1, Franziska 10, Rosina 1.
(a) Joseph Sielber 72, son of Jakob, from Dambach, Alsace.
WIFE: Marianna Boltz, 61, daughter of Johann, from Bietigheim, Baden.

33. **Anton Fröhlich** 29, son of Philipp, from the colony of Landau.
WIFE: Barbara Weber, 27, daughter of Wendelin.
CHILDREN: Jakob 6, Elisabeth 8, Konstanzia 3.

34. **Philipp Klug** 31, son of Johann, from Schwanheim, Rhinepalatinate.
WIFE: Katharina Mayer, 30, daughter of Johann.
CHILDREN: Michael 7, Katharina 3, Barbara 1.

35. **Franziska Andres** 55, widow, daughter of Peter Schmalz, from Salmbach, Alsace.
CHILDREN: Georg 21, Theresia 13, Margaretha 9.
FATHER'S NAME: Hubert Andres.
(a) Philipp Andres, 26, son of Hubert.
WIFE: Ludowika Vogel, 22, daughter of Adam.

36. **Philipp Gerhardt** 30, son of Jakob, from Obersimten, Rhinepalatinate.

WIFE: Barbara Geiger, 28, daughter of Dominik.
CHILDREN: Johann 9, Sebastian 7, Adam 1, Margaretha 6, Katharina 4, Apolonia 3.
(a) Johannes Geiger, 27, son of Dominik.
WIFE: Annamaria Gerhardt, 28, daughter of Jakob.
CHILDREN: Magdalena 1.
37. **Anton Eret** 36. son of Georg, from Salmbach, Alsace.
WIFE: Margaretha Schuster, 31, daughter of Michael.
CHILDREN: Anton 9, Augustin 5, Benedict 2, Joseph 1.
(a) Georg Eret 75, son of Johann, from Salbach, Alsace.
WIFE: Margaretha Rerich, 65, daughter of Lorenz.
(b) Theresia Bilmann 64, daughter of Michael Schäfer, widow.
38. **Adam Winschel** 46, son of Michael, from Hatzenbühl, Rhinepalatinate.
WIFE: Franziska Völker 41, daughter of Dominik, from Germersheim, Rhinepalatinate.
CHILDREN: Domian 19, Joseph 15, Johann 12, Vinzenz 3, Michael 1, Elisabeth 18, Rosalia 5.
39. **Peter Buhlinger** 63, son of Adam, from Herxheim, Rhinepalatinate.
WIFE: Katharina Rau 52, daughter of Michael, from Lohrbach, Baden.
CHILDREN: Michael 16, Marianna 14, Franziska 12.
40. **Michael Wetzstein** 61, son of Johann, from Kuhardt, Rhinepalatinate.
WIFE: Marianna Heck, 58, daughter of Joseph, from Bietigheim, Baden.
CHILDREN: Martin 20, Peter 12, Ferdinand 10, Michael 6, Barbara 14.
(a) Matthias Wetzstein 24, son of Michael.
WIFE: Ludovika Gerhardt, 21, daughter of Adam.
CHILDREN: Johann 2, Katharina 1.
(b) Lorenz Bühlmann 28, son of Egidius.
WIFE: Christina Wetzstein, 26, daughter of Michael.
CHILDREN: Simon 2, Margaretha 1.
41. **Matthias Wagner** 42, son of Andreas, from Siegen, Alsace.
WIFE: Eva Bär 40, daughter of Philipp, from Kuhardt, Rhinepalatinate.
CHILDREN: Matthias 21, Jakob 15, Bernhard 10, Franz 7, Barbara 16, Rosa 4, Christina 2, Martina 1.
42. **Joseph Gantz** 33, son of Martin, from Bietigheim, Baden.
WIFE: Rosina Vogel 26, daughter of Adam, from Steinfeld, Rhinepalatinate.
CHILDREN: Michael 6, Peter 1, Ludovika 3.

Maria-Josepha Gantz 61, widow of Martin Gantz, daughter of Peter Würtz.
CHILDREN: Nikolaus 24, Johann 18.

43. **Anton Milius** 38, son of Jakob, from Walburg, Alsace.
WIFE: Magdalena Broszmann, 41, daughter of Johann, from Surburg, Alsace.
CHILDREN: Jakob 19, Peter 16, Margaretha 13, Theresia 2.

44. **Adam Gerhardt** 46, son of Jakob, from Obersimten, Rhinepalatinate.
WIFE: Elisabeth Hörner, 25, daughter of Dominik.
CHILDREN: Jakob 18, Anton 14, Joseph 12, Johann 6, Maria 16, Elisabeth 10, Angela 3, Katharina 1.

45. **Jakob Gerhardt** 46, son of Jakob, from Obersimten, Rhinepalatinate.
WIFE: Katharina Lanz, 37, daughter of Franz, from Odenheim, Baden.
CHILDREN: Philipp 14, Peter 10, Friederika 12, Katharina 8.
Margaretha Gerhardt 63, daughter of Martin Westermaier, from Wingen, Alsace.

46. **Georg Mühl** 48, son of Jakob, from Hatzenbühl, Rhinepalatinate.
WIFE: Margaretha Wünschel, 44, daughter of Michael.
CHILDREN: Maria 14, Luzia 11, Katharina 6, Magdalena 4.
Kaspar Mühl 56, brother.

47. **Kaspar Romburg** 28, son of Joseph, from Surburg, Alsace.
WIFE: Magdalena Bär 38, daughter of Philipp, from Kuhardt, Rhinepalatinate.
CHILDREN: Magdalena 16, Barbara 11, Margaretha 9, Katharina 6, Maria-Eva 3, Matthias 15, Martin 2, Anton 1.
(a) Jakob Lochbaum 25, son of Andreas.
WIFE: Christina Hoffmann, 20, daughter of Jakob.
CHILDREN: Adam 1.

48. **Jakob Stockert** 33, son of Ferdinand, from Minfeld, Rhinepalatinate.
WIFE: Antonia Klein, 33, daughter of Anton, from Langenbrücken, Baden.
CHILDREN: Martin 11, Balthassar 9, Johann 7, Katharina 4, Cäzilia 2.
Martin Heck, 21, stepson, son of Lorenz.

49. **Bernhard Schaf** 46, son of Andreas, from Jockgrim, Rhinepalatinate.
WIFE: Margaretha Jahner, 34, daughter of Adam.
CHILDREN: Anton 22, Philipp 20, Dominik 19, Martin 9, Franz 7, Jakob 5, Prokobius 2.

50. **Michael Wagner** 48, son of Andreas, from Hatzenbühl, Rhinepalatinate.
WIFE: Rosina Kaiser, 52, daughter of Georg from Siegen, Alsace.
CHILDREN: Johann 15, Katharina 17, Maria-Eva 13.
(a) Jakob Decker, 24.
WIFE: Rosina Wagner, 23, daughter of Michael.
51. **Adam Vogel** 65, widower from Steinfeld, Rhinepalatinate.
CHILDREN: Damian 22, Katharina 15.
(a) Dominik Vogel, 25, son of Adam.
WIFE: Katharina Hatzenbühler, 20, daughter of Joseph.
CHILDREN: Katharina 2.
52. **Ludwig Schwöbel** 55, son of Paul, from Kapsweyer, Rhinepalatinate.
WIFE: Elisabeth Ekert, 59, daughter of Joseph.
CHILDREN: Adam 14, Philipp 11.
(a) Joseph Schwöbel, 27, son of Ludwig.
WIFE: Katharina Wolf, 24, daughter of Michael.
CHILDREN: Adam 3, Jakob 2, Marianna 1.
53. **Damian Heinz** 58, son of Georg, from Dahn, Rhinepalatinate. Rhinepalatinate.
WIFE: Marianna Bühlmann, 68, daughter of Georg, from Winzenbach, Alsace.
(a) Philipp Mock 32, son of Sebastian from Kapsweyer, Rhinepalatinate.
WIFE: Marianna Heinz, 33, daughter of Damian.
CHILDREN: Ludwig 11, Jakob 1, Elisabeth 9, Katharina 4.
54. **Valentin Jahner** 34, son of Adam from Hayna, Rhinepalatinate.
WIFE: Magdalena Jakobi, 30, daughter of Johann.
CHILDREN: Martin 5, Annamaria 7, Franziska 3, Elisabeth 2.
Adam Jahner 70, son of Jakob, from Hayna, Rhinepalatinate.
55. **Martin Makelke** 65, son of Jakob, from Lendweder, Prussia.
WIFE: Elisabeth Schmidt, daughter of Martin from Neudorf.
CHILDREN: Philipp 12, Rosina 16, Barbara 2.
56. **Elisabeth Immel** 51, widow of Joseph Immel, daughter of Georg-Adam Weisz, from Hambach, Rhinepalatinate.
CHILDREN: Martin 23, Magdalena 17.
57. **Johann Maier** 37, son of Johann.
WIFE: Regina Schwarz, 30, daughter of Johann.
CHILDREN: Valentin 8, Franz 4, Georg 2, Joseph 1.
58. **Augustin Dilschneider** 28, son of Michael.
WIFE: Helena Wünschel, 26, daughter of Georg.
CHILDREN: Jakob 1, Katharina 2.
59. **Johann Schlosser** 27, son of Michael, from Mothern, Alsace.

WIFE: Katharina Kunz, 21, daughter of Martin.
CHILDREN: Martin 2, Goerg 1, Ludwina 3.

60. **Friedrich Klug** 35, son of Johann, from Salmbach, Alsace.
WIFE: Katharina Gerber, 31, daughter of Johann.
CHILDREN: Maria 11, Maria-Eva 2, Apolonia 1.
STEP-CHILDREN: Franz Riesz 13, Klara Rieger 14.

61. **Michael Jantzer** 53, son of Michael, from Rülzheim, Rhinepalatinate.
WIFE: Barbara Hilmann, 56, daughter of George.
(a) Adam Schafer 22, son of Michael.
WIFE: Maria-Eva Jantzer, 21, daughter of Michael.
CHILDREN: Friederika 1.

62. **Martin Kunz** 38, son of Martin from Bietigheim, Baden.
WIFE: Margaretha Stokert, 30, daughter of Ferdinand from Minfeld, Rhinepalatinate.
Margaretha 15, adopted; daughter of Ferdinand Stokert.

63. **Augustin Kunz** 31, son of Martin.
WIFE: Margaretha Völker, 31, daughter of Dominik, from Hatzenbühl, Rhinepalatinate.
CHILDREN: Joseph 8, Bruno 3, Elisabeth 2, Margaretha 1.

64. **Georg Keller** 62, son of Johann from Obersteinbach, Alsace.
WIFE: Marianna Schwarz, 76, daughter of Michael.
CHILDREN: Marianna 14.
(a) Jakob Keller, 20, son of Johann.
WIFE: Magdalena Stroh, 19, daughter of Johann.

65. **Georg Keller** 30, son of Johann.
WIFE: Barbara Förderer, 25.
CHILDREN: Johann 7.

66. **Peter Schmalz** 45, son of Peter, from Salmbach, Alsace.
WIFE: Marianna Keller, 60, daughter of Johann, from Obersteinbach, Alsace.
(a) Michael Popp 34, son of Anton, from Surburg, Alsace.
WIFE: Katharina Kirzinger, 24, daughter of Joseph.
CHILDREN: Valentin 3, Katharina 2, Theresia 1.
(b) Christian Kastner 19, son of Johann.
WIFE: Franziska Schmalz, 18, daughter of Peter.

67. **Georg Gerber** 26, son of Christian, from Salmbach, Alsace.
WIFE: Katharina Deutsch, 23, daughter of Adam, from Jockgrim, Rhinepalatinate.
CHILDREN: Marianna 4, Monika 3, Franziska 1.
Maria-Eva Steif 15, adopted daughter; mother, Maria-Eva Gerber, maiden name, Erich.

68. **Martin Kunz** 70, son of Martin from Bietigheim, Baden.
WIFE: Katharina Kunz, 56, from Rülzheim, Rhinepalatinate.

(a) Matthäus Kunz, 25, son of Martin.
WIFE: Margaretha Schlosser, 24, daughter of Michael.
CHILDREN: Jakob 2, Johann 1.
(b) Johann Hörner 23, son of Dominik.
WIFE: Maria-Eva Kunz 19, daughter of Martin.
69. **Martin Makelke** 27, son of Martin, from Lendweder, Prussia.
WIFE: Annamaria Assel, 27, daughter of Friedrich.
CHILDREN: Friedrich 4, Martin 2, Elisabeth 7.
(a) Friedrich Makelke, 25, son of Martin.
WIFE: Marianna Assel, 20, daughter of Friedrich.
70. **Dominik Völker** 62, son of Franz, from Germersheim, Rhinepalatinate.
WIFE: Ludwiga Möbel, 58, daughter of Johann from Steinfeld, Rhinepalatinate.
CHILDREN: Regina 15, Maria 11.
(a) Joseph Jantzer 23, son of Michael from Rülzheim, Rhinepalatinate.
WIFE: Rosina Völker, 21, daughter of Dominik.
CHILDREN: Katharina 1.
71. **Friedrich Assel** 72, son of Jakob, from Hatzenbühl, Rhinepalatinate.
WIFE: Katharina Wünschel, 48.
CHILDREN: Friedrich 13, Stephan 10.
(a) Matthaus Assel, 22, son of Friedrich.
WIFE: Elisabeth Glensch, 22, daughter of Bartholomaus.
CHILDREN: Magdalena 2.
(b) Johann Assel 21, son of Friedrich.
WIFE: Marianna Schlosser, 22, daughter of Michael.
CHILDREN: Magdalena 1.
72. **Matthaus Schanz** 35, son of Anton from Lingenfeld, Rhinepalatinate.
WIFE: Elisabeth Martin, 31, daughter of Johann, from Käfertal, Baden.
CHILDREN: Stephan 12, Paul 5, Elisabeth 10, Margaretha 8, Theresia 1.
73. **Johann Gerber** 61, son of Adam from Salmbach, Alsace.
WIFE: Annamaria Keller, 55, daughter of Leonhard.
CHILDREN: Regina 18, Ludowika 12.
(a) Johann Gerber 23, son of Johann.
WIFE: Maria-Eva Keller, 22, daughter of Georg.
CHILDREN: Regina 2.
(b) Christian Geiger, 22, son of Dominik.
WIFE: Marianna Gerber,20, daughter of Johann.
CHILDREN: Regina 1.

74. **Friedrich Wünschel** 24, son of Georg from Hatzenbühl, Rhinepalatinate.
WIFE: Rosina Gerber, 24, daughter of Johann.
CHILDREN: Joseph 1.
MOTHER: Maria Dreyer, 63,daughter of Georg, from Odenbach, Rhinepalatinate.

75. **Melchior Kunz** 40, son of Michael, from Bietigheim, Baden.
WIFE: Barbara Hechler, 39, daughter of Matthias, from Pfortz, Rhinepalatinate.
CHILDREN: Martin 17, Joseph 6, Philipp 3, Matthias 1, Marianna 5.

76. **Franz Aemter** 36, son of Franz.
WIFE: Theresia Wünschel, 40, daughter of Michael.
CHILDREN: Georg 17, Michael 16, Johann 11, Valentin 8, August 6, Katharina 13, Elisabeth 4.

77. **Dominik Hörner** 53, son of Michael from Kuhardt, Rhinepalatinate.
WIFE: Elisabeth Koz, 51, daughter of Matthias, from Ranschbach, Rhinepalatinate.
CHILDREN: Joseph 19, Christian 17, Philipp 15, Valentin 12.

78. **Joseph Frank** 31, son of Nikolaus, from Kapsweyer, Rhinepalatinate.
WIFE: Magdalena Assel, 28, daughter of Friedrich.
CHILDREN: Martin 9, Friedrich 3, Maria 6, Elisabeth 1.
(a) Martin Frank 32, son of Nikolaus.
WIFE: Katharina Hechler, 28, daughter of Matthias.
CHILDREN: Matthias 4, Marianna 5, Elisabeth 6, Margaretha 2.

79. **Dominik Geiger** 52, son of Johann, from Kuhardt, Rhinepalatinate.
WIFE: Elisabeth Schaf, 48, daughter of Andreas, from Leimersheim, Rhinepalatinate.
CHILDREN: Anton 13.
(a) Matthias Fleck, son of Christian, from the colony of Landau.
WIFE: Marianna Geiger 19, daughter of Dominik.

80. **Michael Weichel** 41, son of Johann, from Büchelberg, Rhinepalatinate.
WIFE: Marianna Schmalz, 35, daughter of Peter, from Salmbach, Alsace.
CHILDREN: Andreas 12, Albin 8, Martin 2, Elisabeth 6.

81. **Joseph Rambur** 30, son of Joseph, from Surburg, Alsace.
WIFE: Katharina Bechtel, 28, daughter of Matthias.
CHILDREN: Johann 9, Adam 4, Margaretha 2.
(a) Michael Rambur, 24, brother.
MOTHER: Margaretha, 59, daughter of Franz Streifel, from Mothern, Alsace.

82. **Ferdinand Stockert** 37, son of Ferdinand, from Minfeld, Rhinepalatinate.
WIFE: Theresia Schmidt 40, daughter of Lorenz, from Bietigheim, Baden.
CHILDREN: Joseph 16, Christian 11, Martin 8, Franziska 9, Maria-Eva 5, Praxedis 3, Theresia 1.
83. **Johann Vogel** 33, son of Adam from Steinfeld, Rhinepalatinate.
WIFE: Annamaria Schmidt 30, daughter of Lorenz, from Bietigheim, Baden.
CHILDREN: Joseph 8, Michael 1, Katharina 5, Anna 3.
84. **Michael Schäfer** 60, son of Michael, from Bietigheim, Baden.
WIFE: Margaretha Herdwick 50, daughter of Joseph.
(a) Michael Schäfer 26, son of Michael.
WIFE: Angela Weisgerber, 18, daughter of Anton.
CHILDREN: Klara 1.
85. **Johann Maier** 57, son of Andreas, from Bietigheim, Baden.
WIFE: Annamaria Holz, 58, daughter of Johann.
(a) Matthias Maier 23, son of Johann.
WIFE: Elisabeth Andres, 23, daughter of Hubert.
CHILDREN: Juliana 1.
(b) Michael Hörner 28, son of Dominik.
WIFE: Maria-Eva Maier, 28, daughter of Johann.
CHILDREN: Matthias 4, Johann 2.
86. **Philipp Hörner** 55, son of Johann, from Kuhardt, Rhinepalatinate.
WIFE: Katharina Wolf, 48, daughter of Michael.
CHILDREN: Johann 18, Dominik 15, Jakob 10, Elisabeth 13, Franziska 6.
(a) Bernhard Hörner 25, son of Philipp.
WIFE: Marianna Hatzenbühler 19, daughter of Joseph.
CHILDREN: Annamaria 1.
87. **Michael Schlosser** 55, son of Jakob, from Mothern, Alsace.
WIFE: Annamaria Silber, 53, daughter of Joseph, from Dambach, Alsace.
CHILDREN: Joseph 18, Katharina 12, Franziska 9.
(a) Philipp Schlosser 25, son of Michael.
WIFE: Magdalena Völker, 19, daughter of Dominik.
CHILDREN: Michael 1.
88. **Jakob Martin** 28, son of Anton, from Kandel, Rhinepalatinate.
WIFE: Annamaria Bühlmann, 29, daughter of Egidius, from Winzenbach, Alsace.
CHILDREN: Michael 4, Maria-Eva 8, Franziska 6, Christina 2.

(a) Georg Buschol 28, son of Joseph.
WIFE: Franziska Martin 28, daughter of Anton.
CHILDREN: Anton 7, Philipp 3, Georg 1.

89.**Anton Popp** 37, son of Anton, from Surburg, Alsace.
WIFE: Angela Bauman, 32, daughter of Michael, from Rheinzabern, Rhinepalatinate.
CHILDREN: Georg 9, Adam 7, Johann 5, Katharina 3.
(a) Michael Baumann 56, son of Georg, from Rheinzabern, Rhinepalatinate.
WIFE: Katharina Kuhn 52, daughter of Balthassar.

90. **Joseph Heck** 38, son of Joseph, from Bietigheim, Baden.
WIFE: Annamaria Bast 36, daughter of Johann, from Steinfeld, Rhinepalatinate.
CHILDREN: Michael 15, Georg 11, Maria-Eva 10, Annamaria 1.

91. **Martin Senn** 34, son of Michael, from Oberseebach, Alsace.
WIFE: Eva Margaretha Fäth, 37, daughter of Johann, from Rheinsheim, Baden.
CHILDREN: Johann 15, Philipp 8, Michael 6, Franziska 17, Elisabeth 13, Maria 10, Katharina 4, Magdalena 1.
MOTHER: Elisabeth Fäth 69, daughter of Valentin Wischler.

92. **Philipp Schaf** 49, son of Michael.
WIFE: Barbara Schmidt 44, daughter of Johann, from Queichheimbach, Rhinepalatinate.
CHILDREN: Johann 9, Martin 7, Jakob 1, Anastasia 15.
STEP-CHILDREN: Christian Dilschneider, 16, Barbara Dilschneider, 13.
(a) Georg Schaf 22, son of Philipp.
WIFE: Magdalena Rieger, 24, daughter of Joseph.

93. **Jakob Dietrich** 38, son of Peter, from Blankenborn, Rhinepalatinate.
WIFE: Katharina Schardt 32, daughter of Michael from Leimersheim, Rhinepalatinate.
CHILDREN: Maria 14.
MOTHER: Elisabeth Schardt, 61, daughter of Johann Wischler.

94. **Karl Dietrich** 43, son of Peter (as above).
WIFE: Maria-Eva Jochim, 38, daughter of Heinrich, from Rülzheim, Rhinepalatinate.
CHILDREN: Jakob 5, Basilius 4, Eva 15, Katharina 12, Marianna 10, Magdalena 7, Elisabeth 1.

95. **Adam Deutsch** 49, son of Adam-Joseph from Jockgrim, Rhinepalatinate.
WIFE: Katharina Berger 51, daughter of Matthias, from Freckenfeld, Rhinepalatinate.
CHILDREN: Peter 22, Valentin 18, Matthias 10, Margaretha 14.

(a) Franz Krastel 34, son of Georg, from Kuhardt, Rhinepalatinate.
WIFE: Maria-Eva Deutsch 27, daughter of Adam.
CHILDREN: Wendelin 5, Franz 3, Katharina 8, Rosina 6, Franziska 4, Maria-Eva 1.

96. **Matthäus Berger** 39, son of Matthäus from Jockgrim, Rhinepalatinate.
WIFE: Barbara Ferderer, 30, daughter of Anton.
CHILDREN: Matthias 11, Dominik 11, Jakob 2, Karolina 9, Elisabeth 6.
(a) Johann Berger 21, son of Matthäus.
WIFE: Margaretha Bast, 21, daughter of Martin.

97. **Valentin Denius** 37, son of Adam, from Hatzenbühl, Rhinepalatinate.
WIFE: Rosina Pfau 32, daughter of Anton.
CHILDREN: Philipp 12, Georg 2, Annamaria 11, Maria-Eva 6, Klara 1.
(a) Matthias Berger 80, son of Jakob from Jockgrim, Rhinepalatinate.
WIFE: Katharina Hüner 77, daughter of Johann, from Frankenfeld, Rhinepalatinate.
(b) Martin Judt 23.
WIFE: Franziska 17.

98. **Adam Fäth** 40, son of Sebastian, from Leimersheim, Rhinepalatinate.
WIFE: Theresia Weibel 26, daughter of Franz.
CHILDREN: Valentin 6, Michael 2, Elisabeth 14, Margaretha 12, Franziska 10, Theresia 1.

99. **Wendel Schardt** 30, son of Michael from Leimersheim, Rhinepalatinate.
WIFE: Eva Geiger 32, daughter of Dominik.
CHILDREN: Heinrich 2, Marianna 1.
(a) Georg Schardt 23, son of Michael.
WIFE: Maria Berger, daughter of Johann.
CHILDREN: Matthias 1.

100. **Philipp Böhm** 28, son of Joseph from Bühl, Baden.
WIFE: Marianna Hechler 25, daughter of Matthias.
CHILDREN: Wendel 1, Maria 3.
(a) Georg Schäfer 28, son of Michael.
WIFE: Franziska Hechler 32, daughter of Matthias.
CHILDREN: Philipp 4, Ludwig 1.

101. **Ferdinand Judt** 25, son of Matthaus from Freckenfeld, Rhinepalatinate.
WIFE: Katharina Wingerter 21, daughter of Franz.
CHILDREN: Peter 1, Anna Hördner 8, (adopted).
(a) Bernhard Judt 26, son of Matthaus.

WIFE: Elisabeth Schuh 16, daughter of Franz.
(b) Peter Andres 24, son of Hubert, from Schwanau.
WIFE: Elisabeth Judt, 19, daughter of Matthaus.
(c) Adam Gräf 65, son of Jakob.
CHILDREN: Franz 14, Jakob 11.

102. **Johann Marthaler** 49, son of Johann from Leimersheim, Rhinepalatinate.
WIFE: Margaretha Helbling 47, daughter of Johann, from Wingen, Alsace.
CHILDREN: Christian 15, Franz 12, Joseph 5, Barbara 10, Franziska 8.
(a) Johann Berger 23, son of Johann.
WIFE: Maria-Eva Marthaler 20.
CHILDREN: Margaretha 1.

103. **Christian Helbling** 48, son of Johann from Wingen, Alsace.
WIFE: Elizabeth Schmidt 40, daughter of Joseph from Queichheimbach, Rhinepalatinate.
CHILDREN: Christian 17, Franz 16, Johann 12, Ludwig 6, Joseph 2, Elisabeth 3, Margaretha 1.

104. **Franz Renner** 50, son of Martin from Steinweiller, Rhinepalatinate.
WIFE: Annamaria Schmidt 48, daughter of Joseph from Queichheimbach, Rhinepalatinate.
CHILDREN: Franz 17, Johann 11, Margaretha 13, Franziska 9, Maria-Eva 6.
(a) Christian Renner 21, son of Franz.
WIFE: Magdalena 18, daughter of Joseph.

105. **Georg Schmidt** 43, son of Joseph, from Queichheimbach, Rhinepalatinate.
WIFE: Marianna Bast 40, daughter of Johann, from Steinfeld, Rhinepalatinate.
CHILDREN: Christian 11, Martin 1, Barbara 9, Magdalena 7, Marianna 2, Katharina 1.
(a) Franz Sebald 42, son of Johann, from Freckenfeld, Rhinepalatinate.
WIFE: Angela Scholl 24, daughter of Michael.
CHILDREN: Adam 2, Barbara 5, Margaretha 1.

106. **Franz Wingerter** 47, son of Anton, from Herxheim, Rhinepalatinate.
WIFE: Margaretha Müller 47, daughter of Johann, from Leimersheim, Rhinepalatinate.
CHILDREN: Franz 15, Joseph 9, Michael 5.
(a) Egidies Bühlmann 23, son of Egidies, from Winzenbach, Alsace.
WIFE: Elisabeth Wingerter 21, daughter of Franz.

CHILDREN: Katharina 1.
MOTHER: Eva Müller 80, daughter of Martin Horn.

107. **Jakob Schaf** 24, son of Peter, from Leimersheim, Rhinepalatinate.
WIFE: Elisabeth Mischel 24, daughter of Joseph, from Rülzheim, Rhinepalatinate.
CHILDREN: August 2, Marianna 1.
(a)MOTHER: Margaretha Schaf 52, daughter of Adam Müller.
CHILDREN: Johann 23, Martin 20, Bernhard 18, Peter 16.

108. **Jakob Stumpf** 52, son of Michael, from Riedselz, Alsace.
WIFE: Maria-Eva Schardt 49, daughter of Johann, from Leimersheim, Rhinepalatinate.
CHILDREN: Peter 11, Johann 6, Maria-Eva 15, Dominika 4.
STEP-CHILDREN: Elisabeth Heinz 10, Katharina Heinz 13.

109. **Michael Scholl** 38, son of Georg, from Walldorf, Baden.
WIFE: Karolina Stolz 42, daughter of Christian, from Theresia, Prussia.
CHILDREN: Michael 3, Joseph 1, Elisabeth 16, Katharina 10.
STEP-CHILDREN: Michael Dekele 16.
(a) Georg Scholl 23, son of Georg.
WIFE: Elisabeth Blech 22, daughter of Franz.
CHILDREN: Nikolaus 1, Johann 2.
(b) Friedrich Hiesermann 28, son of Johann, from Unteressendorf, Würtemberg.
WIFE: Katharina Scholl 28, daughter of Michael.
CHILDREN: Katharina 8, Margaretha 5, Marianna 2.
(c) Georg Mock 22.
WIFE: Philippina Ehret.
CHILDREN: Jakob 2, Marianna 4.

110. **Nikolaus Aspenleiter** 62, son of Anton, from Birkenhördt, Rhinepalatinate.
WIFE: Magdalena Lang, 60, daughter of Gabriel.
CHILDREN: Joseph 22, Jakob 17, Anton 16.
(a) Johann Aspenleiter 32, son of Nikolaus.
WIFE: Johanna Heck 30, daughter of Lorenz, from Elchesheim, Baden.
CHILDREN: Joseph 4, Peter 2.
MOTHER: Nothburga Heck, 62, daughter of Johann.

111. **Michael Wanner** 38, son of Jakob, from Schweighhofen, Rhinepalatinate.
WIFE: Karolina Helbling 34, daughter of Johann, from Wingen, Alsace.
CHILDREN: Michael 10, Johann 7, Joseph 1, Eva 4.

112. **Michael Kary** 40, son of Jakob, from Elchesheim, Baden.

WIFE: Maria Storck 42, daughter of Johann, from Kapsweyer, Rhinepalatinate.
CHILDREN: Stephan 12, Michael 3, Angela 10, Johanna 1.
(a) Jakob Kary 22, son of Michael.
WIFE: Julianna Meyer 18, daughter of Johann.
113. **Matthias Schanz** 39, son of Johann, from Lingenfeld, Rhinepalatinate.
WIFE: Katharina-Theresa Schaf 32, daughter of Lorenz, from Leimersheim, Rhinepalatinate.
CHILDREN: Jakob 12, Johann 9, Michael 8, Kaspar 6, Christian 2 Elisabeth 11, Katharina 3, Marianna 1.
114. **Jakob Barth** 41, son of Georg, from Rheinzabern, Rhinepalatinate.
WIFE: Magdalena Scholl 34, daughter of Michael, from Waldorf.
CHILDREN: Thomas 15, Martin 13, Eva 11, Katharina 9, Magaretha 5, Maria 2.
115. **Georg Kuhn** 34, son of Johann, from Leimersheim, Rhinepalatinate.
WIFE: Franziska Deutsch 28, daughter of Adam, from Jockgrim, Rhinepalatinate.
CHILDREN: Michael 9, Franz 1, Katharina 7, Franziska 5.
(a) Michael Kuhn 32, son of Johann.
WIFE: Elisabeth Schulz 23, daughter of Johann.
CHILDREN: Franz 5, Georg 1.
116. **Philipp Hörner** 29, son of Philipp, from Kuhardt, Rhinepalatinate.
WIFE: Magdalena Jonas 27, daughter of George, from Steinfeld, Rhinepalatinate.
CHILDREN: Johann 1, Elisabeth 5.
Johann Krinitzsky 15, hired man, son of Ludwig.
117. **Elisabeth Holfinger** 46, widow, daughter of Peter Frenzel, from Berg, Rhinepalatinate.
CHILDREN: Philipp 7, Elisabeth 17, Michael 19, Matthias 28.
STEP-CHILDREN: Johann Krinitzsky 16, Regina Krinitzsky 14, Elisabeth Krinitzsky 12.
(a) Johann Andres 29, son of Johann.
WIFE: Apolonia Krinitzsky 24, daughter of Martin.
CHILDREN: Sylvester 2, Georg 1, Elisabeth 3.
118. **Michael Helbling** 54, son of Johann, from Wingen, Alsace.
WIFE: Maria-Eva Fried 49, daughter of Valentin, from Berg, Rhinepalatinate.
CHILDREN: Christian 20, Jakob 17, Valentin 15, Michael 13, Ludwig 9, Franz 8.
119. **Karl Mösmer** 26, son of Joseph, from Birkenhördt,

Rhinepalatinate.
WIFE: Katharina Friedrich 23, daughter of Lorenz, from Prussia.
CHILDREN: Egidius 1, Franziska 8, Gunemunda 2.

120. **Franz Philipp Gotting** 53, son of Franz, from Albersweiler, Rhinepalatinate.
WIFE: Margaretha Kühlmeier 47, daughter of Michael.
CHILDREN: Franz 18, Philipp 16, Joseph 14, Ludwig 4, Barbara 13, Johanna 10, Maria 7.
(a) Johann Koffler 28, son of Matthäus, from the colony of Rastadt.
WIFE: Maria Gotting 24, daughter of Philipp.
CHILDREN: Michael 6, Eva 5, Katharina 1.

121. **Jakob Melinger** 37, son of Joseph, from Steinfeld, Rhinepalatinate.
WIFE: Katharina Förderer 27, daughter of Anton, from Oestringen, Baden.
CHILDREN: Adam 1, Marianna 9, Maria 6.

122. **Joseph Rieger** 47, son of Martin, from Durlach, Baden.
WIFE: Barbara Klug 40, daughter of Johann, from Schwanheim, Rhinepalatinate.
CHILDREN: Friedrich 15, Angela 19, Klara 15, Katharina 9, Marianna 6, Annamaria 4, Eva 1.
(a) Joseph Eret 24, son of Joseph.
WIFE: Margaretha Dilschneider 19, daughter of Michael.
CHILDREN: Johann 2.

The beginning of
Speier Colony

The colony of Speier was founded during the years of 1809-1810. There were three groups who came to Odessa from the border city of Radzivilov. The leader of the first group was Michael Fischer; the leader of the second group was Martin Zimmermann, and of the third group, Johannes Bosch. As previously mentioned, the first group came to the present site during harvest and the father of each family built a hut in which they spent the winter. In the spring, when the other parties arrived, the Crown houses were built. The head of the household of each family received a sum of money from the Crown to buy implements and cattle. The advance loan for this amounted to 308 rubles, 57.25 kopeks in silver for each householder. This had to be repaid in yearly installments of 7 rubles, 14.25 kopeks in silver. Those who had received daily allowances during their journey from the Russian border also received flour and other necessities when they arrived at their designated location.

Only 41 householders brough some means from their homeland, amounting altogether to 2910 rubles of silver. The purchases at that time were all made in the city of Sokolo *(Vosnesensk). The two noblemen, Ignatowicz and Malaschewicz, loaned and sold many necessities to the Beresan people such as salt, flour, wheat, reeds and other things.

By the 1 January 1811 most of the Crown houses were finished. There were 102 families, with 212 males and 236 females; altogether 448 souls, all of Catholic denomination. Every family had one or two horses, one cow and the other necessities to start with. When ploughing, it was sometimes necessary for four, or even six farmers to work together because the unbroken land was so firm. Some of the settlers had never done this type of work before because many of them were tradesmen or day labourers in the cities where they did not have occasion to see a plough. The colonists who had knowledge of ploughing, were approached by the authorities and asked to teach their colleagues and supervise their work.

In the fall of 1811 the colony of Speier sowed 204 chetvert of winter wheat; in the spring, they sowed 102 chetvert of Arnaut wheat and 102 chetvert of oats, equalling a total of 408 chetvert for the harvest year of 1811/12.

Tradesmen in Speier in 1811, were as follows:

CARPENTER: Dominik Völker.
TAILORS: Philipp Hörner, Michael Wetzstein and Jakob Gleisenberg.
SHOEMAKERS: Christian Samtmann and Friedrich Assel.
MILLER: Johann Helbling.
WEAVER: Christian Gerber, Johann Gerber, Ferdinand Stocker, Adam Heinrich, Adam Denius, Peter Müller and Adam Hellmer.
BRICKLAYERS: Adam Vogel and Jakob Schwarber.
BUTCHER: Johann Stark.
BLACK-SMITH Michael Schardt.
STONE-MASON Andreas Amann.

The statistics for the colony of Speier in 1818 were as follows: there were 89 families, 213 males and 230 females, a total of 443 souls.

The real property of the community at this time was: 417 horses, 779 horned cattle, 404 pigs, 91 ploughs, 117 harrows, 98 wagons, 54 distaffs, and 2 weaving looms. Craftsmen were: 1 carpenter, 1 cabinet-maker, 3 barrel-makers, 3 millers, 3 tailors, 3 weavers, 3 shoemakers, and 3 bricklayers.

---

*The colonists still call it Sokolai even today.

Seeded in 1817/1818 was:

	Tschetwert	Tschetwerik*
Winter wheat	1	2
Summer wheat	285	5
Rye	97	6
Barley	119	4
Oats	116	1
Potatoes	103	5
Buckwheat	2	3.5
Corn	5	6.5
Millet	7	1
Peas	12	3
Lentils	1	7.5
Beans	4	7.5
Hemp	1	5
Flax	4	6

The Community Land of the Colony of Speier

There were 7895.5 dessiatines in the community land of Speier. It forms an irregular square and lies on both sides of the Beresan River. The south border is formed by the Landau community land; the west border is formed by the colony of Johannestal and Rohrbach; in the north, by the land of Waterloo and the land of the Beresan sheep herders; in the east, is the land of the colony of Katharinental. The surface of the land is mostly level. Only the Beresan, the valley of the forest and the Stuttgart valley cause insignificant indentations. The soil is good black loam with an underlay of yellow clay.

In 1848 there was a small spring in the Beresan near Speier, which was well cribbed and contained good water. I do not know whether it is still there. The land was very productive. In spite of the fact that the first settlers worked the land poorly, they often received good harvests. The old people also maintain that more kinds of grass grew on their land than at the present. They also tell of the colourful flowers and plants that grew over the whole steppe in the early days. The flowers gave off such a pungent, pleasant perfume that one could imagine himself in paradise.

---

*1 tschetwerik = 1/8 of a tschetwert.

1 tschetwert = 10 pud.

1 pud = 36.1 lbs. (Canadian).

Lately, the land is less productive because it has been cultivated for 100 years without any replacement of fertilizer, either natural or artificial, in order to increase the productivity of the soil.

In 1842 a woodland and gardens for plants, fruits and grapes were laid out. In 1871, when the Fürsorge Committee was dissolved and the planting in the colonies was no longer supervised, the people started to cut and destroy this lovely forest. However, the colony of Speier must be complimented because they have maintained at least part of this nice woodland.

The Parish of Speier

The colony at present has 338 lots and 4410 souls of both sexes, all of Catholic denomination. Other denominations live in Speier only temporarily. The parish of Speier has been here since 1837. Earlier it was affiliated with the Landau parish.

The estates of Marianovka and Stadnaja-Balka are included in the parish of Speier. Speier belongs to the deanery of Nikolayev in the diocese of Tiraspol. It is 4 versts from the post and telegraph office at Landau.

History of the Parish

For almost 50 years the colonies of Landau, Speier, Karlsruhe, Sulz and the somewhat later founded colony of Katharinental, formed a single parish, but as a result of their steady growth they became too much for a single priest. The church authorities, therefore, asked the parishioners of the Landau if they were prepared to pay for the salary of a vicar who would reside in the Landau rectory. The community could not come to an agreement on this point. Most of the colonists did not want to assume new expenses with the result that no vicar was installed in the parish of Landau.

During the war of 1854-1856, typhus and other diseases were prevalent in the colonies. Sometimes there were 10 to 15 drivers waiting at the rectory to take the priest to their sick or to bury their dead. Many people died without receiving the last sacraments and, consequently, the parishioners realized that one priest could no longer provide the necessary services for the large parish of Landau. The first to begin to organize its own parish was the colony of Speier.

As a result of a community consensus, it was decided to send a petition to Ferdinand Helanus Kahn, the new Bishop of Tiraspol, asking that a new parish be founded in the colony of Speier and that a priest be sent as soon as possible. There was a great scarcity of priests for the large Catholic dioceses of Russia and since the newly formed diocese of Tiraspol did not yet have a seminary, it took a long time to comply with this request. Permission was first obtained from the Russian authorities in 1857 for Speier to have their own parish. In October 1857 Father Johannes Thiel was sent to Speier as the first priest. On the 7 October 1857 he performed the first priestly duties there.

Order of Succession of Priests
in Speier

FATHER JOHANNES THIEL
7 October 1857 to 7 October 1862

Father Johannes Thiel was born in Poland in 1807. He was Polonized German who understood German very poorly. As a youth he entered a seminary and, on completing his studies in 1832, he was ordained to the priesthood. When Bishop Kahn took over the administration of the Tiraspol diocese, he attemped to find German priests, or others who understood German, to post in the German colonies. Father J. Thiel fitted into this category, and in 1854 he was assigned to the newly formed parish of Franzfeld. Here he worked as a diligent and faithful servent for his Master. In 1857 he was moved to Speier as the first priest of the newly formed parish.

A new and heavy workload awaited him at Speier. The parish had to be organized and put in order. There was not yet a rectory available and, consequently, the priest had to live in a private home. The church or so-called prayer-house was already too small for this large community; therefore, they soon had to consider building a church. This caused the new priest considerable worry and hard work. He prevailed upon the community to acquire a house next to the prayer-hall and there the rectory was subsequently built. He also took a lot of trouble to get the community to accept the idea to build a new church. The church was finally completed in 1863 when Father Thiel was retired to Nikolayev. The reason for his removal is not known. He was a pious, diligent, cultured priest, who strived constantly to fulfill his duties. He died in Nikolayev in 1880. From 1863 to 1864 Speier was once more supervised from Landau.

FATHER ZENON KALINOWSKY *Ord. Preachers-Curate*
2 August 1864 to 1 July 1865

Father Zenon Kalinowsky was born in Poland in 1809. As a youth, he entered a Dominican Monastery, completed his studies there, and in 1833, he was ordained. He understood German well and so he was sent to the Crimean Peninsula by the church authorities. Here he worked for 6 years in the German colony of Rosental. From here he was sent to Novorossisk as military chaplain, where he remained for 18 years. Following this he was the priest in Stavropol for one year after which he went to Speier for one year.

From 1866 to 1867 he was the priest in Landau. Later, he spent a year in Marienfeld and Marienberg. Tired and weary because of work, old age, and illness, he returned to the Dominican Monastery at Petersburg where he died an edifying death a few years later.

Father Kalinowsky was a pious and cultured priest, pleasant and good natured. He was decorated by the Czar with the distinguished Golden Cross.

FATHER JOHANNES GARTZ *Franciscan Order*
5 July 1864 to 31 January 1865

Father Johannes Gartz was born in 1800 and ordained in 1832. (More about Father Gartz in Vol. I trans., 137, 140).

After Father Gartz, the parish was looked after by Father Anton Simnoch and Father Leibham from Landau.

FATHER PHILIPP DORZWEILER *Administrator*
5 August 1868 to 23 February 1872

Father Philipp Dorzweiler was born in Katharinenstadt on the Volga in 1844. His first position was in the parish school of his own home. He received his education in the Seminary at Saratov and was ordained by Bishop Vinzentius Lipsky on the 30 March 1868. His first posting as a priest was to the colony of Pfeifer, where he remained for only a short time. In 1868 he became the administrator at Speier, where he remained until 23 February 1872. Father Dorzweiler was always convivial; he liked gay company, and consequently was very much liked by his parishioners. He performed his duties conscientiously and according to precept.

In 1873 he was moved to the large parish of Köhler. Here he soon became ill because of fatigue from over-exertion, and the bishop of the diocese moved him back to the parish of Pfeifer. It seems that he died there in 1878.

From 1872 to 1876 Speier was once again supervised from Landau.

FATHER NIKOLAUS MITZIG *Administrator*
8 January 1876 to 30 September 1879

Father Mitzig was also the administrator of Rastadt. From 1876 to 1878 Speier was administered from Katharinental.

FATHER JOSEPH IHLY *Administrator*
6 January 1878 to 12 July 1903

Father J. Ihly was also administrator of Karlsruhe. From 1903 to 1905 Speier was supervised from Katharinental.

FATHER LUDWIG RISZLING
6 February 1905 to 17 September 1908
(See Vol. I, transl., 209).

FATHER ANDREAS ZIMMERMANN *Administrator*
17 September 1908 to 20 September 1910

Father Andreas Zimmerman was born on the 22 October 1879 in the colony of Seelmann on the Volga. He received his education in the provincial school in his home and graduated with distinction. In August 1894 he entered the Seminary in Saratov, and completed his training in the spring of 1903. After completing his examinations at the seminary, he and six other fellow students were lucky enough to accompany Bishop Ropp on his round of visits in the Caucasus. There, in this beautiful country where God created the highest mountains and the deepest valleys and nature at that time had put on its most beautiful coat, Father Zimmermann was ordained on the 5 May 1903 in the beautiful seaport of Batum.

On 22 May 1903 he said his first Holy Mass in his home, and soon thereafter was sent as vicar to Mariental on the Karamann. Here he carried out his duties diligently until 10 May 1904. From this date until the 15 September 1908, he worked as vicar in Klosterdorf. This was a new but very difficult field of activity for the young priest for he had to organize everything from the beginning. Since the people of Klosterdorf had been without the services of a priest for 100 years, they were pretty unruly. It required a great deal of effort on his part to persuade them to once more lead a Christian life. Still, the people were obliging and obedient so that his administration soon bore fruit.

He left Klosterdorf on the 15 September 1908 to go to Speier. Here he worked diligently, again with good results. But the people of Speier were not as manageable or pliable as those in Klosterdorf. When the priest wished to bring in a sexton of his own choice the people protested, wishing to have authority of approval of the choice.

On 1 December 1911 the bishop moved Father Zimmermann to the seminary as spiritual advisor. He was made a domestic prelate and on the 1 June 1912 he was named the Bishop's Secretary. In spite of these duties, he was also posted as a religious instructor at a secondary school. In June 1913 he was named a penitential canon.

From 1910 to 1913 the parish of Speier was administered from Landau.

FATHER MARTIN FIX

Father Martin Fix was administrator from June 1913. There is information about him in the section on SULZ.

Parish Endowment

The priest received a salary of 650 rubles and firewood. The surplice fees were: baptism 1 ruble, weddings 3 rubles, proclamation of banns 1 ruble, burial 1 ruble, low mass 1 ruble, high mass 1 ruble, 50 kopecks.

The Parish Church

It would appear that the first prayer house in Speier was built in 1812 and was used as such until 1824. In 1824 a new prayer house was built, located where the present community chancellory office is situated. This prayer house was 60 feet long, 30 feet wide and approximately 12 feet high, with the altar facing west. The roof was covered with reeds. The inside of the church contained only an altar, a pulpit, a confessional and several Holy pictures. The bell tower was outside on the north. It was 24 feet high and contained 3 bells. The church (prayer house) was enclosed by a nice stone wall.

The New Parish Church

The present parish church was built of cut field stone in 1863-1864. Every household was obligated to haul a specified amount of stones and those living nearby also had to provide labour. The church, with just the rough brick, cost 14,000 rubles. It was consecrated by His Grace Bishop Zerr, on the 5 October 1896.

The patron of the church is St. Martin. The church is 140 yards from the main street on the east, located on a small elevation. It is 120 feet long, 36 feet wide and 24 feet high.

The bell tower is 90 feet high and is built onto the church. There is a single entrance to the church below the steeple. On either side of the nave, there is a half round chapel. There is no space provided for the sacristy, but instead there is a room behind the main altar for the priest to put on his vestments.

The roof of the church is covered with tin and painted green. In the tower there is a nice clock and three bells which call the people to prayers. The church is surrounded by a massive stone wall, laid out in a square with a chapel in every corner for the Feast of Corpus Christi.

As one enters the church, one sees benches on either side. On the walls there are small, but attractive, stations of the cross. A little further on, in the first side chapel, there is an altar dedicated to St. Clemens Romanus. From here one stands in front of the main altar which is built of stone and looks very plain. The tabernacle is made of marble and is surmounted by a beautiful woodcarved vestibule for the blessed Sacrament. Above the altar is a beautiful crucifix.

On the right of this is the picture of St. Martin and on the left, that of St. Wendelinus. Besides these, there is a statue of St. Agnes in a small niche on the right and on the left is a statue of St. Aloysius. As one leaves the sanctuary, one finds himself on the second side chapel, in the front of the altar to the Mother of God. Above it there is a lovely picture of Our Lady, copied from Murrillo. Across from this altar there is a plain pulpit and under this, a plain baptismal font. In the choir loft one finds the organ, manufactured by the firm of Sauer at a cost of 4000 rubles.

In the middle of the church there are two small chandeliers which are lit only on the highest feast days or extraordinary celebrations. In comparison with other churches in the Beresan, Speier is still very poor.

The Grave Yard

It would appear that the graveyard is the same as was set aside at the original settlement, but it was enlarged as necessity required. At the present time it is enclosed by a nice high stone wall.

The Parsonage

When Father Johannes Thiel came to Speier in 1857, a parsonage was not yet available. The community then bought a house from Jakob Dietrich for 1560 rubles. This house served as the parsonage until 1879. At this time the present rectory was built, with seven rooms and a kitchen, which cost the community 4000 rubles to build.

Lately, large cracks are appearing in the walls. If it is not tended to, the whole building will be in ruins. The yard of the parsonage is 140 yards long and 30 yards wide, enclosed by a nice stone wall.

School Business

There is no record of the first school house in Speier. The second school was built in 1828. It contained a single large room without any living quarters for the school teacher. This schoolhouse remained until 1902 when the present large, attractive school was built. This new school has six (6) class rooms and cost 12,000 rubles. At the present time there are four (4) teachers, each receiving 330 rubles. The total number of children is 241. The first school teacher, apparently, was Christian Sandmann.

After 1817, the teachers were: Ludwig Helbling, Christian Sandmann, Matthias Fleck, Christian Schmidt, Nikolaus Immel, Joseph Kunz, Franz Wanner. The lady teachers were Margaretha, Ottilie, and Rosa Böhm.

FATHER RAPHAEL SCHÄFER

Father Raphael Schäfer was born in Speier on the 14 November 1872, the son of Friedrich Schäfer and Lucia Mühl. His father died when he was still young. After this misfortune, he came to Nikolayev as a 10 year-old-youngster to attend the church school. He was a good student and after having prepared himself well there, he entered the Seminary at Saratov to continue his studies. After many years of diligent studying, he finally obtained the necessary requirements to be a priest and was ordained on the 4 May 1899 by Bishop Antonius Zerr.

His first posting was to Blumenfeld in the Odessa district; he remained here for 4 months. From Blumenfeld he returned to Nikolayev as vicar to his old patron, Prelate Tschernjachowicz, who introduced him into the art of pastoral activity. This training by a practical-minded and versatile man was of incalculable value to this young priest and a useful guide to his future activities in the priesthood. Unfortunately, he had to give up his position after 2 1/2 years. Having become chilled, he developed a very serious illness which made it necessary to look for a warmer climate. He hurried to Yalta in the Crimea. Under the careful nursing attention of his dear sister, he soon recovered sufficiently to look after the small parish of Yalta. In 1905, after having been in Yalta for 2 years, he was sent to Taganrog as administrator where he remained for 5 years.

In 1910 he was sent to the parish in Jekaterinoslav and was made dean of that district, which position he still holds today.

FATHER STEPHAN PORUBSKY

Strictly speaking, Father Stephan Porubsky's name does not belong here as his father was a foreigner. However, his mother was a colonist in Speier and thus his name must be included.

Father Porubsky was born in Speier in 1880. After having completed his studies in the parish school there, he entered the Seminary in Saratov, finishing his studies there in 1904. At the present time he is the administrator in the Novorossiisk parish.

FATHER OTTO BÖHM

Father Otto Böhm was born in 1873 and ordained on the 27 July 1898. He obtained his Masters degree in Theology in the Academy at Petersburg and spent a short time in the Seminary at Saratov. However, he eventually lost his faith and became a teacher in a German grammar school.

KASPAR WANNER *Teacher*

Kaspar Wanner was born on the 14 October 1861 in the colony of Speier, the son of Michael Wanner and Marianna Schardt. He attended the parish school in Karlsruhe where his father was the teacher at that time. After completing his studies at the school in Karlsruhe and having received his first communion, he returned to Speier with his family. Here he attended private schools for several winters conducted at that time by corrupt high school graduates.

In these schools he learned very little and therefore cherished the wish to attend the Seminary at Saratov. Eventually, after many years when he had already reached his manhood, his wish was fulfilled. In 1881 he entered the second class in the above-named seminary where he prevailed in his studies in the quiet rooms of this institution. Since he did not receive the call to the priesthood, he left the Seminary in 1885 and returned to his home. In the fall of 1885 he took the position of teacher in Speier, which position he holds to this day. In 1887 he received the diploma of public school teacher.

On the 12 November 1890 he married Marianna Kopp from Karlsruhe. They had 6 boys and 5 girls; the three oldest boys died. On the 6 December 1905, Kaspar Wanner received the Order of the Silver Medal on the Alexander sash from the Czar, with the inscription, "For Zeal."

CHRISTIAN BARTH *Teacher and Secretary*

Christian Barth was born in Speier on the 14 June 1858, the son of the colonists, Peter Barth and Elisabetha Berger. After completing his studies at the parish school, he continued his studies as secretary. From 1874 to 1876 he was the teacher and secretary in Halbstadt in the Odessa district. In 1876 he became the secretary in Katharinental, which duty he carried out with devotion and diligence until the 14 June 1893.

At his urging and as a result of his acquaintance with the superintendent of orphanages, Johann-Sebastian Butsch, he laid the ground work for an orphan's bank in Karlsruhe. Here the orphans received proper entitlement of their money, which had not been the case up until now. He resigned in 1893, acquired a small estate in the Crimea and administered it efficiently.

NIKODEMUS SCHMALZ *Teacher*

Nikodemus Schmalz was born on his father's estate, not far from Speier, on the 25 August 1886, the son of Christian Schmalz and Audenia Bopp, both from the colony of Speier. His first education was received at Speier after which he attended the central school in Grossliebental which he successfully completed. He wrote the examinations as a public school teacher in 1905 in the Alexander High School. Subsequently, he obtained a position as teacher in München where he still is today.

JAKOB KUHN *Teacher*

Jakob Kuhn was born in Speier on the 6 February 1885, the son of Georg Kuhn and Marianna Gerhardt. After completing his studies at the parish school, he attended the private school of teacher Kaspar Wanner for a time, and in 1898 he entered the Seminary at Saratov. After having completed three classes there, he left the seminary and wrote the public school examinations for teacher at Nikolayev. In 1904 he received a position as teacher in the colony of Landau.

In 1907 he came to Speier as teacher and remained until 1911. On the 3 August 1911, he went to America where he married Rosa Renner, following which he returned to his position of teacher at Speier. In 1912 he took teacher training courses in the teacher's college in Grossliebental.

NIKODEMUS DIETRICH Teacher

Nikodemus was born in Speier in 1861. He studied in the Seminary at Saratov, following which he wrote the public school examinations for teacher and obtained a position in Katharinental. Not long thereafter, he went to Landau and from there to Rastadt as teacher where he is still working.

JAKOB GERHARDT *Officer*

Jakob Gerhardt was born in Speier on the 15 January 1860, the son of Peter Gerhardt and Annamaria Heck. He received his first education from an old soldier of Napoleon's time, Schäfer, who had a private school in Speier. Later he went to the school of teacher Karl Schneider, in preparation to attend High school. In 1872 he went to Odessa, but since he could not get into the non-classical secondary school there, he attended the small boarding school of W. Schreibel where there were several other students from the colonies. As he was unsuccessful in getting into an officers' school from there, he discontinued his studies and in 1873, went to Katharinental to his step-father, Theodor Jochim, and devoted himself to farming. In Katharinental he became a machinist, then a teacher, and for a time, a community secretary.

In 1877 he was for a time a tutor for a private landowner and then became a teacher and sexton in New Landau. In 1878 he returned to Odessa and wrote the examinations for a commission in the army; he was accepted in the number 15 Rifle Regiment. After a year of training in the military school, he became a non-commissioned officer, then an officer cadet, and in 1884, a sub-lieutenant. In 1884 he was transferred to the 43rd Rifle Regiment. Here he received various assignments from his superiors which he carried out, diligently and punctually. In 1887 he was transferred to the 55th Reserve Battalion in Nikolayev. In this same year he married Anna Heinemann; they had 5 children. He received his pension in 1890 and bought an estate containing 335 dessiatines in the district of Elisabethgrad moving there with his family.

After a crop failure and various other problems, he sold his estate in 1902 and moved to Odessa so that his children, now of school age, could receive a suitable education. In Odessa he became an administrator in the local government, where he distinguished himself by his zeal and special knowledge.

In 1905, along with Father Neugum, he founded the newspaper "Deutsches Leben" of which he became editor and publisher for some time. However, this paper did not succeed for various reasons, and in its place came the "Deutsche Rundschau" published by the Clemens Society. Gerhardt also took great interest in this paper and obtained many advertisements for it. He was constantly on hand to help and advise. In recognition of his services, the Society of Clemens appointed him chairman at one of its general meetings, which position he held until 5 September 1912.

WOLDEMAR GERHARDT *Officer*

Woldemar Gerhardt was born on his father's estate in Elisabethgrad on the 6 November 1892, the son of Jakob Gerhardt and Anna Heinemann. He completed the course in the St. Paul's Secondary School and then entered the military school on 7 August 1912, succeeding in obtaining the rank of 'officer cadet.' He joined the 56th Shitomir Infantry Regiment where he is still serving. He received two medals, one as a souvenir of the 100th anniversary of his regiment, and one as a memorial of the 300th year of the origin of the Russian Czars of the House of Romanov.

ANTON GERHARDT *Engineer*

Anton Gerhardt was born in Speier on the 19 September 1863, the son of Peter Gerhardt and Annamaria Heck. After having prepared himself through private instruction, he entered St. Paul's Secondary School where he successfully completed his course in 1884. He then entered as a volunteer in the 42nd Rifle Regiment to complete his military training. Later he left the country and entered the Polytechnical School in Zürich, Switzerland. He was very conscientious and received his diploma as an engineer in 1890.

For a while he worked on the Zürich railroad, but he soon gave this up when he received a call to come home.

After tending business, he left for Germany and received an appointment on the Höllental Railroad near Freiburg in Breisgau where he worked for 15 years. At this time the big Siberian railroad was started and Gerhardt was invited to work on the Blagoveschchensk branch line. Later, he received an appointment in Odessa to the South-West Railroad. Eventually, he was made chief engineer in Perm and then in Baku, to supervise the building of the Petrovsk-Baku line. From there, he again went to Siberia where, as engineer, he performed various duties. However, he became ill and had to go to Petersburg. Later he had brief appointments in various cities because he had never completely recovered from his illness. Since 1905 he has not been working.

He married Lucy Heinemann who was a teacher of German in various institutes in Odessa. They have two daughters, the oldest Helena, an actress, and the younger one, Aloysa, in the eighth grade in the grammar school.

LUISE GERHARDT *Teacher*

Luise Gerhardt, daughter of Jakob Gerhardt and Anna Heinemann, was born on the 1 February 1889. She received her first instruction in her home under the guidance of her mother. In 1902, she attended the girls' grammar school in Odessa and finished the 7th class there in 1906.

In the fall of 1906 she went to Bavaria with her sister, Hildegard, and entered the ladies Institute for higher education in order to learn more about the German language and other matters of higher education. In 1907 both sisters attended the Girls Institute in Morsch, Switzerland in order to become proficient in the French language. After returning to Odessa, Luise completed the 8th class in the secondary school and received a diploma as teacher of German, Russian and Mathematics. After completing her studies, she gave instruction in several ladies' schools in Odessa and also in several families of high officials. In 1912 she married Counsellor N. Letkin of Moscow.

HILDEGARD GERHARDT *Teacher*

Hildegard Gerhardt was born in Nikolayev on the 18 March 1890. She received a similar education to her sister, as indicated above. Since finishing, she has been a teacher of German in the Grammar School in Wiskovata.

There are others who did not submit their curriculum vitae: Commissioner Philipp Wingerter; Secretary, Friedrich Hörner; Teacher, Matthias Maier; Sexton, Melchior Marthaller; Sexton, Nikodemus Marthaller; Sexton, Franz Schmidt; and Sexton, Peter Geisz.

The present wealth and condition
of the Colony of Speier

In Speier there are at present 338 houses and adobe huts. There are 798 Catholic families with 4410 people; two Lutheran families with 9 people; 28 Russian families with 92 people; 43 Jewish families and 4 families of gypsies with 17 people. There are 400 Russian hired men, each receiving 100 rubles per year; 70 Russian maids, each receiving 80 rubles each year. There are 97 families who do not own land. There were 357 families who went to America and 143 who went to Siberia.

Tradesmen in Speier were as follows: Coopers 2; locksmiths 5; blacksmiths 5; wagon builders 4; carpenters 4; shoemakers 6; tailors 2.

There were 2 steam flour mills and 2 beer parlours.

The community land amounted to 7896.5 dessiatines utilized as follows: Yard lots 100 dessiatines; vegetable gardens 31, vineyards 28, woods 29.5, underwater (dams) 10, roads 30, under cultivation 5638, under pasture 2000, hay 126.

Rent for 1 dessiatine of cultivated land for 1 year is 16 rubles. There are approximately 47,022 dessiatine of bought land, 1799 horses, 1176 cows and 529 pigs.

Agricultural implements and other utilities; 9 steam thresh-machines, 3 motors, 25 self-binders, 130 mowers, 410 ploughs, 1060 harrows, 1 phaeton (coach), 1 automobile; the number of wagons is unknown.

Planted in 1913 were 2467 dessiatines in wheat, 704 in rye, 2107 in barley, and 360 dessiatines in corn and potatoes.

For the year 1913 the community paid 5495 rubles, 59 kopeks in dues; land taxes, 6210 rubles, 49 kopeks; community income taxes, 867 rubles, 49 kopeks.

The Colony of Sulz

The colony of Sulz, located in the Province of Kherson, is 100 versts from the city of Kherson and the same distance from the capital city of Odessa, and 7 versts from the community of Landau. The colony is located on the left bank of the Beresan River. The main street is more than 2 versts long with one side street. There are rows of houses on either side of Main Street which runs in a north-south direction. In the early days there were only 6 houses in the north part of the colony, along with the stone windmill of Jakob Meckler. At the present time there are 15 earth houses and 7 more in the hollow near the cow well. In the mill hollow, where in the early days only cattle ranged, one now finds a small street named "Stehleritz-sky" on which there are small houses, mostly owned by the landless cotters (tenant farmers).

Just to the east of the main street there is a back street with a single row of houses extending to the lower colony. From the lot of Peter Heidt (now Marzellius) is the so-called "small street" extending in an east-west direction with two rows of houses. At the end of the lower colony there are some earth houses, which in no way add to the appearance of the colony.

From mill hollow to the yard of Jakob Segmüller the colony is flat. From here the hill of the lower colony begins and extends to the end of the colony. In the early days the mill creek was fairly deep and had a bridge over it, but lately it is quite shallow.

The main building in the colony is the church, already too small for this large community. To the right of the church is the old school house which is now the community chancery. Adjacent to the chancery is the rectory, and across from this, the very fine new, two story school house.

Privately owned buildings are the brick factory of Michael Stöbner & Co. and that of Georg Köhler beyond the Beresan.

There are also the houses of Dominik Sattler, Martin Weber, Johann Kupper, Joseph Ehly, and the community co-operative building.

The houses in Sulz are similar in construction to those in other colonies, but most of the buildings have tile roofs. The lots are all enclosed by stone walls and the side facing the street is white-washed. In front of each house is a flower garden, acacia trees and different types of shrubs which provided shade and present a very pleasant appearance.

Recently, storehouses for chaff have been built in Sulz which had not been the custom previously. There is plenty of water, but of varying quality. In the lower colony the water is safer and better tasting than in the upper colony; only the cow well is an exception. There are many stones but they are not suitable for larger buildings. They can only be used for walls or for burning in the lime kilns. Near Sulz there is a kind of limestone which is very good for white washing the houses.

When the first settlers came in 1809, the area was desolate and uninhabited. All one could see was a well for sheep and the traces of flocks of sheep. This well had abundant water, but the surface was covered by a greenish color which in turn affected the taste of the water. Many people became sick and died from the use of this water. As a result of this and other illnesses, 24 families had died by 1814.

The settlers of Sulz obtained their passports in Frankfurt on the Main and left for Russia in various groups, but without guides. In the border city of Radzivilov, where they usually had a rest period of one month, they joined other migrating parties and enrolled with the groups of colonist going to Odessa. The leader of one transport was Theodor Brücker. The leader of the second group was Franz Scherer and the third was led as far as the city of Odessa by a soldier.

In the fall of 1809 the first party was led to its destination by the mayor of Liebental, Franz Brittner.

Adjacent to the new school, in the valley where the old horse well is located, is the place where the first settlers stopped. After receiving their instructions, they unloaded their few belongings.

In the slope behind the threshing place of Joseph Braxmeier, they dug square holes in the ground, covered them with wood and reeds, and in this manner constructed living quarters for the approaching severe Russian winter.

These poor settlers were not as well adapted as their neighbours, the well furred foxes and wolves who lived in their dens in the near-by ravines. Our dear grandparents had brought only cotton coats from their homeland. Something warmer was necessary to face this fierce cold. They were expected to live in these inadequate huts, dying of cold, illness and hunger. These same burdened German immigrant colonists were expected to bring culture to this wild Russia. Not a single Frenchman or Englishman answered the call.

In spite of all the handicaps, these poor immigrants and those who came after them brought civilization to South Russia by their industry, perseverance and intelligence, so that this province eventually became the richest in all of Russia. At the present time, the German colonists occupy approximately 40% of the land in the Odessa region, a very commendable showing.

In the spring of 1810 the other parties came. They had spent the winter in the Liebental and Kutschurgan colonies. Soon the building of the Crown houses was started. The material was brought to the colony from Odessa by a contractor named Hermann. This was immediately divided among the heads of the families by Mayor Brittner who had guided the colonists. The money which they had received as small daily allowances was now used to buy flour, meat and other necessities. The name "Sulz" was given to the colony by the colonist Matthias Kress who had come from the village of Sulz in Alsace.

The occupation of the people of Sulz is agriculture, cattle and, of late, some industry. The people are strong, muscular and well built, but of a light complexion. The weather in summer is very hot and for this reason many of them built dams in the Beresan River, using manure and garbage, in order to have water for the geese and ducks. As a result of these dams, the entrapped water became a hot-bed for bacterial growth and many 'became ill during the summer. The public health authorities should not permit dams built with manure.

The language of the people of Sulz is mostly of the Palatinate, as is spoken in Kandel and Annweiler, the people say, "Ich geh a mitt," (I will go along) and "Sisch emol e Mann un e Frä gewest," (Once there was a man and a woman).

They are early risers and industrious people. During harvesting they usually only have four hours of sleep, some even less. The people are rather rough but approachable and friendly, especially the men, but this could not always be said about the women.

The Settlers of the Colony of Sulz
and their original homes
1839-1840

1. **Karl Roshau** Lutheran.
WIFE: Elisabeth Külmeier 46, daughter of Michael, from Albersweiler, Rhinepalatinate.
CHILDREN: Karl, Friedrich, Anna 11, Katharina 5.

2. **Philipp Ring** 30, son of Georg, from Mannweiler, Rhinepalatinate.
WIFE: Franziska Meuchel 22, daughter of Johann.
CHILDREN: Georg 1, Barbara 4, Marianna 1, Katharina 2.
   3. **Jakob Bernhard** 33, from Rheinzabern, Rhinepalatinate.
WIFE: Magdalena Wetsch 32, daughter of Johann, from Weidental.
CHILDREN: Franz 9, Stephan 2, Franziska 5, Barbara 5, Seraphina 1.
   4. **Konrad Fix** 51, son of Franz, from Albersweiler, Rhinepalatinate.
WIFE: Annamaria Engel 47, daughter of Martin.
CHILDREN: Katharina 16, Elisabeth 14, Annamaria 4, Johannes 9, Konrad 6, Jakob 2.
(a) Joseph Fix 22, son of Konrad.
WIFE: Theresia Stöbner 24, daughter of Peter.
CHILDREN: Katharina 1.
(b) Elisabeth Lauberspacher 61, daughter of Franz Fix (widow).
   5. **Johannes Kupper** 24, son of Johann, from Mühlbach, Rhinepalatinate.
WIFE: Katharina Segmüller 22, daughter of Peter.
CHILDREN: Nikomed 3, Jakob 1, Susanna 1.
   6. **Martin Bisan** 66, son of Michael from Bellheim, Rhinepalatinate.
WIFE: Margaretha Hüfner 48, daughter of Sebastian, from Riedselz, Alsace.
CHILDREN: Barbara 22, Elisabeth 20, Katharina 15, Marianna 13, Annamaria 11.
   7. **Ferdinand Weiss** 53, son of Georg from Aschbach, Rhinepalatinate.
WIFE: Katharina Fleck 48, daughter of Johann, from Wingen, Alsace.
CHILDREN: Katharina 13, Margaretha 11.
   8. **Lukas Weber** 26, son of Michael.
WIFE: Margaretha Ehly 24, daughter of Martin.
CHILDREN: Menna 1, Annamaria 5, Margaretha 3.
   9. **Andreas Gabriel** 65, son of Andreas from Scheibenhart,* Alsace.
WIFE: Margaretha Zimmermann 63, daughter of Joseph, from Kröttweiler, Alsace.
(a) Martin Gabriel 24, son of Andreas.
WIFE: Annamaria Bruckner 28, daughter of Theobald.
CHILDREN: Jakob 4, Joseph 1, Elisabeth 2.

---

*Scheibenhart is located on both sides of the Lauter, and is half Alsatian and half Palatinate.

10. **Stephan Ehly** 41, son of Stephan from Schaidt, Rhinepalatinate.
WIFE: Elisabeth Lorenz 37, daughter of Michael from Siegen, Alsace.
CHILDREN: Georg 16, Martin 8, Peter 4, Philipp 2, Sebastian 1, Marianna 14, Katharina 12, Elisabeth 6.

11. **Anton Bauer** 32, son of Kaspar from Hölschloch, Alsace.
WIFE: Gertrud Sacky 30, daughter of Matthaus.
CHILDREN: Dominik 11, Elisabeth 9, Annamaria 4, Katharina 1, Margaretha 1.
(a) Kaspar Ehrenpreis 32, son of Matthias, from Schwetzingen, Baden.
WIFE: Margaretha Kornely, daughter of Anton, from Berg, Rhinepalatinate.
CHILDREN: Gottlieb 5, Maria-Eva 14, Elisabeth 11, Franziska 7, Annamaria 1, daughter of Kaspar Bauer.

12. **Franz Scherer** 41, son of Andreas, from Hagenbach, Rhinepalatinate.
WIFE: Juliana Zentner 37, daughter of Franz.
CHILDREN: Gabriel 10, Jakob 6, Elisabeth 13, Genovefa 1.
(a) Simon Staudinger 22.
WIFE: Barbara Scherer 19, daughter of Franz.

13. **Christian Breidenreicher** 57, son of Karl, from Lembach, Alsace.
WIFE: Maria-Eva Warter 53, daughter of Martin, from Surburg, Alsace.

14. **Martin Ehly** 55, son of Sebastian, from Schardt, Rhinepalatinate.
WIFE: Barbara Zimmermann 51, daughter of Joseph.
CHILDREN: Barbara 16, Elisabeth 14, Marianna 9.
(a) Martin Ehly 3, son of Martin.
WIFE: Margaretha Weitzstein 18, daughter of Michael, from the colony of Speier.

15. **Matthias Scherer** 30, son of Franz, from Hagenbach, Rhinepalatinate.
WIFE: Magdalena Badinger 30, daughter of Jakob, from Albersweiler, Rhinepalatinate.
CHILDREN: Joseph 7, Franz 5, Hilar 2.

16. **Joseph Braxmeier** 53, son of Johann from Walburg, Alsace.
WIFE: Margaretha Hoffmann 56, daughter of Christoph from Hatzenbühl, Rhinepalatinate.
CHILDREN: Georg 22, Elisabeth (?), Elisabeth Breitenbach 8 (orphan).

17. **Jakob Reinhardt** 83.
WIFE: Katharina Weber 65, daughter of Joseph.

(a) Joseph Zimmermann 25, son of Michael.
WIFE: Margaretha Reinhardt 23, daughter of Jakob.
CHILDREN: Margaretha 1.
(b) Joseph Schaf 28, son of Peter.
WIFE: Margaretha Hutmacher 21, daughter of Anton.
CHILDREN: Hyazint 1, Villana 3.

18. **Joseph Fix*** 42, son of Franz from Albersweiler, Rhinepalatinate.
WIFE: Annamaria Kühlmeier 46, daughter of Michael.
CHILDREN: Konrad 15, Andreas 3, Franz 9, Jakob 6, Jordan 2.

19. **Margaretha Hutmacher** 35, widow, daughter of Philipp Bär.
CHILDREN: Jakob 14, Katharina 12, Anna 9, Thekla 8, Elisabeth 5, Emerenzia 3.
(a) Joseph Hutmacher 23, son of Anton.
WIFE: Katharina Ehly, 21, daughter of Martin.
(b) Anton Hutmacher, 23, son of Anton.
WIFE: Margaretha Heinert 22, daughter of Jakob.
CHILDREN: Regina 2.

20. **Julianna Kupper** 52, widow, daughter of Karl Konrad from Dörrenbach, Rhinepalatinate.
CHILDREN: Georg 14, Peter 12, Anton 10.
(a) Jakob Kupper 20, son of Johann.
WIFE: Magdalena Braxmeier 21, daughter of Joseph.
(b) Markus Braxmeier 21, son of Joseph.
WIFE: Genovefa Kupper, daughter of Johann.

21. **Joseph Meckler** 39, son of Franz from Rohrbach, Baden.
WIFE: Johanna Seitz 37, daughter of Sebastian, from Bundental, Rhinepalatinate.
CHILDREN: Jakob 16, Sebastian 14, Johannes 12, Johann 10, Daniel 8, Joseph 6, Erasmus 6, Anna-Elisabeth 12.
(a) Maria-Eva Seitz, widow; age 60, daughter of Anton Semann from Pfarrhausen, Württemburg.

22. **Peter Schaf** 29, son of Peter.
WIFE: Theresia Masset 38, daughter of Johann Baptista.
CHILDREN: Joseph 6, Johann 4, Peter 2, Johanna 15, Elisabeth 14, Margaretha 10, Marianna 9, Kreszenz 1.

23. **Siegfried Helfrich** 32, son of Jakob from Weidental, Rhinepalatinate.
WIFE: Katharina Baumann 30, daughter of Christian, from Kirchhart, Baden.
CHILDREN: Joseph 12, Franz-Joseph 3, Philipp 1, Magdalena 10, Marianna 6.

---

*Moved to Rumania.

24. **Georg Kunz** 44, son of Friedrich from Spechbach, Baden.
WIFE: Ursula Knoll 35, daughter of Anton, from Büchelberg, Rhinepalatinate.
CHILDREN: Peter 15, Jakob 12, Joseph 6, Johann 6, Didakus 2, Katharina 10, Elisabeth 8, Agnes 3, Barbara 1.

25. **Andreas Scherer** 36, son of Franz.
WIFE: Annamaria Fried 47, daughter of Valentin.
CHILDREN: Dominik 12, Franz 10, Rosina 8, Elisabeth 6, Thomas 3.
Michael Armbrust 22, Annamaria Armbrust 18, from wife's first husband.

26. **Jacob Knittel** 53, son of Adam from Oberseebach, Alsace.
WIFE: Regina Luber 54, daughter of Georg, from Altenstadt, Alsace.
CHILDREN: Martin 17.
(a) Johannes Knittel 24, son of Jakob.
WIFE: Maria-Eva Fitterer 19, daughter of Anton from the colony of Katharinental.
CHILDREN: Katharina 1.

27. **Philipp-Adam Heidt** 41, son of Franz, from Leimersheim, Rhinepalatinate.
WIFE: Katharina Knittel 27, daughter of Jakob.
CHILDREN: Peter 12, Klemens-Nikolaus 8, Marzellius 3, Annamaria 9.

28. **Johannes Heinert** 38, son of Jakob from Ranschbach, Rhinepalatinate.
WIFE: Apolonia Herdy 34, daughter of Johann, from Herxheim, Rhinepalatinate.
CHILDREN: Franz 13, Blasius 4, Adam 1, Annamaria 11, Brigitta 8, Katharina 6, Barbara 1.

29. **Katharina Rebsam** 64, widow of Peter, daughter of Peter Schmalz, from Steinfeld, Rhinepalatinate.
DAUGHTER: Sophia Blumenschein 30, from first husband, Joseph Blumenschein.
(a) Franz Blumenschein 25, son of Joseph.
WIFE: Barbara Derschan 22, daughter of Nikolaus.

30. **Anton Stöbner** 22, son of Peter.
WIFE: Barbara Sattler, 31, daughter of Paul.
CHILDREN: Joseph 6, Michael 1, Franzeska 8, Willana 3.

31. **Adam Morell** 40, son of Matthias from Rheinzabern, Rhinepalatinate.
WIFE: Elisabeth Breitenreicher 27, daughter of Christian from Surburg, Alsace.
CHILDREN: Peter 8, Regina 14, Margaretha 1.
STEP-CHILDREN: Johannes Wetsch 8, Franziska 5, children of Friedrich Wetsch.

(a) Anton Mildenberger 24, son of Joseph from Kirchhardt, Baden.
WIFE: Maria-Eva Morell 19, daughter of Adam.

32. **Jakob Schlosz** 35, son of Joseph from Jockgrim, Rhinepalatinate.
WIFE: Annamaria Staudinger 25, daughter of Franz from the colony of Karlsruhe.
CHILDREN: Simon 1, Annamaria 8, Brigitta 3.

33. **Franz Wetsch** 33, son of Johannes from Weidental, Rhinepalatinate.
WIFE: Marianna Heinert 27, daughter of Jakob, from Ranschbach, Rhinepalatinate.
CHILDREN: Wilhelm 12, August 10, Jakob 7, Thomas 1.

(a) Matthias Schmidt 34, son of Valentin, from Brühl, Baden.
WIFE: Klara Bachert 18, daughter of Matthias, from the colony of Katharinental.
CHILDREN: Joseph 1.

34. **Barbara Derschan** 42, daughter of Philipp Rollwacher from Oberseebach, Alsace, widow of Nikolaus Derschan.
CHILDREN: Anton 16, Michael 13, Jakob 10, Peter 7, Johanna 11, Katharina 6.

(a) Adam Heck 30, son of Joseph, from Bietigheim, Baden.
WIFE: Sophie Schloss 22, daughter of Joseph, from the colony of Sulz.
CHILDREN: Stanislaus 2, Margaretha 1.

35. **Johannes Schmidt** 28, son of Valentin, from Brühl, Baden.
WIFE: Katharina Heidt 26, daughter of Franz.
CHILDREN: Joseph 5, Franz 1, Veronika 3.

(a) Eva Stein 43, daughter of Valentin Schmidt.
CHILDREN: Ignaz 3.

(b) Peter Kunz 38, son of Friedrich, from Weidental, Rhinepalatinate.
WIFE: Susanna Sakke 36, daughter of Matthias from the colony of Landau.
CHILDREN: Ludwig 17, Kajetan 5, Gertrude 12, Regina 3, Marianna 1.

(c) Anton Lefrank 24, son of Joseph from Zabern, Alsace.
WIFE: Annamaria Hatz 23, daughter of Michael from the colony of Baden.
CHILDREN: Rosina 4, Margaretha 2.

36. **Michael Sigwart** 39, son of Johann from Lembach, Alsace.
WIFE: Barbara Kriegsmeyer 30, from Bornheim, Rhinepalatinate.
CHILDREN: Ludwig 16, Michael 9, Peter 6, Magdalena 18, Johanna 12, Barbara 2.

(a) Joseph Schuschu 43, son of Peter from Rheinzabern, Rhinepalatinate.

WIFE: Magdalena Sigwart 36, daughter of Johannes.
CHILDREN: Johann 11, Wendelin 3, Elisabeth 13, Marianna 7.
(b) Georg Fischer 67, son of Kaspar from Obersteinbach, Alsace.
WIFE: Margaretha Klemens 67, daughter of George.
37. **Demetrius Weber** 22, son of Michael.
WIFE: Katharina Armbrust 21, daughter of Anton.
CHILDREN: Adam 1, Elisabeth 2.
38. **Michael Weber** 61, Lutheran, from Hechingen, Baden.
WIFE: Elisabeth Schmidt 28, daughter of Valentin from Brühl, Baden.
CHILDREN: Christian 9, Michael 4, Jakob 1, Katharina 7, Magdalena 1.
Margaretha Zumkehr 60, widow of Vanentin Schmdit, and daughter of Wilhelm.
39. **Sebastian Ehly** 34, son of Stephan from Schaidt, Rhinepalatinate.
WIFE: Theresia Wetsch 24, daughter of Johann.
CHILDREN: Joseph 13, Ludwig 6, Katharina 10, Elisabeth 8, Seraphina 4, Katharina 2, Franziska 1.
40. **Peter Stöbner** 62, son of Jakob from Wernersberg, Rhinepalatinate.
WIFE: Sophia Weinert 51, daughter of Adam from Arzheim, Rhinepalatinate.
CHILDREN: Michael 16, Juliana 13.
(a) Johannes Brucker 20, son of Theobald from the colony of Karlsruhe.
WIFE: Margaretha Stöbner 20, daughter of Peter.
41. **Christian Keller** 66, son of Joseph from Bindersbach, Rhinepalatinate.
WIFE: Annamaria Stöbner 64, daughter of Jakob from Wernersberg, Rhinepalatinate.
CHILDREN: Leonhard 40, Peter 32.
(a) Elisabeth Keller 22, daughter of Johannes Frank and widow of Jakob Keller.
DAUGHTER: Regina 1.
(b) Joseph Keller 22, son of Christian.
WIFE: Juliana Thomas 18, daughter of Georg.
42. **Georg Heinert** 33, son of Jakob from Arzheim, Rhinepalatinate.
WIFE: Elizabeth Schell 31, daughter of Michael from Schleital, Alsace.
(a) Michael Gartner 23, son of Georg.
WIFE: Regina Roll 18, daughter of Martin.
43. **Jakob Heinert** 44, son of Jakob from Arzheim,

Rhinepalatinate.

WIFE: Magdalena Rözle 25, daughter of Joseph from Grombach, Baden.

CHILDREN: Franz 20, Jakob 13, Joseph 1, Apolonia 11, Marianna 8, Katharina 6, Annamaria 2, Barbara 1.

44. **Dominik Deiss** 37, son of Johann from Schönenburg, Alsace.

WIFE: Barbara Bauer 33, daughter of Kaspar from Altstadt, Rhinepalatinate.

CHILDREN: Franz 7.

MOTHER: Katharina Deiss 63, daughter of Georg Kay.

(a) Franz Weinert 27, son of Adam.

WIFE: Annamaria Rink 20, daughter of Georg.

CHILDREN: Andreas 3, Sebastian 1.

(b) Theresia Freidig 39, widow of Peter Freidig, and daughter of Johann Deiss.

CHILDREN: Peter 19, Karl 16, Maria 11, Margaretha 7.

45. **Wilhelm Köhler** 39, son of Karl, from Schwetzingen, Baden.

WIFE: Ursula Heinert 34, daughter of Jakob, from Anspach, Baden.

CHILDREN: Joseph 11, Johannes 8, Sebastian 3, Sigfried 1, Katharina 17, Elisabeth 1.

46. **Johann Baptista Knoll** 26, son of Anton, from Büchelberg, Rhinepalatinate.

WIFE: Barbara Immel 20, daughter of Joseph, from the colony of Speier.

CHILDREN: Barbara 2, Hyazintha 1.

(a) Peter Fischer 27, son of Georg, from Steinbach, Rhinepalatinate.

WIFE: Margaretha Knoll 25, daughter of Anton.

CHILDREN: Joachim 2, Sigfried 1, Dominik 1.

47. **Peter Schilling** 46, son of Joseph from Schluchtern, Baden.

WIFE: Elisabeth Blech 40, daughter of Franz.

CHILDREN: Franz 16, Petronella 2.

(a) Franz Blech 26, son of Franz from Konstanz, Baden.

WIFE: Elisabeth Ott, 19, daughter of Johann.

48. **Johannes Wetsch** 57, son of Jakob from Weidental, Rhinepalatinate.

WIFE: Elisabeth Bauer 46, daughter of Kaspar from Surburg, Alsace.

49. **Georg Tremmel** 31, son of Wenzeslaus from Brühl, Baden.

WIFE: Annamaria Lorenz 31, daughter of Michael from Siegen, Alsace.

CHILDREN: Stephan 12, Erasmus 3, Joseph 1.

Barbara Tremmel 58, daughter of Michael Werner from Brühl, Baden, and widow of Wenzeslaus Tremmel.

50. **Wendelin Heidt** 33, son of Franz from Leimersheim, Rhinepalatinate.

WIFE: Franziska Straub 34, daughter of Johann from Oestringen, Baden.

CHILDREN: Adam 6, Joseph 1, Annamaria 12, Marianna 10, Margaretha 1.

51. **Georg Thomas** 43, son of Peter from Siegen, Alsace.

WIFE: Margaretha Blumenschein, daughter of Joseph from Steinfeld, Rhinepalatinate.

CHILDREN: Heinrich 19, Johannes 14, Anton 12, Joseph Michael 9, Georg 7, Franz 5, Konrad 2, Katharina 1.

(a) Franz Wurm Lutheran, from Groszliebental.

WIFE: Katharina Wetsch 26, daughter of Johannes.

52. **Michael Zimmermann** 54, son of Joseph from Kröttweiler, Alsace.

WIFE: Margaretha Brettmeier 48, daughter of Konrad from Büchelberg, Rhinepalatinate.

CHILDREN: Anton 17, Stephan 5, Sophie 15, Annamaria 13, Scholastika 9.

53. **Ludwig Zentner** 42, son of Franz from Kandel, Rhinepalatinate.

WIFE: Eva Ehly 38, daughter of Stephan from Schaidt, Rhinepalatinate.

CHILDREN: Jakob 12, Konrad 4, Margaretha 14, Julianna 7, Salomea 1.

54. **Joseph Nachbauer** 27.

WIFE: Annamaria Müller, 23, daughter of Jakob.

ORPHAN: Joseph Müller.

55. **Michael Geiger** 59, son of Michael, from Ettenheim, Baden.

WIFE: Katharina Reis 50, daughter of Georg, from Wollmesheim, Rhinepalatinate.

(a) Johannes Geiger, 28, son of Michael.

WIFE: Ursula Masset 19, daughter of Johann Baptista.

56. **Joseph Forster*** 28, son of Adam, from Herxheim, Rhinepalatinate.

WIFE: Annamaria Knittel 25, daughter of Jakob.

CHILDREN: Elisabetha 5, Susanna 3, Margaretha 1.

MOTHER: Margaretha Forster 68, daughter of Johann Fritz.

57. **Johannes Frank** 49, son of Martin, from Kapsweyer, Rhinepalatinate.

WIFE: Elisabeth Gress 47, daughter of Matthaus, from Reimersweiler, Alsace.

CHILDREN: Kaspar 20, Joseph 13, Albin 7, Katharina 16, Magdalena 10.

---

*All the Forsters went to America.

58. **Joseph Weber** 52, son of Kaspar, from Albersweiler, Rhinepalatinate.
WIFE: Annamaria Herdy 36, daughter of Johann, from Herxheim, Rhinepalatinate.
CHILDREN: Anton 18, Joseph 11, Jakob 9, Konrad 1, Barbara 16, Katharina 7.
59. **Peter Segmüller** 51, son of Michael from Rheinzabern, Rhinepalatinate.
WIFE: Annamaria Weber 43, daughter of Kaspar from Albersweiler, Rhinepalatinate.
CHILDREN: Johann 25, Michael 18, Johann(II) 5, Jakob 3, Eva 12, Margaretha 15, Brigitta 10, Annamaria 7, Ottilia 1.
STEP-CHILDREN: Martin Weisgerber 17, Elisabeth Weisgerber 15, children of Heinrich Weisgerber of Josephstal in Liebental District.
60. **Johannes Sattler** 42, son of Paul from Bornheim, Rhinepalatinate.
WIFE: Franziska Ehly 36, daughter of Martin.
CHILDREN: Joseph 13, Dominik 10, Daniel 6, Barbara 16, Katharina 3, Margaretha 1.
61. **Jakob Weber** 39, son of Kaspar from Albersweiler, Rhinepalatinate.
WIFE: Katharina Lorentz 34, daughter of Michael from Kröttweiler, Alsace.
CHILDREN: Jakob 4, Jordan 1, Elisabeth 14, Annamaria 11, Margaretha 5.
62. **Katharina Meuchel** 46, daughter of Johannes Kuhn from Leimersheim, Rhinepalatinate, widow of Johannes Meuchel.
CHILDREN: Jakob 12, Genovefa 9.
(a) Philipp Stumpf, son of Jakob from the colony of Speier.
WIFE: Katharina Meuchel 16, daughter of Johannes.
(b) Franz Meuchel 26, son of Johann.
WIFE: Marianna Engel 20, daughter of Anton.
CHILDREN: Philipp 2, Lukas 1.
63. **Johannes Ehlis** Lutheran from Rohrbach colony.
WIFE: Katharina Forster 30, daughter of Adam from Herxheim, Rhinepalatinate.
CHILDREN: Anton 10, Johannes 8, Sebastian 6, Joseph 1, Elisabeth 11, Anna-Eva 4, Franziska 3.
(a) Joseph Braxmeier 24, son of Joseph.
WIFE: Anna-Eva Meuchel 19, daughter of Johann.
CHILDREN: Philipp 1.
(b) Joseph Scherer 25, son of Valentin from the colony of Baden, Kutschurgen.
WIFE: Elisabeth Sattler 24, daughter of Paul.

STEP-CHILDREN: Franz-Joseph Brücker 5, Johanna Brücker 5, children of Daniel Brucker.

64. **Georg-Jakob Brucker** 36, son of Theobald from Offenbach, Rhinepalatinate.
WIFE: Katharina Staudinger 33, daughter of Franz from Wanzenan, Alsace.
CHILDREN: Johann 12, Joseph 9, Sebastian 6, Villana 4, Annamaria 3.
Simon Staudinger 20, hired man, son of Franz.
Juliana Lefrank 12, maid, daughter of Joseph.
(a) Joseph Brucker 25, son of Theobald from the colony of Karlsruhe.
WIFE: Annamaria Hellmann 22, daughter of Michael.
CHILDREN: Georg 1, Annamaria 1.
(b) Theobald Brucker 60, son of Christopher from Offenbach, Rhinepalatinate.
WIFE: Apolonia Garrecht 62, daughter of Georg-Jakob.
(c) Johannes Brucker 22, son of Theobald.
WIFE: Margaretha Stöbner 21, daughter of Peter.
CHILDREN: Joseph 1.
(d) Joseph Schoch 21.
WIFE: Regina Stöbner 20, daughter of Peter.
(e) Johannes Helfrich 26, son of Jakob.
WIFE: Katharina Deck 20, daughter of Ulrich.
CHILDREN: Jakob 3, Dominik 2.
(f) Georg Rebsam 23, son of Peter.
WIFE: Regina Heinert 18, daughter of Jakob.
(g) Johannes Wetsch 27, son of Johann.
WIFE: Elisabeth Weisgerber 17, daughter of Heinrich.
(h) Jakob Bretzer 61, son of Martin from Baden.
WIFE: Magdalena Schaf 40, daughter of Peter.
CHILDREN: Michael 4.

The beginning of
the Colony of Sulz

The colony of Sulz was settled in the years 1809 and 1810. As previously indicated, one group came in the fall of 1809 and built themselves huts in which they spent the winter under the most unfavourable conditions. The other group came in the spring of 1810 and construction of the Crown houses started immediately, directed by experienced persons from the Liebental colonies. Built of stamped earth, the houses contained one living room, one bedroom and a kitchen with a porch. The roof was covered with reeds. One such Crown house is still standing in Speier, and three years ago celebrated its one hundredth jubilee.

The head of every household received an advance loan for house construction and other essentials. Each proprietor also received a cow, and those who did not bring horses with them from Germany received some from the Crown. Every three households also received one plough, one harrow, and seed wheat, but by the spring of 1810 the settlers had not yet done any seeding.

The Sulz settlers were mostly tradesmen or day labourers and had no knowledge of agriculture. Only one man had experience in this, Peter Stöbner Sr. from Wernersberg in the Palatinate.

After they were settled in their houses, Inspector Strohmeier took a census of all of the Beresan colonies. When he arrived in Sulz he commanded the bailiff to ring the bell, advising every head of the family to stand at the gate of his yard so that he may be interviewed by the inspector. The inspector, accompanied by the bailiff and the village mayor, made the rounds through the colony from one end to the other. The inspector asked the first man, "What is your trade?" "Stocking weaver, your Excellency,*" he answered. The inspector received many answers to his question, e.g. soap-maker, silk-weaver, furrier, etc. He became very indignant and said, "Where in the devil are the farmers?" Finally they came to Peter Stöbner Sr. whose reply to the inspectors question was, "I am a farmer, Excellency." The inspector patted him on the shoulder and said, "At last I have found my man. Please show me your farm." After the inspector had seen it all and found it in good condition, he appointed Stöbner overseer and instructor for the farmers of Sulz.

The first census in January 1811 showed 63 Catholic families with 117 men and 105 women and one Lutheran family with two males and one female.

The amount seeded in 1811 amounted to 128 tschetwert of winter wheat. Spring wheat in 1812 was 64 tschetwert and oats 64 tschetwert. The total amount seeded in 1811-1812 was 256 tschetwert.

The tradesmen in Sulz in 1811 were:

HARNESS MAKER: Georg Nagel.
CARPENTERS: Matthias Morell, Philipp Kirchheimer, Joseph Schimpf, Johann Kupper.
BLACKSMITH: Jakob Helfrich.
NAIL-MAKER: Christian Breitenreicher.
MILLER: Johannes Laubersbacher.
BAKER: Jakob Lefrank.

---

*So as not to be wrong, the colonists called all supervisors, "Excellency."

SHOE-MAKER: Franz Zentner.
RAKE-MAKER: Michael Weber.
SHEPHERD: Leonard Tutt.

In 1818, the census in Sulz was as follows: 49 families with 108 men and 113 women, altogether 221 people. The community owned 309 horses, 267 horned cattle, 15 sheep, 243 pigs, 41 ploughs, 38 harrows, 47 wagons, 16 distaffs.

Tradesmen were: carpenters 1, cabinet maker 1, tailors 2, weaver 1, shoemakers 2, and one mason.

The amount seeded for the year 1817-1818 was as follows:

	tschetwert.	tschetwerik.
Rye and winter wheat	48	2
Summer wheat	104	
Barley	36	
Oats	32	4
Potatoes	54	
Buckwheat	1	
Corn	2	1
Millet	2	4
Peas	2	1
Lentils	3	
Beans	2	1
Flax		1
Hemp		1
Total:	286.0	15.0

The Community Land of the
Colony of Sulz

The community land of Sulz amounted to 4402.75 dessiatines. The land was a long rectangle, its width bordering on the Beresan for approximately 6 versts and its long side, approximately 12 versts was across Fox Valley. All of the other colonies were situated on both sides of the river, but the colony of Sulz was only on the left side.

The elders of the community tell the following story about the land division. During the general survey of the land, the surveyor was making a furrow with the plough in a westerly direction near Sulz. A rider from the land owner, Yeschitzsky, came up in great haste, whispered something in the surveyors ear, squeezed something into his hand and then rode away. The surveyor then yelled, "Go back, one may go no further."

The land of Sulz was bounded by the land of the Tartars in the south which has now been bought by the people of Sulz. On the west is the so-named Keller steppe. On the north, Sulz is bounded by the land of the colonies of Landau and Karlsruhe and on the east, by the estate of nobleman, Kirijakow.

The land is mostly uneven and in addition to the banks of the Beresan on the east, the Fox Valley (Karlsruhe Valley) runs through its midst. Also, to the east of Fox Valley, there are several valleys and ravines of which Wolf Valley is the deepest.

The soil is varied. From the Beresan (river) east and around the colony, the black soil is approximately 14 inches deep. On the west bank and from Fox Valley north towards the Karlsruhe border, the black soil is much thinner and very sandy. In Fox Valley itself, particularly near the river bed, the black soil is very deep and forms a rich, productive garden soil on the many small meadows. Until recently, the people of Sulz have not planted any gardens there as they are not knowledgeable about soil science. The steep north banks would protect the fruit gardens from the frost. Towards the south, on the west bank of Fox Valley, there is mostly a reddish yellow, loamy soil which is excellent for vineyards, but until now, no one has tried to plant a vineyard there.

From Fox Valley east, one finds the best soil, especially where the "Deerfield" and the "Oxenfield" used to be.

In 1823, on the orders of the authorities of the colonies, fruit trees were planted in the area adjacent to the river and to the east of the colony a vineyard was started on the so-named "Little Street." Since most of the colonists had no experience with growing fruit trees or vineyards, nearly all of those planted, died. When the authorities enquired about the success of the planting, the village officials answered, "Nothing grows here."

General Eugen Hahn did not consider this reason valid in 1842 and gave strict orders that in all of the colonies, trees, gardens and orchards "must grow." He made the mayor and councillors responsible and subsequently the trees started to grow, creating a forest and gardens, which became the fairest ornament in the Beresan colonies.

The forest was planted in the southern part of the colony. To every head of the household was given 1/2 dessiatine of land. The trees along the rich soil of the river bed grew to magnificent splendour and through their pleasant fragrance, created a bird sanctuary in the surrounding steppe. On a beautiful, quiet May evening, it created a 'little bit of Paradise'. But after the supervision by the Fürsorge Committee ceased in 1871, this beautiful forest became a victim of the greed and ignorance of several settlers.

The orchards also did very well. The pears and apricots were extraordinarily large and tasty. The best orchards keepers in Sulz were

Jakob Weber, the old "Bastel," (Sebastian Ehly), and Georg Wetsch. Recently the people planted fruit trees where previously the forested part had been. Also, on the 'little street' where the first fruit trees were planted and did not want to grow, new small plants have been set out which are growing well. However, many of them were damaged by the red louse and other insects.

The Parish of Sulz

The colony of Sulz comprises 200 lots with 1915 inhabitants, all Catholics. Other denominations remain only temporarily. The parish of Sulz was founded in 1869. Previous to that it was affiliated with the parish of Landau. The hamlets of Benderhof and Wowtsche, and those Catholics settled in the Beresan valley, all belong to the parish of Sulz. The Sulz parish belongs to the Nikolayev deanery of the diocese of Tiraspol. For the past two years Sulz has had its own post office.

The Story of the Parish

As the people in the Beresan colonies became settled and took on the responsibilities of colonists, they wished to separate from the mother church at Landau and to organize their own parishes. The colony of Speier was on its own. Karlsruhe, along with Katharinental, had founded their own parishes with permission from the authorities. The desire for their own church grew, along with the wish to be separated from Landau. It was the unanimous wish of the community that a properly worded, written petition be forwarded to the church authorities with the request for founding their own parish. Permission was soon granted for the founding of the Parish of Sulz. However, things did not move very quickly because there was a great shortage of priests in the Tiraspol diocese at that time. The parish of Sulz was finally established in 1869, but for a time the new parish had to be supervised from Landau until a priest could be sent there. They did not have long to wait as the authorities had already designated one, whom we shall now introduce.

Sequence of Priests in Sulz

Father Julian Michalsky *Vicar 1871-1882*

Father Julian Michalsky was born in 1837 in the province of Radom in the kingdom of Poland. He received his classical education in a so-called district school. Following this, he entered the religious seminary in the diocese of Wlatzlaw. After successfully completing his studies here, he was ordained a priest in 1860 in the parish church of Petrikau, where he worked for 3 years.

When the Polish revolution broke out in 1863, the suspicion of participation was pointed at the young priest. He was immediately placed in solitary confinement for 5 months. After his case was investigated and he remained suspect, he was deported, along with political criminals, to the province of Kostroma where he ate the bitter bread of banishment and exile for 8 years. One can easily imagine what a difficult 8 years this young priest endured under these rude people. Sacrifices of all kinds were his daily lot. The thing that hurt him most was the complete denial of any priestly functions such as reading the Holy Mass. The dear Lord did not forget his faithful servant in his exile, but rather endowed him with the comfort of rich grace in the resignation to his Holy Will.

These eight years of suffering in exile laid the foundation for 'pious living' for this young priest and his future blessed activities. 'He who has borne such a heavy cross has received a certificate from God. On entering public life he will not waver nor swerve from the road of truth, and under all circumstances will stand fast as the rock in a stormy sea.'

After having graduated from this school of horrors, Father Michalsky came to Sulz where a difficult task awaited him. At this time, Sulz stood on a very low level of morality. The whole colony had become divided over a quarrel about a school teacher. Nothing could ever be decided at a community meeting. The two sides would not compromise.

Village law and order had disappeared. When the mayor was from the lower colony, the people in the upper colony would not obey him, and vice versa. On Sundays the old people went to the taverns and quarrelled and the younger ones collected in someone's yard or in the street and played the much liked "Oriol."

This was the situation in which Father Michalsky found himself. He brought good will and a great religious zeal but did not understand German very well. He did, however, make every effort to learn German. Through diligence and perseverance, he was soon able to read his sermon from a manuscript. He took great pains to teach the people the commandments of love of God and one's neighbour, and to practice this virtue in their daily living. His fiery sermons, coming from his heart, impressed the people and resulted in a better way of life for them. The people began to realize that they were not created to fight with each other, but rather to live in love and peace as it becomes every Christian. After two years Sulz was completely changed as a result of the work of the zealous Father Michalsky. Through his humility and example, through his modesty and unassuming ways, his courteous manner to rich and poor alike, he won all to his heart. The people knew that he was a strict priest who worked only for the honor of God and the salvation of souls. Since all loved him, seldom were any of his requests refused.

With childlike trust, the people clung to him, came to him with their problems and sought his advice, help, and consolation. Like a father, he walked among his parishioners and was a good friend of the children, like his divine Master. The youngsters loved him and always brought him presents, whereupon the good priest gave them pretty pictures or crosses. Father Michalsky also did much to beautify and adorn the church. He loved good singing and church music. He became famous through out the Beresan for introducing a new variety of potato, which spread throughout the community and among the Russian neighbours. Today they are still known as Father's Potatoes."

Father Michalsky worked in Sulz for 10 years and, for reasons which I can not relate here, he was moved to Kleinliebental in 1883. Here he worked diligently at his duties for two years. Later he became vicar in Odessa, which place he administered officially after 1892.

In January 1902 he was named curate of the Polish Nation. He had not been well of late and requested permission from his superiors to be sent to Pyatigorsk in the Caucasus in order to undergo treatments in the mineral waters. His request was granted and he worked in that parish for four years. In 1906 he requested permission to leave the diocese of Tiraspol. He moved to his home and presently is a priest in Zlozew 'where he is helping the vicar while awaiting his call to Heaven.

In 1882 to 1883 Sulz was supervised by Father J. Dobrowolsky from Landau and also by Father J. Ihly from Speier.

FATHER ADAM GUTOWSKY

From 29 June 1884 to 25 July 1884, Father Adam Gutowsky was the administrator. He was born in Lithuania in 1860. He finished four classes in the highschool in Mitau and then entered the seminary in Saratov. While a student, he was also business manager in the seminary and could therefore only fulfill his duties as a candidate to the priesthood with difficulty.

He was ordained a priest by Bishop Zottmann on the 24 April 1883 and was then sent to Sulz as the administrator. He was a conscientious worker and was well liked.

In 1884 he was sent to Rostov on the Don as the administrator. Here he worked for several years until he died of cancer at a very young age.

It is of some interest to note that in his home Father Gutowsky had seven uncles who were all priests. When Father Gutowsky died,

Sulz was administered from Speier for one month.

FATHER JOHANN UNGEMACH *Administrator*
12 October 1884 to 28 October 1890

Father Johann Ungemach was born in Josephstal in 1860 and ordained as a priest in 1883. The story here is that Father Ungemach provided the initiative for the separation of Blumenfeld from Sulz and also obtained permission to build a church in Blumenfeld. In Elsass he built a new church and organized the founding of a new parish. In 1893 he built a new school in Mannheim and in 1896, the parish church. He also obtained permission to build a church in Georgental. He built schools in Georgental, Johannestal and Mandrovka. He also built a parish school, a rectory and three church houses in Berdyansk and obtained land for a cemetery.

From all this, one can see that Father Ungemach was indeed a leader and builder. He was nicknamed the 'engineer priest.' Since 1911 Father Ungemach has been the dean in the Berdyansk deanery.

After Father Ungemach left, Sulz was again supervised from Landau until 1891.

FATHER JOHANN KOBERLEIN *Administrator*
4 October 1891 to 27 April 1895

Father Köberlein was born in 1863. He completed his course in the seminary in Saratov and was ordained on the 12 August 1890. He came to Sulz in 1891, where he worked as a priest for four years. Later he became ill and went into retirement. He died on the 17 August 1910.

For several months thereafter, Sulz was administered from Landau.

FATHER JOSEPH KESSLER
Pastor from 8 July 1895 to 23 September 1899.
Presently Bishop of Tiraspol.

Father Joseph Kessler was born on the 12 August 1862 in Louis on the Karaman, in the province of Samara. He was baptised on the same day.

Although the education of our colonists at that time left something to be desired, there were some well educated individuals. The families of Kessler and Schneider, from which Father Joseph descended, were among these. Suffice it to say that his grandfather, Joseph Kessler, was the community secretary in Mariental for many years and his great-grandfather, Anton Schneider, was the editor of the well known "Volga Chronicle." Education was an heirloom the ancestors had brought with them from the German homeland.

When the first county school opened in the German colonies in 1871, the curriculum was under the jurisdiction of the Minister of

143

Education. Joseph was one of the first pupils, and after five years he successfully passed the examinations and was granted a shorter term of military service. He was diligent, intelligent, and loved to study. His parents, however, were poor and could not pay for any advanced education. In his youth he had indicated interest in the priesthood, but even the cost of attending the seminary was beyond their means.

Such an unfavourable situation overshadowing his calling would have been the end for most people. The decision was made that the boy was to learn his father's trade. After a year everyone gave up the notion of any further education for the young tradesman, except Joseph. A little voice within him kept saying that he would one day be a priest, but how this would come about he himself had no idea. With this purpose in mind, he studied Latin grammar diligently. How thankful he would have been if there had been someone who could have helped him resolve the uncertainties he had about the numerous rules. Unfortunately, he could not find a teacher who knew Latin. The local priest, because of his numerous duties, did not have the time. Those others who had graduated from the seminary did not have the desire to help. No doubt this 13-year-old boy wondered whether his desire to be a priest was but a vain self-deception.

At this time, many colonists were migrating to America. This caused a business slump and Joseph's parents, though people of untiring industry, became very poor. Presently, through the workings of the Lord, his parents obtained the means to pay for his education. He was overjoyed at the prospect of starting his training as a priest. After writing the entrance examinations, he was placed in the second year of the boy's seminary. At the end of three years, he finished his preparatory schooling and was admitted to the clerical seminary. After completing his courses at the seminary, the young cleric was sent by the diocesan authorities to the Clerical Academy at Petersburg to pursue post-graduate studies.

Here he was the only German among 60 Polish and Lithuanian students. This was a great opportunity for him to learn Polish, which came in very handy in his later calling. He was ordained a priest on the 4 March 1889 by Archbishop Gintowt with the consent of his own bishop. On the feast of St. Joseph, he said his first mass at St. Stanislaus Church in Petersburg.

After four years of study, he received the degree of Master of Theology. He was returned to his home as vicar in charge of the Cathedral and appointed Professor of Latin in the diocesan seminary.

At the end of two years he had to exchange these positions with that of an administrator of the parish of Simpheropol. The 6000 Catholics here were of various nationalities and were scattered over an area of 600 square versts. Normal pastoral activity was not possible. There were instances when the priest had sick calls from three places at the same time.

In Simpheropol he restored the rather poor church, built a rectory, gathered the Catholics from Sevastopol, persuaded the community of Alexandrovka (where through some foolishness, two chapels were built under one roof) to build another church. Permission for this, however, was granted only after he became bishop.

He fought against the public lack of faith of some Catholics who blasphemed what they had never learned, against heresy, freethinking, religious obscurantism, and the prevalence of mixed marriages.

After four years of arduous and painful activity, he was removed to a German parish. The governor of Crimea had denounced him as a religious fanatic to the Minister of the Interior. So it came about that Father Joseph Kessler was sent to Sulz in the summer of 1895. Sulz at that time was one of the disreputable parishes in the diocese. This rumour was not true as was proved by the friendly reception given to the priest by the parishioners. The good relationship between the priest and the parish was never disturbed.

The community raised his salary and on their own initiative constructed a number of new buildings on the church grounds. They spent generous amounts of money towards a new organ and tower clock, which the priest imported from abroad.

Among his favorite occupations was the religious instruction in the schools. As in earlier days, he himself instructed the children daily. After the difficult pastorate in Simpheropol, where today there are four priests posted, his work in Sulz was relaxing. Here he could study theological writings to his heart's content. He had plenty of spare time from his routine duties. At this time the weekly newspaper "Klemens" was established through the efforts of Prelate Kruschinsky. Father Joseph was one of the active promoters and collaborators.

On the 15 September 1899 Father Joseph Kessler was appointed administrator of the parish of Kischinev. When the day of his departure arrived it became obvious how the pastor and the parish loved one another. At his farewell sermon everyone was in tears. In Kischinev he built a parish school and constructed a chapel in Bendery, where there was not yet a priest.

As a result of the raw weather he caught frequent colds while making his rounds in the communities and colonies. His health was severely affected so that he was no longer able to do his duties in the large parish of Kischinev. But, because of the shortage of priests, there was no chance of getting any assistance. At the urgent request of the new Ordinary of the diocese, Bishop Baron Von der Ropp, Father Kessler accepted the responsible post of Inspector and Professor at the Seminary. He left the parish on the 10 January 1903. The Polish Catholics still have great love and respect for this priest even today.

His new appointment required all his energy and in no way provided peace and quiet for his convalescence. After the first school year he became seriously ill and was confined to bed. A short rest in the Caucasus brought him only slight relief. He faced the second school year with considerable anxiety. However, Providence had called him to a still more difficult task. He was to become Bishop of the diocese. Judicious men, whose counsel he sought in this serious matter, advised him to accept the burden, for they regarded his priestly career and the circumstances of his appointment as evident signs of divine providence.

On the 28 October 1904, on the feast of the Apostles Simon and Jude, he was consecrated a bishop in St. Catherine's Church in Petersburg. He said his first Pontifical High Mass on the 7 November 1904 in the presence of many priests and laymen, on the Feast of the Assumption of the Mother of God. He was now in charge of the diocese which he had often administered during the absence of his predecessor.

The time when Bishop Kessler took over the guidance of the diocese was, without a doubt, one of the most ill-fated to hit the Russian Fatherland. In the far east there was the unfortunate war. At home there was obstruction and open rebellion against the legal government. Crop failures, hunger and pestilence among men and beasts had a damaging effect not only on ordinary citizens, but on many Christians and some priests.

That some forsook their religion and some of the priests gave up their priestly duties is a sad truth. Bishop Kessler realized that to remedy this situation it was necessary to reform the seminary. His predecessor had already made plans to enlarge the small seminary building. For this purpose he had collected 18,672 rubles in the diocese. The new Ordinary (Bishop) took the money and immediately planned a new building. He also proposed to expand the seminary for boys into a fully accredited high school.

The minister in charge of high schools informed him that his program was not acceptable. But he received the assurance that permission to open a high school would be granted if he adopted the regular program of studies and placed the school under the control of the Ministry of Enlightenment. On this point he wished first to obtain the counsel of the Holy Father before making a decision.

He obtained the best teachers in the diocese for the institution, increased the class hours in the most important subjects and appointed a priest to help the inspector to better supervise the discipline.

Soon after his consecration he sent his first pastoral letter to his clergy and the faithful, which was widely accepted without dissension. Since that time he has sent out a pastoral letter to the clergy and the people every year. The second letter dealt with 'Christian Instruction,' others with marriage, the harmful interference by the laity in church affairs, church property and its administration. The letter dealing with frequent Holy Communion and about drunkenness was written only in Polish. All other letters were written in both German and Polish. He organized a society to publish the church paper, 'Klemens.' He also started the periodical, "Deutsche Rundschau" (German Review), and for this purpose donated 1356 rubles. The society obtained a printing press and bookstore with the hope that once the publications became known to the people it would pay for itself. For half a year he had the bookstore in his own residence, having to take over this new undertaking because of poor circumstances. Even today the bookstore with devotional materials is located in a rent-free room in the bishop's home near the Cathedral in Saratov.

He was the first to succeed in separating the Armenians from the diocese. He obtained for them a priest as administrator with the headquarters in Tiflis.

He confirmed 75,000 people, consecrated 31 churches and travelled almost everywhere in the vast diocese. He preached the word of God everywhere, in German and Polish. In 1907 he had four foreign missionaries come to conduct missions in the deanery of Odessa. He himself travelled with three Franciscan Polish missionaries whom he had brought from Galicia to conduct missions for the Polish people in the diocese. He had planned to have the sons of St. Alphonsus preach the word of God in other parts of the diocese, but he could not obtain permission from the government.

In order to improve the singing in the seminary and in the Cathedral, he sent a young priest to the church music school in Regensburg. In 1908, when the Pope celebrated his 50th jubilee in the priesthood, he made his visit "ad limina" and, on this occasion, delivered the "Peter's Pence" to the Pope and best wishes on behalf of the clergy and faithful of the diocese. In this same year, he visited Lourdes for the second time, where he again and again witnessed astonishing cures.

The summer air in Saratov, for the most part, is not good for older people. the bishop therefore found it impossible to remain for the summer months, particularly since he did not wish to injure his health and be unable to perform his duties. Consequently, he built a summer villa for the bishops of Tiraspol at a cost of 15,000 rubles, on 5 dessiatines of land.

The seminary made considerable progress under his guidance. Not far from the city it acquired an estate of 149 dessiatines of land of which 15 dessiatines was forest. The seminary operated a farm there. In 1906 a large new hospital was built from the profits at a cost of 11,500 rubles. Near the Cathedral, on the grounds of the old school, the parish of Saratov founded a nice new school. This was due to the initiative and support of the pastor of the diocese. May he live to see the building of the new seminary and the development of the fully accredited high school. The collection of 132,000 rubles for this purpose makes prospects good that this goal will be realized in the near future.

He attended two bishops' conferences in Petersburg, one in 1905 and one in 1911. In a memorandum to the Government in 1905, he asked for greater freedom of communication with the Apostolic See, for the admission of religious men and women to his diocese and for the abolition of various religious restraints.

In the last two years he summoned the priests from the northern deaneries to spiritual exercises in Saratov, in which he himself participated and chaired the conference. Last September during harvest he went to Vienna where he took part in the 23rd Eucharistic World Congress. During the solemn procession, he presented the heart-felt wishes and prayers of the diocese to the Redeemer.

On the 22 September 1913 he consecrated the beautiful Church of St. Clemens in Odessa. On the 25 September 1913 he left Odessa for Rome in order to deliver the "St. Peter's Pence" of the diocese of Tiraspol to the Pope. In the year 1914 his Grace Bishop Kessler will celebrate two jubilees, his 25th anniversary to the priesthood and his 10th anniversary as Bishop of the diocese of Tiraspol.

FATHER GEORG SAUER *Administrator*
4 September 1899 to 8 April 1902

Father Georg Sauer was born in the colony of Solothurn on the Volga in the year 1864. He studied in the Seminary in Saratov and on completion of his course he was ordained a priest on the 10 May 1887. He served in several parishes on the Volga and in the south. At present he is administrator in Rohleder on the Karaman.

FATHER MARKUS MARSAL *Administrator*
17 April 1902 until 18 July 1904
(See section on Landau, page 69)

FATHER JOHANNES VETSCH *Curate*

Father Johannes Vetsch was born in Josephstal on the Baraboi on the 25 January 1861 and ordained a priest on the 11 June 1884. Presently, he is in Severinovka. (See Vol. I, transl., p. 185)

FATHER CONSTANTIN STAUB, Ph.D.

Father Constantin Staub was administrator from 2 September 1907 until 7 December 1908. He was born on the 8 July 1872 in the colony of Katharinenstadt on the Volga River. His father, Johannes, was the district secretary and his mother's name was Barbara, nee Küstner. He received his classical education in the local high school. He entered the seminary in Saratov in 1885. On completing his course, he was ordained on the 14 May 1895. His first position was that of administrator in Neukolonie on the Volga, where he remained for 3 1/2 months. In August 1895 he was sent as curate to Strassburg in the Kutschurgan. On the 16 December 1899 he went to Freiburg in Switzerland, where he studied philosophy and history. Later he went to Munich to continue his studies in Philosophy. He wrote his examinations on the 16 June 1901. After submitting his thesis on the Russian poet, L. Tolstoy, he received the diploma of Doctor of Philosophy. This thesis was published by the Kösel press in Kempten in 1908 and has been acclaimed by the critics as the best work on Tolstoy written in German. Father Staub also wrote a treatise on Pedagogy and Philosophy in the monthly publication of "Hochland and Pharus."

In 1904 he returned to Russia and was appointed vicar at Novocherkask. Soon thereafter he was made religious instructor in the Central High School at Prischib. In September 1907 he was made administrator in Sulz. Here he constructed a fine two-story parish school and obtained various objects for the church. For building the school in Sulz, he received a letter of thanks from the Superintendent of Education of the Odessa district, Cherbakov. In 1908, because of illness, he submitted his resignation and since then has lived in Odessa. In 1913 he wrote the State Examinations for the German language and literature in Petersburg.

From the 7 December 1908 to the 24 September 1909 Sulz was supervised from Karlsruhe.

FATHER MICHAEL HATZENBÖLLER
Curate from the 27 September 1909 to the present time.

Father Michael Hatzenböller was born on the 26 September 1878 in the colony of Neubaden. He was the son of Valentin Hatzenböller, from the colony of Selz, and his wife Magdalena Zerr. After completing his studies there, he felt run down and returned to his home to recuperate. After having rested and regained his strength he continued his studies in the same seminary. On completing his studies he was ordained by Bishop Edward Von Ropp on the 25 April 1904. His first appointment was as vicar in Kostheim. Soon thereafter he was sent to Obermonjou as administrator. In 1907 he was made the religious instructor in the Junior High School in Karlsruhe by Father Scherr and from there he was moved to Klosterdorf in 1908. Since the 27 September 1909 he has been at Sulz, where he was made a curate in December 1912.

Father Hatzenböller is a diligent, devout priest who strives to do his duties well. He has already done many things to improve the appearance of the church and is a great admirer of good church music and singing. He hoped to open a trades school in Sulz, something that has been lacking in the Beresan for a long time. He is also a poet of considerable talent.

Parish Endowment

The priest receives 600 rubles, living accommodation and fire wood. The surplice fees are: for baptism 1 ruble, wedding 3 rubles, to publish banns 1 ruble, funeral fees 1 ruble, low mass 1 ruble, high mass 1 ruble, 50 kopecks.

The Parish Church

It is not known where the people of Sulz had their religious services prior to 1819. The first church in Sulz was located just across from the present parish church in the yard of Joseph Braxmeier. The church was built in 1819 by Father Franz Scherer, S.J. It was 57 feet long, 24 feet wide and 12 feet high. It contained a single atlar which faced to the west. Besides the altar, the confessional and a single holy picture, there was no furniture. In the centre of the church there was a partition. It is likely that the church was used as a school for some time, until a schoolhouse was built in 1827. The church was built of fieldstones and the roof was shingled. The bell tower, some distance to the north, was 24 feet high and also had a roof of shingles. During the war (1855) the church was already run down. The soldiers who were stationed in Sulz used the church to manufacture ammunition.

Of all the Beresan colonies, Sulz was the first to build a church. In 1820 Commissar Krüger wrote a circular letter to all the Beresan colonies in which he made this fact known and praised the people of Sulz for their diligence in building the church. Before the church was built, services were conducted in the new school which now is actually the old schoolhouse.

The New Parish Church

The present parish church, which is located in the centre of the colony facing in an east-west direction, was built of fieldstone in 1863.

It was decreed that every head of the household was to deliver a specific amount of cut stone and to provide labour to build the church. The brickwork cost approximately 9000 rubles. The church is of mixed architecture and was built at the parishioners' own expense. It was consecrated by Bishop Anton Zerr on the 20 October 1896. The patron of the church is the Virgin Mary, dedicated to her on her birthday.

The church is approximately 60 feet long, 36 feet wide and 24 feet high. There are two doors, one in the front under the steeple and the other in the left sacristy. There are seven windows on either side. The roof is covered with tin and is painted green. The steeple is incorporated into the church and is 72 feet high. In the bell tower there are 3 very nice bells and one clock. The church is surrounded by a massive stone wall with an iron railing on the part facing the street.

On entering the church one sees several rows of seats on either side with pictures of the stations of the cross starting on the right wall. Between the second and third windows there is a beautiful wood carving of the Pieta. The confessional is placed between the third and fourth windows. Beside the fourth window is the side altar made of nice carved wood on which there are four figurines of angels. The 'Holy Sepulcher' is on the front of the altar below the antipendium. A wood carving of St. Joseph is immediately adjacent to this side altar. From here, on entering the sanctuary, one finds oneself facing the main altar which rests on a platform with two steps. It is built of stone and is 7 feet long and 3 1/2 feet wide. The tabernacle and the vestibule for the blessed sacrament, resting thereon, are made of marble. Above the altar is a lovely old picture of the Queen of Heaven, guardian of the church consecrated to Her. To the right, on leaving the sanctuary, one sees the beautiful statue of the Virgin Mary. Immediately adjacent to this is the second side altar, also carved of wood and displaying many sacred figures. Above the altar table is a picture of the shepherds and the wise men, praying to the child Jesus in the stable in Bethlehem. Beside this altar, one finds the pulpit and overhead sound reflectors. On four panels there are pictures of the four Evangelists. Below the pulpit is the marble baptismal font. Between the second and third window is a beautiful statue representing the "Ecce Homo."

There are two very nice chandeliers. The choir loft is supported by 6 pillars and is large enough for the choir and organ. The floor is made of heavy boards and is painted red. The church is already too small and plans are being made to build a larger one.

The Graveyard

The graveyard has remained unchanged since the founding of the colony. Presently there are 2 nice chapels with family vaults in the graveyard. One belongs to the Konrad Zentner family, the other to the family of Jakob Gabriel. Father Valentin Weber is also buried here. There are several beautiful monuments and the entire graveyard is enclosed by a large stone fence.

The Rectory

When permission was granted by the authorities for the parish of Sulz to be established, the community bought the house of Nikomed Kupper, with plans to build a new rectory onto it. However, since this house was the second one from the church, it was not suitable for a rectory. Consequently, the community exchanged this house for that of Markus Braxmeier, whose house was adjacent to the church. This did not come about until 1883 and meanwhile the priest lived in the house of Nikomed Kupper.

The present rectory was built of cut stone and cost the community 4000 rubles. The rectory contained 6 rooms, a hall and kitchen. The roof was covered with tin. There were also small stables and other buildings. The yard was approximately 120 yeards long and 30 yards wide and surrounded by a stone wall. Lovely acacia trees were planted in the back yard which provided shade in the summer.

The School

The first school was apparently held in the prayer house, as there was a dividing partition centrally, the Jesuits being too poor to do it any other way.

The first school was built in 1828 at the site where the present community cattle barns are located. It was 48 feet long and 24 feet wide and contained one large and one small room.

The second school, which is now the community chancery office, was built of cut stone and the roof was covered with reeds. It contained two large rooms with one hallway. As the old church deteriorated, services were held in this new school house, until 1863 when the new church was built.

The present two-storey school house, built in 1908, is also made of cut stone and the roof is covered with tin. It is 72 feet long, 36 feet wide and 27 feet high. It contains 6 large classrooms and a corridor and cost 11,500 rubles. Presently there are 4 teachers in the school, three receiving 350 rubles each and the fourth, who is also the sexton, receives 400 rubles. There are 188 children attending school.

The first school teacher in Sulz was Georg Warter. Following him were Joseph Keller, Peter Schmidt, Franz Meuchel, Lukian Meuchel, Franz Domansky, Karl Schneider, Adam Gratz, Erasmus Tremmel, senior sexton, Johann Kupper, Peter Usellmann, Anton Wald, Peter Lekstoff, Jakob Kupper, Franz Braxmeier, Johan Braxmeier, Martin Braxmeier, Rudolf Böhm, Rochus Böhm, Jakob Hörner, Andreas Loran, Jakob Weber, Michael Geiger, Nikolaus Immel, Anton Jäger and Jakob Meckler.

The present teachers are Johannes Weber, Raphael Wetsch, Erasmus Tremmel Jr. and Raphael Stein.

People from the Parish of Sulz
who became Priests

FATHER VALENTIN WEBER

Father Valentin Weber was born in Sulz on the 28 February 1843, the son of Lukian Weber and Margaretha Ehly.

After completing his education in the school in the colony and after receiving private instruction, he entered the seminary in Saratov in 1861. In 1863 he was allowed to return to his home where he taught in the community school during the winter.

In 1864 he returned to the seminary and finished his studies in 1867. He was ordained on the 11 June 1867 by Bishop V. Lipsky. On the 9 October 1867 he was posted to the newly formed parish of Strassburg in the Kutchurgan.

As a young priest, he was endowed with considerable energy and inspiration in trying to lead his parishioners along the path of righteousness.

At this time the Kutchurgan Central School was being founded. Father Weber became very interested in this very important project. When the school could not be placed in Selz or Baden, he persuaded the school authorities to build the school in Strassburg and to place him in charge. He took great care to obtain good teachers for the school and to improve the teaching salaries.

In 1870 he was appointed religious instructor in the Central School, and in 1879 he was made pastor of Strassburg.

In 1882 he received the Gold Pectoral Cross from the authorities in recognition of his services, and in 1890 he received the Order of Stanislaus third class.

Father Weber was very interested in orchards and in bee-keeping. He developed a nice orchard with many varieties of fruit trees, in Strassburg, throughout which he had many beehives.

In 1891 he was moved to Severinovka, where he again developed a nice garden and vineyard. In the last few years he was ill a great deal and lived a quiet, lonesome life. In 1907 he became seriously ill and, after receiving the last sacraments, died an edifying death on the 23 July 1907. A beautiful monument adorns his grave in his birthplace of Sulz.

He left almost his entire estate of 18,000 rubles to the orphanage in Karlsruhe. He will receive credit in Heaven for his kindness.

FATHER FRANZ SCHERER

Father Franz Scherer was born in Vosnesensk in 1849 and ordained on the 11 February 1879. Father Scherer was in the parish of Katharinenstadt on the Volga, in Husaren, Rosental, Göttland, Strassburg, Franzfeld and also Karmin. (More in Vol. I transl., 209-210)

FATHER KONRAD KELLER

(See Vol. I transl., 210-211)

Father Konrad Keller was born in Sulz on the 1 March 1857 and ordained a priest by Bishop Zottmann on the 23 November 1883. Because of illness, he resigned from the parish of Franzfeld in 1904. Wanting a purpose in life, he began to do research on the German colonies in Russia. His first book, "The German Colonies in South Russia," was published in 1905. Thereafter he wrote many articles in various publications.

1. In *Hausfreund Kalender:*
   1904: Noteworthy Events in the Early History of the Diocese of Tiraspol.
2. In *Wirtschafts-Kalender:*
   1906: The Colony Landau.
   1907: The Selz Volost District.
   1907: The Beresan German Colonies.
3. In *Odessaer Zeitung:*
   1905: The Catholic Colonies of the Liebental District.
   1907: The Kutschurgan Colonies.
4. In *Deutscher Volkskalender:*
   1909: The Beresan German Colonies.
   1910: The Hundred Year Jubilee of the Beresan Colonies.
   1911: The Catholic Colonies Heidelberg, Kostheim, Leitershausen and Waldorf on the Molotschna and the Colony of Kamenka.
   1912: The Catholic Colonies on the Volga Bergseite.
   1913: The Colony Krasna in Bessarabia and Blumenfeld near Odessa.
   1914: The Colony Rosental in the Crimea and the Colony Klosterdorf.
5. In the periodical *Deutsche Erde*, published by Prof. Langhans in Gotha;
   1909: The Kutschurgan German Colonies.
   1910: The Hundred Year Jubilee of the Beresan Colonies.
   1911: The Catholic Volga Colonies.

The article on the Hundred Year Jubilee of the Beresan Colonies was published in many foreign newspapers, such as "Landauer Zeitung," "Heidelberger Tagenblatt," "Pfälzisches Museum,"

Caritas and many other periodicals.

In 1909 Father Keller was made an honorary member of the Klemens Society. In 1910 he was invited to the Tenth International Geographic Congress in Rome. At the regular meeting of the Bibliographic Society of the Imperial New Russian University on 30 September 1913 Father Keller was chosen as an actual member of this society.

FATHER MARTIN FIX

Father Martin Stephan Fix was born in the colony of Sulz on the 18 June 1883, the son of Peter Fix and Barbara Derschan. He received his first schooling from his uncle, Sebastian Derschan, who prepared him for entry into the Seminary.

In 1898 he wrote the examinations set by Father Scherr and in August of the same year he entered the seminary in Saratov. He completed his studies there in 1909 and, on the 2 August of the same year, was ordained by his Excellency Bishop Kessler.

His first appointment was as vicar in Katharinenstadt. In addition to his ordinary duties, he also spent 28 hours a week teaching religion in the schools. This heavy load undermined his health so that he had to ask for a two months 'leave of absence.'

After having recuperated in his home in Sulz, he was made administrator in Franzfeld in October of the same year. He remained here for nineteen months, working hard and diligently at his duties. He liked particularly to keep the church clean, decorated and in good order, for which he was complimented by his Bishop.

In May 1912 he was sent as vicar to Klosterdorf, where he again worked very diligently at his duties.

In August 1913 he was made administrator of the somewhat neglected parish in Speier, where we hope he is still carrying on his work. Father Fix did not enjoy good health but, in spite of this, he did not lose his enthusiasm for he knew that since God had called him, he would also provide him with the strength, comfort and vigor to perform his duties. In Speier he started immediately to decorate the church. There are three new altars, a new organ and other essentials already on order.

Lay People who were born in Sulz
or worked there

GEORG WARTER *Teacher*

Georg Warter was born in 1789 in Surburg, Alsace. He came to Russia in 1809 and settled as a colonist in Sulz where he became the first school teacher. He returned to Germany in 1820 to bring his blind mother back with him. On his return they were set upon by robbers near Radzivilov and he and his mother were killed.

About the same time Konrad Fix, also coming from Germany, was found to be carrying a Bible which the Warters had intended to bring with them. Consequently, suspicion of murder fell on Fix. He was arrested and held in jail for a long time, until the murder was solved by the Austrian authorities and the news reached the Fürsorge Committee. Only then was Konrad Fix, who was on bail in Rohrbach, able to obtain his freedom.

In 1823 the widow, Walburga Warter, nee Geroldstein, returned to Germany with her children from her first marriage, namely, Stanislaus and Margaretha Ries. Her brother, Georg Thomas, has not heard from her since. Whether she ran into the same misfortune as her husband no one knows. Her home was in Siegen, Alsace.

MICHAEL WEBER *Secretary and Fire Marshal*

Michael Weber was born in Hechingen in 1779 and went to Sulz in 1811. Because he was a Lutheran, he did not intend to stay in Sulz. He was a very capable and well educated man. At first he was appointed mayor, then judge, and later fire marshal for all of the colonies of the Beresan, which position he fulfilled satisfactorily for many years. In 1819, when the Lutheran colonies of Johannestal and Waterloo were founded, he wished to move to one of these colonies. In order to keep him in Sulz, he was given a lot and also appointed secretary. He accepted this position and remained.

His first wife was Katharina Mummert. They had three sons, Heinrich, Lukian and Demetrius. The eldest son, Heinrich, was Lutheran, and late in life he moved to America with his sons. The two younger boys, Lukian and Demetrius, were Catholics and remained in Sulz.

After his first wife died, he married the single girl, Elizabeth Schmidt. They had seven sons and two daughters. He died in Sulz on the 14 December 1851. He was the grandfather of Father Valentin Weber.

JOSEPH BRAXMEIER *Teacher*

Joseph Braxmeier was born in Walburg, Alsace on the 30 July 1786. He came to Russia in 1809 and settled in Sulz. He was the second school teacher in 1820. He was strict but his students loved and respected him, an exemplary Christian. He died an old man on the 14 December 1861 in Sulz.

JAKOB WEBER *Teacher*

Jakob Weber, son of Kaspar, was born on the 25 August 1799 in Albersweiler, Rhinepalatinate. He came to Sulz in 1809, where his father settled as a colonist. Jakob Weber was a very capable fellow and had a wonderful memory. As an example, even though he was only a boy when he left home, he could talk all day about things there and relate his own experiences of the journey from his home and the poor circumstances in which the new settlers found themselves. He was the school teacher for many years and, for a time, also the mayor in Sulz. He was very progressive and particularly interested in fruit growing and agriculture. He also owned the first 'samovar' in Sulz. Later he was rather poor and lived with his daughter Elisabeth Helbling, in Kapustina, where he died in 1900 at the age of 100 years.

MICHAEL GEIGER *Teacher*

Michael Geiger was born in 1781 in Ettenheim, Baden. He went to Sulz in 1820 and taught for a while.

JOSEPH KELLER *Teacher*

Joseph Keller was born on the 19 January 1819 in the colony of Bindersbach near Annweiler in the Rhinepalatinate. His parents were Christian Keller and Anna Stöbner, who moved to Sulz on 10 December 1819 and settled as colonists. During the war of 1854-1856 he was mayor of Sulz. Thereafter, he was the school teacher for many years in Sulz, Halbstadt and other places. He died in Felsenburg in 1906. He was a capable, well-read man and endowed with a good memory.

JAKOB MECKLER *School Teacher*

Jakob Meckler was born in Sulz in 1824, the son of Joseph Meckler and Johanna Seitz. The eldest of nine boys, he was a capable, diligent fellow who was very well-read and a good conversationalist. He died in Sulz, survived by several sons and daughters and his widow, Katharina (née Mosbrucker), who is now 88 years old.

FRANZ MEUCHEL *Teacher*

Franz Muechel was born in Sulz in 1814. He was a capable, serious, diligent, hard working school teacher. He died in his home in Sulz at an advanced age.

LUKIAN MEUCHEL *Teacher*

Lukian Meuchel, son of Franz, was born in Sulz in 1840. He attended the Parish school and then received private instruction until he had a passable education. He was an industrious school teacher and served as such in Sulz, Karlsruhe and other places. He was a good singer and was familar with choral singing. Some time ago he moved to America with his family.

FRANZ DOMANSKY

Franz Domansky was born in Odessa and received his education in one of the high schools there. There was a big argument in Sulz at this time about the school teacher. The people of the lower colony had selected a candidate as teacher and the people in the upper colony would not accept him, wishing to select their own candidate. As a result of this, the community became divided and the peace was disturbed.

The people of the upper colony hired their own school teacher who taught in the school house. The people of the lower colony had their own school teacher who carried on instruction in a private school. There were, however, some families in the upper colony who wished to send their children to the lower colony school and, similarly, some families in the lower colony wished to have their children included in the upper colony school. Consequently, these children had to pass the hostile school of the lower colony on their way to school in the upper colony. This usually resulted in fighting among the unfortunate youngsters. Repulsive insults were exchanged daily, snowballs or mud were thrown at both schools every day. The parents, instead of trying to correct the children, praised them and advised them of what more they should do.

Father L., who was the priest at the time, sympathized with the people of the lower colony and from the pulpit he accused the people in the upper colony of causing all the trouble. The people of the upper colony would not accept this and sent a complaint to the Fürsorge Committee. A magistrate was subsequently sent to investigate the matter.

In his report to the Fürsorge Committee, the official scolded the priest because he did not endeavour to establish peace. The Fürsorge Committee removed both school teacher candidates and appointed Franz Domansky as the "privileged" school teacher of Sulz. It was wrong to appoint this young man who could not speak the language of the colonists and was not familiar with their teaching methods. It became absolutely necessary for him to have one of the old school teachers to help him and, consequently, the old fight started all over again.

He tried his utmost to do what was right for both parties and tried to win the favour of the people in the upper colony, but the people of the lower colony became even more hostile and insubordinate. He realized that, under the circumstances, his position was intolerable and he left Sulz, taking the position of secretary in Rastadt. He worked there for many years but then became seriously ill and died.

When Franz Domansky left, Adam Gratz came to Sulz as the school teacher. He has previously been reported on.

ERASMUS TREMMEL (1) *Teacher and Organist*

Erasmus Tremmel was born in Sulz on the 25 February 1858, the son of Erasmus Tremmel and Margaretha Scherer. In 1872 he came to the seminary in Saratov where he completed several classes and then returned home. After this, he received private instruction and then went to Odessa to the famous organist, Swirowitsch, to study music. He remained in Odessa for 6 months and studied a large amount of church music. As a result of his extraordinary talent and diligence, he progressed so rapidly that he wrote one of his own compositions called, "Frühlings Marsch" (Spring March). During his time, this composition was played in various cities by the military band.

In 1878 he was appointed organist in Sulz, which position he fulfilled to everyone's satisfaction until 1883 when he went to Rosental in the Crimea as teacher and organist for one year. Later he returned to Sulz and formed an orchestra, which continued for one year. From Sulz he went to Alexandrovka (Korojevo) where he remained for four years.

After this he quit teaching and returned to Sulz, where he became a partner in a brick factory. After twelve years he sold his share and began farming. After farming for seven years, he bought 300 dessiatines of land but sold this again and bought a rolling mill. In 1910 he was appointed mayor of the Beresan district, but soon asked the authorities to relieve him from the appointment.

JOHANN KUPPER *Teacher*

Johann Kupper, son of Johannes, was born in Sulz in 1857. He went to the seminary in Saratov in 1872 where he completed some classes. Following this he was appointed teacher and sexton in Kronental in the Crimea where he worked for twelve years. Later he was in Sulz for five years. At the present time he is a partner in the brick factory.

ROMUALD (Roman) DERSCHAN *Teacher*

Romuald Derschan, son of Anton, was born in Sulz in 1856. He entered the Catholic Seminary in Saratov in 1872. However, he was not a good student. He then entered a hat factory where he advanced rapidly and soon was made an associate. He married a non-Catholic girl there who left him soon after. He returned to Sulz, where he was a teacher for one year and then he emigrated to America.

SEBASTIAN DERSCHAN *Teacher*

Sebastian Derschan, son of Michael, was born in Sulz in 1863. He entered the minor seminary in Saratov completed his studies there and then accepted an appointment as teacher in Karlsruhe. Later he became involved in farming but was not at all successful. After a few years he moved to America, but soon died there.

ERASMUS TREMMEL (ii) *Teacher*

Erasmus Tremmel was born in Sulz on the 21 December 1890, the son of Erasmus Tremmel and Katharina Sattler. After completing his studies at the community school, he entered the high school in Karlsruhe under Father Scherr. After completing the courses of study there, he wrote and succeeded in passing the examinations for teaching in 1911. His first appointment as teacher was in Blumenfeld, but after 6 months there he moved to Sulz where he still is at the present time.

PHILIPP NIKOLAUS HEIDT *Teacher*

Philipp Nikolaus Heidt, son of Nikolaus, was born on the 6 April 1890. After completing his studies at the parish school in Sulz, he entered the high school in Karlsruhe under Father Scherr where he completed his course in 6 years, receiving high honors. After this, he wished to enroll in the Imperial High School in Vosnesensk but was refused as he was too old for the class enrolled at that time. In 1909 he accepted a teaching position in Ausz-Kirk in the Crimea where he taught for one year. In the summer of 1910 he wished to enter the Teacher Training Institute in Theodosia but, because of overcrowding, he was not accepted. In the winter of 1910 he took a position as private instructor in Korsunzy on the Baraboi. In the fall of 1911 he wrote the examinations for teacher in Aleschky in the Crimea. He succeeded in passing these and soon thereafter was appointed a teacher by the inspector in the community school in Katharinenfeld, in the parish of Georgsburg. On the 15 May 1912 he was made teacher, sexton and secretary in Rosenfeld in the parish of Georgsburg, where he is at the present time.

JOHANNES WEBER *Teacher*

Johannes Weber born in Sulz on the 16 December 1884, the son of Martin Weber and Mariana Braxmeier. He completed his education in the Beresan Central School in Neufreudental and then went to Odessa, where he enrolled in a course in pedagogy. He obtained his teaching diploma there. In 1903 he was appointed teacher of religion and German in Sulz, which appointment he maintained for seven years. In 1910 he became ill and had to stop teaching in order to regain his health. After he was well again, he accepted the position of teacher of Russian in Sulz.

RAPHAEL WETSCH *Teacher*

Raphael Wetsch was born in Sulz on the 28 October 1886, the son of Stephan Wetsch and Marianna Kupper. He took four classes in the non-classical school in Nikolayev, wrote the examinations for teacher and in 1904 was appointed teacher in Halbstadt, in the district of Odessa. After one year he moved to Landau as teacher and, in 1906, was appointed teacher in Sulz, where he still is today.

JOHANNES FIX *Teacher*

Johannes Fix was born in Sulz in 1882, the son of Anton Fix and Anna Hellmann. After completing his studies at the parish school, he entered the Beresan Central School which at that time was located in Neufreudental. He was a good student and successfully completed his courses. After obtaining his teaching certificate, he was appointed as teacher in Karlsruhe where he remained for 2 years. He then resigned, married and started farming.

ERASMUS TREMMEL *Secretary*

Erasmus Tremmel, son of Georg, was born in Sulz on the 1 March 1836. After completing his studies in the parish school, his father, realizing that he was a bright and industrious boy, apprenticed him to Anton Riedinger, the secretary for the district of Landau. He soon learned the essentials of bookkeeping and, as a youth of 18, he was made secretary for the community of Sulz. During the war of 1854 — 1856 he performed his duties energetically and very successfully, to the satisfaction of both his superiors and the community. He was a quiet, unassuming and industrious type of individual, but died at the prime of life in the year 1863. He was survived by his wife, Margaretha, nee Scherer, and his son, Erasmus.

FRANZ KUPPER *Secretary*

Franz Kupper was born in Sulz in 1843, the son of Johannes Kupper and Katharina Segmüller. Because he was a talented fellow, his father took him to the Fürsorge Committee in Odessa where promising young colonist boys were accepted for training as secretaries. After completing his studies there he was appointed secretary in Sulz where he remained for several years. He was knowledgeable about the laws and was a good speaker. He died in Sulz on the 9 March 1873 survived by his wife, Christina, nee Zerr, and two children. His wife remarried and migrated to America.

JOSEPH ROSHAU *Secretary*

Joseph Roshau, the son of Friedrich, was born in Sulz in 1857. He spent several years with his uncle, Father Valentin Weber, in Strassburg where he received instruction. He was the secretary in Sulz for a few years.

GEORG WEBER *Teacher and Secretary*

Georg Weber, son of Jakob, was born in Sulz in 1851. After finishing his studies in the community school, he entered in the seminary in Saratov. After completing several classes, he left and took over a teaching position. Presently, he is the District Secretary in Heidelberg in the Molotschna.

LUKAS (LUKIAN) WETSCH *Artist*

Lukas Wetsch was born in Steinberg on the 28 April 1885, the son of Johannes Wetsch and Marianna Weber. His mother died when he was only five years old. Even though he could not comprehend his bereavement, he felt a dreadful emptiness in his heart and searched for support for his childhood emotions. He found this support from his oldest sister and her husband, H. G. Thauberger, who was teaching in Steinberg at this time. The latter managed to interest the boy in a love for nature and in the destiny of mankind as sketched in the "Universal History," the big book of the Creator.

When his brother-in-law was posted to Kleinliebental as teacher, he went along and attended the Central School in Grossliebental. At the end of one year, he wrote the entrance examinations for the non-classical school in Nikolayev, where he showed a preference for sketching. Since the instructor's method did not appeal to him, he spent his spare time in drawing according to his own inclination. After completing the non-classical school, his brother-in-law advised him to go abroad in order to study art. His father was in agreement with this suggestion and he was soon on his way to Munich, the 'German Athens.' He first entered the technical high school in the course of building engineer, but destiny had something else in store for him. As he strolled about Munich and saw all sorts of beautiful art treasures in the Art Museum, he became enraptured with both the new and the old schools and became inspired not only to look but to draw for himself. He spent many hours viewing the pictures of the best artists and attempted to reproduce them with his paint brush. In this he spent a long time before he learned the techniques, but finally became a determined artist.

On the advice of the young artist, Korthaus, he left the Technical High School and began to study art seriously under his instruction. After overcoming these first hurdles, he attended the private academy of Professor H. Knerr where he learned the technique of modern art.

Instruction here was frequently about the French artists and, for this reason, he went to Paris. He found the French art was beautiful, but did not find the contemporary art of the French in any way better than the creations of the artists of Munich. After two years in Paris, he returned to Munich on his way home, where he is presently completing his military duty in the army.

FRIEDRICH WEBER *Engineer*

Friedrich Weber was born in Sulz in 1888, the son of Martin Weber and Marianna Braxmeier. After finishing at the local parish school, he entered the Central School in Neufreudental. After completing the courses here, he took private instruction and then entered the High School in Odessa. After diligent study, he received his certificate and entered the Poly-Technical School in St. Petersburg. He completed his studies in 1910 and awaited his appointment as an engineer.

JAKOB ZENTNER *Rancher*

Jakob Zentner was born in Sulz on the 2 April 1857, the son of Konrad Zentner and Regina Keller. After completing his studies in the local parish school, he received some private instruction from the district secretary, Nikolaus Stroh.

He married Elisabeth Braxmeier on the 19 November 1879. Soon thereafter, he leased land on the Steppes near Woltschy. Because he was industrious and a hard worker, he soon accumulated enough wealth so that in 1900 he was able to buy his own land. Besides farming, he was particularly interested in cattle raising. He noticed that the heifers from the Molotschna breed were getting smaller and producing less milk. He crossed these with the Holland breed and as a result produced a crossbreed of strong cattle that were also good milkers. Subsequently, he crossed this mixed breed with the Simmental breed and the result was further progress in size and milk production. As a result of this, he received a commendation and medal from three Agricultural Exhibitions. He also raised pigs for which he was famous throughout the district.

Jakob Zentner is the father of a large family of 3 boys and 6 girls. The eldest boy, Kornelius, is a good farmer. His second son, Joseph, is at the present time a student in the Poly-Technical School in Charkov. The youngest son, Raphael, has completed five years in the St. Paul non-classical school in Odessa, but because of illness had to discontinue his studies. Klementine, the youngest daughter, is taking her fifth year in the Girl's Commerical School. The second youngest daughter, Anna, is completing her fourth year in the same school.

HEINRICH ZIMMERMANN *Rancher*

Heinrich Zimmerman was born in Sulz on the 7 March 1850, the son of Anton Zimmerman and Alexandra Lopuskaja. He attended the school in Sulz and then in Nikolayev, and later in the Swiss colony of Schaba near Ackermann. Here he learned to speak French.

In 1862 he again returned to Sulz where he received his first Holy Communion. Soon thereafter, he moved with his parents to the estate of Schostack where his father farmed and raised sheep on rented land.

He married Katharina Schardt, daughter of Johannes Schardt, on the 6 November 1872 and then started farming for himself. He bought 600 dessiatines of land in the province of Ekaterinoslav and began to raise cattle. Because of his experience and knowledge of cattle, he was appointed supervisor of the Government Imperial Breeding Station at Verchnedneprovsk.

He remained there for 15 years and supervised it to everyone's satisfaction, receiving a medal on a Stanislaus ribbon in 1903 in recognition for his services.

In 1904 he bought 3170 dessiatines of land near Parutino which he had to sell after the revolution at a great loss. Presently he is farming in Novo-Ukrainka, raising cattle of the Swiss breed and also English and Tombov breeds of horses. He has 4 boys and 5 girls. His two sons, Viktor and Joseph, are presently studying at the Nikolayev non-classical school.

PETER BÖHM *Bookkeeper*

Peter Böhm was born in the colony of Brabander in the province of Samara on the 18 February 1867. After finishing at the local community school, he entered the Central School in Katharinenstadt. After completing his courses there, he took over the position of secretary in Bangert where he remained until 1891.

From 1891 to 1904 he was a teacher in one of the colonies near Mariupol. In 1904 he was invited to Sulz in the Beresan where he was the manager and bookkeeper for the Co-operative there. In 1909 he was made business manager of the Klemens Society in Odessa where he still is today.

In 1894 he married Maria Grunsky, who died on the 29 November 1909, leaving seven children.

The oldest son, Eugene, is attending art school in Odessa and promises to become a very good artist.

JOSEPH EHLY *Mayor*

Joseph Ehly was born in Sulz in 1862, the son of Anton Ehly and Regina Fix. He attended the parish school and finished with honours. He lived on rented land for a long time and, through his industry and diligence ran an exemplary farm as a result of which he became quite wealthy.

On returning to his home in Sulz, he received more community duties which he performed with prudence and intelligence.

In 1911 he was nominated as a candidate for the office of mayor for the district of Landau and in 1914 he was elected mayor of Landau in the Beresan.

JOHANNES KELLER *School Master*

Johannes Keller was born on the 14 August 1846 in the colony of Sulz, the son of Joseph Keller and Juliana Thomas. He graduated from the community school with a good report. Anton Jäger was the school master. Later Keller was the school master in Steinberg, then in Sebastianfeld, Halbstadt and in other places.

DOMINIK KELLER *Schoolmaster*

Dominik Keller was born in Sulz on the 20 November 1852, the son of Joseph Keller and Julianna Thomas. He was an intelligent, industrious student in the community school. After completing his schooling there, he received private instruction in order to further his learning.

For some years he was the schoolmaster in Neukarlsruhe where he married Annamaria Schmidt. After a few years he moved to Orenburg where he bought a small farm of 400 dessiatines. Soon he became homesick, sold his land and returned to Sulz where he farmed some community land.

He became ill and died in Sulz in 1907.

JOHANNES SCHERER *Merchant*

Johannes Scherer, son of Franz-Anton, was born in Sulz on March 3, 1818. After completing his education in the community school he went to Vosnesensk as an apprentice to a baker. After a few years he opened his own bakery. Business was good and he soon became quite wealthy. He was very charitable and often helped his countrymen in Sulz when things did not go well for them. His two sons, Karl and Friedrich, were also merchants and hotel owners.

JOSEPH TREMMEL *Merchant*

Joseph Tremmel was born in Sulz on the 5 February 1838, the son of Georg Tremmel and Maria Lorentz. After he was married he moved to Korojevo with some other people from Sulz. They rented land and started farming. As a result of hard work and diligence, he became quite rich and bought the land which he had been renting. Later he became a merchant in the city of Majaky.

DANIEL SATTLER *Merchant*

Daniel Sattler was born in Sulz in July 1861. For a long time he farmed and raised cattle and, as a result, became quite wealthy. He owned 3200 dessiatines of land and three fine homes in Nikolayev. In 1898 he joined the second guild of merchants in Otschakov.

The present Wealth and Conditions
of the Colony of Sulz

There are 200 lots in Sulz with 1915 people, all of the Catholic faith. There are also 26 German families from the province of Samara, 8 Russian families, 35 Jewish families and 3 gypsy families.

During the winter there are 150 Russian hired-men, but in the summer this number increases to five or six hundred. The annual salary for a hired man was 125 rubles.

Russian maids usually number 50 during the winter and 200 to 250 in the summer. They receive an annual salary of 90 to 100 rubles.

There are 77 families in Sulz who do not own any land. There are 240 families who went to America and Siberia and 53 families who moved elsewhere.

The community land amounted to 4402.75 dessiatines. Bought land in Sulz amounted to 28,709 dessiatines.

On the community land there were 23 families living on a full allotment of 60 dessiatines, 24 families on only 30 dessiatines, 49 families on 15 dessiatines and 25 families on 7.5 dessiatines.

The community land is divided as follows: house lots 83 dessiatines, vineyards 73 dessiatines, vegetable gardens and orchards 27 dessiatines, agriculture 2930 dessiatines and pasture land 1294 dessiatines.

Hay land cost 200 rubles, land in the vicinity of Sulz cost 250 to 300 rubles and rented land cost 12 to 15 rubles per year.

Animals in the colony are: horses 1480, cows 1250, calves and pigs 840.

Winter and summer wheat planted in 1912 amounted to 8450 dessiatines. The farm equipment is not given.

There are 4 automobiles.

Tradesmen are as follows: blacksmiths 4, cabinet maker 1, tailors 2 (both Jewish), shoemakers 3.

There are 2 steam flour mills, one Co-operative Society Store, 10 small shops and 1 tavern. There are also 2 brick factories that make roofing tiles and glazed tiles, as well as 2 cement brick works.

The newspapers read in Sulz were about 41 copies of "Deutsche Rundschau," 3 copies of "Odessaer Zeitung," some Russian newspapers, as well as several small weekly and monthly publications.

Freight or shipping charges are 5 kopecks per pud from Nikolayev, when there is a good road, and 8 to 10 kopecks per pud when the road is bad.

The community pays the following taxes and rents: Crown taxes 322 rubles, 86 kopecks; payments for land purchased 506 rubles, 34 kopecks; rent 1340 rubles, 41 kopecks; community takes 2447 rubles, 5 kopecks.

The Colony of Karlsruhe

The colony of Karlsruhe is located in the province of Kherson, 100 versts from the city of Kherson, 110 versts from the capital of Odessa and 5 versts from the community of Landau. It is located on both sides of "Fox Valley Creek," which runs in a north-south direction. Fox Valley River originates approximately 15 versts to the north of the colony and empties into the Beresan 10 versts to the south, near the colony of Sulz.

Main Street, on the left side of the river bank, is only 1.5 verst long, running in a north-south direction. Where the colony is located, the land is very uneven. There are three ponds, Goose Pond, Reed Pond and Calf Pond, which join on the east side of the upper colony (also called Matzenberg) and divide the main street, separating it from the middle colony.

To the north-west one finds "Mill Hollow" with a dam on the Fox Valley Creek. On the right side of the creek is Hill Street, running north and south, with a side street named "Wojeny." South of Hill Street is Pig Hill, which runs from the east to the west. On the east side of the main street the so-called "Gassel" (alley) originates and runs easterly.

The main buildings in the colony are the lovely Gothic church, the rectory, the lower classical school (on the 2 February 1914 this was made into an 8-classroom high school by Father Scherr), the parish school with the chancery, the co-operative society store, the community tavern, and some fine private homes.

The architecture of the homes is similar to that of the other colonies, but of late there have been some very large, beautiful homes built which would even grace a city.

In front of the houses there are usually small flower gardens and lovely acacia trees which form an avenue throughout the length of the colony.

Until 1871 there were lovely orchards at the back of the lots near the threshing places, which later were sadly neglected and have been largely replaced by potatoes and vegetables.

The main occupations of the people are agriculture and cattle raising. Lately they have again started some vineyards, but until now they have not really amounted to anything.

There are many field stones on the south side of the colony, but these are of inferior quality.

There is plenty of water in all of the wells and most of it is quite palatable.

The weather is relatively healthy, the people strong and muscular.

The vernacular is largely the dialect of Baden; the people of Karlsruhe say, "Ich geh aach mit" (I'll also go along).

There are 12 people over the age of 80. The people of Karlsruhe are industrious, cheerful people, and are distinguished for their hospitality among the people of the Beresan. But, they are also bluff in speech, quick to ridicule, and often use coarse proverbial expressions.

The name "Karlsruhe" was given to the colony by Franz Brittner, Mayor of Liebental, because most of the colonists came from the Grand Duchy of Baden of which Karlsruhe is the capital.

The colonists of Karlsruhe migrated to South Russia as a result of the Ukase of Alexander I on the 20 February 1804. In 1809 they received passports from the Russian Consul, Bethmann, in Frankfurt on the river Main. They left their homes without guides and travelled to the Russian border town of Radzivilov, where they rested for a while.

After they left Radzivilov they moved on into South Russia, arriving in Odessa in the fall. As it was too late to move to the site of the colony, they were quartered for the winter with the people of the Liebental and Kutschurgan districts.

In the spring of 1810 they all gathered in Odessa. From here they were led under the guidance of the mayor of Liebental, Franz Brittner, to their site in the Beresan. As they arrived at their destination, they saw only the vast uncultivated steppe covered with tall fox-tails (grass) and shrubs. There were two trees that were large enough to provide shade; an indication that people had lived here previously.

Most of the new colonists were completely destitute and the Crown had to provide them with everything. Only a few of the colonists had brought some money from home, amounting to 4060 silver rubles. As soon as the settlers arrived at their destination, they started to build the Crown houses and by the time winter came, most of them were finished.

List of the Settlers
of the
Colony of Karlsruhe in the Beresan
in the years 1839 and 1840
with notation of their original homes in Germany.

1. **Joseph Aman** 27, son of Joseph.
WIFE: Maria-Eva Gugert 26, daughter of Philipp.
CHILDREN: Joseph 1, Katharina 4.
2. **Joseph Garecht** 58, son of Jacob, from Offenbach, Rhinepalatinate.
WIFE: Barbara Uhl 54, daughter of Jakob.
CHILDREN: Jakob 12, Katharina 17.
(a) Johannes Garecht 25, son of Joseph.
WIFE: Barbara Schüler 21, daughter of Nikolaus, from Mörlheim, Rhinepalatinate.
CHILDREN: Annamaria 1.
3. **Franz Hatzenbühler** 30, son of Franz, from Mietesheim, Alsace. Another record shows him as having come from Knittelsheim, Rhinepalatinate.
WIFE: Barbara Brittner 32, daughter of Joseph, from Offenbach, Rhinepalatinate.
CHILDREN: Valentin 9, Johann 6, Genovefa 10.
4. **Sebastian Förderer** 33, son of Joseph, from Offenbach, Rhinepalatinate.
WIFE: Carolina Bleyle 26, daughter of Joseph, from Kenzingen, Baden.
CHILDREN: Jakob 7, Johann 5, Georg 3, Rosalia 9.
HIRED MAN: Adam Röller 16.
5. **Friedrich Kopp** 47, son of Georg, from Steinweiler, Rhinepalatinate.
WIFE: Karolina Geisz 44, daughter of Peter from Hagenau, Alsace.
CHILDREN: Johann 11, Simon 6.
(a) Nikolaus Bechler 24, son of Michael from Malsch, Baden.
WIFE: Marianna Kopp 23, daughter of Friedrich.
CHILDREN: Magdalena 6, Susanna 4, (children of Johann-Philipp Geiger), Elisabeth 2.
6. **Valentin Klein** 68, from Rülzheim, Rhinepalatinate.
WIFE: Eva Meuchel 58, daughter of Johann, from Schindhart, Rhinepalatinate.

STEP-SON: Franz Helfrich 20.

7. **Johannes Hatzenbühler** 37, son of Martin from Knittelsheim, Rhinepalatinate.
WIFE: Elisabeth Hopfauf 33, daughter of Andreas, from Klosterhausen, Baden.
CHILDREN: Stanislaus 9, Georg 6, Joseph 2, Katharina 14, Karolina 11.
FATHER: Johannes-Martin Hatzenbühler 76, son of Konrad.

8. **Johannes Anton** 47, son of Georg-Jakob, from Morlheim, Rhinepalatinate.
WIFE: Annamaria Hatzenbühler 48, daughter of Johann Thomas, from Ottersheim, Rhinepalatinate.
CHILDREN: Georg-Jakob 17, Johann 8.
(a) Friedrich Anton 22, son of Johann.
WIFE: Katharina Röther 19, daughter of Johann.
CHILDREN: Joachim 1.

9. **Heinrich Loran** 54, son of Sebastian, from Queichheim, Rhinepalatinate.
WIFE: Maria-Eva Horter 52, daughter of Peter, from Mörlheim, Rhinepalatinate.
CHILDREN: Sebastian 18, Nikolaus 16, Margaretha 14, Apolonia 13, Marianna 10.
(a) Michael Loran 21, son of Heinrich.
WIFE: Klara Stumpf 18, daughter of Jakob.

10. **Ludwig Paul** 40, son of Philipp, from Kapsweyer, Rhinepalatinate.
WIFE: Katharina Fried 39, daughter of Valentin, from Berg, Rhinepalatinate.
CHILDREN: Valentin 16, Joseph 14, Jakob 12, Peter 5, Johann 3, Helena 9, Barbara 7.

11. **Ferdinand Anton** 35, son of Jakob, from Mörlheim, Rhinepalatinate.
WIFE: Magdalena Garecht 22, daughter of Joseph, from Offenbach, Rhinepalatinate.
CHILDREN: Rosalia 9, Maria-Eva 4, Salomea 2, Katharina 1.
STEP-FATHER: Franz Koch 69, son of Nikolaus from Ottersheim, Rhinepalatinate.

12. **Peter Hopfauf** 37, son of Andreas, from Klosterhausen, Baden.
WIFE: Katharina Bleyle 33, daughter of Joseph, from Sesenheim, Alsace.
CHILDREN: Johann 13, Peter 12, Ferdinand 9, Franz 3, Philipp 1.

13. **Franz Steckler** 51, son of Valentin, from Sondernheim, Rhinepalatinate.

WIFE: Katharina Schreck 50, daughter of Valentin, from Lingenfeld, Rhinepalatinate.
CHILDREN: Jakob 17, Martin 14, Alexander 7, Barbara 9.
(a) Jakob Bär 30, son of Philipp, from Kuhardt, Rhinepalatinate.
WIFE: Magdalena Steckler 25, daughter of Franz.
CHILDREN: Johann 2, Emilie 1.

14. **Joseph Ihly** 53, son of Joseph, from Malsch, Baden.
WIFE: Marianna Reuter 49, daughter of Franz, from Sulzbach, Baden.
CHILDREN: Joseph 9, Katharina 13.
(a) Jakob Ihly 27, son of Joseph.
WIFE: Walburga Renner 25, daughter of Martin.
CHILDREN: Michael 2, Friedrich 1.
(b) Johann Philipp Ihly 23, son of Joseph.
WIFE: Barbara Heidt 17, daughter of Adam, from the colony of Sulz.

15. **Thomas Martin** 58, from Nussdorf, Rhinepalatinate, son of Thomas.
WIFE: Maria-Eva Nebel 44, daughter of Georg, from Knittelsheim, Rhinepalatinate.
CHILDREN: Thomas 11, Johann 8, Leonhard 6, Margaretha 4, Annamaria 2.
(a) Johann Deck 25, son of Ulrich, from Winzenbach, Alsace.
WIFE: Maria Thomas 20, daughter of Martin.
CHILDREN: Jakob 1.

16. **Simon Baron** 77, son of Valentin, from Deutsch-Chemnitz, Prussia.
WIFE: Katharina Filikis 64, daughter of Adam, from Neukirch, Baden.
(a) Karl Baron 35, son of Simon.
WIFE: Karolina Siegel 34, daughter of Valentin, from Klingenmünster, Rhinepalatinate.
CHILDREN: Joseph 14, Peter 8, Jordan 5, Magdalena 12, Margaretha 9, Maria-Eva 2.
(b) Michael Ruf 26, son of Johann, from Mörlheim, Rhinepalatinate.
WIFE: Marianna Baron 25, daughter of Simon.
CHILDREN: Martin 5, Franz 2, Gabriel 1.

17. **Andreas Hopfauf** 61, son of Peter, from Klosterhausen, Baden.
WIFE: Walburga Gallion 63, daughter of Friedrich.
(a) Georg Hopfauf 27, son of Andreas.
WIFE: Elisabeth Röther 25, daughter of Johann.
CHILDREN: Philipp 5, Katharina 1.
(b) Ludwig Schmidt 25, son of Paul.
WIFE: Barbara Hopfauf 23, daughter of Andreas.

CHILDREN: Peter 3, Franz 2, Georg 1.

18. **Margaretha Baron** 36, widow, daughter of Georg Nebel, from Knittelsheim, Rhinepalatinate.
CHILDREN: Michael 17, Friedrich 15, Valentin 12, Franz 5, Magdalena 9.

19. **Jakob Fried** 51, son of Valentin, from Berg, Rhinepalatinate.
WIFE: Elisabeth Hoffmann 48, daughter of Georg.
CHILDREN: Peter 14, Franz 13, Ludwig 11, Annamaria 9.
(a) Johannes Messer 22, son of Bernhard from Rohrbach, Baden.
WIFE: Elisabeth Fried 20, daughter of Jakob.
CHILDREN: Valentin 1.

20. **Michael Bechler** 63, son of Johann, from Malsch, Baden.
WIFE: Elisabeth Hoffmann 56, daughter of Johann.
CHILDREN: Gregor 20, Klara 25.

21. **Valentin Brittner** 37, son of Joseph, from Offenbach, Rhinepalatinate.
WIFE: Margaretha Jonas 32, daughter of Georg, from Steinfeld, Rhinepalatinate.
CHILDREN: Georg-Jakob 14, Anton 3, Katharina 9, Barbara 6.
Leokadia Abele 60, daughter of Anton from Jöhlingen, Baden.

22. **Valentin Braun** 52, son of Peter, from Offenbach, Rhinepalatinate.
WIFE: Margaretha Brittner 52, daughter of Joseph.
CHILDREN: Jakob 19, Peter 17, Leonhard 14, Karl 12, Johann 5, Margaretha 9.
(a) Joseph Braun 23, son of Valentin.
WIFE: Katharina Fried 21, daughter of Joseph.
CHILDREN: Margaretha 1.

23. **Annamaria Hellmann** 48, daughter of Georg-Jacob Anton and widow of Michael Hellmann, from Mörlheim, Rhinepalatinate.
CHILDREN: Peter 16, Jakob 14, Franz 6, Katharina 12.
(a) Johann Hellmann 24, son of Michael.
WIFE: Sophie Helfrich 20, daughter of Jakob.
CHILDREN: Valentin 1.
(b) Nikolaus Hellmann 22, son of Michael.
WIFE: Elisabeth Ihly 18, daughter of Joseph.

24. **Bernhard Messer** 53, son of Anton, from Rohrbach, Baden.
WIFE: Katharina Muth 57, daughter of Konstantin.
CHILDREN: Anton 28, Johann-Georg 18, Valentin 17, Jakob 13, Margaretha 15.
(a) Valentin Dörr 27, son of Daniel, from the colony of Landau.
WIFE: Katharina Messer 24, daughter of Bernhard.
CHILDREN: Maria-Eva 1.

25. **Joseph Pfaff** 26, son of Jakob, from Elchesheim, Baden.

WIFE: Annamaria Höpfner 24, daughter of Aloys, from Ettlingen, Baden.

(a) Rosina Kelmel (or Kimmel) 69, widow of Jakob Pfaff, daughter of Peter, from Steinmauern, Baden.

CHILDREN: Helena 36.

(b) Adam Ekrott 29, son of Adam, from Waldrems, Baden.

WIFE: Gertrude Pfaff 22, daughter of Jakob.

CHILDREN: Apolonia 3.

26. **Friedrich Renner** 57, son of Friedrich, from Ixheim, Rhinepalatinate.

WIFE: Barbara Nebel 42, daughter of Georg, from Knittelsheim, Rhinepalatinate.

CHILDREN: Joseph 16, Margaretha 14, Katharina 10, Barbara 7.

(a) Johannes Renner 22, son of Friedrich.

WIFE: Magdalena Matz 19, daughter of Jakob.

27. **Franz Heck** 54, son of Martin from Lohrbach, Baden.

WIFE: Philippina Drescher 34, from Freiburg.

CHILDREN: Kaspar 13, Jakob 11, Christian 7, Michael 3, Anton 1.

(a) Michael Sprung 37, son of Peter, from Eussertal, Rhinepalatinate.

WIFE: Margaretha Drescher 32, daughter of Andreas from Freiburg.

CHILDREN: Johann 11, Oswald 7, Michael 1, Elisabeth 9.

28. **Magdalena Landeis** 40, widow of Anton, and daughter of Franz Humel from Birkenau, Baden.

CHILDREN: Philipp 9, Raphael 7, Karl 2, Elisabeth 18, Barbara 17, Katharina 14, Marianna 5.

(a) Karl Schuh 38, son of Bernhard from Schwetzingen, Baden.

WIFE: Franziska Humel 35, daughter of Franz.

WIFE: Katharina 13, Elisabeth 8, Franziska 2, Marianna 1.

29. **Leonhard Wander** 33, son of Johann from Erlenbach, Rhinepalatinate.

WIFE: Katharina Gugert 21, daughter of Philipp, from Lorsch, Hessen.

CHILDREN: Margaretha 7, Eva 1.

30. **Johannes Schardt** 51, from Leimersheim, Rhinepalatinate.

WIFE: Katharina Hammer 51, daughter of Jakob.

CHILDREN: Johann 14, Peter 10, Andreas 7.

(a) Michael Schardt 22, son of Johann.

WIFE: Marianna Ihly 21, daughter of Joseph.

CHILDREN: Euphemia 2.

31. **Johannes Heintz** 25, son of Georg, from Leimersheim, Rhinepalatinate.

WIFE: Barbara Loran 22, daughter of Heinrich, from Queichheim, Rhinepalatinate.

CHILDREN: Aloys 2, Elisabeth 1.
BROTHER: Andreas 15.
(a) Joseph Böhm 54, son of Michael, from Bühl, Baden.
WIFE: Maria-Josepha Ihly 59, daughter of Philipp.
    32. **Georg Schüler** 34, son of Nikolaus, from Mörlheim, Rhinepalatinate.
WIFE: Barbara Mayer 31, daughter of Johann, from Dahn, Rhinepalatinate.
CHILDREN: Johann 9, Jakob 4, Philipp 3, Margaretha 10, Annamaria 6, Katharina 1.
    33. **Friedrich Renner** 33, son of Friedrich, from Kandel, Rhinepalatinate.
WIFE: Marianna Kitzel 26, daughter of Joseph, from Ranschbach, Rhinepalatinate.
CHILDREN: Marianna 5.
(a) Joseph Heck 26, son of Veith, from Lohrbach, Baden.
WIFE: Elisabeth Kitzel 21, daughter of Joseph.
CHILDREN: Jakob 2.
    34. **Jakob Hoffmann** 35, son of Johann, from Offenbach, Rhinepalatinate.
WIFE: Annamaria Frank 31, daughter of Martin, from Kapsweyer, Rhinepalatinate.
CHILDREN: Ludwig 7, Johann-Georg 5, Paul 3, Ferdinand 1, Annamaria 12, Marianna 10, Margaretha 1.
    35. **Joseph Schmidt** 45, son of Paul, from Röschwoog, Alsace.
WIFE: Barbara Brucker 40, daughter of Theobald, from Offenbach, Rhinepalatinate.
CHILDREN: Ludwig 9, Joseph 5, Stanislaus 1, Barbara 15, Elisabeth 13.
(a) Philipp Schoch 23, son of Jakob.
WIFE: Philippina Schmidt 21, daughter of Joseph.
CHILDREN: Emilie 2, Marianna 1.
    36. **Georg Brittner** 40, son of Joseph, from Offenbach, Rhinepalatinate.
WIFE: Barbara Koch 38, daughter of Franz, from Ottersheim, Rhinepalatinate.
CHILDREN: Johann 13, Kajetan 8, Annamaria 13, Elisabeth 7, Marianna 5, Anna Katharina 2.
    36(a) Andreas Martin 26, son of Michael, from Nussdorf, Rhinepalatinate.
WIFE: Elisabeth Heinrich 22, daughter of Adam, from the colony of Speier.
CHILDREN: Heinrich 2, Elisabeth 1.
BROTHERS OF ANDREAS: Thomas 23, Paul 22.

37. **Heinrich Mayer** 30, son of Johann, from Freudental (?).
WIFE: Katharina Deibig 25, daughter of Philipp.
CHILDREN: Johann 6, Maria-Eva 4, Luzia 2, Barbara 1.

38. **Paul Steckler** 28, son of Franz, from Sondernheim, Rhinepalatinate.
WIFE: Margaretha Geiger 25, daughter of Johann.
CHILDREN: Philipp 4, Jakob 2, Michael 1.
SISTER OF MARGARETHA: Elisabeth Geiger 13.

39. **Philipp Schardt** 26, son of Johann from Leimersheim, Rhinepalatinate.
WIFE: Elisabeth Steckler 23, daughter of Franz, from Sondernheim, Rhinepalatinate.
CHILDREN: Margaretha 2, Katharina 1, Elisabeth Dockendorf 14, (orphan).

40. **Thomas Braun** 29, son of Valentin, from Offenbach, Rhinepalatinate.
WIFE: Maria-Eva Loran 24, daughter of Heinrich, from Queichheim, Rhinepalatinate.
CHILDREN: Vinzenz 2, Elisabeth 4, Barbara 1.

41. **Valentin Muth** 36, son of Konstantin, from Rohrbach, Baden.
WIFE: Elisabeth Lanz 35, daughter of Franz, from Odenheim, Baden.
CHILDREN: Johann 6, Ferdinand 1, Antonina 9, Rosina 4, Stephania 2.

42. **Johannes Loran** 30, son of Heinrich, from Queichheim, Rhinepalatinate.
WIFE: Maria-Elisabeth Schardt 29, daughter of Johann, from Leimersheim, Rhinepalatinate.
CHILDREN: Philipp 9, Heinrich 3, Maria-Eva 7, Barbara 1.

43. **Georg Lanz** 38, son of Franz, from Odenheim, Baden.
WIFE: Margaretha Fischer, 32, daughter of Michael, from the colony of Landau.
CHILDREN: Jakob 6, Johann 4, Georg 1, Elisabeth 10, Theresia 8, Maria Elisabeth 2.
Elisabeth Weingärtner 55, daughter of Jakob (presumably the mother of Georg Lanz).

44. **Konrad Bösherz** 26, son of Daniel, from the colony of Landau.
WIFE: Maria-Elisabeth Wolf 29, daughter of Michael.
CHILDREN: Marianna 8, Magdalena 5, Johanna 4. These are all children of Franz-Peter Rewels, (first husband of Maria-Elisabeth Wolf).

45. **Heinrich Fried** 23, son of Jakob, from Berg, Rhinepalatinate.
WIFE: Elisabeth Deibig 20, daughter of Philipp.
CHILDREN: Heinrich 1.

Philipp Deibig 57, father, and son of Peter, from Leimersheim, Rhinepalatinate.

46. **Johannes Geiger** 54, widower, son of Valentin, from Leimersheim, Rhinepalatinate.
CHILDREN: Theresia 14, Elisabeth 12, Marianna 5.
(a) Michael Geiger 23, son of Johann.
WIFE: Margaretha Steckler 19, daughter of Franz.
CHILDREN: Rosa 1.
(b) Aloys Geiger 20, son of Johann.
WIFE: Elisabeth Siegel 19, daughter of Wilhelm.

47. **Philipp Gugert** 54, son of Bartholomaus, from Lorsch, Hessen.
WIFE: Gertrud Schütz 53, daughter of Michael, from Birkenau, Baden.
CHILDREN: Johann 10.
(a) Lorenz Gugert 23, son of Philipp.
WIFE: Annamaria Dillmann 19, daughter of Adam.
CHILDREN: Katharina 1.

48. **Andreas Drescher** 48, son of Andreas, from Freiburg, Prussia.
WIFE: Theresia Millius 48, daughter of Jakob, from Walburg, Alsace.
CHILDREN: Johann 12, Joseph 10, Maria-Eva 15, Elisabeth 8, Magdalena 3, Katharina 1.

49. **Marianna Böhm** 48, widow of Franz Böhm, and daughter of Michael Wolf, from Weingarten, Rhinepalatinate.
CHILDREN: Johann 20, Elisabeth 14, Katharina 12.
BROTHER: Georg Wolf 15. (brother of Marianna).
(a) Theobald Ihly 25, son of Joseph from Malsch, Baden.
WIFE: Gertrud Böhm 21, daughter of Franz.
CHILDREN: Johann 2, Philippina 1.

50. **Joseph Gärtner** 35, son of Sebastian, from Kirchhausen, Württemberg.
WIFE: Maria-Eva Fried 25, daughter of Jakob.
CHILDREN: Joseph 1.
Barbara Busch 54, daughter of Jakob Braun, and her son, Joseph Braun 14.

51. **Augustin Stolz** 46, son of Christian, from Teresia, Poland.
WIFE: Elisabeth Muth 48, daughter of Konstantin, from Rohrbach, Baden.
CHILDREN: Michael 9, Katharina 16, Christina 14, Theresia 12, Elisabeth 7.

52. **Joseph Böchler** 25, son of Michael.
WIFE: Johanna Frank 20, daughter of Karl.

53. **Lorenz Geiss** 63, son of Lorenz, from Rohrbach, Baden.

WIFE: Marianna Lehr 55, daughter of Anton, from the same place.
CHILDREN: Zyriak 16, Johann 12, Elisabeth 8.
(a) Georg Jungmann 27, son of Adam, from Spechbach, Baden.
WIFE: Apollonia Geiss 25, daughter of Lorenz.
CHILDREN: Katharina 1.
(b) Joseph Geiss 35, son of Lorenz.
WIFE: Elisabeth Ruf 30, daughter of Johann.
CHILDREN: Karl 4, Margaretha 14, Elisabeth 12, Karolina 8.

    54. **Andreas Reisenauer** 36, son of Johann, from Malsch, Baden.
WIFE: Annamaria Nebel 31, daughter of Georg, from Knittelsheim, Rhinepalatinate.
CHILDREN: Michael 3, Marianna 10, Barbara 9, Apollonia 6, Katharina 1.
(a) Johann Reisenauer 74, son of Georg, and father of Andreas (above).
WIFE: Barbara Ihly 66, daughter of Joseph.

    55. **Jakob Loran** 25, son of Heinrich, from Queichheim, Rhinepalatinate.
WIFE: Marianna Blumenschein 22, daughter of Ludwig, from Zeisigheim, Alsace.
CHILDREN: Johann 1, Barbara 3.
Joseph Blumenschein 20, brother of Marianna, and her sister, Krescentia 18.

    56. **Joseph Messer** 30, son of Bernhard, from Rohrbach, Baden.
WIFE: Margaretha Hellmann 27, daughter of Michael.
CHILDREN: Michael 7, Johann 5, Ludowika 9, Eva 2.

    57. **Nikolaus Schüler** 58, son of Ferdinand, from Mörlheim, Rhinepalatinate.
WIFE: Margaretha Hoffmann 59, daughter of Georg-Jakob.
CHILDREN: Johann 14.
(a) Valentin Garecht 32, son of Joseph, from Offenbach, Rhinepalatinate.
WIFE: Annamaria Schüler 25, daughter of Nikolaus.
CHILDREN: Peter 3, Johann 1.

    58. **Adam Landeis** 46, from Hördt, Rhinepalatinate, son of Jakob.
WIFE: Maria-Antonia Hely 44, daughter of Jakob, from Malsch, Baden.
CHILDREN: Peter 15.
(a) Jakob Pfaff 18, son of Anton.
WIFE: Katharina Landeis 19, daughter of Adam.
(b) Daniel Landeis 38, son of Jakob.
WIFE: Katharina Jungmann 24, daughter of Adam, from Spechbach, Baden.

CHILDREN: Philipp 10, Jakob 5, Pius 5, Katharina 9.
59. **Jakob Schoch** 50, from Malsch, Baden.
WIFE: Katharina Reisenauer 30, daughter of Johann.
CHILDREN: Johann 18, Jakob 15, Florian 3, Helena 12, Barbara 6, Katharina 1.
60. **Johann Schweikert** 25, son of Adam, from Spechbach, Baden.
WIFE: Theresia Bühler 28, daughter of Oswald, from Obertsrot, Baden.
CHILDREN: Benedict 3, Michael 1, Apolonia 4.
(a) Friedrich Martin 21, son of Thomas.
WIFE: Maria Josepha Waibel 20, daughter of Franz.
(b) Johann Hild 26, son of Matthaus.
WIFE: Maria-Eva Schweikert 20, daughter of Adam.
CHILDREN: Klara 2.
61. **Philipp Helfrich** 31, son of Jakob, from Weidenthal, Rhinepalatinate.
WIFE: Elisabeth Höpfner 30, daughter of Aloys, from Rheinzabern, Rhinepalatinate.
CHILDREN: Stanislaus 7, Jakob 2, Margaretha 4.
Margaretha Ekrott 53, widow, daughter of Anton Führer.
CHILDREN: Joseph 20, Johann 11.
62. **Johann Förderer** 27, son of Joseph from Malsch, Baden.
WIFE: Gertrud Krank 21, daughter of Joseph.
CHILDREN: Katharina 3, Carolina 1.
63. **Matthias Schmidt** 33, son of Paul, from Röschwoog, Alsace.
WIFE: Elisabeth Messer 26, daughter of Bernhardt.
CHILDREN: Philipp 5, Joseph 4, Andreas 2, Valentin 1, Helena 8.
BROTHER: Jakob Schmidt 39.
64. **Jakob Geiss** 37, son of Peter, from Wanzenau, Alsace.
WIFE: Margaretha Ruf 35, daughter of Johann, from Mörlheim, Rhinepalatinate.
CHILDREN: Lorenz 8, Wilhelm 1, Magdalena 6, Brigitta 3.
BROTHER: Johann Geiss 20.
65. **Joseph Bleyle** 70, son of Bernhard, from Kenzingen, Baden.
WIFE: Martha Grieb 65, daughter of Bartholomäus, from Dettingen, Wurtemberg.
(a) Michael Bleyle 20, son of Joseph.
WIFE: Annamaria Anton 18, daughter of Peter.
CHILDREN: Sophia 1.
65(b) Jakob Bleyle 23, son of Joseph.
WIFE: Barbara Martin 23, daughter of Thomas.
CHILDREN: Peter 1.
66. **Peter Anton** son of Jakob 42, from Mörlheim, Rhinepalatinate.

WIFE: Annamaria Hatzenbühler 47, daughter of Theobald, from Ottersheim, Rhinepalatinate.
CHILDREN: Barbara 12, Helena 9.
(a) Andreas Renner 22, son of Martin, from Steinweiler, Rhinepalatinate.
WIFE: Maria-Eva Messer 20, daughter of Bernhard.
CHILDREN: Katharina 1.
(b) Theobald Renner 27, son of Martin.
WIFE: Salomea Anton 25, daughter of Johann.
CHILDREN: Thomas 5, Johann 1, Magdalena 3, Emilia 1.
(c) Johannes Anton 21, son of Peter.
WIFE: Marianna Schmidt 17, daughter of Joseph.
67. **Valentin Fried** 36, son of Valentin, from Berg, Rhinepalatinate.
WIFE: Elisabeth Marthian 31, daughter of Valentin, from Knittelsheim, Rhinepalatinate.
CHILDREN: Joseph 11, Franz 9, Peter 4, Katharina 13, Rosina 6, Margaretha 1.
Valentin Fried 76, father, son of Jakob.
WIFE: Margaretha Sörbel 72, daughter of Jakob.
68. **Valentin Siegel** 64, widower, son of Johann, from Klingenmünster, Rhinepalatinate.
(a) Magdalena Geiss 42, daughter of Peter, from Wanzenau, Alsace.
CHILDREN: Michael 16, Jakob 3, Nikolaus 2, Marianna 13, Margaretha 11, Magdalena 9, Annamaria 5, Franziska 1.
69. **Johannes Röther** 58, son of Ernst from Offenbach, Rhinepalatinate.
WIFE: Katharina Baron 42, daughter of Simon, from Neukirch, Baden.
CHILDREN: Johann 11, Stanislaus 9, Karl 7, Vinzenz 2, Barbara 13, Susanna 5, Margaretha 1.
(a) Joseph Röther 21, son of Johann.
WIFE: Carolina Siegel 20, daughter of Wilhelm.
CHILDREN: Katharina 1.
70. **Johann Ruf** 64, son of Jakob, from Mörlheim, Rhinepalatinate.
WIFE: Barbara Matzer (or Schmutzer) 59, daughter of Lorenz.
CHILDREN: Maria-Eva 18, Katharina 16.
(a) Martin Schmitt 27, son of Paul.
WIFE: Annamaria Ruf 23, daughter of Johann.
CHILDREN: Peter 6, Magdalena 3.
71. **Joseph Mildenberger** 26, son of Joseph from Kirchen, Baden.
WIFE: Karolina Millius 22, daughter of Jakob.
CHILDREN: Maria-Eva 5.

MOTHER: Maria Millius 60, daughter of Joseph Werner from Dörrenbach, Rhinepalatinate.

72. **Abraham Anton** 39, son of Jakob, from Mörlheim, Rhinepalatinate.
WIFE: Eva Katharina Klein 32, daughter of Valentin, from Rülzheim, Rhinepalatinate.
Lambert Keller 17, hired man.

73. **Joseph Förderer** 60, son of Sebastian, from Offenbach, Rhinepalatinate.
WIFE: Elisabeth Röther 60, daughter of Johann (as above).
CHILDREN: Joseph 18.
(a) Andreas Förderer 21, son of Joseph.
WIFE: Katharina Popp 20, daughter of Anton, from the colony of Speier.
CHILDREN: Georg 1.

74. **Peter Sprung** 62, son of Peter from Eussertal, Rhinepalatinate.
WIFE: Annamaria Baudy 55, daughter of Sebastian (as above).
CHILDREN: Jakob 19, Martha 25.
(a) Johann Sprung 31, son of Peter.
WIFE: Barbara Böhm 27, daughter of Franz.
CHILDREN: Sebastian 4, Gertrud 5, Annamaria 2, Katharina 1.

75. **Franz Schuh** 40, son of Bernhard, from Schwetzingen, Baden.
WIFE: Juliana Mayer 53, daughter of Friedrich, from Albersweiler, Rhinepalatinate.
CHILDREN: Joseph (adopted) son of Andreas Anton, Simon 19, Katharina 15.
(a) Philipp Aman 26, son of Andreas.
WIFE: Magdalena Billmann 22, daughter of Johann.
CHILDREN: Maria-Eva 2.
(b) Sebastian Fäth 27, son of Sebastian, from the colony of Landau.
WIFE: Franziska Schuh 21, daughter of Franz.
CHILDREN: Magdalena 2.

76. **Oswald Bühler** 49, son of Michael, from Oberschrot, Switzerland.
WIFE: Margaretha Götz 50, daughter of Michael (as above).
CHILDREN: Joseph 15.
76.(a) Philipp Bühler 25, son of Oswald.
WIFE: Maria-Eva Schüler 20, daughter of Albert, from Dahn, Rhinepalatinate.
CHILDREN: Jakob 2, Joseph 1.
(b) Michael Bühler 21, son of Oswald.
WIFE: Katharina Bechler 19, daughter of Michael.

77. **Michael Martin** 38, son of Johann, from Kandel,

Rhinepalatinate.

WIFE: Elisabeth Billmann 25, daughter of Egidius, from Winzenbach, Alsace.

CHILDREN: Johann 8, Oswald 1, Katharina 9.

78. **Ulrich Deck** 46, son of Lorenz, from Winzenbach, Alsace.

WIFE: Margaretha Fried 44, daughter of Ferdinand, from Berg, Rhinepalatinate.

CHILDREN: Georg 16, Albin 8, Theresia 14, Barbara 12, Elisabeth 5, Bibianna 3.

79. **Joseph Heinzmann** 60, son of Georg, from Kollnau, Baden.

WIFE: Katharina Humel 47, daughter of Franz, from Philippsburg, Baden.

CHILDREN: Jakob 11, Franz 4, Andreas 2, Philippina 8, Johanna 6. Franz Staudinger 20, son of Franz (hired man ?).

80. **Jakob Schüler** 30, son of Nikolaus, from Mörlheim, Rhinepalatinate.

WIFE: Marianna Schoch 29, daughter of Jakob, from Bornbacherhof, Rhinepalatinate.

CHILDREN: Annamaria 6, Kunigunde 4, Bibianna 1.

81. **Franz Bender** 26, son of Johann.

WIFE: Margaretha Baron 23, daughter of Simon.

CHILDREN: Franz 2, Magdalena 4, Gertrud 1.

82. **Johann Heck** 46, son of Martin, from Lohrbach, Baden.

WIFE: Katharina Deibig 44, daughter of Peter, from Leimersheim, Rhinepalatinate.

CHILDREN: Franz-Adam 19, Veith 16, Michael 4, Albert 2, Regina 12, Katharina 8.

83. **Michael Wander** 25, son of Johann, from Erlenbach, Rhinepalatinate.

WIFE: Christina Pfoh 23, daughter of Michael, from the colony of Rastadt.

CHILDREN: Katharina 2.

84. **Sebastian Schwartz** 43, son of Johann, from Mingolsheim, Baden.

WIFE: Josepha Metz 42, daughter of Jakob, from Hayna, Rhinepalatinate.

CHILDREN: Michael 16, Joseph 11, Johann 3.

85. **Franz Humel** 64, son of Anton, from Rohrbach, Baden.

WIFE: Barbara Meckler 44, daughter of Franz (as above).

CHILDREN: Joseph 1, Marianna 5.

86. **Johann Hoffmann** 58, son of Heinrich, from Offenbach, Rhinepalatinate.

WIFE: Apolonia Ekrott 37, daughter of Adam, from Waldürn, Rhinepalatinate.

CHILDREN: Johann 12, Heinrich 10, Adam 2, Franziska 6, Gertrud 4.
    87. **Jakob Bläth** 51, son of Joseph, from Pfaffenroth, Baden.
WIFE: Marianna Becht 47, daughter of Franz (as above).
CHILDREN: Gregor 16, Margaretha 10, Marianna 8.
    88. **Johann Helfrich** 25, son of Jakob.
WIFE: Katharina Deck 18, daughter of Ulrich.
CHILDREN: Jakob 1.

The Beginnings of the
Colony of Karlsruhe

As indicated previously, the people of Karlsruhe came to their settlement in the spring of 1810 and started to build the Crown houses immediately. The houses were made of stamped earth and their construction was supervised by experienced people from the Liebental district. The head of each household received 100 bank rubles to buy draft animals and a wagon, and 35 rubles for a cow.

Each family also received some wood and reeds to build their homes. The colonists received other essentials, namely, hoes, shovels, scythes, scythe sharpeners, and three or four spinning wheels.

The first Crown house completed were allotted as follows: in the bottom row of houses, Johann Schardt (now young Johann Schardt lives there); Johannes Heinz (now Raphael Schardt); Joseph Knoll (now Father Scherr). In the other row of houses, Franz Lanz (now Andreas Loran); Philipp Deubich (now Jakob Höpfner); John Geiger (now Valetin Ruf); Theobald Brucker (now Philipp Höpfner).

On the 1 January 1811 there were 71 families, 147 males and 156 females, a total of 303 people. The families had 72 horses, 215 horned cattle, 69 wagons, 782 loads of hay, 10.35 tschetwert wheat, and 38.5 tschetwert of oats.

Tradesmen were as follows:
TAILORS: Joseph Ihly, Franz Lanz, Georg Rebel.
PLASTERERS: Veith Heck, Lorenz Geiss, Jakob Pfaff, Joseph Jung.
MILLERS: Franz Eberts (who moved to Rastadt), Adam Schweigert, Joseph Frank.
ROPE-MAKER: Oswald Bühler.
CARPENTERS: Simon Baron, Johann Reisenauer.
WEAVERS: Franz Steckler, Johann Röther, Adam Röther.
BLACK-SMITH: Michael Hellmann.

In the year 1812, they seeded 284 tschetwert of winter and summer wheat.

Six years after the founding, there was the following progress: in the year 1817-1818 there were 68 families with 161 males and 173 females, a total of 334 people. They had 309 horses, 347 horned cattle, 395 pigs, 51 ploughs, 37 harrows, 69 wagons, 6 distaffs, and one weaving chair.

Tradesmen were as follows: 1 carpenter, 1 miller, 1 tailor, 1 shoemaker, 1 watchmaker, and 1 plasterer.*

In 1817-1818, the colonists seeded;

	Tschetwert	Tschetwerik.**
Rye	98	2
Summer Wheat	196	4
Barley	67	5
Oats	81	2
Potatoes	68	5
Buckwheat	2	0
Corn	4	2.5
Millet	7	0.5
Peas	7	1.5
Lentils	1	3.0
Beans	1	5
Hemp	0	2.5
Flax	6	0
Total	538	33.0
	tschetwert	tschetwerik

Converted total = 542 Tschetwert, 1.0 tschetwerik.

The Community Land of Karlsruhe

The community land of the colony of Karlsruhe totalled 5450 dessiatines. The land formed an irregular square and was located on both sides of the Fox Valley (river). In the south the land extended to that of the district of Sulz, on the west it bordered on the land of the district of Landau, in the north by the land of Katharinental, and on the east, the estate of Kortschinsky. The land is quite flat. Only the Fox Valley, with its connecting valleys, make the surface irregular and give it the appearance of waves.

On the east side of the river the soil is good, black loam, 14 to 21 inches thick with a base of clay. On the south side of the Fox Valley, the black surface soil is thinner and the base is stony. In this location, the people of Karlsruhe have their best field stones.

In the early years the land was very fertile so that after two or three rains at the right time, they obtained a good harvest.

*Nearly all of the original tradesmen are still living, but they no longer list their trade.
**1 tschetwert = 8 tschetwerik.

In 1823, on instructions from the authorities, they also planted trees, orchards and vineyards. Unfortunately, the colonists had no experience with culturing trees or orchards and they soon died.

In 1842 a stricter directive was sent by the authorities stating that 'In all German colonies, trees, orchards and vineyards must be planted.' At this time there were also the so-named 'district gardens' planted and nursed by horticulturists. From these gardens, the other colonists obtained seedlings for their community and private gardens at very reasonable prices. They were also ordered by the authorities to cultivate tobacco and some of the Karlsruhe colonists were particularly good at this.

The "Unterhaltungsblatt" quoted the following: "In 1846 the colonial authority of the colony of Karlsruhe of the Beresan district had a trial at cultivating tobacco and undertook this project with praiseworthy care. Their success exceeded all expectations. The tobacco realized a very high price. The samples sent to St. Petersburg were highly praised by the assayer and the factory there declared outright that it would pay 10 rubles silver per pud."

The tobacco which was 10 rubles per pud at that time, is today priced at 60 to 70 rubles. "Good people of Karlsruhe, plant tobacco again."

The Parish of Karlsruhe

The parish colony of Karlsruhe at present has 260 lots and 1932 people, all Catholics. Non-Catholics remain in the colony for only a short time and will be mentioned elsewhere. The parish was founded in 1861. Prior to this it was supervised from the Landau parish.

Karlsruhe belongs to the deanery of Nikolayev in the diocese of Tiraspol. The hamlet of Antonowka belongs to this parish. Karlsruhe is 5 versts from the postoffice and telegraph station in Landau.

The Parish Story

After the colony of Speier separated from the mother church of Landau in 1857 and formed its own parish, subsequently having its own priest, the people of Karlsruhe and those of Katharinental also became desirous of having their own parish. The two communities of Karlsruhe and Katharinental got together, reached a common decision, and sent a representative with a written petition to the diocesan bishop, Ferdinand Helanus Kahn. In the petition the reasons were given for founding a parish in Karlsruhe with the added request to take the necessary steps to obtain the confirmation of the secular authorities.

The permission was soon forthcoming and a priest was sent there. Since the Fürsorge Committee supported the requests of both communities, the sanction for the new parish of Karlsruhe was received in a short time. The first priest arrived on the 15 December 1861, Father Michael Stankewicz.

The Sequence of Priests in Karlsruhe

FATHER MICHAEL STANKEWICZ
15 December 1861 to 7 March 1877

Father Michael Stankewicz was born in 1798 in the province of Vilna and was ordained a priest in 1828.

On the 4 April 1835 he was sent to Josephstal to take over the position of Father Kaspar Borowsky, who was appointed assistant in the Academy in Vilna. He was a diligent worker in Josephstal in the cause of Christianity and set a good example by his moral conduct and piety. Still, after many years, a change came about within him. On the 17 October 1853 Bishop Kahn wrote to Prelate Rasutowicz in Petersburg stating that he wished to sentence the two disobedient priests, Ch. Pietkewicz and M. Stankewicz, to one month's penance.*

After this episode, Father Stankewicz was moved from Josephstal to Kleinliebental where he remained until 1861.

In 1861 he came to Karlsruhe as parish priest. Here he worked for the well-being of his parishioners, with prudence and diligence. He did not speak German very well and was very slow in all of his ministrations. He was also a poor singer and, consequently, was never able to gain the full support of his parishioners. He also managed a big farm in Karlsruhe where he cultivated flax extensively. His greatest problem in Karlsruhe was caused by the big, unruly boys.

When he realized that his pastoral work was bearing little fruit and that he was weakening with old age, he sent a request to the authorities for his retirement, which was granted to him. He lived for a few more years and died, I believe, in Simferopol in the eighties of the last century.

FATHER JAKOB SEELINGER
7 March 1877 and 22 March 1886

For information about him see Rastadt, page 252. From 1886 until 1888, Karlsruhe was supervised from Katharinental.

---

*Archives of the Church of Odessa, 1853.

FATHER JAKOB SCHERR

Father Scherr was born on the 3 July 1863 in Strassburg, Kutschurgan, the son of Joseph Scherr and Barbara Held. He was a good student and attended both the Parish and the Central School in Strassburg.

As a result of his good preparation in the Central School, he passed the elementary teacher's examinations set by the examining board in Odessa and entered the Seminary in Saratov.

As a result of diligent study, he finished his course and was ordained a priest on the 1 May 1888. He said his first mass in the chapel of the seminary on the 10 May 1888.

His first posting was as vicar to the colony of Mariental on the Karaman, where he worked for three months.

In September 1888 he was appointed administrator in the colony of Karlsruhe, where he remained until 27 May 1908. He worked hard in the duties of Christian ministrations to his people. His activities in Karlsruhe were numerous. In addition to his priestly functions in the pulpit, in the confessional, and his teaching of religion in the schools, he also founded an orphanage and a boy's junior high school. These two projects are still under his guidance today and have the Lord's blessing. As a result of his work, there are more and more benefits accruing to the general welfare of the Beresan colonies as well as to more distant regions.

He started his zealous activities in Karlsruhe by renovating the interior of the church. He had terra cotta tile placed on the church floor and put stained glass in all the windows, as designed by the Franciscan priest, Father Johann-Marra Reiter. He also ordered an organ from the workshop of Steinmeier. He introduced the Eucharistic Society, the Perpetual Adoration, and the Third Order of St. Francis in the Beresan. He reformed the church music according to the statutes of the St. Cecilia Society and initiated many other activities in the church and school. In addition, he was often the retreat master for the priests in the Beresan at their conventions. He also held several spiritual retreats for the pupils in the seminary in Saratov. Lately he is concentrating all his efforts on the lower classical school, where he sees his life's work in the role as educator of the young.

FATHER JOSEPH WOLF *Vicar and Religious Instructor*
from the 2 August 1905 until the 9 September 1906

Father Joseph Wolf was born in the colony of Wolkovo on the 24 May 1882, the son of Joseph Wolf and Karolina Deschle. He received his first instruction in the colony school in his home.

In 1896 he entered the seminary in Saratov. After completing his courses of study, he was ordained a priest on the 26 May 1905. His first position was as vicar and German preacher in Odessa. Here he founded a library for the German community and the Marian Aid Society. On the 3 August 1909 he was sent to Saratov to the clerical seminary as spiritual advisor and in 1910 was made the prefect of the seminary. Since the 20 July 1912 he has been the administrator in the Turgai district in Siberia where there are many German Catholic settlers from the diocese of Tiraspol.

FATHER MICHAEL HATZENBÖLLER *Administrator*
from 27 May 1908 to 31 August 1908

See under Sulz, page 149

FATHER JOSEPH BEILMANN *Administrator*
from 21 September 1908 until 9 October 1910

Father Joseph Beilmann was born in the colony of Vollmer in 1873. He was ordained a priest in 1897. He was in various parishes of the diocese of Tiraspol and is at the present time the religious instructor in Rovnoye.

FATHER JOHANNES BACK *Administrator*
from 22 October 1910 until now

Father Johannes Back was born in 1884 and ordained a priest in 1908. No further information is available on him.

FATHER FRANZ RAU *Teacher of Religion*

Father Franz Rau was born in 1888 and ordained in 1911. Since then he has been administrator in Marienfeld.

Parish Endowment

The salary of the priest amounts to 600 rubles. The community provides the firewood. The surplice fees are baptism 1 ruble, wedding services 2 rubles, publishing of banns 1 ruble, funeral 1 ruble, low mass 1 ruble, high mass 1 ruble, 50 kopecks.

The Parish Church

The first church building was started in 1820 and completed in 1830. The building was approximately 60 feet long, 36 feet wide and the roof was covered with reeds. The inside was pleasantly decorated and contained an altar, a pulpit, a confessional, and some holy pictures. The church was located on the same spot as the present church is located.

Since its original construction, the church has been frequently remodelled and also enlarged. When Father M. Stankewicz came to Karlsruhe in 1861, he realized that the church was too small for this large community. Consequently, he tried to obtain permission from the authorities to build a new church in Karlsruhe. In answer to this request, Prelate Rasutowicz replied on the 12 February 1864 that a new church in Karlsruhe could be built only with permission from the Fürsorge Committee. This permission would only be granted if the community had the necessary money to build the church and to guarantee the necessary funds. Since they had only 500 rubles on hand in the church revenue, the matter was deferred. This situation remained unchanged until 1878 when Father Stankewicz moved away from Karlsruhe and the young, energetic Father Jakob Seelinger took his place.

At a community meeting on the 19 November 1879, a decision was finally made to build the church, and they guaranteed payment for this purpose to the amount of 35,000 rubles.

On the 7 March 1881 the community elected a building committee and obtained a plan from the architect, Korf, to build the church. On the 15 May 1881 the community signed an agreement with the German building contractor, Herman Wulfken, whereby Wulfken agreed to build the church for 17,000 rubles and to have it completed by the 15 May 1883.

The work was started and until October 1882 all went well. At this time, the work came to a halt because the contractor, Wulfken, would not continue with the building under any circumstances. The community was obligated to turn the work over to the contractor, Artjomov. Unfortunately, this man died in the latter part of 1883 and the contract had to be turned over to a third contractor, namely Pentjuchov. He finally completed the work in 1885.

The New Parish Church

The large and impressive, new Gothic church is located in the middle of the colony. It is built of field stone and extends in an east-west direction.

The brickwork cost 70,000 rubles and was completely paid for by the parishioners: The church was blessed by Prelate N. Tschernjachowicz on the 29 June 1885 and consecrated by Bishop Zerr on the 4 October 1887.

The patrons of the church are the Holy Apostles, Peter and Paul.

The church consists of three naves and is located approximately 48 feet from the main street. It is 120 feet long, 57 feet wide, and the roof in its central portion is 63 feet high. There are four entrance doors, three at the front under the steeple and one on the left, leading to the sacristy chamber. Each of the two outer naves has five windows shaped in the form of pointed arches. They are 30 feet high and 70 inches wide. The central nave, which rises above the two lateral naves, also has five windows on either side, but they are round. The windows on the facade are of various size and form, but without any ornamentation.

The steeple contains two stories and is built on the church. The bottom story is square and extends above the roof of the central nave with an ogival window facing to the front.

The top story is an equi-angular octagon, decorated with cornices and eight small buttresses. This story contains the bell tower, with four louvred windows, the tower clock, and three fine bells to call the faithful to prayers. Above this story projects the pointed peak of the tower roof, with a large cupola and a cross extending several faden high.

The church roof is covered with tin and is painted green. The church yard is enclosed by a massive stone wall. There are twelve stone steps leading to the main door, where one enters the church through the four faden high portal.

The appearance of the inside of the church is as follows: the church consists of three naves, the central nave being twice as high as the lateral naves and separated from them by a row of five large, square pillars on either side. These pillars are 12 feet high and are joined to each other by pointed arches. These arches are continued into the transverse vaults that extend over the entire length of the lateral naves. In this same way, the pillars of the central nave are joined to the wall pillars of the side extension by pointed arches, and divide the ceiling of the side extensions into four areas.

The side naves are 21 feet high, 12 feet wide and approximately 78 feet long. They are not decorated and run parallel on either side of the central nave.

On the east end of the side naves, adjacent to the communion bench, there are two shallow niches containing two side altars, essentially of simple design.

The central nave is 66 feet long, 24 feet wide, 45 feet high, and opens into the large presbytery, 30 feet long and 24 feet wide. On either side of it there is a sacristy.

The presbytery obtains its light through two stained glass windows with ogival arches mounted into niches. The Gothic altar rests on a platform reached by four steps. It is 24 feet high, and was designed by the architect, W. Dombrowsky, who had designed the two side altars. It was built by J. Kaiser, a cabinet maker in Odessa.

The observer is very favourably impressed by the main altar as it extends upwards, supported by ornamental, carved turrets and pillars to which the statues of Peter and Paul are attached. The turrets and pillars are grouped to form three steeples, one main central steeple and two side steeples. They are joined at the bottom by two niches, but at the top they are free and project upwards. The two side altars are smaller but of simpler design. The side altar on the right is dedicated to Saint Joseph, the one on the left, to the Blessed Virgin Mary, queen of the Holy Rosary. The lovely oak carved pulpit is attached to one of the pillars in the central nave and rests on a smoothly polished oak pillar.

Affixed to every free pillar, and in the recesses on either side of the altar, there are statues from the workshop of Adolf Vogel in Hall. There are eight statues which have been placed in the following order, proceeding from the right side of the altar towards the entrance door: a Pieta, the Blessed Heart of Jesus, Saint Aloysius, and Saint Paul. To the left there is an Ecce Home, the Holy Mother of God, the Immaculate Conception, and St. Peter. Each one of the statues cost 200 rubles.

The main choir loft rests on the four pillars of the central nave near the entrance and contains an organ from the factory of Steinmeyer. The organ was bought in 1897 at a cost of 5,400 rubles. Nine Stations of the Cross were bought in 1901 from the firm of Adolf Vogel in Hall at a cost of 3000 rubles. These are among the most beautiful adornments in the church. In 1902 Father Scherr ordered stained glass windows from the firm of Neuhauser, Jele and Company. The money for these windows, generously donated by many of the parishioners, amounted to 6,000 rubles.

In 1909 the artist, Raphael Thaler, from Innsbruck decorated the interior of the church. The work was executed in an artistic style and especially the two large-scale paintings on the ceiling must be regarded as eminently successful. The first one is a picture of the Descent of the Holy Ghost and the second, a picture of the Preaching of Saint Peter. There are also many smaller pictures which cannot be described here. The entire cost of the paintings amounted to 6,000 rubles.

When one adds the cost of the decoration of the interior to the original cost of 70,000 rubles for the building, it comes to well over 100,000 rubles. Through the construction of this magnificent church, Father J. Seelinger and Father J. Scherr left a lasting memorial for themselves, and the people of Karlsruhe left a worthy memorial for their faith and their exemplary generosity.

The Graveyard and Chapel

The graveyard is approximately 200 yards to the south of the church and has been in the same place since the founding of the colony. A cemetery chapel built by Michael Schardt in 1893 serves the family as a burial place. The remains of the late Father Jakob Schardt rest in the chapel. The graveyard is enclosed by a massive stone wall and contains some fine monuments.

The Parish Rectory

Father M. Stankewicz lived in a private home when he first came to Karlsruhe. The people of the community of Karlsruhe approached the district mayor's office of Beresan for permission to build a rectory, on the 20 February 1867. The plan, which included the over-all cost of 1417 rubles, was approved by the Fürsorge Committee. The community had 800 rubles from rent obtained from the liquor dispenser. The other 617 rubles was to be donated by the people. The rectory was completed in 1869. It was built of field stone and the roof was covered with tin. The rectory contained five rooms, a kitchen and a corridor. The necessary barns and wells were also provided.

School Affairs

On searching the archives, no record could be found of the first school in Karlsruhe. The second school was apparently built in 1827 or 1828. The present schoolhouse, built in 1873 was constructed of field stone and contained three large class rooms and a large hall for the community chancery. At the present time there are three teachers employed, each receiving a salary of 350 rubles. There are 135 children in attendance.

The first school teacher was Nikolaus Schüler, who was followed by his son, Georg-Jakob Schüler. From approximately 1850 on, the following were the school masters and teachers: Kaspar Jäger Sr., Kaspar Jäger Jr., Michael Stankewicz (later became Father M. Stankewicz), Michael Wanner, Lukas Meuchel, Johannes Gärtner, Philipp Schardt, Ludwig Loran, Georg Schardt, Rudolf Gratz, Joseph Kunz, Franz Ochs, Sebastian Derschan, Zachaus Dechant, Michael Bertsch, Joseph Hopfauf, Raphael Schardt, Johannes Fix, Erasmus Thomas, Jakob Rink, Joseph Reisenauer, Peter Barthle, and a lady teacher, Anna Matkowskaja.

THE HIGH SCHOOL
FOUNDED BY FATHER SCHERR

A bright spot in the cultural development of the Beresan district and a glorious page in its history is the founding of the highschool by Father J. Scherr. This school is of great interest to all the people of the Beresan; consequently, a few words on the origin and development of the school are in order.

It was the mishandling of school affairs in the colonies of the Beresan that provided the motive for founding the high school in Karlsruhe. Approximately twenty years ago there were various inadequate schools in the colonies of the Beresan, founded by unqualified private teachers of questionable morals. These small private schools interfered with the development of the church schools, took many children away from the proper religious instruction and sowed the seeds of moral and religious ruin. To counter the bad influence of these small private schools, Father P. Scherr decided to found a community school in Karlsruhe. As a result of having received his teacher's diploma, even before entering the seminary, he was qualified to undertake such a task.

The plan for founding the school was completed in the spring of 1900. He took the necessary step of applying to the school authorities for permission. His request was granted and the school was established without delay.

In the summer of 1900 the savings from the orphanage, which at that time was privately run by Father Scherr, were made available to construct the much needed school. The school was opened on the 1 September 1900 and instruction started. The program was that of an expanded elementary school. There were 36 students, including some from the orphanage, who were enrolled immediately. Instruction was given by two good teachers.

The enrollment increased every year. The students who came from a distance took up residence in a boarding house near the orphanage. The good reputation of the school soon spread throughout the whole district and students eager to learn came from all directions to Karlsruhe in order to enroll in Father Scherr's school. In a period of five years the enrollment increased from 36 to 215 pupils. This rapid increase in enrollment was a reminder that some thought should be given to founding an intermediate school. In order to obtain permission to establish a secondary school, Father Scherr, in spite of the fact that he was forty-one years old, undertook to write the private tutor examinations. After he obtained the necessary diploma, he took further steps to accomplish his desire. He bought two lots from his neighbour and in the summer of 1905 started to build a large boarding school. He received permission from the authorities to build a four classroom school on the 26 April 1906, with a view to expanding its facilities into a Junior High School.

During the school term of 1906-1907, the enrollment in both the elementary and the Junior High Schools increased to 260 pupils. After the schools were divided, their enrollment, with slight fluctuations, has remained high until today.

Permission for the secondary highschool was given by the Minister of Education on the 4 February 1908. The yearly school examinations, conducted under the chairmanship of a deputy from the school authorities, provided proof of the highly qualified performance of the school. In 6 years, 116 pupils obtained their certificates and were eligible to enter the fifth class of a government Highschool.

As a result of this success, Father Scherr resolved to enlarge his school into a complete 8-class high school and submitted the necessary request to the school authorities. The first request was submitted in 1908; two further requests were submitted, but they were all refused.

In the summer of 1913 he obtained permission to open a 5-class highschool and finally, on the 2 February 1914, a telegram was received from Petersburg sanctioning an 8-class highschool for Father Scherr and his pupils. So Karlsruhe and the whole Beresan district had the good fortune of having a full highschool course with permission for examinations. Undertaking the construction of a new institution is indeed still a formidable task. It is to be hoped that the initiative displayed until now, as indicated by their obvious success, will continue. With good fortune and God's blessing, the academy will be completed.

The aims of Father Scherr's present secondary school were to teach his pupils the high ideals of obedience to the church and and the Creator, to provide subjects who are loyal to the Emperor and citizens who are useful to the State. May the new highschool continue to implant in its pupils the highest ideals of man, religion, knowledge, love of the Fatherland, and true humanity.

The main promoters and benefactors of the new institution in Karlsruhe were: Nikolaus Theodorowitsch Suchomlinov, noble marshal and member of the council of the Government; other members of the council who donated were P. W. Nowitzsky, G. Lutz, Thomas Zentner, and Jakob Kaiser.

Father J. Scherr, the founder of the school, considered its construction to be the work of divine providence and attributed the success to the blessings of the Sacred Heart of Jesus and the prayers of his dear orphan children.

List of the Teachers
at the Institute of Father Scherr
for the school year 1912-1913.

1. Father J. Scherr—founder of the school and religious instructor.
2. Stefan Burakow—Russian Orthodox religious instructor.
3. Vladimir Awdiew—Head Master, instructor of mathematics, natural history and geography; has a university degree.
4. Heinrich Krüger—teacher of Latin and Russian, world history, has a university degree.
5. Amalia Krüger—teacher of Russian, has a diploma as teacher.
6. Lidia Dupon—teacher of French, has her teacher's diploma.
7. George Neugum—teacher of German, has his teacher's certificate.

8. George Poliansky—supervisor and instructor in physical training, has a high school education.
9. Philipp Jundt—teacher, has his diploma as an elementary teacher.

*List of Graduates
of the
Secondary School of Father Scherr
1908 to 1913*

1908
1. Peter Josephowitsch Hammel. 2. Johann Friedrichowitsch Hörner. 3. Philipp Nikolajewitsch Heidt. 4. Philipp Petrowitsch Hopfauf. 5. Joseph Jakowlewitsch Rosshau. 6. Stanislaus Antonowitsch Skwiretzky. 7. Ignatius Matwejewitsch Fischer. 8. Anton Stanislawowitsch Schardt. 9. Gregorius Josephowitsch Schardt.
1909
1. Johannowitsch Georg Adler. 2. Joseph Michaelowitsch Berger. 3. Johan Franzewitsch Hammel. 4. Aloysius Jakowelewitsch Höpfner. 5. Johann Adamowitsch Hopfinger. 6. Alexander Christianowitsch Dauenhauer. 7. Pius Jakowlewitsch Sänger. 8. Johann Franzewitsch Immel. 9. Martin Jewgenijewitsch Kiefel. 10. Anton Franzewitsch Mitzel. 11. Paul Benhardtowitsch Meier. 12. Alexius Michaelowitsch Rihl. 13. Raphael Antonowitsch Fleck. 14. Joseph Johannowitsch Schefer. 15. Otto Michaelowitsch Stein. 16. Peter Schmidt.
1910
1. George Antonowitsch Bart. 2. Peter Antonowitsch Welk. 3. Anton Antonowitsch Weninger. 4. Georg Georgijewitsch Wolf. 5. Kaspar Johannowitsch Kedack. 6. Kaspar Johannowitsch Heisser. 7. Johan Johannowitsch Höpfner. 8. Franz Josephowitsch Köhler. 9. Georg Petrowitsch Lebold. 10. Eduard Wilhelmowitsch Lust. 11. Eduard Kiprionow Monkewitsch. 12. Marian Pawlowsky. 13. Joseph Jakowlewitsch. 14. Erasmus Erasmowitsch Tremmel. 15. Jakob Jalowlewitsch Ferderer. 16. Johann Johannowitsch Vetsch. 17. August Friedrichowitsch Fuchs.
1911
1. Philipp Petrowitsch Anton. 2. Philipp Jakowlewitsch Anton. 3. Leon Johannowitsch Biegler. 4. Valentin Josephowitsch Blank. 5. Andreas Josephowitsch Bartle. 6. Sebastian Johannowitsch Haag. 7. Thomas Johannowitsch Darscht. 8. Matthias Antonowitsch Ihly. 9. Johann Johannowitsch Imberi. 10. Franz Johannowitsch Job. 11. Johann Ignatijewitsch Lipinsky. 12. Joseph Johannowitsch Mack. 13. Georg Franzewitsch Materi. 14. Alexander Michaelowitsch Alexander. 15. Anton Wladislawitsch Pawlowsky. 16. Joseph Andrejewitsch Ribel. 17. Johann Michaelowitsch Rombs. 18. Valentin

Jakowlewitsch Rutkowsky. 19. Anton Josephowitsch Simon. 20. Franz Frank. 21. Damian Zentner. 22. Johann Schardt. 23. Johann Schefer. 24. Adam Schmidt. 25. Johann Schmidt. 26. Christian Steckler. 27. Adolf Ehli.

1912

1. Friedrich Anton. 2. Jakob Anton. 3. Baltazar Bachmann. 4. Eugenius Biegler. 5. Johann Hardock. 6. Jakob Dauenhauer. 7. Johann Karch. 8. Zachäus Deibele. 9. Leo Reisser. 10. Michael Köhler. 11. Raphael Kellerman. 12. Nikolaus Kimejew. 13. Johann Riefel. 14. Anton Kupper. 15. Stephan Martin. 16. Peter Mein. 17. Leo Meckler. 18. Wladislaus Monkewitsch. 19. Lukas Pawlowsky. 20. Ignatius Potemkowsky. 21. Anton Prochaska. 22. Klemens Renner. 23. Christian Renner. 24. Aloysius Röther. 25. Alexander Rische. 26. Woldemar Usatjuck. 27. Aloysius Feisst. 28. Eugenius Zentner. 29. Eduard Zentner. 30. Raphael Schardt. 31. Jakob Schardt. 32. Jakob Schlosser.

1913

1. Johann Adler. 2. Stanislaus Boguschewsky. 3. Valentin Wolf. 4. Aloysius Heim. 5. Eduard Selinger. 6. Jakob Sattler. 7. Joseph Ihly. 8. Klemens Job. 9. Michael Keller. 10. Joseph Kupper. 11. Leo Kuhn. 12. Joseph Fix. 13. Thomas Fischer. 14. Raphael Ehrenpreis.

The Orphanage
Founded in Karlsruhe by Father Scherr.

The most important good deed which a Christian can do for his fellow men is, without a doubt, to care for poor orphans. The Lord himself has spoken on this subject; "He who accepts one of these children, accepts me." This admonition was heard by Father Scherr and acted upon as an example for all good Christians to follow. He founded an orphanage in Karlsruhe dedicated to the Sacred Heart of Jesus.

In 1892 Heinrich Hoffmann, a colonist from Karlsruhe who has since died, donated a house to be used for an orphanage.

To adapt it for its use, two parishioners, Johannes Anton and Thomas Martin, each donated 100 rubles. With these modest means, the new institution was founded. It opened in the same year with six orphans being accommodated. Two good-hearted young ladies, Gertrud Keller from Selz and Paulina Wolf from Mariental, acted as matrons and took over, without pay, the supervision and education of the poor orphans. Today, the institution can look back over 22 years of good work under the guidance of the Sacred Heart of Jesus.

At the present time, the orphanage is divided into two units. The first unit, the House of Mercy, called the "House of St. Joseph," with five sick, retarded wards, is a two-story house with 12,000 rubles founding capital. The second unit is the main orphanage with 75 orphans, occupying three houses and 12,000 rubles founding capital, 21 dessiatines of land and a model farm under the supervision of the orphan mother and co-foundress, Fräulein Gertrud Keller. The main benefactors of the institute are His Excellency Bishop Kessler. Father M. Marsal, Father I. Hoffmann, Father L. Eberle, Father I. Beilmann, Father V. Weber, Father A. Baier, Father A. Keller. The lay people benefactors were R. Monte, J. Anton, Th. Martin, M. Schardt, L. Geiss, J. Schardt and P. Beile.

Priests born
in the
Parish of Karlsruhe

FATHER JOSEPH IHLY

Father Joseph Ihly was born in Karlsruhe on the 5 June 1851, the son of colonist Theobald Ihly and Gertrud Böhm. He received his first instruction in his parents home and in the parish school. In 1868 he entered the Seminary in Saratov. After completing the necessary courses there, he was ordained a priest by Bishop Franziskus Zottmann on the 29 June 1875. He was first posted to Rothammel as administrator where he remained until the 31 August 1876 when he was moved as administrator to Katharinental in the Beresan. On the 19 August 1880 he was sent to Speier as administrator and on the 13 May 1882, he was named vicar and officially installed.

Father Ihly worked hard in Speier, particularly with reference to Christian teaching in the schools. There are still some of his pupils who are able to repeat the catechism from cover to cover.

As a result of his hard work in the community, he developed a severe laryngitis which made it difficult for him to carry on his work. He applied to the authorities for his retirement. His request was granted on the 4 July 1903 by Bishop Ropp and this was later confirmed by the bishop of the diocese, Joseph Kessler. Since then, Father Ihly has been in Nikolayev in retirement.

FATHER JAKOB SCHARDT *Priest and Dean*

Father Jakob Schardt was born in the colony of Karlsruhe on the 13 August 1857. He received his first instruction in the parish school. In 1872, along with several other boys from the Beresan, he went to Saratov to enter the Seminary.

As he was a good, bright student he progressed rapidly in his studies. After completing his studies in the minor seminary, he decided to become a priest and requested permission to enroll in the Clerical Seminary.

In his theological studies he again made very good progress and excelled in dogmatics. After completing his courses at the seminary, he was ordained by Bishop Zottmann on the 27 April 1880. He was sent as curate vicar to Kischinev, relieving Father R. Zwikla who was seriously ill. The latter priest died shortly thereafter and Father Schardt took over the administration of the parish of Kischinev.

In 1884 he was made dean of the Bessarabian deanery and appointed religious instructor in the secondary school there. The duties assigned to him were too heavy for this young, somewhat sickly priest and therefore he requested an assistant vicar. His request was granted and Father Jansky was sent as vicar.

Unfortunately, not long after, Father Jansky died quite suddenly and Father Schardt had to work alone once more. As a result of a severe cold, he became seriously ill and he died in Kischinev after receiving the last sacraments on the 24 July 1891. His body was taken to Karlsruhe where he was buried in the presence of a large number of the faithful. A lovely chapel was built over his grave. Father Schardt had been corresponding for a long time with the priest in Leimersheim in the Palatinate from where his grandfather, Johann Schardt had emigrated to Russia. Shortly before his death he had expressed a wish to visit the home of his forefathers but, unfortunately, God called him too soon to his heavenly home.

FATHER JOSEPH RÖTHER

Father Joseph Röther was born in the colony of Karlsruhe on the 24 June 1854, the son of Johann Röther and Helena Anton.

He received his first instruction in the local parish school. In 1872, this 18 year-old joined a group of young people seeking further education and went to the Seminary in Saratov. He was a good student and, because of his pleasant personality, he was well liked. As a result of his secondary education, he was able to help the younger and weaker students with their studies. After completing his studies at the seminary, he was ordained by Bishop Franz Zottmann on the 15 March 1881.

His first appointment was as administrator in Göttland where he remained for 2 1/2 years. From here he was sent as administrator to Bergtal where he remained for 10 1/2 years, struggling with the many problems of the newly founded parish.

In 1895 he was transferred to the parish of Eichwald. Here he is still carrying on in his own quiet, friendly but vigorous fashion, tending to the needs of his parishioners.

FATHER JOSEPH LORAN

Father Joseph Loran was born on the 23 May 1859 in the colony of Karlsruhe. He received his first instruction from his father, a man of considerable education and an excellent organist. Subsequently, he attended the local parish school.

In 1872 he went with the above-mentioned group of students from the Beresan district to attend the Seminary in Saratov. In addition to the required courses, he studied music so that he soon became an excellent, deeply engrossed violinist. Whenever he had a free moment, he would go to a separate room to play his beloved violin. It gave him great pleasure when he was able to find someone with whom he could play a duet. Father Loran was kind and obliging and ready with a helping hand whenever the need arose.

His first appointment was to the newly founded parish of Graf on the Karaman. He was here only a short time when he was moved to the large parish of Mariental on the Karaman, where he had a great deal of work.

In 1886 he was appointed administrator at Rosental in the Crimea where he worked for five years at his duties as a priest. In 1891 he was moved to Göttland, where he became ill and died on the 8 January 1892.

FATHER JOHANN HOFFMANN

Father Johann Hoffmann was born in Karlsruhe in 1868. He was ordained on the 19 September 1893. Since 1897 he has been working as the priest in the colony of Heidelberg.

FATHER RAPHAEL LORAN

Father Raphael Loran, son of Michael, was born in 1872 in Karlsruhe. He was ordained in 1897 and is presently the curate in the parish of Baden.

FATHER FRANZ LORAN

Father Franz Loran, son of Heinrich, was born in Karlsruhe in 1873 and was ordained in 1897. He was the curate in Kleinliebental for several years.

FATHER VALENTIN BÖCHLER

Father Böchler was born in Karlsruhe in 1874 and ordained in 1900. Since then he as been the parish priest in Strassburg in the Kutschurgan.

FATHER EDUARD HOPFAUF

Father Eduard Hopfauf was born in 1880 in the colony of Karlsruhe. He completed his studies in the Seminary in Saratov in 1906 and was ordained the same year. He was a pious and diligent priest. He worked in Hekovka for one year, tending to the needs of the parishioners.

Unfortunately, although he was still very young, he became seriously ill and died quietly on the 16 February 1912 and was buried in Hekovka. His life was short, but rich in suffering.

FATHER KARL HOPFAUF

Father Karl Hopfauf was born in the colony of Karlsruhe in 1881 and was ordained in 1905. He was the vicar in Mariental, where he founded a trade school and worked hard for the betterment of society. Because of illness, his activities soon came to an end.

FATHER NIKODEMUS IHLY

Father Nikodemus Ihly was born on the 8 February 1882, in the colony of Karlsruhe, the son of colonist Philipp Ihly and Barbara Hopfauf. After his parents both died, he entered the Seminary in Saratov. He completed his courses in 1910 and was ordained on the 8 September 1910 by his Excellency Bishop Joseph Aloysius Kessler.

His first appointment was to Mariental in the Karaman, where he worked as vicar for several months. On the 1 December 1911 he was sent to Hölzel as administrator, where a heavy assignment awaited him. However, he was healthy and of good spirit and carried out his duties diligently.

FATHER NIKOLAUS HELLMANN

Father Nikolaus Hellmann was born in 1885 and ordained in 1910. Further information is not available.

Important Lay People
who were born in Karlsruhe
or worked there

NIKOLAUS SCHÜLER *Schoolmaster*

Nikolaus Schüler was born in 1780 in Mörlheim in the Rhinepalatinate, went to Russia in 1809, and settled as a colonist in Karlsruhe. He was the first schoolmaster. He was intelligent, had a good sense of humour, and was a natural poet. He was always ready with rhymes and proverbs and had many anecdotes and stories about the old home in Germany. He promoted the old folk traditions and customs of his ancestral homeland. He also provided the speeches and customs of the races at Pentecost in the Beresan, most of which are still in use today. He wrote a satirical poem about all of the Beresan colonists, but the original text of this could not be found.

Nikolaus Schüler, far advanced in years, died in his home in Karlsruhe. His son, Georg-Jakob Schüler, was also a schoolmaster for several years.

LUDWIG LORAN *Teacher*

Ludwig Loran was born in Karlsruhe in 1859. After completing his studies in the local parish school, he entered the Seminary in Saratov. He completed his studies in the so-called "Little Seminary" and accepted a position as teacher in his home colony. Later he moved to Nikolayev where he ran a bookstore for a while. After a few years he bought some land and started farming.

VINZENZ SCHUH *Teacher*

Vinzenz Schuh was born in Karlsruhe on the 15 November 1861, the son of Franz Schuh and Maria-Eva Ruf. After finishing his studies at the parish school, he attended the Seminary in Saratov. After completing four classes he accepted a position as teacher in Zürichtal in the Crimea, where he remained until 1888. From 1888 on he became teacher, sexton and secretary in the colony of Mirnowka in the Crimea.

From Mirnowka he moved to Felsenbach, in the province of Poltawa, where he was teacher, sexton and secretary until 1903. From here he moved to Rosenfeld, in the province of Jekaterinoslav, where he again held the three positions of teacher, sexton and secretary until 1905.

From there he returned to his hometown of Karlsruhe, where he remained for two-and-one-half years as teacher and bookkeeper in the Co-operative Society there.

He then had the desire to migrate to America, but he had some ill luck. The first time he got as far as Libau, where he was turned down by the doctor because his children contracted some eye infection and therefore they had to return. He went to Professor Erdberg in Nikolayev, where the infection was cured, and he felt assured that they would now be permitted to go to America. He proceeded on his way for the second time and got as far as Liverpool, where the doctor once more rejected him, necessitating his return to Russia.

Presently, he is the teacher, sexton and secretary in Nikolaital.

PETER SCHARDT *Teacher*

Peter Schardt was born in Karlsruhe on the 30 September 1888, the son of Valentin Schardt and Barbara Baron. After completing the studies in the local parish school, he entered the Secondary School of Father Scherr, which he completed in due course. Later he wrote the examination as elementary teacher in Beresovka and accepted a position as teacher in München, in 1909. He is still there today.

HIERONYMUS FRIEDT *Organist*

Hieronymus Friedt was born in Karlsruhe on the 27 September 1881. He was the organist in Katharinental, München and Heidelberg, and also played in the colony of Kandel in the Kutschurgan district.

JOSEPH HOPFAUF *Teacher and Organist*

Joseph Hopfauf was born on the 7 February 1884 in the colony of Karlsruhe. At the age of six, he started to take music lessons. After completing his studies in the local elementary school, he entered the school of Father Scherr. After completing his studies there, he wrote the examinations for his teacher's certificate in 1904. For six years he taught as an elementary teacher.

From 1904 to 1909 he taught music in Father Scherr's secondary school. On two occasions he went abroad to Freiburg in Switzerland, where he studied music in the Gregorian Academy.

He married Monika Dauenhauer in 1910. From 1910 to 1912 he was the organist in his home colony of Karlsruhe. From 1912 to 1914 he was the organist and choral director in the Catholic church in Nikolayev.

He wrote many short religious compositions and is presently a member of the Imperial Russian Music Society.

ALEXANDER PAUL *Organist*

Alexander Paul was born in August 1880 in the Jewish colony of Dobroje, the son of Michael Paul and Magdalena Wanner.

He attended school in Korojevo where his father had settled. After completing his studies at the school, he took music lessons from the organist, Edmund Schmid, in Karlsruhe. He was a good student. Subsequently he attended the Seminary in Saratov, following which he returned to E. Schmid. He then joined the army in the orchestra of the Minsk Regiment. After four years of military service, he returned to continue his studies with his old teacher.

In 1906 he was appointed organist in the colony of Kandel, where he married Pauline Kessler. For the past three years, he has been the organist in Selz.

EDMUND SCHMID *Organist and Music Teacher*

Edmund Schmid was born on the 29 September 1862 in Obergünzburg in Bavaria, the son of Anton Schmid and Josephina Ruf. After completing his studies in the local parish school, he attended a preparatory school for three years and then a teacher's training college. After completing his studies here, he went to Regensberg to attend the music school, which at that time was under the direction of Dr. Haberl who was famous throughout Europe.

After completing his musical studies here in 1892, he was invited to the colony of Karlsruhe near Odessa. Here he remained for five years as organist and music teacher. He had many students in Karlsruhe, some of whom are still organists today. Some of these are listed here: Georg Schönfeld, Father Leo Weinmaier, Nikodemus Marthaller, Michael Stolz, Alexander Paul.

From Karlsruhe, Edmond Schmid went to Odessa as organist, where he remained for five years. Subsequently, along with Father J. Neugum, he founded the newspaper, "Deutsches Leben," and was the editor for two years. He also composed some music such as, "O Salutaris Hostia," "Marian Antiphons," and "Responses for the Corpus Christi procession." E. Schmid did much to enhance songs and music in the Catholic colonies of South Russia and to introduce changes in accord with church directives.

GEORG NEUGUM *Teacher and Physician*

Georg Neugum was born in Franzfeld in the Crimea on the 6 January 1884. He attended the community school in Kronental in the Crimea until he was 13 and then was sent to the Seminary in Saratov by his parents.

After completing the third course in the clerical seminary and not feeling the call to the priesthood, he left the seminary and went to Berlin in order to study medicine there. He entered a private institute of treatment by natural remedies and completed the course with considerable success.

In 1907 he returned to Russia with the intention of taking the State Examination in Medicine at the New Russian Imperial University. However, as a result of various obstacles, he had to give up this idea.

In 1908 he wrote the examinations for a tutor's diploma in the German language.

In 1910 he was invited to Berlin by his old teacher and was his assistant for 2 years. During this time he attended the lectures in the Humbolt Academy in Berlin. Since 1912 he has been teaching German in the Father Scherr Highschool and, in his spare time, practicing his art of natural healing.

NIKOLAUS SCHARDT *Merchant*

Nikolaus Schardt, son of Nikolaus, was born in Larievka, not far from Nikolayev on the 20 February 1879.

He entered the Seminary in Saratov in 1892. After two years he left and went to Odessa to enter the School of Commerce. He completed his studies there in 1900 and then volunteered for military service for 1 year.

He married Ann Tremmel on the 6 November 1901 and moved to his father's estate in the district of Alexandria, where he worked for three years. After the agrarian unrest, he moved back to Nikolayev.

In 1908 he moved to Odessa to join his brother-in-law in a hardware store under the firm name of "Bakosch and Schardt." This firm annually had a gross business of approximately one million rubles.

GERTRUD KELLER *Matron at the Orphanage*

Gertrud Keller was born in the colony of Selz on the 6 April 1862. She attended the local parish school as well as the private school which Father Georg Rissling had founded at Selz while he was a seminary student.

After completing her studies, she strove to increase her knowledge by reading in various fields. She lived quietly with her parents in Selz until she was 27 years old, after which she kept house for her brother Father Andreas Keller.

In 1892 she came to Karlsruhe, where Father Scherr had founded an orphanage, and was made matron of the institute. She opened the orphanage with 6 children and cash assets of 25 rubles. It obviously required considerable thrift and hard work to keep the institute solvent. However, through gifts from generous donors and the Lord's blessing, the institute began to flourish so that, at the present time, there are 75 orphans in attendance being trained and educated.

Fraulein G. Keller was also manager of the large farm which was established near the highschool by Father Scherr.

MARIANNA KELLER *Teacher*

Marianna Keller was born on the 2 July 1884 in the colony of Selz.

She attended the local parish school and after this received private instruction from her brother, Father Andreas Keller. Later she attended private school in Nikolayev for a year and then went to Elizabetgrad where she resumed her studies and wrote the examinations for a teacher's certificate.

From 1904 to 1912 she taught German and Russian in Father Scherr's junior highschool. In 1912 she married Anton Seelinger from Rastadt.

RAPHAEL LORAN *Reserve Officer*

Raphael Loran, son of Jakob, was born in 1887 in the new colony of Christina, where his parents had moved from Karlsruhe. He completed his studies in the non-classical secondary school in Nikolayev and then volunteered for the Officer Corps.

Nothing more is known about him.

The present Wealth and Status of the Colony of Karlsruhe

The colony of Karlsruhe contains at present 220 houses and 40 adobe huts with 1932 people, both male and female, all of Catholic denomination. Other denominations were 135 Russians, 90 Jews, and 3 families of gypsies. The Russians who live there are mostly hired men and hired girls working for the colonists. A hired man's wages are 120 rubles and a hired girl receives 100 to 110 rubles per year. The day wage in the winter time is 50 kopecks and in summer, 1 ruble, 20 kopecks. Approximately 300 families have moved elsewhere.

The community land owned by the colony is 5450 dessiatines while bought land, near and far, amounts to 46,564 dessiatines. Of the community land, 3189 dessiatines are for agriculture, 15 dessiatines for hay, pasture land 1972 dessiatines, home yards 86 dessiatines, vineyards 89 dessiatines, forest 14 dessiatines, unusable land 85 dessiatines.

The land seeded in 1913 was: winter wheat 1621 dessiatines and summer wheat 85 dessiatines.

There are 1794 horses, 1021 cows, 448 calves and 584 pigs. The horse herder receives 40 kopecks per head and the swine herder receives 60 kopecks per head.

There are four stallions owned by the community and 12 bulls. Rent for one dessiatine of land for one year is 13 to 22 rubles. The people of Karlsruhe annually rent approximately 3000 dessiatines of land in Trechata and Solonicha.

Tradesmen there are as follows: Wagon makers 2, cabinet makers 2, blacksmiths 2, shoemakers 3, tailors 2, carpenters 2, and locksmiths 1.

In addition, there is a small Credit Institute, 1 Consumers' Cooperative Society, 5 general stores, 1 steam flour mill, 1 tavern and 3 beer halls.

The annual salaries of the community officials are for the mayor 122 rubles, the treasurer 14 rubles, the secretary 650 rubles, and the amount paid the beadle is unknown.

The community receives 825 rubles rent for water and fishing. Freight charges to Nikolayev, when the road is good, are 5 kopecks per pud and 8 to 10 kopecks per pud when the roads are bad.

Taxes paid by the community are: Crown taxes and land taxes 3674 rubles 52 kopecks, community taxes are 5150 rubles 65 kopecks.

Additional information is lacking.

The Colony of Katharinental

The colony of Katharinental is located in the province of Kherson, in the district of Odessa. It is one hundred versts from the city of Kherson, one hundred and ten versts from the capital city of Odessa, and six versts from the district of Landau. The colony is located on the left bank of Fox Valley Creek, approximately 10 versts from its origin. It is surveyed in the shape of a cross.

In the centre of the cross is the lovely parish church. The upper colony with the so-named, Heidelberg, extends from the north to the south as far as the church. From here it continues as "Schwanzgasse" for a distance of two versts. Schwaben Street runs from the west to the east as far as the church. The portion on the east side is called Joseph Street and is approximately one verst long. To the north of Schwaben Street is Cat Street and behind the upper colony, towards the valley, is the new Mud Street. To the south of Schwaben Street is Musician Alley.

The landscape of the colony is fairly level, its surface broken by three ponds, two in the upper colony, and one in Joseph Street. The main buildings in the colony are the parish church, the rectory, the nice new school, the chapel in the graveyard, the chancery, the Co-operative Society Store and some lovely private homes. The architecture of the homes is similar to that of the other colonies.

Behind the threshing places there were orchards in the early days, but now they have nearly all been converted to vegetable gardens. In the early days the lots were marked by a line of earthwork because of the lack of stone, but now all of the better lots are surrounded by stone walls. On both sides of the streets, the lovely acacia trees are planted. In the summer time when they are blooming, they make the colony quite picturesque.

In the early days of the colony there was a severe water shortage so that they frequently had to buy their water from the neighbouring colony of Karlsruhe. Presently, they have a number of wells and dams with sufficient water for the people and their livestock.

There are no fieldstones in Katharinetal. When needed, they are bought from Landau or from the nobleman, Maleschewicz.

The main occupations of the colonists are agriculture and cattle raising, and lately also vineyards. The climate is healthy as the colony is located at a high elevation. They have seldom been afflicted with an epidemic. The people are not very tall, but are of strong stature and quite muscular.

The people of Katharinental are hard workers, and say, "Eile mit weile" (make haste slowly.) By nature they are more conservative than progressive in their farming operation. They stick tenaciously to old methods and check new ideas very carefully to see whether they may benefit by them.

Family life is more patriarchal than in other colonies and the children have more respect for their elders. The language is a mixture of Palatinate and Swabian. Schwaben Street is completely settled by Swabians from Württemberg. The people say "Ich hab, du host, er hot," (I have, you have he has,) but some seem to pronounce host, "hoist." There are 12 or more people between the ages of 70 and 80.

The name of Katharinental was given to the colony by General Inzov and was confirmed by the authorities on the 13 December 1819. When the first group of 17 families came to this settlement in 1817, they found nothing but the desolate prairie, the so-called "Crown Steppe," where there were neither homes nor other buildings. Consequently, the colonial authorities quartered them in the colony of Karlsruhe for the winter. This first group of settlers came from the kingdom of Württemberg. Several families came from the Duchy of Baden and went via boat on the Danube as far as Ismail. From here they went to Odessa by the land route. In 1818 there were 17 families who came from the Palatinate via land, through Radzivilov to the new settlement. In 1919 there were 17 families from Baden who came via the same land route as those previously. These 51 families were the original settlers of the colony. There were additional settlers who came during the next ten years until all of the lots were filled.

List of the Settlers
in the Colony of Katharinental
in the Beresan
1839-1840
(and the names of their homes from which
they migrated)

1. **Jakob Daub** 38, son of Franz from Neupfotz, Rhinepalatinate.
WIFE: Elisabetha Bernhard 30, daughter of Franz from Eussertal, Rhinepalatinate.
CHILDREN: Adam 5, Franz 3, Jakob 1, Magdalena 11, Katharina 8, Emerenzia 4.
   2. **Wilhelm Böhm** 30, son of Nikolaus from Rülzheim, Rhinepalatinate.
WIFE: Theresia Kastner 31, daughter of Johannes from Malsch, Baden.
CHILDREN: Magdalena 8, Marianna 5, Christina 3.
   3. **Peter Jochim** 31, son of Heinrich from Rülzheim, Rhinepalatinate.
WIFE: Margaretha Böhm 21, daughter of Nikolaus.
CHILDREN: Ignaz 9, Maria-Eva 7, Franziska 5.
   4. **Kaspar Haff** 67, son of Valentin from Rittersbach, Baden.
WIFE: Katharina Schweigert 56, daughter of Bernhardt.
(a) Andreas Haff 30, son of Kaspar.
WIFE: Marianna Krieger 25, daughter of Wendelin from Hördt, Rhinepalatinate.
CHILDREN: Georg 5, Peter 2, Margaretha 1.
MAID: Julianna Hornstein 17.
(b) Simon Haff 20, son of Kaspar.
WIFE: Gertrude Helfrich 18.
CHILDREN: Andreas 1.
   5. **Kaspar Sturm** 56, son of Nikolaus from Mühlhausen, Baden.
WIFE: Eufemia Geissel 54, daughter of Johannes.
CHILDREN: Joseph 15, Magdalena 9.
(a) Joseph Kunz 25, son of Jakob from Rülzheim, Rhinepalatinate.
WIFE: Kreszentia Sturm 22, daughter of Kaspar.
CHILDREN: Simon 4, Adam 2.
MAID: Elisabeth Jochim.
   6. **Adam Rung** 55, son of Franz from Herxheim, Rhinepalatinate.
WIFE: Apolonia Mühl 55, daughter of Peter, also from Herxheim.
CHILDREN: Margaretha 17.
(a) Bernhard Rung 23, son of Adam.
WIFE: Cäcilia Hof 22, daughter of Johannes.

CHILDREN: Joseph 2.
    6. (b)**Peter Haff** 24, son of Kaspar.
WIFE: Margaretha Rung 18, daughter of Adam.
    7. **Franz Böhm** 36, son of Michael from Rülzheim, Rhinepalatinate.
WIFE: Elisabeth Gerhardt 41, daughter of Jakob from Simten, Rhinepalatinate.
CHILDREN: Franz 14, Adam 8, Johann 4, Gertrud 1.
(a) Adam Böhm 31, son of Michael from Rülzheim, Rhinepalatinate.
WIFE: Gertrud Dietrich 37, daughter of Peter.
CHILDREN: Erasmus 4, Franz 1, Elisabeth 1.
    8. **Adam Jochim** 41, son of Heinrich from Rülzheim, Rhinepalatinate.
WIFE: Eva Mischel 36, daughter of Joseph.
CHILDREN: Theodor 13, Jakob 2, Barbara 15, Irlanda 11, Katharina 8, Eva 4.
    9. **Nikolaus Böhm** 56, son of Adam from Rülzheim, Rhinepalatinate.
WIFE: Elisabeth Jochim 53, daughter of Georg.
CHILDREN: Stephan 18, Adam 13.
(a) Adam Böhm 27, son of Nikolaus.
WIFE: Christina Stroh 21, daughter of Michael.
CHILDREN: Katharina 2, Magdalena 1, Karolina 1.
(b) Jakob Stroh 29, son of Michael.
WIFE: Barbara Böhm 23, daughter of Nikolaus.
    10. **Ludwig Gräff** 27, son of Adam from Albersweiler, Rhinepalatinate.
WIFE: Susanna Hörner 26, daughter of Christophor, from Kirchardt, Baden.
CHILDREN: Dorothea 6, Maria-Eva 1.
(a) Adam Gräff 64, son of Jakob from Albersweiler, Rhinepalatinate.
CHILDREN: Jakob 8, Franz 11.
    11. **Anton Fitterer** 56, son of Adam from Mörsch, Baden. He was a widower.
CHILDREN: Sylvester 23, Johann 15.
(a) Joseph Fitterer 28, son of Anton.
WIFE: Margaretha Roll 22, from the colony of Sulz.
CHILDREN: Maria-Eva 1.
(b) Egidius Fitterer 21, son of Anton.
WIFE: Barbara Sturm 18, daughter of Kaspar.
CHILDREN: Sylvester, Creszentia 2.
(c) Sylvester Fitterer 24, son of Anton.
WIFE: Magdalena Deck 24, daughter of Ulrich.
    12. **Sebastian Weiler** 56, son of Jakob from Herxheim,

Rhinepalatinate.

WIFE: Margaretha Böhlin 49, daughter of Wendelin from Elsenz, Baden.

CHILDREN: Anton 18, Katharina 16.

(b) Peter Klein 26, son of Georg from Elsenz, Baden.

WIFE: Margaretha Dillmann 24, daughter of Georg.

CHILDREN: Georg 5, Rosalia 2, Julianna 2, Annamaria 1.

(b) Georg Klein 22, son of Georg.

WIFE: Rosalia Weiler 19, daughter of Sebastian.

CHILDREN: Franz 1, Adam 1, Barbara 2.

13. **Johann Dietz** 58, son of Christian from Kirchardt, Baden.

WIFE: Philippina Wolf 58, daughter of Georg (Lutheran).

(a) Franz Dietz 22, son of Johann.

WIFE: Eva Hörner.

CHILDREN: Peter 1.

(b) Martin Weiler 23, son of Sebastian.

WIFE: Maria-Eva Dietz 18, daughter of Johann.

CHILDREN: Maria-Eva 1.

14. **Johann Härdy** 72, son of Paul from Herxheim, Rhinepalatinate.

WIFE: Annamaria Reichert 51, daughter of Peter.

CHILDREN: Markus 14.

14.(a) Franz Braun 28, son of Valentin from the colony of Karlsruhe.

WIFE: Margaretha Härdy 22, daughter of Johann.

CHILDREN: Sebastian 1, Magdalena 2.

15. **Karl Keller** 34, son of Michael from Steinhilben, Baden.

WIFE: Regina Messmer 34, daughter of Michael from Rülzheim, Rhinepalatinate.

CHILDREN: Joseph 1, Marianna 7. (daughter of Elisabeth Krieger?)

(a) Wilhelm Keller 30, son of Michael from Steinhilben, Baden.

WIFE: Magdalena Sauter 26, daughter of Georg from Ilshofen, Württemberg.

CHILDREN: Pius 2, Franz Xaver 1, Maria-Eva 1.

16. **Franziska Steiner** 55, widow of Michael and daughter of Heinrich Lorenz from Langenkandel, (= Kandel,) Rhinepalatinate.

CHILDREN: Friedrich 16.

(a) Sebastian Weiler 28, son of Sebastian.

WIFE: Barbara Steiner 27, daughter of Michael.

CHILDREN: Georg 4, Christophor 1, Barbara 2.

17. **Peter Mildenberger** 50, son of Peter from Schlüchtern, Baden.

WIFE: Katharina Huck 30, daughter of Karl, from Herxheim, Rhinepalatinate.

CHILDREN: Joseph 7, Peter 3.

(a) Adam Bullinger 28, son of Johann.
WIFE: Elisabeth Mildenberger 22, daughter of Peter.
(b) Anton Mildenberger 24, son of Joseph.
WIFE: Maria-Eva Morell 20, daughter of Adam from Sulz.
CHILDREN: Katharina 1.
18. **Ferdinand Krieger** 27, son of Wendelin from Hördt, Rhinepalatinate.
WIFE: Luise Wagner 25, daughter of Michael from the colony of Speier.
CHILDREN: Andreas 3, Johann 1, Margaretha 1.
(a) Martin Schmalz 51, widower, son of Peter from Steinfeld, Rhinepalatinate.
CHILDREN: Elisabeth 25, Katharina 12.
19. **Sebastian Butsch** 30, son of Fidelis from Wurmlingen, Württemberg.
WIFE: Theresia Lanz 27, daughter of Anton from the colony of Karlsruhe.
CHILDREN: Johann 1, Franz-Xaver 1, Franziska 4.
(a) Joseph Butsch 33, son of Fidelis.
WIFE: Margaretha Röther 30, daughter of Johann from Offenbach, Rhinepalatinate.
CHILDREN: Stephan 10, Joseph 6, Johann 1, Adam 1.
20. **Simon Mayer** 59, son of Jakob from Plankstadt, Baden.
WIFE: Rosina Edinger 59, daughter of Peter.
(a) Franz Mayer 38, son of Simon.
WIFE: Kunigunde Keller 24, daughter of Michael.
CHILDREN: Joseph 8, Franz 4, Friederika 11, Franziska 9, Katharina 6.
(b) Christoph Mayer 28, son of Simon.
WIFE: Maria-Eva Steiner 28, daughter of Michael.
CHILDREN: Franz 7, Georg 1, Barbara 5.
21. **Christoph Hörner** 49, son of Christian from Kirchardt, Baden.
WIFE: Johanna Kappes 49, daughter of Georg.
CHILDREN: Ludwig 17, Franz 14, Johann 14, Philipp 10, Thomas 8, Georg 3.
22. **Jakob Dilger** 50, widower, son of Philipp from Schweighofen, Rhinepalatinate.
HIS SECOND WIFE: Marianna Martin.
CHILDREN: Franz 9, Katharina 13, Margaretha 4.
(a) Johannes Heid 23, son of Joseph.
WIFE: Annamaria Dilger 21, daughter of Philipp.
CHILDREN: Simon 1.
23. **Xaver Kohler** 30, son of Fidelis from Steinhilben, Baden.
WIFE: Annamaria Gerber 28, from the colony of Speier.

CHILDREN: Joseph 6, Marianna 7, Magdalena 4, Maria-Eva 1.

24. **Joseph Baumann** 29, son of Christian from Kirchardt, Baden.
WIFE: Katharina Völker 22, daughter of Kominikus from the colony of Speier.
CHILDREN: Gottfried 3, Franz-Xaver 2, Franz 1.
Franziska Steidig 56 (maid?).

25. **Franz Schilling** 37, son of Joseph from Schluchtern, Baden.
WIFE: Martha Kappes 38, daughter of Georg from Kirchardt, Baden.

26. **Georg Janzer** 47, son of Michael from Rülzheim, Rhinepalatinate.
WIFE: Barbara Mischel 40, daughter of Joseph.
CHILDREN: Adam 13, Franz 4, Karl 2, Helena 10, Margaretha 7.

27. **Anton Merz** 68, son of Joseph from Sulzbach, Baden.
WIFE: Marianna Unser 58, daughter of Franz, from Sulzbach.
(a) Gottfried Veitenheimer 22, son of Paul from Kirchardt, Baden.
WIFE: Marianna Merz 17, daughter of Anton.
CHILDREN: Joseph 2, Anton 1.

28. **Jakob Bernhard** 28, son of Franz from Eussertal, Rhinepalatinate.
WIFE: Apolonia Weibel 22, daughter of Franz.
CHILDREN: Martin 1.
(a) Franz Bernhard 23, son of Franz.
WIFE: Annamaria Butsch 20, daughter of Fidelis.
CHILDREN: Joseph 2, Gottfried 1.
Katharina Bernhard 58, widow, daughter of Adam Schildberger.
Georg Butsch 16, hired man.

29. **Friedrich Schutzmann** 27, son of Johann from Hasterov, Posen.
WIFE: Apolonia Röther 29, daughter of Johann.
CHILDREN: Adam 1, Margaretha 1, Johann Reisenauer 4, Thimothaus 3, (presumably step-children).

30. **Johann Bullinger** 48, son of Johann from Herxheim, Rhinepalatinate.
WIFE: Magdalena Reichert 48, daughter of Nikolaus.
CHILDREN: Elisabeth 14, Maria-Eva 13, Katharina 10.
(a) Adam Bullinger 26, son of Johann.
WIFE: Katharina Bernhard, daughter of Franz.
CHILDREN: Franz 1, Apolonia 4, Katharina 1.
(b) Franz Kohler 25, son of Fidelis from Trochtelfingen, Hohenzollern.
WIFE: Katharina Bullinger 21, daughter of Johann.
CHILDREN: Adam 1.
(c) Peter Bullinger 21, son of Johann.
WIFE: Annamaria 19.

31. **Matthias Bauer** 38, son of Joseph from Landshausen, Baden.

WIFE: Regina Imhof 38, daughter of Anton.
CHILDREN: Andreas 6, Philippina 10.

32. **Johann Stroh** 49, son of Jakob from Landhausen, Baden.
WIFE: Barbara Makerdt 49, daughter of Adam from Epfenbach, Baden. Her mother was Susanna Mehr, 70.
CHILDREN: Elisabeth 13.
(a) Dietrich Schuh 25.
WIFE: Katharina Stroh.

33. **Johann Doll** 58, son of Nikolaus from Neuhausen, Baden.
WIFE: Barbara Hunkel 57, daughter of Michael.

34. **Peter Häufer** 47, son of Michael from Herxheim, Rhinepalatinate.
WIFE: Marianna Dörr 48, daughter of Georg.
CHILDREN: Georg 12, Nikolaus 8, Adam 5.

35. **Franz Weiler** 32, son of Sebastian from Herxheim, Rhinepalatinate.
WIFE: Katharina Sturm 31, daughter of Kaspar.
CHILDREN: Johann 7, Sebastian 1, Barbara 9, Elisabeth 5, Bibianna 3, Kreszentia 1.

36. **Franz Zentner** 37, son of Franz from Kandel, Rhinepalatinate.
FIRST WIFE: Elisabeth Sturm 33, daughter of Nikolaus.
SECOND WIFE: Katharina Stroh.
CHILDREN: Johann 13, Sebastian ?, Katharina 4, Christina 1.
Joseph Heinzelmann 56, step-father, son of Anton from Mühlhausen, Baden.
(a) Alexander Engel 24.
WIFE: Franziska Zentner 17, daughter of Franz.

37. **Peter Hammel** 54, son of Joseph from Rohrbach, Baden.
WIFE: Margaretha Ehmann 54, daughter of Joseph.
CHILDREN: Lorenz 18.
(a) Joseph Hammel 24, son of Peter.
WIFE: Marianna Wander 20, daughter of Johann from the colony of Karlsruhe.
CHILDREN: Johann 2, Joseph 1.
(b) Johannes Hammel 26, son of Peter.
WIFE: Elisabeth Wolf 23, daughter of Michael.

38. **Franz Häuser** 49, son of Michael from Herxheim, Rhinepalatinate.
WIFE: Julianna Mohr 46, daughter of Stephan.
CHILDREN: Martin 20, Stephan 9, Franz 4, Elisabeth 12.
(a) Martin Häuser — son of Michael.
WIFE: Katharina Janzer, daughter of Georg.
(b) Simon Häuser 20, son of Franz.
WIFE: Magdalena Berger 17, daughter of Peter.

CHILDREN: Lorenz 1.

(c) Joseph Braumbeck 20, son of Joseph from Stanorgan, Hungary.
WIFE: Franziska Häuser, 18, daughter of Franz.
CHILDREN: Katharina 1.

39. **Joseph Messer** 47, son of Adam from Landshausen, Baden.
WIFE: Annamaria Merz 32, daughter of Anton.
CHILDREN: Gottfried 1, Elisabeth 14, Magdalena 8, Eva 6, Theresia 4.

40. **Adam Dillmann** 43, son of Peter from Eschbach, Rhinepalatinate.
WIFE: Elisabeth Sturm 33, daughter of Kaspar from Mühlhausen, Baden.
CHILDREN: Johann 15, Christoph 12, Andreas 2, Joseph 1, Carolina 16, Elisabeth 8, Katharina 6, Kreszentia 4.

40(a) Johannes Dillmann 40, son of Peter.
WIFE: Katharina Hordy 40, daughter of Johannes.
CHILDREN: Johann 3, Johanna 9.

41. **Joseph Deubele** 36, son of Johann from Sulz, Alsace.
WIFE: Franziska Steiner 30, from Kandel, Rhinepalatinate.
CHILDREN: Johann 8, Jakob 4, Magdalena 10, Barbara 1.

42. **Joseph Heid** 50, son of Joseph from Berg, Rhinepalatinate.
WIFE: Katharian Braun 41, daughter of Johann.
CHILDREN: Franz 20, Michael 11, Katharina 17, Annamaria 10, Rosina 5.

(a) Johannes Heid 22, son of Joseph.
WIFE: Annamaria Dilger 19, daughter of Jakob.
CHILDREN: Simon 2, Franz 1.

43. **Daniel Makert** 39, son of Adam from Epfenbach, Baden.
WIFE: Apolonia Bühler 35, daughter of Oswald from Oberschrot, Switzerland.
CHILDREN: Stanislaus 10, Peter 4, Katharina 12, Theresia 8, Apolonia 6, Magdalena 2, Margaretha 1.

44. **Michael Flink** 49, son of Johann from Spechbach, Baden.
WIFE: Magdalena Eichstetter 35, daughter of Jakob.
CHILDREN: Johann 6, Stephan 1, Philippina 1.

(a) Georg Flink 25, son of Michael.
WIFE: Paulina Doll 26, daughter of Johann.
CHILDREN: Theresia 4, Gertrud 2, Elisabeth 1.

45. **Georg Klein** 45, son of Georg from Kirchardt, Baden.
WIFE: Elisabeth Hermann 38, daughter of Philipp, from Kirchardt.
CHILDREN: Peter 16, Paul 13, Johann 8, Andreas 4, Marianna 11, Barbara 6, Elisabeth 2, Katharina 1.

46. **Johann Kastner** 66, son of Michael from Malsch, Baden.
WIFE: Magdalena Ehrlich 53, daughter of Joseph from Svonsdorf,

Austria.

(a) Paul Kastner 24, son of Johann.

WIFE: Apolonia Federer 22, daughter of Joseph from the colony of Karlsruhe.

CHILDREN: Georg 2, Wendelin 1, Barbara 1.

(b) Simon Kastner 22, son of Johann.

WIFE: Magdalena Firen 20, daughter of Andreas.

CHILDREN: Klara 2.

47. **Konrad Doll** 33, son of Johann from Neuhausen, Baden.

WIFE: Elisabeth Klein 29, daughter of Georg from Elsenz, Baden.

CHILDREN: Franz 7, Georg 5, Marzellinus 3, Peter 1.

(a) Simon Doll 30, son of Johann.

WIFE: Katharina Anton 28, daughter of Johann from the colony of Karlsruhe.

CHILDREN: Konrad 6, Theobald 2.

48. **Theobald Thierin** 24, son of Andreas from Hördt, Rhinepalatinate.

WIFE: Regina Roll 23, daughter of Jakob from the colony of Sulz.

CHILDREN: Magdalena 2, Marianna 1.

49. **Adam Mischel** 27, son of Joseph from Rülzheim, Rhinepalatinate.

WIFE: Marianna Schwebel 25, daughter of Ludwig from the colony of Karlsruhe.

CHILDREN: Marianna 4, Katharina 2, Columba 1.

(a) Elisabeth Schwebel 53, widow, daughter of Peter Ekert.

CHILDREN: Philipp 12.

50. **Jakob Kunz** 52, son of Peter from Rülzheim, Rhinepalatinate.

WIFE: Katharina Mesmer 52, daughter of Michael, from Rülzheim.

CHILDREN: Jakob 29, Adam 17, Valentin 11, Katharina 14, Elisabeth 6.

(a) Peter Kunz 27, son of Jakob.

WIFE: Margaretha Wanner 25, daughter of Jakob from the colony of Landau.

CHILDREN: Simon 2, Magdalena 4, Barbara 1.

(b) Simon Kunz 23, son of Jakob.

WIFE: Juliana Hornstein 18, daughter of Ludwig.

51. **Michael Steiner** 33, from Kandel, Rhinepalatinate.

WIFE: Barbara Weiler 30, daughter of Sebastian from Herxheim, Rhinepalatinate.

CHILDREN: Sebastian 8, Franz 5, Christoph 2, Nikolaus 1, Georg 1, Marianna 10, Thekla 3.

52. **Valentin Jochim** 34, son of Heinrich from Rülzheim, Rhinepalatinate.

WIFE: Katharina Mischel 34, daughter of Joseph from Rülzheim,

Rhinepalatinate.

CHILDREN: Adam 11, Stephan 9, Barbara 4, Katharina 2.

53. **Johann Röszle** 35, son of Wilhelm from Grombach, Baden.

WIFE: Marianna Stajok, daughter of Michael.

CHILDREN: Karl 11, Wilhelm 4, Elisabeth 9, Katharina 8, Theresia 6.

54. **Jakob Zentner** 30, son of Franz from Kandel, Rhinepalatinate.

WIFE: Elisabeth Steiner 24, daughter of Michael.

CHILDREN: Sebastian 1, Franz 1, Franziska 3.

55. **Michael Jochim** 27, son of Heinrich from Rülzheim, Rhinepalatinate.

WIFE: Marianna Martin 22, daughter of Anton from Kandel, Rhinepalatinate.

CHILDREN: Anton 2, Katharina 1.

(a) Anton Martin 80, son of Michael.

WIFE: Franziska Mock 68, daughter of Johann.

56. **Michael Stroh** 62, son of Jakob from Sandhausen, Baden.

WIFE: Katharina Schatz 58, daughter of Matthäus.

CHILDREN: Ludwig 18, Klara 16, Maria-Eva 15.

(a) Jakob Stroh 31, son of Michael.

WIFE: Katharina Klein 19, daughter of Georg.

(b) Philipp Stroh 27, son of Michael.

WIFE: Franziska Dillmann 20, daughter of Adam.

(c) Franz Neukircher 58, son of Andreas from Presnitz, Austria.

WIFE: Regina Zentner 33, daughter of Ludwig from Kandel, Rhinepalatinate.

(d) Johann Martin 62, son of Leonhard.

WIFE: Katharina Binzmann 61, daughter of Jakob.

CHILDREN: Thomas 21, Johann 19, Nikolaus 16, Sophia 23.

(e) Peter Stein 25, son of Peter.

WIFE: Jakobina Martin 25, daughter of Johannes.

CHILDREN: Katharina 1.

Beginnings
in the
Colony of Katharinental

The settlers of the colony of Katharinental had considerable advantage over the other Beresan colonists. By the time they arrived many of their countrymen, whom they knew in the old country, had preceded them and settled in the neighbourhood. They were able to live there and borrow the needed implements.

On the 8 March 1819, General Inzov wrote to the old Beresan colonist requesting that they be hospitable to the new colonists and give each agricultural family a tschetwert of wheat, but to the tradesmen only one half a tschetwert from the community granary. As a result of this request the people of Katharinental received help from various places. The people of Karlsruhe loaned them grain from their storage bins for bread and various tools for building their houses.

Each family of the first two groups that arrived received from the Crown 544 rubles to build their homes and acquire some implements. The third group, who came in 1819, received no help from the Crown, but had to build their houses at their own expense.

The lumber for the houses was bought in Kherson by Commissar Krüger who had laid out the colony initially. The lumber was sent by boat to Nikolayev and the colonists picked up the lumber from there themselves. Until the Crown houses were finished, the new settlers lived in the colony of Karlsruhe which was only three versts away from their own settlement. From here they went to work in the new colony every day. The most serious handicap was the scarcity of water. They had already dug eight wells, all 36 to 84 feet deep, but found no water. The colonial authorities were giving serious thought to moving the settlers to another location. Eventually, they found water in the ninth well, that was plentiful and quite tasty. It was an occasion for celebration for all of the settlers of Katharinental. This was the only well until 1834 that had sufficient water. After 1834 there were six more wells dug, of which five produced good water. The sixth however, had poor water. Later the community built three dams in the fields, which usually held sufficient water for the cattle.

On the 1 January 1820, fifty-one families with their oxen and necessary implements for cultivation, were settled in the new colony. Until now it had been called the fourth division, now it was called Katharinental.

Accurate statistics of the material wealth of the new colony and the actual number of tradesmen, unfortunately, is not given in the records, as was the custom in the other colonies.

The Community Land of Katharinental

The land of the community of Katharinental according to the records totals 5816.5 dessiatines. This property forms an irregular square and is located on both sides of Fox Valley Creek. On the south, the land borders on the Karlsruhe community land; on the west, the Speier land; on the north, the estate of Nobleman Erdeli; on the east, by some Russian farmers. The land is reasonably level but its surface becomes broken by the Fox Valley Creek and some ponds.

The soil is composed of good black earth about 14 to 28 inches thick with an underlay of loamy clay. In the early days the soil was very fertile, but this is no longer so. If it does not rain at the right time during the month of May and if there is a shortage of rain in June, crop failure is certain. The people do not seem to understand that they must replenish the soil, either by natural or artifical means. The Beresan people lack the technical training for agriculture and other rural trades. Trees and orchards were planted in Katharinental in 1842 but lately these have been sadly neglected. Only one woodland remains as a memorial to the olden days, where the forest well is, without which the people of Katharinental could not live.

In recent years the people have planted some fine vineyards.

The Parish of Katharinental

At the present time there are 179 lots in the colony of Katharinental in which 1500 Catholics live. People of other religious denominations such as Orthodox maids or hired men live here only at certain times.

From its founding in 1817 until 1861, Katharinental was affiliated with the Landau parish. From 1861 until 1871 it was affiliated with the Karlsruhe parish, and in 1871 it was officially made an independent parish.

Katharinental belongs to the Nikolayev deanery of the diocese of Tiraspol. The communities of Biswanje, Schmalz, Schlosser and the Catholics of the Russian colony of Pokrovskaja, all belong to this parish.

Katharinental is 9 versts from the postoffice and the telegraph station located in Landau.

History of the Katharinental Parish

As all of the other colonies of the Beresan had their own parish, the people of Katharinental also wished to establish their own parish rather than being affiliated with Karlsruhe. On two occasions they applied to the authorities for permission to separate from Karlsruhe and establish their own parish, but their requests were refused on the grounds that their reasons were not well founded.

The third request, in 1870, received a favourable reply and in 1871, the new parish of Katharinental was founded. The first official records start on the 9 May 1871 and were recorded by Father M. Stankevicz, who was there until 6 November 1871.

Sequence of Priests in Katharinental

FATHER NIKODEMUS TSCHERNJACHOWICZ *Administrator* from 6 November 1871 until 2 September 1874

Father Nikodemus Tschernjachowicz was born on the 14 September 1841, the son of Jakob and Anna Tschernjachowicz, in Werbetzkji-Maidan, Poland, in the parish of Novokonstantinovka.

He received his first instruction in his own home. In 1856 he entered the second class in the Second High School in Odessa, where he completed seven classes.

When Bishop Kahn died in 1864 auxiliary Bishop V. Lipsky, who was residing in Odessa at that time, was moved to Saratov as the vicar capitular of the diocese of Tiraspol. Bishop Lipsky knew that the young student was intending to study for the priesthood and invited Tschernjachowicz to come along to Saratov to enter the seminary there. As he was in full agreement, he made the necessary preparations and, with the position of attache, left from Odessa with Bishop Lipsky in January 1865. They first proceeded to Petersburg, where Bishop Lipsky had to present himself to all dignitaries of the department for religious affairs and also receive the necessary instructions and authorization for the administration of the diocese of Tiraspol.

On the way Bishop Lipsky stopped in the cities of Kursk, Oriol, etc. in order to confirm the Catholics living there. In Petersburg Bishop Lipsky met Franz Zottmann, the inspector of the Seminary in Saratov, and professors Michael Glossner and Willibald Zottmann who had been recruited by him in Germany, along with the Capuchin monk, Beda Sebald. They had just heard of the death of Bishop Kahn when they arrived in Petersburg and were now awaiting further instructions from Bishop Lipsky. As soon as Bishop Lipsky had accomplished his work in Petersburg he left for Saratov, accompanied by professors Franz Zottmann, Michael Glossner, Willibald Zottmann, and the student N. Tschernjachowicz.

In Saratov, N. Tschernjachowicz entered the seminary to study theology and philosophy. After completing his studies there, he was ordained a priest on the 21 December 1869 by Bishop V. Lipsky. His first appointment was as chaplain to the Bishop and vicar at the Cathedral. Because of illness he was obliged to give up both positions and go to the Crimea for a rest cure. He recuperated rapidly and on the 11 October 1871 he was sent as administrator to the newly founded parish of Katharinental. Here the young priest worked hard as a prudent pastor and soon won the love and respect of his parishioners. To the great sorrow of all of the parishioners of Katharinental, he was moved to Nikolayev after two years, where he is still doing pastoral duties at the present time.

Nikolayev at this time had 4000 Catholics, most of whom were poor labourers. The parish church was small, poorly kept and looked more like a store than a place of worship.

The first thing the new priest undertook was to build a new church. The Gothic edifice stood large and majestic in the center of the city of Nikolayev. This Catholic parish church added to the appearance of the city and served as a memorial to the energy, work and determination of a single priest. Father N. Tschernjachowicz. One could write a book about the methods and skill with which this priest collected the means to build this magnificent church. He did not build a rectory for himself but used the money to build a beautiful home for the poor and helpless. He also built a large school beside the church and founded a benevolent society in Nikolayev. He built homes for all the needy in his parish except himself. He still lives in the decrepit rectory with its primitive door latches and worn out floors. For this, he receives considerable praise.

As recognition for his services he received various distinctions from the Russian Government; the golden cross on the Stanislaus sash, second and third order, and the Order of Anne, third-class.

In 1880 he became a dean of the Landau (now Nikolayev) deanery and in 1883 he was named a canon. His work was also recognized in Rome in that the Pope made him domestic papal prelate a few years ago.

FATHER NIKOLAUS MITZIG *Administrator*

Father Mitzig will be included under Rastadt.

FATHER JOSEPH IHLY *Administrator*
16 September 1872 to 21 August 1880

Father Ihly was already referred to under Karlsruhe, page 197.

FATHER KASPAR JÄGER *Administrator*
25 October 1880 until 18 June 1884

See under Landau, page 68. From 19 June 1884 until 1 May 1885, Katharinental was supervised by Father Seelinger from Karlsruhe.

FATHER JOHANNES SCHNEIDER *Senior*
Pastor from 1 May 1885 until 15 October 1894

Father Johannes Schneider was born in the colony of Semenovka in 1855.

He entered the Seminary in Saratov and, when he completed his courses, he was ordained a priest on the 14 September 1880 by Bishop Franz Zottmann. In Katharinental he worked diligently at his pastoral duties. He visited the school often, giving Christian instruction. He was indefatigable in hearing confessions and in delivering sermons.

Following this he worked in other parishes, but, as a result of over-exertion, he became ill. He requested retirement from the bishop of the diocese, which was granted.

From 15 October 1894 until 27 June 1895, Katharinental was supervised from Speier by Father Ihly.

FATHER JOHANN WASINGER *Administrator*
27 June 1895 to 11 July 1898

Father Johann Wasinger was born on the 8 December 1870 in the colony of Graf, in the province of Samara.

In 1885 he entered the boys' seminary in Saratov and completed the courses there in 1890. He then entered the clerical seminary and, after completing his courses, he was ordained on the 20 March 1894. Immediately thereafter he was sent to the parish of Liebental.

On the 2 May 1894 he was sent to Semenovka in the Caucasus on a temporary basis. In 1895 he received an appointment as administrator in Katharinental, where he worked hard for three years.

In 1898 he was moved to Zug on the Volga and soon thereafter was moved to Rohleder on the Karaman. Unfortunately, he contracted tuberculosis and died on the 19 February 1901 in his birthplace of Graf having received the last sacraments.

FATHER PHILIPP BECKER *Administrator*
2 August 1898 to 8 June 1903

Father Philipp Becker was born on the 15 August 1868 in the colony of Selz in the Kutchurgan.

He entered the seminary in Saratov in 1884 and was ordained a priest by Bishop Zerr on the 18 August 1891.

His first appointment was as vicar in Freudenfeld in the parish of Heidelberg on the Molotschna, where he worked for one year.

In 1892 he was sent to Blumenfeld in the parish of Sulz, where he remained for ten months.

In 1893 he was made administrator of the large Köhler parish in the deanery of Kamenka. Through his initiative, the parish was divided into two. The two affiliates of Leichtling and Hildmann separated from Köhler and formed their own parish with Hildmann as the centre of the new parish. After one-and-a-half years in Köhler, he was moved to Zug on the Volga, as administrator.

In Zug there were 400 school children and only one teacher. The community did not wish to hire another teacher, so Father Becker worked with the teacher for three to four hours every day. In addition, he gave Christian instruction and conducted a night school. He also instructed the colonists how to grow corn with greater success.

In 1898 he was sent to Katharinental as administrator. He worked hard in Katharinental at his pastoral duties and soon gained the trust and respect of his new parishioners. He was also able to influence the people to more economical organization. In order to counter the high prices of the Jewish tradesmen, he persuaded the community to start a co-operative society, the first society of this type of organized in the Beresan. He also founded a reading society in Katharinental. In addition, he persuaded the people to plant vineyards, which example was subsequently followed by other colonies.

In 1904 he was sent to Katharinenstadt on the Volga as priest and administrator.

In 1906 he was appointed the editor of the paper, "Klemens," and was moved to Saratov. He also played a large part in the founding of the "Klemens Society," for which purpose he raised 13,000 rubles from various parishes.

When the newspaper "Deutsche Rundschau," was founded the next year in addition to the "Klemens," its publication was moved from Saratov to Odessa and Father Becker went along as its editor. After one year, he resigned the position of editor and took the position of religious teacher in the secondary schools in Odessa, where he is still working.

FATHER PETER RIEDEL *Administrator*
from 3 July 1903 until 8 September 1906

Father Riedel was born in the colony of Herzog on the Karaman in 1880.

He entered the Seminary in Saratov, completing his courses there, and was ordained in 1903.

Further information is not available.

FATHER JOHANNES VON PAUER
Pastor from 8 September 1906 until 1913

Father Johannes Von Pauer was born on the 26 May 1864 in the glass works town of Annenhütte in Courland where his parents had moved from Germany.

His father, Franz-Joseph Von Pauer, was a knight and squire in Wollsbach and his mother, Franziska Prechtl, came from the Upper Palatinate (Bavaria).

At the age of 12 he entered the highschool in Goldingen, where he persevered diligently in his studies of the humanities and matriculated in June 1883. After this he recuperated for one year in a health resort. He then moved to the University of Dorpat, where he studied philology and philosophy under the professors Horschelmann, Mendelsohn-Bartholdy and Teichmuller for a year-and-a-half.

All this knowledge of nature did not satisfy his soul as he wished to know something about the Creator himself. With this thought in mind, he entered the seminary in Saratov where he studied the courses for four years. He was ordained on the 12 August 1890 by Bishop Zerr. Following this he was the vicar in Kamenka for a short time and on the 20 October 1890, he was sent to the parish of Pfeifer as administrator. He worked hard at his priestly duties and soon gained the trust and respect of his parishioners.

In 1898 he was named parish priest. As a result of over-exertion he became weak and run down. Once again he went to a health resort abroad. In the town of Deggendorf on the blue Danube, in lovely Bavaria, he often visited his sisters and his aged father.

In 1906 he was sent to Katharinental as the parish priest, where he fulfilled his duties in spite of illness.

In 1906 he was made lecturer in Latin in the seminary in Saratov, where he is still working.

On the 1 March 1914 he was made a domestic prelate. Presently (1914) Katharinental is supervised from Speier.

Parish Endowment

The priest receives 600 rubles from the community, a supply of fuel and twelve drives to Nikolayev in any one year. The surplice charges are: baptism 1 ruble, marriage 3 rubles, publishing of banns 1 ruble, funeral 1 ruble, low mass 1 ruble, high mass 1 ruble, 50 kopecks.

The Parish Church

It would appear that the first church was built in Katharinental in 1820 and was located in the present parish house yard. It was 72 feet long, 30 feet wide and approximately 18 feet high.

There were three entrances, one at the front and two on the sides. The bell tower was located at some distance from the church. The roof of the church and the steeple were covered with shingles.

The church contained an altar, a confessional, and some Holy pictures.

The New Parish Church

The new church was started in 1868 and completed in 1869. It is made of well cut field-stone and incorporated a variety of styles.

It was consecrated by Bishop Antonius Zerr on the 22 September 1896. The patron of the church is His Holiness Pope Pius V.

The church is located in the centre of a cross, formed by four streets, and is built in a westerly to easterly direction.

It is 96 feet long, 30 feet wide and 24 feet high. The tower is attached to the church and rises to a height of 108 feet. The roof is covered with tin and painted green. The church has only one entrance below the steeple and on either side there are six windows. It is surrounded by a massive stone wall.

Inside the church, and on both sides, are the seats and kneeling benches. On the right wall the stations of the cross begin, made of stone with the relief figurines on a golden background, very impressive workmanship.

Between the fourth and fifth window is the confessional in Gothic style. Beside it is the altar of the Heart of Jesus, above which there is a lovely picture of the Resurrection. Adjacent to the altar, on a high pedestal, is a carved statue of the Heart of Jesus.

On entering the presbytery one finds himself in front of the main altar, which is made of stone and adorned with artificial flowers. The tabernacle is made of wood and decorated with gold. Above it, the sacrament chamber rests on four small pillars. On the right side of the altar there is the statue of St. Peter; on the left, the statue of St. Paul.

High above the altar is an oil painting of the church patron, Pope Pius V. After leaving the presbytery one finds the statue of the Mother of God on the right and, immediately adjacent to it, the Marian Altar. Above this is a picture of the Immaculate Conception. Beside the altar is the baptismal font and further on, the pulpit without an echo reflector. Above the pulpit, there is a picture of the Multiplication of the Loaves.

The choir loft rests on four stone pillars and has room for the organ and the choir. The floor of the church is made of wood and is painted red with oil paint.

The Graveyard and the Chapel

The graveyard is in the same locality as when the colony was founded and is surrounded by a high stone wall. In the graveyard there is a chapel with family vaults, built by Adam Bullinger. The chapel is 36 feet long, 24 feet wide and 24 feet high. There is an entrance at the front and on either side there are three windows. It cost 5000 rubles. Only stone and iron were used in its construction. The inside of the chapel contains eleven benches and an altar with a picture of the Virgin Mary of Perpetual Help.

The Rectory

The rectory was built of good fieldstone in 1870. It contains five rooms and a kitchen and corridor. There are also the necessary barns and a vegetable garden.

The School Affairs

The first school was built soon after Katharinental was founded in 1820 and had the design of a colonist house.

In 1908 the present school house was built of good cut fieldstone. It is 108 feet long, 36 feet wide and contains a number of classrooms.

The first school teacher in Katharinental was Georg Jantzer, who remained there until 1847. There followed Johannes Martin, Kaspar Jäger, Peter Schmidt, J. Götz, J. Kellermann, Eduard Butsch, J. Melhaff, K. Daub, P. Jundt and others. At the present time, there are three teachers in the school, each receiving 350 rubles. There are 180 school children.

A Priest
from Katharinental

FATHER Kaspar Butsch

Father Kaspar Butsch was born on the 22 April 1880 in Katharinental, the son of Johannes Butsch and Katharina Krank.

He entered the local parish school and in 1894 he entered the Seminary in Saratov.

After completing his studies, he was ordained by Bishop Eduard Von Ropp on the 25 April 1904. He held his first mass in Katharinental on the 10 May 1904 and soon thereafter was made administrator in Franzfeld on the Dniester.

In 1905 he was made a vicar in Nikolayev, where he worked until 1907. On the 16 August 1907 he was made administrator in the parish of Elisabethgrad, where he became a curate in 1912.

It is difficult to believe that such a large parish has had only one person who trained for the priesthood. What can the trouble be?

Lay People who were born, or worked
in Katharinental

EDUARD BUTSCH *Teacher*

Eduard Butsch was born in Katharinental on the 4 September 1884, the son of Sebastian Butsch and Helena Geiss.

His father died when he was two years old and he was raised by his mother who soon married a second time.

After completing his studies at the local parish school, he attended the private school of H. P. Böchler in Karlsruhe in order to prepare himself for admission to the seminary in Saratov. However, since there was not room for him in the seminary, he continued his private instruction with a student in order to write the examinations for elementary school teacher. He received his diploma as a teacher on the 29 October 1903 in Vosnesensk, and accepted a community teaching position while he continued his studies in German and literature.

On the 27 September 1905 he received a position as teacher in his own colony of Katharinental.

In the summer of 1908 he attended teacher's summer school in Grossliebental. Since the 22 January 1911 he has been the principal in the community school in Katharinental.

He also occupied himself diligently with the study of folklore and the writer wishes to thank him for his worthwhile efforts in this field.

STEPHAN BÖHM *Organist*

Stephan Böhm, son of Friedrich, was born in Katharinental on the 28 January 1853.

He finished his studies at the community school at the age of twelve and joined the Katharinental orchestra as flutist. Since he was musically talented and enjoyed it greatly, he took music lessons on the piano and also learned to play the organ. After he had progressed satisfactorily, he took over the position of organist in his home parish in the year 1874. He fulfilled this position for 30 years to everyone's delight and satisfaction. Later he was organist and sexton in Hekovka for six years. He returned to his home in 1906 to spend his last days in retirement. However, in 1907 the community persuaded him to accept the position of church warden, later treasurer, and in 1912, chairman of the Katharinental consumers cooperative. He carried out all his assignments faithfully and intelligently for which he received recognition from the priests and the community.

JOSEPH GÖTZ *Teacher*

Joseph Götz was born on the 11 September 1874 in Baden, Kutschurgan, the son of Matthias Götz and Katharina Kraft.

After completing his studies in the provincial school in Baden and the Central School in Strassburg, he wrote the examinations for the elementary teacher's certificate in Kischinev.

In 1895 he was appointed community teacher in Katharinental where he taught for five years.

In 1900 he moved to Franzfeld as teacher and sexton, where he worked until 1 September 1903. From then until 1908 he was the teacher and sexton at Josephstal on the Baraboi.

Since 1908 he has been the principal in the province school in Jeremejevka in the parish of Elsass.

He married Emilie Kaiser on the 9 August 1899, the daughter of Jakob. They had three sons and two daughters.

The present Wealth and Conditions
of the Colony of Katharinental

The colony of Katharinental at the present time contains 204 lots and 1581 Catholic people of both sexes. There are approximately 150 Russian maids and hired men and a few Jewish families.

The salary per year for a hired man is 100 to 120 rubles and for a maid, 90 to 100 rubles. Many familes migrated to America, but their number is not given; others went to Siberia.

The community land of the colony contains 5816.5 dessiatines. Several farmers own 4144 dessiatines of purchased land in the neighbourhood. Additional land bought is not stated.

The community land is utilized as follows: 4209 dessiatines for agriculture, 1208 for pasture land, 53 dessiatines for hayland, 10 dessiatines for forest, 92 dessiatines for vineyards, and 192 dessiatines for lots. The remaining land is used in roads and dams. There are four dams containing fish and every citizen has permission to fish.

The stock in the colony is as follows: horses 1630, cows 1188, pigs 487, community bulls 9.

In 1913 they sowed approximately 600 dessiatines in both winter and summer wheat.

Tradesmen were as follows: Blacksmiths 4, joiners 3, wagon maker 1, shoemaker 1, cooper 1, saddlemaker 1.

There is one co-operative store, six small shops, two steam flour mills and two beer halls.

The salaries of the administrators are: mayor 126 rubles, treasurer 13 rubles, secretary 550 rubles, bailiff 134 rubles, the horse herder 1 ruble, 5 kopecks per horse, and 1/4 pud of wheat, the cow herder 85 kopecks per had and 1/4 pud of wheat, the calf herder 35 kopecks per head. The cost for shipping freight to Nikolayev was 5 to 10 kopecks per pud.

The community paid the following taxes: Crown taxes 426 rubles, 53 kopecks. For the purchase of the land 1846 rubles, 57 kopecks. Ground rent 1793 rubles 15 kopecks; community taxes, 9940 rubles 68 kopecks.

The District and Colony of Rastadt

The District of Rastadt

The Rastadt local government district includes the German colonies of Rastadt and München. Until 1871 these were included in the Beresan district, although they are not located in the Beresan valley, but on the Chitchekleya river in the County of Ananyev.

The Chitchekleya river originates near the boundary of the provinces of Kherson and Podolia and is fed by a number of springs and creeks. It enters the province of Kherson at the village Bobrick and runs almost parallel to its western neighbor the Tiligul river, in a southeasterly direction as far as the colony of München, where it makes a turn to the east and about 40 versts further on empties into the Bug. A few versts from its mouth it makes a sharp turn to the south and then north again to form a peninsula, on which in the olden days there was the city of Kaptchakley, whose ruins and tombstones can still be seen today. The Chitchekleya has a much wider valley than the Beresan and, as an old book in the Vosnesensk city library tells us, about 150 years ago it still had so much water that sailing ships could travel on it.

The fertile region of the Chitchekleya, as late as 50 years ago was inhabited by Bulgars, Serbs, Arnauts and other Slavic peoples, but today most of the lands here belong to German colonists, for whom the previous owners now work as day laborers or tenants. This shows again that the German colonists are the most progressive people in Russia. Through tireless industry and strenuous work, they have acquired most of the landed estates of the Russian nobility. These became impoverished and bankrupted after 1861, when they lost the serfs who had worked their lands for them at no cost, while they themselves were spending the income in high life activities in Paris. The change took place quietly and in a very natural way, for the German colonist needed land to farm and the noble needed money to live. Then, a few years ago, this honest land acquisition by the German colonists began to be considered a crime and all kinds of improper motives were ascribed to it. There was even a proposal in the Imperial Duma that further land acquisition by the German colonists be prohibited. Until now, however, this so-called "Colonist Bill" has been defeated by the more intelligent of the members.

Sequence of District Mayors
in Rastadt

ANDREAS SEELINGER—1871 to 1876

Andreas Seelinger, son of Andreas, was born in Rastadt on the 20 February 1832. He was a capable, intelligent, industrious man, and was soon noticed by the authorities because of the energy and community spirit which he displayed in his new environment.

His most important undertaking was the introduction of the district school in Rastadt with two certified teachers, and also in München with one certified teacher. These were the first district schools in the German colonies of South Russia. He was considered very upright by his fellow citizens. His death on the 20 June 1885 was mourned by all the good people.

PHILIPP-ERNST SEELINGER—1876-1882

Philipp-Ernst Seelinger, son of Anton, was born in Rastadt in 1840.

He completed his studies in the parish school, obtaining a good record. He then increased his knowledge through constant reading.

In 1870 he was put in charge of orphans' funds, a duty he performed faithfully for six years. For several years he was the magistrate and prosecutor for the district.

His main accomplishment as mayor was the purchase of 697 dessiatines of land for the people of the Rastadt district who did not own land. He was also an active member of the building committee for the church in Rastadt. Two of his sons are presently students in the New Russian Imperial University in Odessa. He died in his home in Rastadt in 1913.

PETER RESCH—1882-1885

Peter Resch, born in Rastadt, was a hard working, industrious type of man, and was elected mayor in 1882. He carried out his duties to the best of his ability.

FRANZ-MICHAEL SEELINGER— 1885-1888

Franz-Michael Seelinger, son of Anton, was born in Rastadt in 1842. For some years he was the district magistrate and prosecutor, and then was elected mayor.

He enlarged the local graveyard and made arrangements to have the old schoolhouse replaced by a new one. He also intended to change the district school from a one-class to a two-classroom school. This resulted in such a serious disagreement in the community that the school inspector took the opportunity to remove all of the German school teachers and replace them with five Russian teachers who could not speak German. This situation continued for almost four years.

Franz-Michael Seelinger died in his home in Rastadt in 1892.

GREGOR EBERLE—1889-1892

Gregor Eberle was a colonist of Rastadt. He was made mayor in place of Jakob Zentner who had been elected but had his confirmation refused. He did his utmost to solve the school problem, the so-called "civil war," but was only partly successful.

JAKOB ZENTNER—1892-1898

Jakob Zentner was born in München on the 13 November 1859. At the age of 13 he entered the Seminary in Saratov for seven years, where he was a capable, industrious student.

When he completed the second year of the clerical seminary and did not feel a calling to the priesthood, he left the seminary and returned to his home. Here he studied law and the 'code of laws' relating to the German colonies in Russia in connection with the laws of the empire. After he had a thorough knowledge of both the theoretical and practical procedures in the practice of law, he took the position of secretary for the district of Rastadt. He was extremely well versed in the Russian language, was a skilled speaker and had a wonderful memory. He often astounded the public officials in Ananyev with his legal and practical knowledge of matters relating to the national welfare, and to the schools. He soon gained the respect of the authorities who admired and feared him. The latter was shown particularly when he was elected as district mayor and the authorities vetoed the election, because they did not want him as mayor. When, however, he was chosen a second time, they let it pass and he was confirmed as mayor in 1892.

His first problem as mayor was to try to solve the intolerable school problem. As a result of his initiative, a nice new five-room school was built, in which the rooms were large. In addition, two German teachers were hired so that the children could once more learn the German language.

His second problem was the welfare of the landless of the community. Through his efforts, the neglected orphans bank was converted into a district bank and the fire insurance was made compulsory for everyone. For two terms he was deputy in the district assembly in Ananyev. For his efforts in his duties to the community he received the silver medallion with the Anne ribbon. Jakob Zentner, throughout his official career, was a faithful defender of the German culture, a very devout Catholic, and a zealous spokesman and sponsor for the poor and needy.

MICHAEL EHRMANTRAUT—1898 to ?

Michael Ehrmantraut, from Rastadt, was mayor for only a short time. He was replaced by Peter Daratha.

No further information is available about these two men.

SEBASTIAN SEELINGER—1902 to ?

Sebastian Seelinger was born in Rastadt in 1846. He had no formal education but was an intelligent, industrious man, who knew his duties as mayor and tried to do his best. He soon got into conflict with the Governor of the district regarding the appointment of the district secretary. He wearied of the quarrel, resigned his appointment, and someone else took his place. Later, Martin Kessel from München was mayor for a time, but nothing is known about his activities.

DOMINIK KOPP—1905 to ?

Dominik Kopp was born in Rastadt. He completed his studies in the minor seminary in Saratov and for some years he was the community teacher and then the district secretary for a short time.

In 1905 he was elected mayor. Much was written in the paper of the time about his administration.

PETER JORDAN—1907

Peter Jordan, son of Karl, was born in Rastadt on the 10 October 1865.

He completed his studies in the local parish school with good reports. He joined the military in 1886 and, as secretary in Kherson, he attended classes there.

In 1887 he was the secretary in Kischinev. After leaving the service in 1891, he returned to his home and was soon appointed cashier of the community bank.

From 1904 to 1907 he presided over the Rastadt district court. Since 1 January 1907 he has been mayor of the Rastadt district.

The Rastadt District Court

Since the 1 September 1891 there has been a district Court of Justice in every district of the province of Kherson, presided over by a chairman and two members. The first chairman of this court was Jakob Zentner; the second Jakob Obrischkewitsch; the third, Michael Kopp; the fourth, Peter Jordan; the fifth, Johannes Schmidt and the sixth, Nikolaus Ehrmantraut. The following were the district secretaries and recorders: Franz Domansky, Peter Schmidt from Baden, Samuel Kludt, Adam Gratz, Jakob Zentner, Jakob Fritz, Dominik Kopp, Christian Seelinger and Andreas Koschkin.

The Colony of Rastadt

The colony of Rastadt is located in the province of Kherson in the district of Ananyev. It is 140 versts from the city of Kherson and 120 versts from the city of Ananyev. It is the administration centre for the district of Rastadt.

The colony, located on the right bank of the Chitchekleya River, runs in an east-west direction and is two versts long.

There are two streets in the colony, the Main Street and the New Street, as well as seven cross streets. The colony is located on a terraced knoll which is encircled on the south by a rocky hill named the Kappellenberg.

The main buildings in the colony are the church, the rectory, the new schoolhouse, and some lovely private homes. The houses are of the same style as those of the other colonies. Most of the lots, but not all of them, are enclosed by massive stone fences.

There is plenty of water as there are 135 wells in the colony. The water in the centre colony is better and more tasty than that in the upper or lower colony.

Field-stones are plentiful on the south side of the hill. When the colonists first came here, the area was wild and uninhabited. But at one time in the past there had been a large settlement here, perhaps Greek. One finds stone foundations almost everywhere throughout the length of the colony, but they are all black from smoke. One can only conjecture that the community was destroyed by fire. Forty years ago colonist M. Merdian found the remains of a walled canal in the yard of L. Eberts. With its origin in the hills, it had the appearance of a Greek or Roman aqueduct. When the government flour mill was built in the early days of the settlement in Rastadt, they found the remains of a huge human skeleton. Parts of a mammoth were also found not far from Rastadt.

Until the Crown houses were finished, the colonists lived in tents or reed huts which proved to be rather unhealthy for the settlers. In order to build their homes, every family received a home grant, as well as the necessary lumber which they received from contractor, Herrmann, in Odessa. Instead of the daily allowances, the colonists now received food rations.

The name "Rastadt" was given to the colony by Johannes Koch. The main occupations of the colonists are agriculture and cattle raising.

The climate in the summertime is not at all healthy and many people contract fevers. The people are of strong stature, medium height with wide shoulders, but are rather pale. They are somewhat sombre by nature, but very kind. The language tends to be more that of Baden than of the Palatinate. This is to be expected as most of the settlers came from the Grand Duchy of Baden, Germany.

Settlers of Rastadt in the Beresan
in 1811
with their homes of origin*

1. **Michael Holzmann** 30, from Rohrbach, Rhinepalatinate.
WIFE: Juliana 33.
CHILDREN: Martin 1, Katharina 4.
2. **Andreas Klein** 30, from Bergzabern, Rhinepalatinate.
WIFE: Christina 28.
CHILDREN: Johann 6, Michael 3, Eva ?.
3. **Cyriak Oswald** 34, from Bischweiler, Alsase.
WIFE: Marianna 41.
CHILDREN: Katharina 5.
4. **Michael Gandermann** 35, from Hördt, Rhinepalatinate.
WIFE: Sophie 31.
CHILDREN: Georg 17, Valentin 3, Katharina 5.
5. **Jakob Hirsch** 41, from Herxheim, Rhinepalatinate.
WIFE: Apollonia 31.
CHILDREN: Martin 13, Valentin 5, Barbara 7.
6. **Georg Bentz** 23, from Hördt, Rhinepalatinate.
WIFE: Barbara 23.
CHILDREN: Konrad 1.
7. **Matthias Asperger** 35, from Flehingen, Baden.
WIFE: Margaretha 28.
CHILDREN: Peter 14, Michael 13, Franz 4, Kunigunde 9, Antonia 8.
8. **Bonifaz Müller** 26, from Rheinzabern, Rhinepalatinate.
WIFE: Katharina 25.
CHILDREN: Margaretha 1.

---

*The information available for Rastadt and München is not as detailed as it was for the other colonies.

9. **Maria Anton** 48, widow, from Mörlheim, Rhinepalatinate.
CHILDREN: Joseph 20, Barbara 13, Maria 10, Margaretha 6.
10. **Johann Belitzer** 37, from Eppingen, Baden.
WIFE: Maria 43.
CHILDREN: Leonard 13, Maria 10.
11. **Gottlieb Zwirner** 38, from Isenheim, Alsace.
WIFE: Johanna 34.
12. **Franz Jos** 39, from Flehingen, Baden.
WIFE: Christina 34.
13. **Anton Gelzinger** 25, from Selz, Alsace.
WIFE: Anastasia 25.
CHILDREN: Joseph 11, Franz 1.
14. **Jakob Seelinger** 31, from Rülzheim, Rhinepalatinate.
WIFE: Apollonia 27.
CHILDREN: Andreas 8, Sebastian 5, Georg 1.
15. **Heinrich Odenbach** 29, from Pleisweiler, Rhinepalatinate.
WIFE: Margartha 29.
CHILDREN: Johann 6.
16. **Franz Wagner** 46, from Insheim, Rhinepalatinate.
WIFE: Eva 47.
CHILDREN: Ferdinand 17, Franz 12.
17. **Georg Kühlwein** 31, from Rülzheim, Rhinepalatinate.
WIFE: Katharina 36.
CHILDREN: Georg 7, Eva 5.
18. **Peter Keller** 27, from Neupfalz, Rhinepalatinate.
WIFE: Magdalena 35.
CHILDREN: Philipp 10.
Katharina Keller 41, mother.
DAUGHTER: Magdalena Ulrich 6.
19. **Augustine Eichhelm** from Selz, Alsace.
WIFE: Juliana 25.
Marianna Fettmann 64, mother.
20. **Johann Fischer** 35, from Hördt, Rhinepalatinate.
WIFE: Marianna 34.
CHILDREN: Adam 18, Andreas 13, Daniel 11, Barbara 10, Margaretha 2.
21. **Adam Daum** 61, widower, from Herxheim, Rhinepalatinate.
CHILDREN: Georg 5, Marianna 25.
(a) Stephan Löbenstein 23, son-in-law.
WIFE: Katharina 31.
CHILDREN: Georg 5.
22. **Adam Sitter** 53, from Jockgrim, Rhinepalatinate.
WIFE: Maria 52.
CHILDREN: Martin 23, Wendel 20, Georg 19, Franz 7, Elisabeth 10,

Theresia 1.
    23. **Anton Kopp** 36, from Bellheim, Rhinepalatinate.
WIFE: Elisabeth 41.
CHILDREN: Franz 3.
    24. **Jakob Kopp** 39, from Queichheim, Rhinepalatinate.
WIFE: Elisabeth 34.
CHILDREN: Anton 6, Johann 4, Jakob 1, Margaretha 8, Apolonia 2.
    25. **Johann Deibele** 53, from Sulz, Alsace.
WIFE: Maria 34.
CHILDREN: Joseph 10, Philipp 7, Marianna 19, Regina 4.
    26. **Ludwig Schmied** from Hördt, Rhinepalatinate.
WIFE: Katharina.
CHILDREN: Joseph 11, Andreas 8.
(a) Rudolf Steiff 27, (son-in-law?)
WIFE: Eva 18.
    27. **Peter Emenet** 31, from Neiderlustadt, Rhinepalatinate.
WIFE: Margaretha 39.
CHILDREN: Lorenz 10, Peter 3, Martin 1, Barbara 14, Margaretha 6.
    28. **Peter Zahnbrecher** 51, from Weissenburg, Alsace.
WIFE: Luisa 37.
CHILDREN: Peter 3.
    29. **Johann Vogt** 30, from Münsterberg, Silesia.
WIFE: Rosalia 37.
CHILDREN: Karolina 10.
    30. **Jakob Sutter** 31, from Auenheim, Alsace.
WIFE: Theresia 36.
CHILDREN: Michael 9, Maria 1.
    31. **Leonard Dürrein** 29, from Hördt, Rhinepalatinate.
WIFE: Agnes 26.
CHILDREN: Maria 2.
Maria Dürrein 21, sister.
    32. **Matthias Wilhelm** 41, from Leutershausen, Baden.
WIFE: Elisabeth 36.
CHILDREN: Johann 24, Margaretha 9, Elizabeth 5.
    33. **Johann Horwat** 41, from Pest, Hungary.
WIFE: Maria 37.
CHILDREN: Johann 17, Friedrich 6, Maria 6.
    34. **Joseph Koch** 34, from Hohweiler, Alsace.
WIFE: Barbara 30.
CHILDREN: Barbara 11, Barbara 6 (printing error?), Friederika 4.
    35. **Karl Eberle** 43, from Blankenborn, Rhinepalatinate.
WIFE: Theresia 43.
CHILDREN: Jakob 13, Heinrich 9, Eva 17, Katharina 12.
    36. **Johann Haag** 37, from Flehingen, Baden.

WIFE: Katharina 35.
CHILDREN: Johann 14, Anton 6, Karl 2, Franziska 5.
37. **Michael Pfoh** 38, from Hilsbach, Baden.
WIFE: Josepha 35.
CHILDREN: Franz 19, Joseph 17, Julianna 6, Maria 3.
38.**Joseph Häuser** 22, from Frost, Saxony.
WIFE: Ursula Paulenz 18.
39. **Sebastian Martin** 51, from Selz, Alsace.
WIFE: Apolonia 41.
CHILDREN: Michael 6, Apolonia 21, Maria 11.
40. **Gottlieb Trost** 41, from Allerhof, Prussia.
WIFE: Constanzia 26.
CHILDREN: Maria 8, Christina 7.
41. **Adam Haag** 39, from Ettlingen, Baden.
WIFE: Magdalena 35.
CHILDREN: Johann 17, Joseph 6, Anton 2, Katharina 11.
42. **Johann Schall** from Heiligenstein, Rhinepalatinate.
WIFE: Apollonia Spanier 28.
CHILDREN: Konrad 18, Elizabeth 16, Magdalena 12.
43. **Thomas Masser** 38, from Schwanheim, Rhinepalatinate.
WIFE: Franziska 37.
CHILDREN: Maria 2.
44. **Melchior Haffner** 30, from Rheinsheim, Baden.
WIFE: Katharina 40.
CHILDREN: Philipp 6, Klara 8.
45. **Christian Fuchs** 28, from Mörlheim, Rhinepalatinate.
WIFE: Magaretha 28.
CHILDREN: Margaretha 4.
46. **Wilhelm Thomä** 47, from Ubstadt, Baden.
WIFE: Magdelena 48.
CHILDREN: Johann 18, Jakob 17, Wilhelm 13, Katharina 16.
47. **Michael Resch** 42, from Ottersheim, Rhinepalatinate.
WIFE: Barbara 37.
CHILDREN: Karl 9, Konrad 7, Sebastian 2, Margaretha 4.
48. **Heinrich Jost** 43, from Rohrbach, Rhinepalatinate.
WIFE: Angelina 27.
CHILDREN: Susanna 18, Katharina 17, Elisabeth 5.
49. **Konrad Rapp** 51, from Volkersweiler, Rhinepalatinate.
WIFE: Christian 37.
CHILDREN: Franz 18, Cyriak 13, Simon 5, Franziska 4.
50. **Friedrich Reichert** 41, from Hilsbach, Baden.
WIFE: Sophia 38.
CHILDREN: Franz 15, Friedrich 13, Karl 9, Josephina 7.
51. **Jakob Segmüller** 37, from Rheinzabern, Rhinepalatinate.

WIFE: Maria 25.
  52. **Johann Gustin** 37, from Wingen, Alsace.
WIFE: Magdalena 31.
CHILDREN: Franz 9, Michael 6, Johann 1, Katharina 16.
  53. **Barbara Stiedner** 35, widow, from Bobental, Rhinepalatinate.
CHILDREN: Philipp 19, Barbara 12, Maria 5.
  54. **Johann Weiss** 37, from Neumarkt, Bavaria.
WIFE: Elisabetha, 23.
  55. **Baltas Meyer** 45, from Breitental, Alsace.
WIFE: Marianna 40.
CHILDREN: Johann 16, Magdalena 21, Margaretha 5.
  56. **Anton Erhard** 29, from Neuhausen, Baden.
WIFE: Walburga 41.
CHILDREN: Marianna 8.
  57. **Christian Singer** 27, from Bebelsheim, Rhinepalatinate.
WIFE: Annamaria 24.
CHILDREN: Katharina 5.
  58. **Franz Moritz** 40, from Bergheim, Alsace.
WIFE: Maria 25.
CHILDREN: Eva 2.
  59. **Peter Winterstein** 41, from Breitenbach, Rhinepalatinate.
WIFE: Christina 31.
CHILDREN: Maria 15.
  60. **Johann Metz** 43, from Seinach, Baden.
WIFE: Katharina 31.
CHILDREN: Johann 3, Margartha 11.
  61. **Peter Weinberger** 47, from Zeiskam, Rhinepalatinate.
WIFE: Marianna 37.
CHILDREN: Joseph 11, Johann 10, Adam 6, Matthias 3, Elisabeth 8, Katharina 2.
  62. **Theobald Wetzel** 46, from Zeiskam, Rhinepalatinate.
WIFE: Katharina 47.
CHILDREN: Martin 12, Magdalena 16.
  63. **Michael Ludwig** 25, from Surburg, Alsace.
WIFE: Margaretha 25.
CHILDREN: Joseph 2.
  64. **Bartholomäus Förderer** from Oestringen, Baden.
WIFE: Maria 53.
CHILDREN: Franz 21, Sebastian 13.
(a) Johann Förderer 34, son of Bartholomäus.
WIFE: Salomea 29.
  65. **Franz Lerner** 52, from Malsch, Baden.
WIFE: Eva 53.
CHILDREN: Michael 17, Bernhard 13.

66. **Ignatz Fritz** 29, from Völkersbach, Baden.
WIFE: Eva 39.
CHILDREN: Benedikt 4, Helena 6, Sabina 2.
67. **Friedrich Schmied** 49, from Durmersheim, Baden.
WIFE: Katharina 46.
CHILDREN: Johann 20, Bernhard 13.
68. **Johann Fröhlich** from Durmersheim, Baden.
WIFE: Anastasia 36.
CHILDREN: Meinrad 4, Magdalena 14, Theresia 8.
69. **Valentin Traub** 33, from Michelbach, Baden.
WIFE: Elisabeth 23.
CHILDREN: Karl 3, Karolina 5.
70. **Matthais Koffler** 47, from Durmersheim, Baden.
WIFE: Maria 37.
CHILDREN: Joseph 21, Anton 14, Eustachius 12, Johann 1, Richarta 10, Katarina 4.
71. **Anton Wirthmüller** 43, from Durmersheim, Baden.
WIFE: Maria 35.
CHILDREN: Konrad 10, Johann 1, Victoria 11, Emerenzia 6.
72. **Joseph Hauer** 37, from Durmersheim, Baden.
WIFE: Maria 30.
CHILDREN: Hubert 2, Matthias 1.
73. **Joseph Oberle** 43, from Durmersheim, Baden.
WIFE: Theresia 32.
CHILDREN: Christina 4.
Michael Metz 56, father of Theresia.
74. **Aloys Arquin** from Sufflenheim, Alsace.
WIFE: Elisabeth 37.
CHILDREN: Katharina 17.
75. **Georg Martin** 42, from Oberottenbach, Rhinepalatinate.
WIFE: Margaretha 21.
CHILDREN: Agnes 1.
76. **Michael Kroll** from Böchingen, Rhinepalatinate.
WIFE: Agnes 31.
CHILDREN: Wilhelm 17, Heinrich 13, August 9, Sophie 10.
77. **Joseph Faininger** 43, from Durmersheim, Baden.
WIFE: Walburga 33.
CHILDREN: Genovefa 10.
78. **Johann Gass** 45. from Malsch, Baden.
WIFE: Katharina 46.
CHILDREN: Ignaz 20, Andreas 13, Peter 4, Walburga 18, Theresia 11.
79. **Johann Koch** 37, from Durmersheim, Baden.
WIFE: Maria 37.

CHILDREN: Johann 8, Dionysius 6.
80. **Nikolaus Schneider** 31, from Völkersbach, Baden.
WIFE: Eva 37.
CHILDREN: Theresia 8, Marianna 6.
81. **Wendel Fäth** 45, from Schleital, Alsace.
WIFE: Barbara 35.
CHILDREN: Martin 13, Ludwig 4, Elisabeth 16, Maria 7.
82. **Anton Förderer** 27, from Oestringen, Baden.
WIFE: Margaretha 20.
CHILDREN: Rudolf 1.
83. **Johann Liska** 38, from Nodendorf, Moravia.
WIFE: Margaretha 37.
84. **Joseph Götzfried** 49, from Dörrenbach, Palatinate.
WIFE: Margaretha 49.
CHILDREN: Philipp 21, Paul 17, Georg 8, Martin 6, Katharina 19, Elisabeth 18.
85. **Johann Hoffer** 35, from Hockenheim, Baden.
WIFE: Katharina 27.
CHILDREN: Eva 4, Barbara 1.
86. **Peter Lehnert** 31, from Sessenheim, Alsace.
WIFE: Maria 33.
CHILDREN: Franz 6.
87. **Daniel Eichstetter** 58, widower, from Hockenheim, Baden.
CHILDREN: Jakob 24, wife — Katharina 20.
88. **Michael Rössle** 31, from Hockenheim, Baden.
WIFE: Katharina 27.
89. **Valentin Wandler** 50, from Hölschloch, Alsace.
WIFE: Magdalena 34.
CHILDREN: Karl 12, Lorenz 11, Martin 9, Joseph 6, Christina 14.
90. **Jakob Eichstätter** 51, from Hockenheim, Baden.
WIFE: Dorothea 41.
CHILDREN: Michael 20, Franz 17, Johann 12.
91. **Joseph Schmied** 41, from Neunkirchen, Baden.
WIFE: Margaretha 39.
CHILDREN: Johann 13, Elizabeth 9, Regina 7, Katharina 3.
92. **Jakob Pretzer** 38, from Söllingen, Baden.
WIFE: Katharina 41.
CHILDREN: Johann 10, Georg 5, Johanna 19, Magdalena 14.
STEP-CHILDREN: Friedrich Reinhard 11, Simon Reinhard 9, Barbara Reinhard 14, Magdalena Reinhard 3.
93. **Michael Brecht** 27, from Neudorf, Baden.
WIFE: Katharina 21.
CHILDREN: Margaretha 1.
94. **Anton Illner** 40, from Hölschloch, Alsace.

WIFE: Katharina 32.
CHILDREN: Katharina 2.
95. **Adam Klein** 26, from Langenbrücken, Baden.
WIFE: Katharina 26.
CHILDREN: Antonia 4.
MOTHER: Katharina Klein (?) 54.
96. **Joseph Dublesier** 43, from Tour, France.
WIFE: Charlotta 31.
CHILDREN: Dorothea 7.
97. **Jakob Ell** 30, from Durmersheim, Baden.
WIFE: Margaretha 26.
CHILDREN: Thomas 5, Ignaz 1.
Joseph Nagel 12, adopted.
98. **Ignaz Fröhlich** 41, from Durmersheim, Baden.
WIFE: Eva 36.
CHILDREN: Bartholomäus 7, Carolina 10.
99. **Franziska Hecht** 44, widow, from Bebelsheim, Rhinepalatinate.
CHILDREN: Lorenz 21.
100. **Franz Burger** 35, from Niederbronn, Alsace.
SECOND WIFE: Katharina Götzfried 19.
CHILDREN: Magdalena 4.
101. **Simon Mayer** 21, from Birlenbach, Alsace.
WIFE: Angelika Jost 27.
102. **Johann Schmidt** 20, from Durmersheim, Baden.
WIFE: Theresia 19.
103. **Anton Stark** 23, from Ottersheim, Rhinepalatinate.
WIFE: Franziska 23.
104. **Leonard Noe** 27, from Bergzabern, Rhinepalatinate.
WIFE: Magdalena 26.
CHILDREN: Marianna 5.
105. **Franz Eberts** 45, from Rülzheim, Rhinepalatinate.
WIFE: Katharina 35.
CHILDREN: Anton 14, Joseph 10, Maria 12, Magdalena 8, Josepha 6.
The following single persons also came:
1. Apollonia Spanier 28, from Kandel, Rhinepalatinate.
2. Margaretha Brünnel 6, from Schwanheim, Rhinepalatinate.
3. Georg Ballweber 21, from Völkersweiler, Rhinepalatinate.
4. Maria Ballweber 18, sister of Georg.
5. Marianna Ballweber 17, also a sister of Georg.
6. Maria Fortmeyer 20, from Hördt, Rhinepalatinate.
7. Stephan Koch 20, from Ottersheim, Baden.
8. Franz Koch 8, as above.
9. Franz Lehnert 18, from Avenheim, Alsace.

10. Georg Epinal 13, from Avenheim, Alsace.
11. Franziska Gottselig 14.

Beginnings of the
Colony of Rastadt

The colony of Rastadt was founded in the spring of 1810. The migrants came in various transports, let by various guides, as far as the border city of Radzivilov where they rested for a considerable time.

From this city they were divided into groups and then transported on to Odessa, arriving there in the fall of 1809. On the orders from Duke Richelieu, they were quartered for the winter with the German colonists in Liebental and Kutschurgan.

In the spring of 1810, under the guidance of Mayor Franz Brittner of Liebental, they moved on to the site of their settlement. The contractor, Herrmann of Odessa, brought materials for building the Crown houses and the founding of the colony was started. Every family received 100 rubles of money to buy the necessary implements and 35 rubles for a cow.

Groups of three families received 3 pair of oxen, 1 plow and one harrow. Instead of the daily money allowance, the colonists received flour, fat and salt.

By the 1 January 1811 there were 100 families and 11 single people, a total of 244 males and 225 females.

The community owned 95 horses, 353 horned cattle, 108 wagons, 527 loads of hay, 60 tschetwert wheat and 24 tschetwert oats.

Tradesmen were:

BAKERS: Michael Holzmann, Valentin Wandler.
SHOEMAKERS: Jakob Seelinger, Johann Metz.
JOINER: Anton Illner.
SADDLEMAKER: Adam Klein.
BELL-MAKER: Jakob Pretzer.
BUTCHERS: Matthias Asperger, Peter Lehnert.
WEAVERS: Johann Belitzer, Dewald Wetzel, Wendel Fäth, Johann Liska.
CARPENTERS: August Eichhelm, Michael Pfoh, Valentin Traub, Joseph Schmied.
BRUSH-MAKERS: Joseph Hag, Daniel Eichstätter.
MILLER: Thomas Masser.
BRICKLAYERS: Christian Fuchs, Joseph Götzfried, Johann Hoffer.
LUMBERMAN: Aloys Arquin.
COMB-MAKER: Joseph Koch.
MUSICIANS: Peter Winterstein, Ignaz Gass.

In the year 1811-1812 they planted 400 tschetwert of winter and summer wheat.

In 1818, after six years, the statistics for the young colony of Rastadt showed 93 families with 222 males and 192 females, a total of 414 people.

They had 256 horses, 714 horned cattle, 31 sheep, 335 pigs, 62 ploughs, 55 harrows, 131 wagons, 42 spinning wheels, and 1 weaving chair.

For the season of 1817-1818 they planted the following:

	Tschetwert	Tschetwerik.
1. Winter Wheat	11.0	2.0
2. Rye	123.0	2.0
3. Summer Wheat	175.0	4.0
4. Barley	43.0	0.0
5. Potatoes	176.0	0.0
6. Oats	75.0	2.0
7. Corn	5.0	4.0
8. Millet	10.0	1.0
9. Peas	5.0	5.5
10. Lentils	3.0	0.
11. Beans	5.0	0.5
12. Hemp	5.0	0.0
13. Flax	1.0	5.0
	637.0	26.0

The Community Land of Rastadt

The community land of Rastadt comprised 5684 dessiatines and in addition there was 120 dessiatines of parish land. The land forms a long rectangle 12 versts long and 2 versts wide and extends southward to the lands of the colonies of Rohrbach and Worms. On the west it borders on München, on the north the land of the nobleman Alexandrowitsch, and on the east the Baumann land.

The land is fairly level, the contour being interrupted only by the Fox Valley and some ponds in one area. The soil is of good, dark loam, and is 21 inches thick with a base of sand and gravel.

In the early days of the settlement, the soil was very fertile and, in spite of improper cultivation, it usually produced a rich harvest which is rarely the case nowadays. At that time there was tall grass (goatsbeard) everywhere which could be used for hay.

In 1823 the colonial authorities advised the colonists to plant trees, community gardens, orchards and vineyards. Unfortunately, these were not tended properly and they soon died.

In 1842 a second strict regulation came from the Fürsorge Committee to plant trees and gardens in the colonies and to have this done by certified intelligent gardeners. Since this order was accompanied by a threat of lashes for the obstinate ones, it succeeded in bringing about the wishes of the authorities.

Trees, orchards and vineyards were planted everywhere in the colonies and, in most cases, they hired people who understood gardening, the results being very good.

When the Fürsorge Committee was abolished in 1871, most of the trees and gardens were uprooted since the new administration did not concern itself with these matters. The people of Rastadt, since that time, have only one plantation in the east end of the colony.

In 1819, because of the inconvenience resulting from the division of the community land, 39 families decided to build new homes on the steppe in order to be closer to their land. General Inzov, who was in charge of the German colonies in South Russia at this time, granted his permission on the proviso that only the houses at the upper and lower ends were to be removed, so that the colony would not become unsightly. As a result, the new colony was located in the fields and called "Neurastadt." Some houses were completed and the people worked hard to finish the others before the harvest of 1819. However, misfortune prevented the completion of the colony. Their first well produced only a limited amount of water. A second well was dug and, at a depth of 60 feet there was a deafening noise such as is heard in an indescribable storm. As a result, the people decided to give up the project and move back to the colony of Rastadt. The place where the well was dug today is known as the "Rumbling Well."

The Parish of Rastadt

At the present time there are 338 lots in Rastadt and 3807 people, all Catholics. Non-Catholics remain in the colony only temporarily.

The parish was founded in 1811 and is under the jurisdiction of the deanery of Nikolayev in the diocese of Tiraspol. Other localities belonging to this parish include the town of Vosnesensk on the Bug, the small market towns of Kantakusenka and Annovka, the hamlets of Novo-Amerika, Alexandrovka one and two, Swenigorodka, Otschakov, Manov, Skarupka, Savidovka and many hamlets in the district of Ananyev. The distance to the postoffice in Mostovoye is 5 versts.

As previously explained in the section under Landau, the people of the Beresan had immediately requested a German priest from the authorities. There was a tremendous scarcity of priests among the

Jesuits who were administering to the Catholics in the Odessa area. Consequently, they had to be served by a Dominican priest from Severinovka.

When the first students graduated in 1811 from the recently opened novitiate in Dvina, the general of the order sent the needed number of priests to the Odessa mission. For Rastadt it was Father H. Reimers. He did not have the right disposition for the people of Rastadt and therefore was soon moved.

Until 1814 Rastadt was administered from Landau. Father Johannes Koervers S. J., a young, industrious priest, came to Rastadt in 1814.

Sequence of Prists in Rastadt

FATHER JOHANNES HUBERTUS REIMERS, S.J.
6 October 1811 to 28 October 1811

Father J. H. Reimers was born on the 21 December 1776. On the 6 September 1810 he entered the novitiate of the Society of Jesus at Dvina to train as a missionary. In 1811 he was sent from here to the mission in Odessa and was the first priest for the newly founded parish of Rastadt. Things generally presented a dismal appearance in Rastadt at that time. There was neither a church or rectory. The people were poor and lived in the newly built, damp Crown houses. As a result of this, and also because of the stale water puddles from the overflow of the Chitchekleya, the poor colonists became ill in epidemic proportions. There was not a home in which people were not either sick or dead. Many times the father or mother died and the children were left as orphans. A priest would have to be specially endowed to carry on his duties in such a situation. Father Reimers did not have these qualities and consequently he soon left, returning to Dvina. The following year he resigned from the order.

After he left, the parish of Rastadt was supervised from Landau until Father Koervers came on the 14 March 1814.

FATHER JOHANNES KOERVERS, S.J.
14 March 1814 to 19 June 1820

Father J. Koervers was born on the 23 December 1773 in Münster-Geleku, Belgium. He entered the Society of Jesus in Dvina on the 6 September 1810.

After completing his studies, he was ordained in 1813, and the following year he was sent to Rastadt.

Father Koervers was a pious and dedicated priest who was always ready to do his duty. He was a good preacher, comforted the people in the confessional and instructed and exhorted the children in Christian teaching as well as in their school education. He tried to win all to Christ. He also visited the sick, comforted them in their suffering, and prepared them for their hour of death. He worked quietly in his assignment of healing the souls until 1820, when all the Jesuits were expelled from Russia.

In his farewell sermon he said, "Hold fast to your religious beliefs, for the priests who succeed me will be wearing horns."

He returned to his home in Belgium where he carried on his duties as a priest until 1836. He died an edifying death at Gravenhage, Holland in 1836.

After he left, Rastadt was supervised from Landau by Father Dominik Bachert and Father Albin Marzinkewicz.

FATHER F. DUKAST *Curate*
27 November 1820 until 2 May 1821

Father F. Dukast previously was a German preacher in Odessa and was sent to Rastadt by Ignaz Lindl. Whether he was a faithful follower of Lindl, I could not ascertain. However, it is recorded that during his time, four families in München left the Catholic faith. About his origin and his destiny, no further information could be ascertained.

FATHER IGNAZ LINDL
9 August 1821 to 1822

Father I. Lindl was born on the 8 May 1774 in Baindelkirchen, in old Bavaria. He was ordained in 1799.

When Lindl was suspended by the investigating commission in Odessa, as explained in volume one, he came to Rastadt in order to propagandize his sect. When Lindl preached his first sermon in Rastadt the people had no complaints. The second one aroused displeasure. His third sermon, in which he denied the perpetual virginity of Mary, the Mother of God, angered everyone. The most educated men in Rastadt, namely Johannes Fischer, the sextons Ignaz Fritz and Aloys Arquin, who had studied in the seminary in Germany, met and notified the authorities. They prohibited Lindl to go on the pulpit and forbade him from carrying on any church functions. Leonard Belitzer threatened to shoot Lindl if he dared to go into the pulpit again.

Since Lindl could no longer preach in Rastadt, he went to München where he held forth in a private home and 30 families left their Catholic faith.

The leading followers of Lindl were Georg Leitner, Michael Leitner, Joseph Kary, Georg Rink and Franz-Michael Flick.

Lindl preached his false doctrine not only in München, but also in the neighbouring Lutheran colonies of Rohrbach and Worms. He also wished to come to Landau but the people blocked his way so that he had to turn back wthout fulfilling his wishes. In the meantime he was relieved of his position as Superintendent of Odessa and excommunicated.

In 1822 he moved to Bessarabia with his followers and founded the colony of Sarata, as described in volume one.

Following Lindl, Rastadt was served by Father Albin Marzinkewicz from Landau, Father Johannes Hammer, and Father Franziskus Hoffmann, Dr. of Theology from Odessa.

FATHER BALTASSAR NIDEZSKY
1 May 1824 to 19 May 1830

Father B. Nidezsky, a Dominican, was born in 1789 and ordained in 1813.

He arrived on 1 May from Poland via private transportation, for which the people of Rastadt had to pay 30 rubles.

Father Nidezsky was a quiet, intelligent, pious priest who strove to carry out his duties conscientiously. However, since he understood German rather poorly and did not understand their customs or needs, he had very little influence among his parishioners. He soon realized his predicament and returned to his home in Poland in 1830.

FATHER CELESTINUS STASCHEWSKY
3 August 1830 to 11 October 1830

Father C. Staschewsky belonged to the Dominican order and was most likely from Volhynia, as he came to Rastadt from Tulschin in 1830 with his nephew Felix.

During 1816 and 1817 Father Staschewsky was the pastor in Severinovka, and in 1819 he went to the newly founded parish of Heidelberg. He was the first priest in Heidelberg and he worked there for 9 years, laying the foundation for Christian life for the people on the Molotchna.

He returned to his home from Heidelberg in 1828, where he spent 2 years recuperating from illness. Even though he had not completely recovered, he went to Rastadt. Here he endeavoured to carry out his duties, but in October he again became seriously ill and died on the 11 October 1830.

When he was being prepared for burial, a penance girdle was found about his loins and the scars of a lash on his body.

He was a worthy son of St. Dominic in regard to his vow of poverty. When his worldly possessions were totalled, they amounted to 24 rubles and 8 kopecks, but he also had a debt of 22 rubles. His nephew, Felix, thus received only 2 rubles 8 kopecks, which was not enough money to pay for his return to his home.

From 11 October 1830 until 27 April 1831, the parish was supervised by Father Maziewsky from Landau.

FATHER DAVID POWROG *Curate*
11 May 1831 until 16 August 1842

Father D. Powrog was apparently an Armenian. Nothing can be found in the records about his arrival or his education. Soon after his arrival on the 20 May 1831, the two communities of Rastadt and München sent a note of thanks to Superintendent Musnitsky for sending Father Powrog to Rastadt. They stated, "He does not speak German very well, but otherwise he carries out his duties zealously."

For two years the priest performed his duties very well, but things soon changed. In 1833 the colonist, Anton Kreidel, reported to the authorities that Father Powrog had bought oats in his presence and was going to send it to Poland (which was having a revolution at this time). He also reported that the priest often met with the administrator, Tschapka, from Kratovka, and that he had spoken disrespectfully about the Czar.

The matter was investigated in November of the same year by the priest, Erasmus Borowsky, from Landau and the official Osterberg from the Fürsorge Committee. The communities of Rastadt and München both confirmed the fact that the priest had bought oats out of compassion. They concluded that Kreidel was a trouble-maker and a back-biting type of individual. Thus having cleared the priest, the matter was dropped.

In 1835 the Beresan Inspector, Pritschenko, started things all over again when he reported that Father Powrog had some imported brandy in his cellar and that he made disrespectful remarks about the Czar from the pulpit. Nothing can be found about the outcome of these accusations. There were further charges made by some of the parishioners, as a result of which the community was divided. Some did not want to let him into the church anymore. He finally left Rastadt and moved to a Russian area where he lived with the landowner, Schukowsky, and his Polish wife.

As the dispute became worse, and since the community found the priest at fault in many matters, he was moved from Rastadt by the church authorities. For a while he lived with Nobleman Schostack, in the district of Elisabethgrad and died there soon after.

After Father Powrog, the parish of Rastadt was served by Father Borowsky from Landau, Father Grizewicz from Kleinliebental, and Father A. Skorulsky from Nikolayev.

FATHER HIERONYMUS SWIENZIZSKY
6 July 1846 to 24 April 1873

Father H. Swienzizsky, a Dominican, was born in 1797 near Lublin in Poland. He was ordained in 1821.

In 1827 he was the vicar in Odessa for a time; then it appears he lived in his home until he went to Rastadt in 1846.

Father Swienzizsky was quite a big, well built man, with a clear sonorous voice. He was a good speaker and a good singer. He was a pious, well educated priest, and an amiable fellow who loved to look after his parishioners. He understood the German language quite well. He fostered and renewed the religious life in Rastadt and impressed upon them the importance of good habits and order in the family and community life.

Father Swienzizsky tried hard to do everything well. There was no event of any importance among the people or the community which he did not counsel or mediate. Even though he was amiable and condescending by nature, he would enter any fray to impose his will and show his authority, which extended as far as the street.

He was very opposed to smoking; pity the fellow he met on the street with a pipe in his mouth. The pipe would be confiscated and the smoker would have to pay 50 kopecks or 1 ruble to the chancery office as a fine.

Father Swienzizsky venerated the Blessed Virgin Mary and the Holy Rosary. He would never preach a sermon without stressing the attributes and virtues of the Mother of God and he requested his parishioners to emulate her way of life. All of the Beresan Catholics were thankful to him for promoting the praying of the rosary.

He translated the small Polish rosary book into German as a result of which the rosary was first sung in Rastadt and later found its way to all of the Beresan colonies.

He also introduced organ music in the Beresan at first hiring Robert Koch (Bärtel) to fulfill this position, and had him take instruction from his sister or niece. Robert Koch in turn taught Joseph Fleck from Landau and Philipp Loran from Karlsruhe, who subsequently taught others throughout the Beresan district.

In 1872 Father Swienzizsky built the present parish church. For almost 30 years he worked as a faithful servant of the Lord in the community of Rastadt, until he became old and senile. He became hard of hearing, his vision began to fail, his speech was difficult to undersand due to a scarcity of teeth. Therefore, he was no longer able to perform his priestly duties adequately.

Regretfully, and with heavy hearts, the people of Rastadt and München requested the bishop of the diocese to send them a younger priest. Their request was soon granted.

Father Swienzizsky retired, and for a while he lived in Nikolayev then he lived with his niece, Kasimira, who had married the landowner, Ignatowicz.

He died there on the 6 July 1887 at the age of 90 and was buried in Rastadt. May he rest in peace.

FATHER NIKOLAUS MITZIG *Administrator*
12 July 1873 to 29 August 1874

Father N. Mitzig was born in 1849 in Göbel and ordained on the 12 April 1873 by Bishop Zottmann. His first position was as administrator in Rastadt. He was enthusiastic about his work and had great plans for his first parish.

During the latter days of the old priest, Christian discipline had dwindled and he wished to rekindle this foundation of all virtues. In his enthusiasm he sometimes became too rough for the people of Rastadt, who had become used to the slower pace of the old priest, and consequently were not pleased. As a result of this, a group organized who were determined to oppose the priest in his efforts. Accusations were made against him. After the inquiry Father Mitzig was declared innocent, but he decided it was best to move to some other parish.

Before he left Rastadt, he made a touching valedictory address; all who heard it were deeply moved and wept. On the 2 September 1874 he moved to Katharinental where he was sent by his Bishop. In Katharinental he carried on courageously, but with more prudence and forethought. After two years of diligent work in his priestly duties, he moved to Rothammel in the deanery of Kamenka where he carried on his work with the same enthusiasm and vigour.

In 1880 he became parish priest and dean in Katharinenstadt on the Volga. This was the last posting of his short life. As a result of the over-exertion in his duties, he became weakened, seriously ill and died in 1881, having received the last sacraments. He was buried in the Catholic graveyard in Katharinenstadt by the vicar-general and now Bishop, Antonius Zerr.

After Father Mitzig left, Rastadt was again supervised by Father Swienzizsky.

GEORGE STRÖMEL
28 February 1875 to the present time

Father G. Strömel was born on the 8 October 1851 in the colony of Kamenka in the province of Saratov.

After completing his studies in the parish school, he attended the famous private school of the teacher, Heinrich Matz, in preparation for entering the seminary in Saratov. The examiners, Father R. Reichert and Father F. X. Klimaschewsky, gave him a good report and in 1867 he entered the boy's seminary. He completed his courses here in 1872 and, feeling the call to the priesthood, he entered the clerical seminary which he completed in good standing in 1875. He was ordained on the 6 January 1875 by Bishop F. Zottmann.

At this time a delegation of two had just arrived from Rastadt requesting Bishop Zottmann to send the young priest there. The request was granted and Father Strömel was sent to the large parish of Rastadt. He was officially installed as a locum tenens on the 1 March 1875 by the Dean of Landau, Johannes Burgardt. The young priest soon realized that some things had to be torn down while others had to be built up. He found the schools were backward in their teaching and too few in numbers. Consequently, he worked in the community with the district mayor, Andreas Seelinger, in obtaining district schools for Rastadt and München with teachers who were certified in their profession. These were the first district schools in Beresan.

Father Strömel conscientiously fulfilled his priestly duties and by his amiable manners gained the respect of the community, not only that of his own parishioners, but also that of the authorities.

In 1882 he was named parish priest and in 1910 he received the golden pectoral cross as a token of appreciation for his service.

Father Strömel is the senior priest of the Beresan district and is an energetic member of the Clemens Society.

Parish Endowments

The priest receives rent from 120 dessiatines of parish land, as well as a small amount of money from the community.

The surplice charges are: baptism 50 kopecks, marriages 3 rubles, publishing of banns 50 kopecks, funerals 50 kopecks, low mass 1 ruble and high mass 1 ruble, 50 kopecks.

The Parish Church

The first church in Rastadt was built of clay in 1812. It was small and rather low containing one altar, some holy pictures and a very peculiar pulpit, the top of which consisted of a barrel that had been cut in two.

The second church was built of fieldstone in 1830 and lasted until 1872. It was located in the same place as the present church. The church was 90 feet long and 42 feet wide. There were two entrances, one from the front and one from the left side (ladies entrance). The church contained an altar, a pulpit, a confessional and some holy pictures. The bell tower stood beside the church.

The New Parish Church

In 1871 the people of the district decided that the parish church was too small for the large number of people in the colonies of Rastadt and München. Some of the men in the community started a proposal to build a new church. The proposal found support in the community and a building committee was appointed.

The church had only 100 rubles on hand, the remaining money having to be raised through donations and by community assessments. A building contractor accepted a proposal to build the church for 21,000 rubles. He would provide the lumber and iron, but the colonists had to provide whatever else was needed. The church was started and finished in 1872 at a total cost of 35,000 rubles.

The patron of the church is St. Francis Xavier. The church is 120 feet long, 48 feet wide and 36 feet high. There are two towers which extend 111 feet in height. In the one tower there is a large bell and in the other, three small bells.

A large stone wall surrounds the church. On the inside of the church there are three altars, one confessional, a pulpit, an organ which cost 4,000 rubles, and many holy pictures. The presbytery has recently been enhanced with wall paintings. Accurate descriptions are lacking.

The Grave Yard

The graveyard is approximately 200 yards south of the church and, as far as is known, has been in the same place since the founding of the colony. Some years ago it was enlarged and surrounded by a large stone wall.

The Rectory

The first rectory, built in 1812, was made of clay brick and was used until 1847. At this tme, the present rectory was built by the community and made of field stone. They obtained a loan from the Fürsorge Committee to be paid back over a 10 year period.

The rectory cost the community 1322 rubles, 95 kopecks. It is 48 feet long, 24 feet wide and 8 1/2 feet high, with seven rooms and a corridor.

School Affairs

The first school was apparently built immediately after the settlers arrived. The second school was built in 1843.

The present school was built in 1894, of good fieldstone, at a cost of 12,000 rubles. It is 120 feet long, 16 feet wide and 12 feet high to the roof. There is a corridor on either side and it contains five large class rooms. There are five teachers and 215 school children.

Each teacher receives 380 rubles, two of the teachers being paid by the Semtsvo. The organist receives 400 rubles.

The first school teacher in Rastadt was Ignaz Fritz. The others who followed were Peter Eberts, Schmidt, Johannes Heck, J. Weinberger, I. Gass, R. Schneider, Guttenberg, Orbritschkewitsch, among others.

Priests who came from the
Parish of Rastadt

FATHER JAKOB SEELINGER *Honorary Canon*

Father J. Seelinger was born in Rastadt on the 30 October 1853. He entered the seminary in Saratov in 1868, completed his studies in 1876 and on the 31 October of the same year he was ordained. He was appointed administrator of the parish of Karlsruhe on the 17 February 1877, where he immediately started to build a new church. The usual plans for the colonist churches did not appeal to him and he went abroad to obtain plans more to his liking.

These plans were altered somewhat by architect, Korf, and subsequently were approved by the authorities. The church was then started and finished as noted previously.

The success for the completion of the rather attractive church must be largely given to Father Seelinger. Through his activity and tenacious energy, and his constant encouragement, he inspired the people of Karlsruhe so that they always brought additional money until the church was completed.

In 1886 he was sent to Eichwald as parish priest and was made dean of the Jekatharinoslav deanery. In 1890 he was made honorary canon. At his own request, in 1895, he was relieved of his position as dean and sent as parish priest to Josephstal on the Baraboi. Here he worked for many years. In the latter years he was often ill and at one time he had to go abroad to recuperate. His recovery being only temporary, he became seriously ill in 1912 and, after much suffering, died on the 20 July 1912 in his home in Rastadt.

FATHER LEONHARD EBERLE

Father L. Eberle was born in Rastadt on the 28 October 1870. His father died when the boy was only 2 years old. He then moved to München to live with his step-father, where he remained until he was 10 years old.

In 1880 he returned to Rastadt to his grandfather, who sent him to the district school and also to private school.

Well educated, but with a rather unhealthy constitution, he entered the seminary in Saratov in 1883. But, after one month, he became ill and had to return home.

In 1886 he returned to the seminary for the second time and completed his studies in 1897. When Bishop Anton Zerr was conducting confirmation in the Beresan in 1897, he also ordained deacon L. Eberle as a priest. On the 7 December 1897 he was sent to the newly founded vicariate of Schönfeld in the parish of Landau. Here he worked hard at his priestly duties until the 12 October 1912.

He travelled considerably, on two occasions going to Jerusalem where he visited the holy places where Jesus lived, worked and suffered.

On the 10 May 1909 he undertook the difficult journey to America to visit his mother, where he met many of their acquaintances who had migrated from his homeland in Russia. (He may write about it in the "Klemens" on his return).

On the 20 September 1912 he was made curate and dean at Kamenka on the Volga and on the 6 December 1912 he was named parish priest.

FATHER ZYRIAK REICHERT

Father Reichert was born in Rastadt in 1871 and ordained a priest on the 19 September 1893.

For many years he worked in Elsass and at the present time he is the religious instructor in the Central School in Beresan and the Girl's School in Landau.

Lay People born in Rastadt
or who worked there

FRANZ-JOSEPH BURGER *Physician*

Franz-Joseph Burger was born in Niederbronn in Alsace, the son of Theobald Burger and Maria-Eva Arnheiter.

After completing his studies in medicine in his home town, he was successful in passing the examinations as a physician. Subsequently, he was invited by the Russian Government to be a physician in the city of Kherson in South Russia. He accepted the invitation and went to Odessa on the 1 October 1808. The colonies of the Kutschurgan had been settled by this time and, since there were many people ill, he was requested to go there. He went to the Kutschurgan colonies and temporarily settled in Baden, from which location he tended to all of the sick people in the district. Unfortunately, his dear wife soon died.

The Beresan colonies were being settled in 1809 and 1810. Since his appointment as physician in Kherson was being delayed, he moved to Rastadt and settled there as a colonist with his only child, Magdalena, who was born on the 2 February 1808.

On the 1 October 1811 he married Katharina Götzfried. At this time there were many epidemics among the colonists and the physician, Burger, did his best to attend to all of the sick, but he himself soon became ill and died.

His widow, Katharina, then moved to Odessa where she became acquainted with Von Lau, the administrator of the Odessa office of the Fürsorge Committee and lived with him as his common-law wife.

The daughter, Magdalena, child of the first wife of the physician, went to live with the Götzfried family. She was married in 1824 to Konrad Bengert from München. After his death she married a Kessel. When he died she married the widower, Rudolf Schulz, on the 16 April 1835. She had a son, Jakob, who is still living. Jakob, in turn, was the father of Father Florian Schulz.

IGNAZ FRITZ *School Teacher*

I. Fritz was born in Völkersbach, Baden in 1781 and went to Russia in 1809. He settled in the colony of Rastadt and was probably the first school teacher there.

He was well educated and was the main opponent of Ignaz Lindl, who was propagating his false doctrines in Rastadt at this time.

PETER EBERTS *School Teacher*

Peter Eberts was born in Rülzheim, Rhinepalatinate in 1797, the son of Franz Eberts and Katharina Hutzler. He came to Russia with his parents in 1809, where his father settled in Karlsruhe as a colonist.

In 1811 the family moved to Rastadt, where his father operated the crown flour mill on a rental basis until his death soon after. His widow, who was a very energetic woman, continued with the rental of the flour mill for many years and also obtained some land. Her eldest son, Peter, was a diligent, capable boy who attended the school of the lay brother Dominik Okulitsch of the Society of Jesus. He was a good student and when not in school he enriched his knowledge by reading in various subjects. He also wrote various articles in the "Unterhaltungsblatt" which show his ability and education, especially the article "The importance of home industry in the life of the German colonists in South Russia."

He taught school for some years and later became the mayor. During the Passion of Holy Week he sang the "Petrus" in church.

A wealthy man, he owned four flour mills, a warehouse, and was a contractor for the military depot at Vosnesensk. He also had many connections with the neighbouring landlords. He died in Rastadt in 1869.

JOHANNES HECK *School Teacher*

Johannes Heck, a colonist of Rastadt, was the school teacher there for many years and a conscientious assistant to Father Swienzizsky as a teacher and religious instructor in the school.

He was a good natured fellow, but the paddling and strappings that he administered to his students for various kinds of mischief were innumerable and remembered by all.

ROBERT KOCH *Organist*

Robert Koch, colonist of Rastadt, was the first organist in Rastadt. He was a capable, industrious man.

He learned to play the organ from the sister or niece of Father Swienzizsky. Later, he himself gave lessons.

He was one of the first estate owners in the Beresan.

SEBASTIAN SEELINGER *Organist and Music Teacher*

Sebastian Seelinger was born in Rastadt on the 24 February 1855, the son of Andreas Seelinger and Margaretha Fischer.

As a student in the parish school, he already showed a love for singing and music. He started to take lessons from his aunt, Theresia Belousova, but on the advice of the district secretary, Franz Domansky, his father sent him to Odessa in 1871. He attended the music school there under the direction of the famous organist, Joseph Swirowitsch.

In 1872 he returned to Rastadt and, along with his brother Georg, he took the position of sexton and organized a group of singers and an orchestra.

From 1873 until 1874 he was also a teacher in the parish school.

In 1882 he was appointed organist at Speier, where he again organized a group of singers and an orchestra and instituted the singing of polyphonic hymns.

In 1888 he was invited to Eichwald as organist and choir director. He again organized an orchestra, with 17 instruments, and inspired the entire district with his music and church songs.

In 1891 he returned to Rastadt and organized a new orchestra. When his brother Georg resigned as sexton, Sebastian took over the position which he held until 1909.

In 1911 he was made sexton in München where he organized a 25 piece orchestra. For some years he has lived in Nikolayev where he has been busy composing church music. Some of his best known compositions are "Alleluia" (1910) with an organ accompaniment (1914), the so-named "Great Mass," the closing vesper hymn, "Alma redemptoris," "Salve Regina, " "Regina coeli," "Veni Creator," "O Salutaris Hostia," "Tantum Ergo" and "Pange Lingua." He also wrote waltzes, marches and other lighter music.

Some of his student organists were Stephan Böhm, Joseph Deibele, Nikolaus Loran, Rochus Böhm, Joseph Zimmerman.

In 1882 he was appointd organ tuner for the firm of Wilhelm Sauer in Frankfurt on the Oder.

GEORG SEELINGER *Organist*

Georg Seelinger was born in Rastadt on the 5 August 1852, the son of Andreas Seelinger and Margaretha Fischer.

He attended the local parish school and then took music lessons from his brother, Sebastian.

In 1871, he accepted the position of sexton in his home in Rastadt, which position he held until 1896.

From 1871 until 1873 he was also the religious instructor in the local parish school.

From 1893 until 1899 he held the position of district judge.

In 1901 he was the mayor of Rastadt. He was a very talented, highly respected man, and an excellent singer.

LEONHARD SEELINGER *Organist*

Leonhard Seelinger was born in the colony of Rastadt on the 4 June 1879, the son of Sebastian Seelinger and Walburga Hirsch.

He attended the local district school and, at the same time, received instruction in music from his father.

After studying music for some time, he accepted the position as organist in Schönfeld in 1897.

In 1900 he was drafted into the army where he served at the front with the regimental orchestra, becoming the band master nine months later.

In 1904 he was appointed the deputy Regimental band leader and was at Santepu and Mukden during the celebrated battles of the Russian-Japanese War.

Here, as the oldest medical orderly in the field hospital, he was praised by his senior officer for his energy and initiative.

During his flight, after the battle of Mukden, all of the equipment of the regimental band was lost. Seelinger performed an almost unbelievable task, rewriting from memory all of the marches and other compositions which they had previously played. He also rewrote some other well known pieces by whistling the tunes to himself. Thus, after several days he restored what was lost. For this he was praised by his superiors and received 300 rubles as an honorarium. He also received the silver medal on the Georgius ribbon, inscribed, "For valiant service," as well as a second silver medal on a Stanislaus ribbon inscribed, "For Zeal." He received a testimonial from Korotkewitsch, Commander of the 56th Zhitomir Infantry Regiment, lauding him for his excellent musical productions.

The Commander wished to take him back to Petersburg with him after the war, but his failing health did not permit this. He accepted his discharge and returned home in 1906 and soon thereafter was appointed organist in München.

Since 1908 he has been the organist in Rastadt, where he has once more organized an excellent orchestra and choral group. He has also written more lovely compositions of which only the march, "Vival," has been published.

ERASMUS SEELINGER *Organist*

Erasmus Seelinger was born on the 10 October 1880 in the colony of Rastadt, the son of Sebastian Seelinger and Walburga Hirsch.

He was taught music and singing by his father, and finished his education at the local district school.

When his brother, Leonhard, had to join the army in 1900, he accepted the position as organist in Schönfeld.

In 1904 he became organist in Landau, where he also taught music in the girls school there.

He distinguished himself during the 100 year jubilee of the Beresan colonies as his songs and music for the celebration were magnificent.

JOHANN SEELINGER *Organist*

Johann Seelinger was born in Rastadt on the 18 October 1882, the son of Sebastian Seelinger and Walburga Hirsch. As his brothers before him, he also received musical instruction from his father.

After completing his military service, he took over the position of sexton in the colony of München. A few years ago he left for America.

JOSEPH FROHLICH *Teacher*

Joseph Fröhlich was born in Rastadt on the 18 February 1885. After completing his studies in the local district school of Rastadt, he attended a private tutor in preparation for the examinations for community teacher.

In 1906 he obtained the diploma as community teacher in Nikolayev and soon thereafter was appointed to the community school in his home.

In 1912 he was appointed principal of the school.

MARKUS KOPP *Teacher*

Markus Kopp, son of Michael, was born in Rastadt on the 22 February 1886.

After completing his studies in the district school he obtained the diploma as community teacher and in 1907 he took a teaching position in Rastadt.

In 1911 he went to Katharinental as teacher, but remained only a short time when he again returned to Rastadt.

CHRISTIAN SEELINGER *Secretary*

Christian Seelinger was born in Rastadt. He completed five classes in the Seminary in Saratov.

For some years he was a house teacher, then secretary for the community and the district of Rastadt. Later he was teacher, sexton and secretary of Neubaden.

Presently, he is the village secretary in Josephstal.

JOHANN HIRSCH *Secretary*

Johann Hirsch, a colonist of Rastadt, learned his trade as apprentice with the Fürsorge Committee and was the secretary of the Rastadt district for many years. When the colonists' rights were taken away from them in 1871 and all the government offices were now conducting their business in Russian, he had to resign. He lived for a few more years and died in his home in Rastadt, a good, righteous Christian.

ANDREAS KOSCHKIN *Secretary*

Andreas Koschkin was born in Moscow in the 15 November 1862. He completed his training in the military army school, entered the service, and in 1901 he was discharged with the rank of Government secretary. Following this he had various positions until 1910, when he was appointed district secretary in Rastadt where he is still working today.

NIKODEMUS SEELINGER *Lawyer*

Nikodemus Seelinger was born in Rastadt in 1888, the son of Johann Seelinger and Barbara Baumann.

He completed his studies in the highschool, then attended the New Russian Imperial University in Odessa where he completed the studies in the faculty of Law. Presently, he is a lawyer in one of the high courts in Odessa.

LUDWIG EBERTS *Veterinarian*

Ludwig Eberts was born in Rastadt in 1857, the son of Paul Eberts and Katharina Weber.

Having prepared himself well, he entered the seminary in Saratov in 1871. After completing the courses at the so-named minor seminary, he entered the University in Dorpat, completing the course in 1881.

After this he worked for some years for the nobleman Martinovsky. In 1887 he entered the Government service in Berdyansk where he is still working. He was a conscientious and trusted official and, after a few years, was appointed Councillor of State.

JOHANN SEELINGER *Merchant*

Johann Seelinger, son of Anton, was born in Rastadt on the 10 May 1864.

He completed his studies in the four class highschool in Vosnesensk and then was the secretary in his home community for some years.

In 1894 he joined the merchants guild in Vosnesensk where he is still living.

At the present time he is the president of the Vosnesensk Credit Society, a member of the town council, honorary member of the four-class Vosnesensk City School where, in the services of the Ministry of Public Education, he was appointed Government Secretary.

For his services he received the Order of Stanislaus, third class. He has a large estate, 2147 dessiatines in all, where he carries on agriculture and cattle raising.

In 1886 he married Miss Barbara Baumann. His eldest son is a lawyer; two younger sons and a daughter are presently in highschool in Vosnesensk.

ANDREAS FISCHER *Shepherd*

Andreas Fischer was born in 1798 in Hördt, Rhinepalatinate, the son of Johann Fischer and Johanna Bertsch.

He came to Russia with his parents, who settled in Rastadt as colonists. He worked for a shepherd to learn the business and, after he received his certificate, he worked as a shepherd for a Frenchman in the Crimea. Later he worked for General Koble in Tiligul in sheep breeding.

Tired of being a subordinate, he returned to Rastadt. As an experienced, good Christian, he was soon appointed mayor by the community. He remained in this position for seven years during the Crimean War (1855) and for some time thereafter.

He performed his duties to the satisfaction of the entire community. For a long time he was a trustee of the church. He died at an advanced age in his home in Rastadt.

The Celebration of the
100 Year Jubilee
of the Beresan Colonies
in the colony of Rastadt on the 10 October 1910

Although many of the colonists of Rastadt had attended the general jubilee for the Beresan colonies held in Landau on the 30 September 1910, they wished to celebrate the occasion in their own locale.

The celebration began at 11 o'clock in the morning by celebration of mass in the parish church of Rastadt. Before the service began, Father L. Eberle ascended to the pulpit and gave a long speech in which he explained the purpose of the celebration. He urged the people to thank God in Heaven for the many favours and graces which He bestowed upon the colonists, in spite of the fact that at times things appeared hopeless and difficult. He also reminded the people of the many favours which were bestowed upon them by the

Russian Government and their debt of gratitude to the ruling family. Following his speech, High Mass was celebrated by Father Strömel with assistance from Fathers Eberle and Hein.

The music and singing, under the direction of organist, Leonhard Seelinger, was elevating and superb.

Following the mass, the priests and the honoured guests led the parade to the Rastadt school house. Among the guests were A. Kraus, member of the provincial assembly, his brother, J. Kraus, J. Seelinger, the Pristaw of Lachoma, the postmaster and many other guests. At the school house they were greeted by the choral group from München and Rastadt, who sang a march for them.

The entertainment committee invited the guests into the school house where dinner for the occasion was arranged in four large rooms. Following the dinner, toasts were proposed to His Majesty the Czar by A. Kraus in Russian and by Father Strömel in German. At its completion, there was a thunderous 'hurrah' from the crowd and the singing of the National Anthem. Following this the celebration continued and, on behalf of those present, a most respectful telegram was sent to His Majesty the Czar. Those present received many congratulatory notes from various places. The celebration was very inspiring due mainly to the very fine music and singing. All of the guests remarked that it was 'beautiful and splendid.'

A telegram was received from His Majesty on the 24 November 1910 in Russian; "To the Governor of the Kherson Province: In response to the expression of true allegiance by the citizens of the Rastadt Wolost (district) as transmitted by the Minister of the Interior in a telegram of October 11, His Majesty wrote down in his own hand; 'Sincere thanks to all.'"

The present Conditions and Wealth
of the Colony of Rastadt

There are 338 lots in the colony and 3807 people, all of Catholic denomination. There are 21 Russian families, 9 Jewish families and 2 families of gypsies. There are 198 families who do not own land. Two hundred and ten families moved to America and 58 families moved to Siberia. There are 48 hired men and 34 Russian maids. The annual salary for a hired man is 130 to 150 rubles, for a maid, 100 to 130 rubles.

Tradesmen are as follows: blacksmiths 11, cabinet makers 7, wheelrights 7, shoemakers 8, tinsmith 1.

There are two steam flourmills and one windmill.

The community land amounts to 5684 dessiatines, of which 5124 dessiatines were for agriculture, 202 dessiatines for pasture, 34 dessiatines were hills, 98 dessiatines were vineyards, 13 dessiatines were under water, and 25 dessiatines were for the Odessa-Bachmatsch Railroad.

A dessiatine of land costs 225 rubles; to rent a dessiatine of land for one year costs 16 rubles. There were 38 farmers on approximately 25,000 dessiatines of bought land.

The stock in the community was: horses 1648, cows 927, oxen 2, sheep 256, pigs 608.

Seeded in the year 1912 was: winter wheat 228 dessiatines, summer wheat 1807 dessiatines, barley 2400 dessiatines, oats 425 dessiatines, rye 272 dessiatines, corn 290 dessiatines, and potatoes 75 dessiatines.

There was also a medical assistant (feldscher), a midwife, and one pharmacist. In addition, there was a small credit bank, a co-operative society warehouse, and six small shops, one bar and four beer halls.

No further statistics are available.

The Colony of München

The colony of München is located in the province of Kherson in the district of Ananyev. It is 141 versts from the city of Kherson, 100 versts from the capital of Ananyev and one verst from the district of Rastadt. The colony is laid out in a northwest to south direction and is located on the right bank of the Chitchekleya River. The main street is 1.5 verst long and there are three side streets. The layout of the colony has the appearance of a ship in that the upper colony is fairly high and the lower colony is quite low, so much so that it is often flooded during high water. It was necessary to move 19 houses to higher ground.

The finest buildings in the colony are the church, the rectory, the new school house and the building of the Co-operative Society.

The architecture of the buildings is similar to that of the other colonies. In front of many of the homes one finds lovely flower gardens and shade trees. In earlier times some of the older colonists had nice orchards, but presently, these are mostly planted with vegetables and potatoes. Most of the lots are enclosed by stone fences. The side facing the street is painted white with calcimine. There is plenty of water in the colony and most of the wells contain good tasting water. There are also many stones near the colony which are of good quality.

The main occupations of the colonists are agriculture and cattle raising.

The climate in the summertime is rather unhealthy and, as a result, there is a great deal of illness, with fever, measles, dropsy and scarlet fever being common. The people are strong and of light complexion. The dialect is Palatinate as in the south Rhinepalatinate. There are many hard working people in München.

The name München, was given to the colony by the colonist Heinrich Adler, who was born in München, the capital of Bavaria. Later he moved elsewhere.

When the first colonists came in the spring of 1910, there was nothing but shrubs and long grass. The promised houses were not built and, as a result, they had to live in reed huts until the Crown houses were finished. It would appear that people had lived here sometime in the past as one found stone foundations in various places, skeletons of people and fragments of pottery, as well as various old kitchen utensils.

The colonists travelled to Russia from Germany over land by way of the city of Radzivillov, where they rested for a time. From here on, they received a daily allowance until they arrived at their destination, where they received food instead.

Those who had their own transportation received a travelling loan from the Crown and the others were transported by the Crown.

From Radzivillov the colonists were separated according to their destination and were led to Odessa under the guidance of soldiers. When they arrived in Odessa in the fall of 1809, they were quartered with the Liebental and Kutschurgan colonists on the orders of the Duke of Richelieu.

In the spring of 1810 they moved to their own settlements.

List of the Settlers in the
Colony of München
and their home of origin
in the year 1811

1. **Nikolaus Riedinger** 25, from Kandel, Rhinepalatinate.
WIFE: Theresia 26.

2. **Martin Becht** 38, from Hördt, Rhinepalatinate.
WIFE: Margaretha 48.
CHILDREN: Joseph 11, Barbara 13, Maria 9.

3. **Michael Weber** 24, from Kandel, Rhinepalatinate.
WIFE: Maria 23.
CHILDREN: Philipp 1.

4. **Rudolf Braun** 31, from Hördt, Rhinepalatinate.
WIFE: Rosina 33.
CHILDREN: Maria 1.

5. **Jakob Thomas** 33, from Offenbach, Rhinepalatinate.
WIFE: Barbara 31.
CHILDREN: Magnus 6, Anna 8, Margaretha 2.

6. **Adam Seifert** 38, from Wörth, Rhinepalatinate.
WIFE: Rosina 28.

CHILDREN: Johann 7, Georg 4.
    7. **Philipp Mayer** 21, from Kuhardt, Rhinepalatinate.
WIFE: Franziska 23.
CHILDREN: Elisabeth 1.
    8. **Heinrich Steiff** 43, from Hördt, Rhinepalatinate.
WIFE: Marianna 39.
CHILDREN: Elisabeth 5.
    9. **Eva Hoffer** 39, widow, from Hasenberg, Rhinepalatinate.
CHILDREN: Johann 11, Eva 19, Her second husband was Joseph Friedmann 33.
    10. **Joseph Karl** 41, from Öftersheim, near Schwezingen, Baden.
WIFE: Elisabeth 38.
    11. **Andreas Stübich** 25, from Hördt, Alsace.
WIFE: Katharina 21.
CHILDREN: Heinrich 1.
MOTHER: Maria Bast 51.
    12. **Georg Leitner** 41, from Birlenbach, Alsace.
WIFE: Eva 45.
CHILDREN: Michael 15, Eva 12, Barbara 4.
    13. **Franz Flick** 45, from Kandel, Rhinepalatinate.
WIFE: Dorothea 45.
CHILDREN: Nikolaus 21, Franz 15, Elisabeth 18, Barbara 6.
    14. **Johann Giesser** 49, from Kusel, Rhinepalatinate.
WIFE: Maria 49.
CHILDREN: Johann 12, Karl 9.
    15. **Georg Kowitz** 43, from Bitschhofen, Alsace.
WIFE: Maria 29.
CHILDREN: Georg 15, Johann 11, Maria 16.
    16. **Georg Hübner** 30, from Lobsann, Alsace.
WIFE: Katharina 29.
CHILDREN: Georg 3.
    17. **Johann Schirner** 37, from Karlsbad, Bohemia.
WIFE: Maria 47.
    18. **Christian Herauff** 57, from Kandel, Rhinepalatinate.
WIFE: Katharina 56.
CHILDREN: Anton 21, Marianna 27.
SISTER'S SON: Adam Herauff 3.
    19. **Andreas Zwickel** 47, from Lauterschwan, Rhinepalatinate.
WIFE: Maria 33.
CHILDREN: Katharina 19, Rosina 5.
    20. **Joseph Stroh** 27, from Kandel, Rhinepalatinate.
WIFE: Elisabeth 23.
CHILDREN: Katharina 1.
    21. **Joseph Kessel** 46, from Hilsbach, Baden.

WIFE: Barbara 36.
CHILDREN: Johann 21, Franz 19, Adam 4, Michael 2, Maria 17, Augusta 7, Elisabeth 1.
    22. **Peter Weiland** 36, from Hilsbach, Baden.
WIFE: Elisabeth 31.
CHILDREN: Adam 4, Sebastian 3, Rosina 17, Regina 15, Elisabeth 8, Franziska 4.
    23. **Georg Dekert** 23, from Steinsfurt, Baden.
WIFE: Barbara 37.
CHILDREN: Christoph 11.
    24. **Benedikt Heck** 49, from Dörrenbach, Rhinepalatinate.
WIFE: Barbara 43.
CHILDREN: Johann 11, Jakob 8.
    25. **Franz Kosak** 33, from Gernenbach, Prussia.
WIFE: Elisabeth 29.
    26. **Anton Wiedmann** 43, from Hilsbach, Baden.
WIFE: Maria 44.
CHILDREN: Franz 17, Margaretha 18, Regina 8.
    27. **Johann Wollbaum** 29, from Mollwitz, Prussia.
WIFE: Maria 29.
CHILDREN: Matthias 13, Anton 3, Christina 11, Maria 6 months.
    28. **Georg Schropp** 56, from Odenheim, Baden.
SECOND WIFE: Julianna 25.
CHILDREN: Sebastian 23, Maria 12.
    29. **Michael Sprauer** 56, from Röschwoog, Alsace.
WIFE: Maria 46.
CHILDREN: Valentin 27, Christina 24.
    30. **Peter Dettler** 24, from Göcklingen, Rhinepalatinate.
WIFE: Bernhardina 20.
CHILDREN: Valentin 1.
    31. **Gottlieb Dettler** 37, from Göcklingen, Rhinepalatinate.
WIFE: Maria 27.
CHILDREN: Johann 1.
    32. **Siegfried Helfrich** 44, from Weidental, Rhinepalatinate.
WIFE: Margaretha 34.
CHILDREN: Jakob 11, Magdalena 7.
    33. **Michael Friedel** 27, from Waldersbach, Alsace.
WIFE: Katharina 25.
CHILDREN: Philipp 2, Margaretha 1.
    34. **Simon Schwan** 29, from Völkersweiler, Rhinepalatinate.
WIFE: Maria 26.
    35. **Anselm Kniel** 43, from Tiefenbach, Baden.
WIFE: Elisabeth 42.
CHILDREN: Georg 15, Elisabeth 17, Marianna 7.

36. **Simon Schäfer** 25, from Völkersweiler, Rhinepalatinate.
WIFE: Marianna 21.
CHILDREN: Simon 1.
37. **Peter Faller** 43, from Steinweiler, Rhinepalatinate.
WIFE: Maria 41.
CHILDREN: Elisabeth 20, Maria 14.
38. **Jakob Schäfer** 37, from Gelnhausen, Hesse.
WIFE: Elisabeth 25.
CHILDREN: Peter 1, Elisabeth 3.
39. **Philipp Hermann** 27, from Steinweiler, Rhinepalatinate.
WIFE: Franziska 27.
CHILDREN: Johann 1, Barbara 2.
40. **Maximilian Ackermann** 23, from Godramstein, Alsace,
Lutheran.
WIFE: Maria 20.
CHILDREN: Margaretha 1.
41. **Jakob Ackermann** 43, from Godramstein, Alsace, Lutheran.
WIFE: Susanna 45.
CHILDREN: Andreas 16, Peter 7, Wilhelm 2, Margaretha 17, Barbara 10, Susanna 5.
42. **Georg Lessinsky** 47, from Kaiserslautern, Rhinepalatinate.
WIFE: Katharina 37.
CHILDREN: Ignaz 5, Katharina 16, Dorothea 7, Margaretha 2.
43. **Georg Heptner** 33, from Lautenbach, Baden, Lutheran.
WIFE: Katharina 35.
CHILDREN: Georg 7, Johann 4, Maria 11.
44. **Franz Scherger** 48, from Hockenheim, Baden.
WIFE: Eva
CHILDREN: Adam 3, Georg 1, Margaretha 21.
ADOPTED: Franz Mayer 10.
45. **Georg Bengert** 31, from Bergzabern, Rhinepalatinate.
WIFE: Friederika 35.
CHILDREN: Konrad 5, Philippina 9, Katharina 7.
46. **Karl Zentner** 35, from Kandel, Rhinepalatinate.
WIFE: Agnes 29.
CHILDREN: Regina 5.
47. **Leonhard Gicherig** 29, from Lauterbach, Rhinepalatinate.
WIFE: Katharina 39.
CHILDREN: Lorenz 7, Leonhard 1, Maria 9.
48. **Konrad Bengert** 28, from Bergzabern, Rhinepalatinate.
WIFE: Barbara 24.
49. **Joseph Nikolaus** 25, from Bergzabern, Rhinepalatinate.
WIFE: Josepha Bengert, 23.
Barbara Bengert 20, sister of Josepha.

(a) Jakob Schreiber 7, orphan, from Klimbach, Alsace.

50. **Katharina Zentner** widow of Joseph Zentner 25, moved to Landau, where she remarried.

The Beginnings
of München

The colony of München was founded in the spring of 1810. The Crown houses were built by experienced men from the Liebental district. Every family received money to purchase oxen and the necessary implements. Most of the colonists were completely destitute and had to be assisted by the Crown. Only a few colonists brought along some essentials from their old homes, the total worth amounting to 1170 rubles.

Most of the Crown houses were completed by January 1811. The colony contained 48 Catholic families, 95 men and 97 women. There were also 8 Lutheran families with 8 men and 8 women, the total amounting to 208 people.

The community owned 47 horses, 149 horned cattle, 45 wagons, 314 loads of hay, 10 ploughs and 10 harrows.

The seed for the year 1811-1812 was winter wheat 102 tschetwert and summer wheat 102 tschertwert.

Tradesmen were as follows:
TAILORS: Nikolaus Riedinger (later moved to Landau), Rudolf Braun, Johann Giesser, Simon Schäfer.
WAGON-MAKER: Georg Hübner.
SHOE-MAKER: Karl Ludwig Zentner.
SHEPHERD: Georg Kowitz.
WEAVER: Jakob Schäfer.
MILLER: Leonhard Giegerich.
BRICKMAKER: Michael Gottselig.
BRICK-LAYERS: Joseph Kessel, Peter Weiland, Anton Wiedmann, Anselm Kniel and Gregor Lesinsky.

In 1817, there were 48 families and 228 people, 118 male and 110 female.

Their property consisted of 126 horses, 298 horned cattle, 92 pigs, 29 plows, 24 harrows, 51 wagons, 26 spinning wheels.

Tradesmen were: Joiner 1, lathe worker 1, miller 1, tailor 1, shoemakers 2, and 6 bricklayers.

Seeded for the year 1817-1818 was as follows:

	Tschetwert	Tschetwerik
Winter wheat	1	0
Rye	57	0
Summer wheat	69	7
Barley	23	5
Oats	33	6
Potatoes	90	2
Buckwheat	0	2
Corn	2	4
Millet	5	5.5
Peas		5.0
Lentils		0.5
Beans		5.5
Hemp		1.5
Flax		0.5

The Community Land of the
colony of München

The community land of the colony of München comprises 2940 dessiatines on the right side of the Chitchekleya River. It forms a rectangle 13 versts long and approximately 1 verst wide. On the south it borders on the community land of Worms, on the west on Bandarevka and the Greeks, in the north on Kratovka (Schardt) and on the east, the river and the colony of Rastadt.

From the hill, in a south-west direction, the surface of the land is nearly level with only a few hollows indenting the contour. The soil is good, black loam from 28 to 42 inches thick. When the weather is suitable most cereals yield well.

In 1820 the colonists wished to extend their colony to the southwest; however, since they could not find any water, they gave up the idea and remained where they were.

On orders from the authorities in 1822, trees and orchards were planted, however, since they were poorly adapted, they did not do well. Still, the colonists who had some knowledge of growing fruit trees and spent more time at it were able to grow unbelievably fine fruit.

In 1842 E. Hahn, the director of the Fürsorge Committee, again gave orders that woods, gardens and orchards were to be planted. Those that were planted properly did well and were soon in bloom. In 1871 all the benefits from these plantings came to naught. München on one occasion was flooded and, as a result, was severely damaged. At least half the colony was under water and the river was 2 versts wide.

The Parish of München

At the present time there are 154 lots in the colony and, including the hamlets, there are 3550 people living there, nearly all of the Catholic faith. The maids and hired men are Orthodox.

Many hamlets belong to this parish, namely: Dvorjanka, Novaselevka, Karlevka, Domanevka, Bagdanovka, Novonikolajevka, Lerisk, Luboalexandrovka, Christoforovka, Kapitanovka, Gardegai, Klundovo, Slepucha, Wolkov, Kavkas, Grisa, Selingera, Kratovka and Heck.

München is 3 versts from the postoffice and telegraph station in Mostovoye.

History of the Parish

At the beginning of the settlement, in 1810, the two colonies of Rastadt and München formed a single parish, which was perhaps the smallest in the Catholic colonies of South Russia.

In the eighties the large colonies on rented land, such as Luisendorf and others on the other side of the Bug, were abandoned. Most of the Catholics from these areas moved to the district of Ananyev, where some settled on rented land and others bought land. The end result was a large increase in the number of parishioners for Rastadt, so much so that it became too large for one priest. The community of München realized the need of founding a parish in their colony. The people agreed and a petition was forwarded to the authorities requesting their permission.

The church authorities concurred in this request and forwarded their petition to the Government. Permission was granted by the Minister of the Interior in 1890.

The first priest came to München on the 6 May 1890.

Sequence of Priests in München

FATHER ANDREAS KELLER
6 May 1890 to 20 August 1891

Father A. Keller was born in Selz in the Kutschurgan district on the 12 January 1867, the son of Johann Keller and Marianna Schwan.

He attended the district school in Selz and later attended the Central School in Strassburg, where the teachers were Jakob Kaiser and Urbanek.

After completing his studies in the Central School, he entered the third class of the boys' seminary in Saratov on the 8 September 1884.

In 1885 he wrote the examinations to enter the first course of the Clerical Seminary. On completing his studies here, he was ordained on the 4 February 1890 by Bishop Antonius Zerr. His first posting was to the newly founded parish of München, where he was taken on the 6 May 1890 by Dean Tscherniachowicz.

Under his direction the church in München was restored, the altar renewed, new vestments obtained, and strict orders maintained in all things.

In 1891 Father Keller, at his own request, moved to New Mannheim where he had to deal with many difficult problems. But, with perseverence and patience, he brought the parish to a tolerable situation.

In 1893 he was sent as administrator to Strassburg, one of the largest parishes in the diocese of Tiraspol, comprising 43 localities. In addition he was the religious instructor in the Central School and taught German, as well as physics and geometry.

On the 21 August 1895 he was sent to Odessa as the religious instructor in the secondary school, where he had 38 to 41 hours of instruction per week.

In 1903 he was sent to Elisabethgrad as the parish priest, where he started religious instruction in the secondary school, restored the church, renovated the rectory and added other necessary buildings.

In 1907 he was sent to Odessa as the religious instructor and in November 1910 he was named the parish priest. His first problem was to establish some order in the finances of the church. He tried to get an increase in the collections in order to pay off the debts. He enlarged the parish school and obtained overseers to supervise the children. Recently, he built 2 nice houses for living quarters and storage. Father Keller administers the parish independently with a board of trustees. At Easter 1912 he received a golden pectoral cross in recognition for his service. From the 24 August 1891 until the 15 May 1892 the parish of München was supervised by Father Strömel.

FATHER FRANZ LÖWENBRÜCK *Administrator*
21 May 1892 to 1 June 1895

Father F. Löwenbrück was born in 1866 in the colony of Herzog (Susly). He was ordained on the 12 August 1890 by Bishop Antonius Zerr. He was the parish priest and dean at Selmann for many years, where he built a new church. He became ill, travelled abroad in search of a cure, and died in Wörishofen in 1913.

From the 10 June 1895 until the 29 January 1897 München was supervised from Rastadt.

FATHER ALEXANDER STAUB *Administrator*
29 January 1897 to 27 September 1898

Father A. Staub was born in May 1870 in Katharinenstadt on the Volga. His father, Johann, who came from Hildmann, was the secretary there for many years.

His first education was in the Central School. He entered the seminary in Saratov in 1884, completed his studies there on the 20 March 1894 and was ordained by Bishop Antonius Zerr.

His first assignment was a temporary one to the parish of Louis (Otrogowka). In the year 1895 he was transferred to Christina as vicar and in the year 1897 to München as administrator. In 1898 he was appointed curate at Kamenka and was made dean of Kamenka deanery. In Kamenka he built a beautiful church and strove always to inculcate good order and discipline. In the year 1906 he was transferred to Zug as curate, where he is still working in the vineyard of the Lord.

FATHER LAURENTIUS WOLF *Administrator*
27 September 1898 to 10 October 1908

Father L. Wolf was born 10 December 1871 in Kleinliebental and ordained to the priesthood on 8 September 1897. (See Vol. I transl., p. 155).

He worked faithfully in München in all aspects of pastoral work. His order in church is particularly praiseworthy. In 1908 he was transferred to Volchov as curate, where he is also a faithful worker in the vineyard of the Lord.

From 10 October 1908 to 1 September 1909, München was again looked after from Rastadt.

FATHER JOSEPH HEIN *Administrator*
1 September 1909 until the present

Father J. Hein was born in Krasna, Bessarabia on the 15 June 1866, the son of the district secretary, Nikolaus Hein, and Katharina Müller.

His first education was in the parish school. Following this he helped his father in the office.

In 1886 he entered the Seminary in Saratov. After completing his studies, he was ordained by Bishop Antonius Zerr on the 30 March 1897.

His first position was as administrator in Köhler, where he also tended to the needs of the parishes of Hildmann and Pfeifer.

In 1897 he was the vicar in Saratov for a while. On the 1 October 1897 he was posted as vicar-expositus to Mariinsk in the Crimea, as well as temporarily administrator of the Polish parish of Konstantinovka. He built a fine rectory in Mariinsk.

On the 8 January 1901 he was moved to New-Mannheim as administrator and in 1909 he was moved to München, where he is the administrator at the present time.

Parish Endowment

The parish pays the priest 500 rubles. The surplice fees are baptism 1 ruble, marriage 3 rubles, publishing of the banns 1 ruble, funeral 1 ruble, low mass 1 ruble, high mass 1 ruble, 50 kopecks.

The Parish Church

The community built a chapel in 1816 but, as a result of floods, it was severely damaged and had to be closed. Eventually the chapel collapsed and had to be removed. On Sundays and religious holidays the people attended services in Rastadt, a distance of 1 verst.

In 1872 they built their own church. The new parish church was built of cut field-stone and cost the community 20,000 rubles. The church was consecrated by Bishop Joseph Aloysius Kessler on the 27 May 1910.

The church is 112 feet long, 42 feet wide and 36 feet high to the roof. The steeple is attached to the church, is 48 feet high and contains 4 bells of various sizes. Inside the church there are 3 altars, one pulpit, one confessional, one organ and some Holy pictures. Further information is not available.

The Rectory

The rectory, built in 1886, was constructed of good field-stone at a cost of 3000 rubles. It contains seven rooms, a kitchen, two front rooms and a corridor.

The Graveyard

The graveyard is located behind Hill Street. It contains some attractive tombstones and is surrounded by a stone wall.

School Affairs

As in the other Beresan colonies, a community school was built at the time of the settlement of the colony.

No information is available about the first school house. The second school was built in 1837 and constructed of field-stone. As a result of repeated flooding it had to be moved. It took some years to build the new school house of cut field-stone, at a cost of 35000 rubles. The building was 54 feet long, 30 feet wide and 12 feet high, containing 3 large class rooms. At the present time there are three teachers in the schoool, with 147 children in attendance. Two teachers are paid by the district and receive 300 rubles. The community pays 30 rubles towards a living allowance. The third teacher is paid by the community and receives 330 rubles.

For general education the community has enough schools, but there are no schools for agriculture or other trades. Since Father Scherr's High School is available to all, it would be worthwhile to convert the Central School to an Agricultural School.

If a trades school is founded in Sulz, it would only be necessary to add a handicraft school. It was desirable to teach crafts to the people so that, instead of being idle during the long winters, they would produce worthwhile products.

The following is a list of the past school masters: Anton Fiwiger, Franz Pfoh, Franz Kessel, Anton Herauf, Johannes Schropp, Max Thomas (taught for 25 years) Johannes Wirtmüller, Nikolaus Gratz.

District Teachers; Thomas Zentner, Al. Trutzsko-Lubetzsky, Johannes Schmidt, Paul Schwoljanskü, Georg Zentner, M. Bukus.

Sextons; Philipp Heck, Franz-Michael Seelinger, Johannes Wagner, Michael Schneider, Georg Schönfeld, Hieronymus Friedt, Leonhard Seelinger, Johann Seelinger, Joseph Zimmermann and Erasmus Benz.

Priests and Lay People who were born
or worked in München

FATHER FRANZ SCHERGER *Honorary Canon*

Father Franz Scherger was born in München in 1869. He entered the Seminary in Saratov in 1887. On completing his courses, he was ordained on the 10 December 1895.

His first appointment was as vicar-expositus in Volchov in the parish of Severinovka, where he worked until 1899.

He was called to Saratov in 1899, where he was made a domestic prelate of the Cathedral and procurator for the Seminary.

On the 24 August 1901 he was sent to Franzfeld as the parish priest, where he remained approximately two years.

On the 14 October 1903 he was made the religious instructor in the secondary school in Tiflis, in the Caucasus, where he remained until 1905. Later he spent some time in Jenakievo, until he was sent to Simferopol as the priest and dean in 1906.

As a result of over-exertion, he soon became ill and died in Yalta on the 31 May 1913. He was buried in Simferopol on the 3 June 1910.

THOMAS ZENTNER *Member of the Imperial Duma*

Thomas Zentner was born in München on the 26 February 1864. He received his education from the St. Paul non-classical secondary school in Odessa, where he completed the 4th class.

After passing the examinations as community teacher, he was accepted in the local school of his home.

From 1889 until 1893 he was the district secretary. In 1893 he was elected president of the Mostovoi Russian district court, which position he held until 1896.

Truly, an unprecedented honor! The Russians did not trust their own people and wanted a German as District Judge.

Later he received other honorary positions and in 1907 he was elected a deputy in the second duma by the landowners of the province of Kherson. He belonged to the Octobrist faction, a party of the left. He was the first member of the duma from the German colonies of South Russia.

For his services to the Clemens Society, he was made honorary member in 1910.

Thomas Zentner owns land in Bachmut region and also in the district of Ananyev, where he has model orchards and vineyards on his estate. He also knows a great deal about the history and archeology of South Russia and often writes original arctiles in the "Deutsche Rundschau." At present T. Zentner is the director of a bank in Vosnesensk and recently has moved his home there.

JOHANNES SCHMIDT *Teacher*

Johannes Schmidt, son of Philipp, was born in München on the 14 November 1870.

After completing his studies in the local district school, he entered the boys' seminary in Saratov in 1883 and completed his studies there in 1888. He received the diploma as community teacher and started to teach in Rastadt.

In 1889 he moved to Katharinental as community teacher. He remained here for 9 years and was very diligent about his work.

In 1898 he moved back to Rastadt where he taught for one more year.

When the Co-operative Society was formed in München at this time, he resigned his position as teacher and took the position as accountant for the Society. Later he presided over the Rastadt District Court for 6 years.

Presently he is a Semstvo deputy in the district of Ananyev.

JOHANNES BRENDEL *Teacher*

Johannes Brendel was born in Selz on the 14 December 1874. He attended the local community school and the courses in pedagogy in the Central School in Grossliebental. After receiving his diploma as teacher, he went to teach in the small colony of Kossakov.

In 1896 he was appointed school master of the community school in München and in 1898 he moved to the colony of Elsass in the same position.

In 1902 he resigned from teaching, moved to Saratov and opened a bookstore. He is the author of some German reading books which have been printed in three parts and are used in the community and secondary schools. He used the pen-name of Konrad Ehlerding and has written a number of articles and papers in the "Deutsche Rundschau" and other papers about school affairs and related subjects.

JOHANNES LAMBOI *Teacher*

Johannes Lamboi was born in Yalta in the Crimea on the 24 December 1889.

In 1904 he entered the second class of the boy's school in Saratov. After completing the 3rd course he entered the clerical seminary.

For the past 3 years he has been a private tutor in Kratovka near München.

*The present Wealth and Conditions
of the Colony of München*

At the present time there are 154 lots and 1828 Catholics. There are 3 Russian and 9 Jewish families. In the summertime there are as many as 140 Russian hired men and approximately 25 Russian maids. There are 35 families who do not own land, 151 families went to America and 19 families went to Siberia.

The community land amounts to 2940 dessiatines, of which 2254 is for agriculture, 550 for pasture, 49 for vineyards, and 14 dessiatines is railroad right of way running between Odessa and Bachmatsch.

The land is divided rather unevenly. Four colonists have over 100 dessiatines, 4 have from 60 to 100 dessiatines, 21 have from 30 to 60 and the rest of the colonists have less than 30 dessiatines. Eleven own bought land, both near and far totalling 6000 dessiatines. One dessiatine of land is priced at 210 rubles and rent for 1 dessiatine is 16 to 18 rubles per year.

Tradesmen in München are; blacksmiths 4, wheelwrights 3, and 1 cabinet maker.

There is also a co-operative store, 4 small shops, 1 steam flour mill and one hotel.

Stock owned; 700 horses, 524 cows and 300 pigs.

Seeded for the year 1913 was; winter and summer wheat 6485 dessiatines.

There are 3 German newspapers and 2 Russian papers read here.

Customs and Folklore in the Beresan

Whenever people had joy in their hearts, a sense of humor and a lively imagination, social life was enriched by proverbs, jokes and aphorisms which were derived from life and illuminated it. Gifted folk poets put these expressions into the form of songs and handed them down as a common heritage to posterity. In this way arose most of the folksongs, the melodies, and the folk traditions which were incorporatd into the cycle of Christian feast days throughout the year.

Many of these traditions have a heathen background because, at the time when Christianity was introduced, the missionaries retained them whenever they were compatible and adapted them to some Christian feast. This was especially true among the Germanic peoples who had many simple and humane customs, including some that were superstitious, in their mythological cycle of feasts. Among no people did the Christian festive year with its meaningful mysteries create such an enduring impression as among the Germans. All important Christian feast-days evoked a responsive echo in the family and in the community and were enhanced by sayings, melodies and dramatic representations. In this way the Germans developed a complete cycle of feasts which could be fittingly called "church-civil" in character.

The German people in the Beresan brought many of these customs from their homeland on the Rhine. However, since they had not been written down, much was forgotten or has come down to the present generation in garbled form. I present the following descriptions of what has remained from the older traditions, without claiming to deal fully with the subject.

Since the folk customs were generally associated with the festival days of the Church, I shall begin the Beresan festive year with the season of Advent.

The Beresan Holidays

The people celebrated the Church feast days. It is best to describe the feasts celebrated in the Beresan with the beginning of the Church year, namely, Advent.

Advent is for Catholics a time of repentance and penance; therefore, weddings and all forms of recreation were prohibited. The password was, "Kathrein stops all music and dancing."

The Feast of the Long Night

It would appear that in the early days, the 9th of December, (old style), the longest night and the beginning of winter, was celebrated only in Sulz. The young people would form groups and, in the evening, would gather in someone's home. The girls would bring flour, eggs, butter and other essentials for baking cakes while the boys would bring wine. This was followed by singing suitable songs for the occasion, such as "Red dawn," "Now I Must Leave My Home," and telling fairy tales.

Christmas Eve

Christmas Eve, the joyous children's feast where the whole of Christianity prays to the Holy child Jesus in the crib, brings joy and ecstacy to all good children, and they receive lovely gifts. The Christmas tree was not used in the Beresan in the early days, but instead, the Christkindel brought gifts to the children, similar to those which are placed on the Christmas tree today. The Christkindel was usually a girl who had a lovely, clear voice and a sense of humor. She was dressed in white, her face covered with a veil, a basket on her arm and a bundle of switches in her hand. Dressed in this fashion and accompanied by other girls or sometimes by Pelzenikel himself, she would appear in front of the windows of homes where the lights had already been lit. One girl would ring a bell in front of the window and the Christkindel would ask, "May the 'Christkindel' enter? With the answer 'yes', the lady of the house would accompany the 'Christkindel' into the room where the children usually awaited her arrival in fear and anguish. Now the examination started with questioning whether the children said their prayers, whether they listen well, etc. After the interrogation, there would be gifts, or blows with the switch. Sometimes, when the Christkindel was very strict about the prayers or had some doubts about whether the children knew their prayers, the whole group would get on their knees, and crying, would say their prayers.

If there were bad unruly boys in the household, Pelzenikel, who until now waited outside, would make his entrance. He was usually a strong young man with a low voice, garbed in a shaggy fur coat, wore a mask with a long nose and sometimes with goat horns, and over his shoulder hung a clattering chain. On one side he had a long sack and in his right hand, a bundle of switches. In such an outfit, which was not much prettier than the devil himself, he entered. The bad boys would scream in fear and trembling and all would attempt to hide, but they would all be found and brought before Pelzenikel to answer to him. He would not say very much but would make his switches whistle, which would resound in the ears of the boys for a long time.

After the Christkindel and Pelzenikel left the house, the children would receive their gifts, which were mostly things to eat such as animal cookies, apples, nuts, etc.

The second feast day, the Feast of St. Stephanus, was formerly called "Bundle Day." On this day the servants left their old masters and moved to their new ones. Hired men and maids tied up their bundles, loaded them on a wagon or sleigh, led the horses decorated with gaily colored ribbons through the street while they sang:

"Today is my bundle day,
Today my time is up,
My boss is sending me away,
He does not pay me enough."

New Year

New Year is a touching scene in the colonies, when the boys and girls wish their parents, uncles and aunts "Happy New Year." After many pretzels, cakes, apples, and nuts, they would return home.

The youngsters New Year's wish was usually as follows, "Parents, aunts and uncles, we wish you a happy New Year, good health, a long life and eternal bliss." While the youngsters were wishing their godparents a happy New Year, the more grown boys would convey best wishes to their godparents, grandparents and lady friends by "shooting" in the New Year. The young man would come to the house with a loaded pistol or gun, knock on the window and say, "Grandparents and godparents, I wish you a happy New Year," then fire his guns so that the windows would rattle. Soon the door would be opened and the shooter would be invited in and treated to some cakes and wine or whisky. After this hospitality he would return to his home. Despite many accidents and the strict police regulations prohibiting shooting, this practice survived in many of the colonies.

Feast of Three Kings

The customs for this feast day were brought from the old country and were carried on in most of the Beresan colonies.

Three boys aged 11 to 13, representing the three kings, would dress in white shirts and decorate crown-shaped hats. Carrying a star, they would go from house to house in the colony and sing the following songs:

No. 1.

1. *Three kings led by God's hand,*
   Come from the East with a star,
   Alle, Alleluja,
   Through Jerusalem, to the Christchild,
   In a stable at Bethlehem.,
   Alle, Alleluja.

2. *In that holy place,*
   His name is Jesus Christ,
   Because of our misdeeds,
   He came down from Heaven,
   Alle, Alleluha.

3. *The star must keep turning,*
   We wish to go further this day,
   Alle, Alleluja.

4. *You have given us a gift,*
   May you spend the year with joy,
   Particularly you and your children,
   Particularly you and your servants.

No. 2.

1. *Three kings are led by God's hand,*
   By a star from the Orient,
   To the Christ child through Jerusalem,
   Into a stable at Bethlehem,
   Alle, alle, alleluja, alle, alle, alleluja.

2. *We have travelled in great haste,*
   In 13 days, 400 miles,
   Over hill and dale through snow and ice,
   We made the distant journey, alle, alleluja, etc.

3. *The star must keep turning,*
   We wish to go further today,
   Alle, Alleluja, etc.

No. 3.

1. *Come, ye wise men, to Jesus in the hard crib,*
   Carry your offerings to Jesus tenderly,
   This has frightened us, and woke us from our sleep,
   Come shepherds, to the crib of the lovely child.
2. *Come ye Wise Men, to anoint the child with ointment!*
   They carry the little child to Mary,
   Bow down 100 times, bow down 1000 times,
   The Lord Jesus Christ is come, truly born.

Shrove Tuesday

In the Beresan there are two occasions when butchering is done. The big butchering is done in November and December when they make sausages, head cheese and hams for the Christmas holiday. The small butchering is done before Lent and provides the housewife with lard to bake the cookies for the night of Shrove Tuesday. On the Monday before Shrove Tuesday, the busy housewife is already at the table rolling the dough to its proper thickness and shaping or cutting it to proper sizes. Then the cookies are put on the stove where all of them are fired in lard. Finally, after a great deal of hard work, they are finished. The table is covered and large bowls filled with glazed white cookies are placed on it. Then the eating begins, usually with many guests invited. In the early years there was dancing on Shrove Tuesday but, of late, the 40 hours devotion is held in many colonies. Formerly, the Shrovetide celebration proved very expensive for many of the colonists, as indicated in this short ditty:

"Hopsa, the Shrovetide celebrations,
Have used up all my money,
If you had rubbed your mouth on the bucket,
Your money would still be in your pocket.

Easter Week

Easter week in all the colonies is a lively and busy time. The ladies, particularly, have a very busy time. Everything in the house and yard had to be cleaned and the essentials for Easter had to be obtained and prepared.

The most important people on this day (at least in their own opinion) are the ratchet ringers. The custom in the Catholic Church is to silence the bells from the singing of the 'Gloria in excelsis' on Maundy Thursday until Holy Saturday, when they are again permitted to ring with the same hymn of praise.

During this period, the ratchet boys replaced the bells. They were usually the oldest students in the parish school. Each one had a ratchet, namely, a little board that could be turned on a sprocket. This wooden instrument would make a grinding sound when it was turned.

The ratchet boys would go down the various streets of the colony and, when they came to the end, they would all twirl their ratchets at the same time, making quite a noise. After continuing this for five minutes, the leader would raise his ratchet, stand still, and all would sing together:

In the mornings:
"The daylight is starting to break,
For the rich and poor alike,
Ave Maria gratia plena."

At noon they sang:
"Dear people, dear people, what do we wish to tell you,
The clock has struck twelve,
Ave Maria, gratia plena."

At night they sang:
"Dear people, dear people, it's time for night prayers!
Ave Maria, gratia plena."

To invite them to come to church, they sang:
"It's the first (second or last) call to church!"

For this service, the ratchet boys would receive donations on Holy Saturday after the church service, by taking a basket from house to house, and singing:
"We rang the ratchet over the Holy Tomb,
So give us also an Easter gift,
Not too large and not too small,
As long as it will go into the basket."

When they received a gift (eggs or some money) they would sing:
"This is the very nicest house,
Three angels are peeking out of the window."

Easter

The Easter rabbit comes early on Easter Sunday, before the youngsters get up, and lays beautifully colored eggs in the mossy nests which the good children have made the previous evening. The idea that the Easter rabbit, which after all is not a bird, but could lay eggs, was in insoluble problem for many of the youngsters. The explanation was usually forthcoming when one of them would see their mother approaching the nest with eggs in her apron.

The most important thing, of course, was to get some eggs for eating and playing games. As soon as one received his share of the eggs from his parents and godparents, he would fill his pockets and go to his friends' place to try his luck in egg-pecking (Eierpicken). If he had good luck, he would return at night with his pockets and jacket full of eggs and gleefully tell his mother about his skill in egg-pecking. However, there were times when his luck was not so good and he would return home in tears to explain his misfortune to his mother.

Egg rolling (Eierschurwle) was still another game. This was played by placing a small board at an incline of approximately 45 degrees and then allowing the egg to roll down. If this egg struck another egg lying in the playing area, the egg that was struck could be claimed by the player.

In the early days it was common practice to play the fascinating game of fortune telling with eggs, in which young men also often participated. There were also several customs in May such as the 'May tree,' the 'May strewing,' etc., but lately nearly all of this has been forgotten.

Pentecost Race in the Beresan

For three to four weeks prior to Pentecost, the bigger boys start getting together their articles of clothing and other things to ensure a successful festivity. On previous Sunday afternoons appropriate rehearsals are undertaken with suitable horses on an open field. It is usually boys from 18 to 21, seldom youngsters and never men, who take part in the Pentecost race. From their midst they choose a colonel, 2 officers, 2 Cossacks, and the remainder are soldiers. The 2 officers and the colonel lead the commando while the Cossacks maintain order. The gypsies who participate are usually hired and have to be very comical fellows. The officers' uniforms have to resemble those of a calvary officer, and similarly for the Cossacks, who had to have Cossack uniforms. The remainder are usually dressed as soldiers, but instead of a uniform, they wore a white shirt with a ribbon around their cap, all the same color. The horses were decorated with various ribbons. The officers and Cossacks had spurs on their shoes, were armed with sabres and their horses had saddles. The soldiers, however, had no saddles but used rugs. They had no weapons. The gypsies were dressed in old rags and looked pretty tattered. Their faces and hands were covered with shoepolish or soot. There were usually 2 to 4 of these participants.

The festivities start on Monday afternoon following the church service. The parade begins at one end of the colony and proceeds through the main street. One horseman rides in front with the Pentecost wreath, followed by the soldiers marching in rows, with the officers and Cossacks at either side. An orchestra plays as the soldiers sing the song, "I am a soldier, and always will be." At the distant rear comes the rickety, two-wheeled gypsy wagon with its tattered top. A gyspy is sitting on the horse backwards and uses every means to get the stubborn animal to move. The second and third come to help him until they finally succeed in following the parade. A crowd of one thousand people follow the parade. The gypsy woman is usually followed by a crowd of children whose function is to tease and make fun of the gypsies until they become angered. Naturally, some may receive an occasional blow with the whip. Little children are often frightened by the gypsies. At the gathering place where they stop, usually a clear area on Main Street, there is a table with beer and several chairs. Here the colonel or one of the officers addresses the public as follows: "We have come from Austria and will not remain here for long. We want to go further today, the road leads us on to Germany." Then they all ride around the table several times and form a circle around it while the colonel and officers take their place at the table. The gypsies are not permitted to come near the circle. Still, they try to get closer and now and then pilfer a bottle of beer from the table or stealthily get on a horse and ride away. If they are caught by the Cossacks, they receive a certain number of whacks, which are ordered by the officers. It is, of course, the role of the gypsies to provide entertainment through their tricks, pranks, and humour. From time to time soldiers get a glass of beer and sing several folk songs; for example "I saw the light of day," "Get up upon a high hill, and gaze on the valley below," "A call resounds like thunder."

Then an officer stands on the table and addresses the gypsies, with them making witty replies. Now they sing the song, "The time has come for me to leave my father's house," and they move out into an open field in an orderly manner, where the festivities come to a close with a horse race for the Pentecostal wreath. The winner is usually exempt from all payments connected with the feast. At the present time there is no dancing, although there was in earlier days. Usually a large number of young people come to this feast from the neighbouring colonies.

Church Dedication Festival (Kerwe*)

The people of the Beresan are fairly serious and sedate but, when the drum sounds announcing the "Kerwe" dance, they forget all about the serious things of life and, with heart and soul, follow the hilarity. Adolescent boys and girls especially were animated at this time by the spirit of hilarity and the pleasure of dancing. However, I must revert to earlier times for, nowadays, "Kerwe" is not celebrated with such great festivity as in the old days (about 50 years ago). On the Friday and Saturday before the festival the women were very busy. The yard was thoroughly cleaned and swept, the stone wall facing the street was whitewashed, the attic, basement and bedrooms were all thoroughly cleaned and tidied. Following this the butchering was done, then came the baking. Without sausages, head-cheese, hams or cakes, the people of the Beresan could not celebrate a "Kerwe." They might eat dry bread and water all year but for "Kerwe," cookies, sausages, and wine had to be on the table for "there's only one 'Kerwe' a year." For this occasion guests were invited from other colonies, and they always came. The invitations were usually given at the annual bazaar in Landau on the 6 October. The bigger boys generally made all preparations prior to this time to celebrate the "Kerwe." A house (usually the tavern) was rented for the dance and musicians were hired. The "Kerwe" bouquet, a red banner and a bottle of wine, was placed on a pole in front of the dance hall. After vespers on Dedication Sunday, the drummer climbed on-to the roof of the dance hall, and by drumming loudly, invited everyone to come to start the "Kerwe." At this signal everone, large, small, young and old, including grandparents, assembled at the dance hall. Here one of the older boys acted as master of ceremonies and invited everyone into the house, assigning them to their place. Then the musicians, who were sitting on a high bench, played some lively music and the dance began. It is said that in previous years the mayor of Landau and his entire staff, along with their wives, would go into the dance hall and one of the officials would dance the first three dances with the mayor's wife.

After this, everyone would dance. The young men usually first danced with their girls, then with different girls or young married

*The most exciting folk festival in the colonies was the annual "Karwe," a traditional celebration that goes back as far as the Middle Ages. Known under the dialect variants of "Kerwe, Kirwe, Kilb and Kirmes, all of which derive from German "Kirchweih," it was originally celebrated on the feastday of the patron saint of the church. Later it became associated with the harvest festival and was widely celebrated in the fall, after the field work was completed. COURTESY OF J. S. HEIGHT.

women. The girls considered it their greatest misfortune if they were not allowed to dance and were regarded as "wall flowers." The girls who danced every dance were praised and envied for having worn out the soles of their shoes at the "Kerwe." The expression, "she has danced her soles through," was the greatest praise and much pride was bestowed upon such a popular dancing girl. The dances were usually waltzes, but other popular dances were the seven step, the schottische or träppler, the Russian polkamasurka, and the kosachok.

As a result of the dancing, those participating became hungry and thirsty. For those who were hungry there were fried sausages with cabbage salad or cooked ham with sour cucumbers. For those who were thirsty, there was a water bucket on the window filled with wine, and anyone who wished could have a drink, using a ladle.

The police declared midnight as the official closing hour and the dancing would stop. On Monday and Tuesday, after the early mass, the festivities would be resumed. The celebration was finally concluded on Tuesday evening. If there was still dancing on Wednesday and Thursday, it was called "After Kerwe." At the "After Kerwe" the dancers were mostly young men and their wives, and often the grandparents. The latter danced old dances from Germany and, consequently, provided considerable amusement for those watching.

The "Kerwe" festival was customarily "buried" on Thursday evening. A chap who was a natural comedian would alter his voice, wear a mask and white sheet and, along with other masqueraders, all festive participants and street urchins marched to the sound of music to the place where the "Kerwe" was to be buried. After a hole was dug in the ground, the wine bottle and the bouquet with the red banner would be lowered into it. While the hole was being covered, the whole group would give a grief-stricken howl, tin cans and kettles would be rattled with an ear-shattering, catterwauling noise. Following this everything would be quiet and they would all return home.

How the three important events
in peoples lives
are celebrated in the Beresan
Birth Days and Baptisms

The birth of a child, particularly the first born, is indeed a joyful event. All the nearest relatives and, particularly the grandparents of the new born, are informed of the happy arrival of the young citizen and are invited to come to the christening. If the baby is healthy, it is usually baptized on the second or third day. The godparents are chosen from among the closer relatives, the brothers and sisters of the parents usually being the first.

For the first baby, one usually names the best man and the bridesmaid as the godparents, as they were the ones who led the happy couple to their marriage. At the baptism the child is usually given the name of the godfather and, if a girl, the name of the godmother.

In former times the infant received two, and sometimes three names; now this rarely happens. If the godparents are single, the godmother wears a white dress and a wreath on her head. The white clothes that the baby wears, and sometimes also a silver or golden cross, are donated by the godparents.

As soon as the child is brought back from the baptism by the godparents and midwife, the baptism celebration begins. They eat a great deal and drink many toasts to the health of the mother and child, who are usually still in bed.

A strange custom, possibly adopted from the Russians, was previously practiced. The midwife must be sweetened with whisky, otherwise as one says, "the child will not grow." This whisky is placed in a glass by the midwife and mixed with brandy and burned sugar. It is then handed around to the godparents and other guests. The guests sip from the glass, place a silver coin therein, and hand it on. The glass, which is soon filled with silver, is given to the midwife for her services.

In earlier days the baptisms were frequently celebrated very exuberantly. Because of the extravagance and boisterousness of the baptisms and weddings, the Fürsorge Committee sometimes forbade them.

The Wedding

As with all Christian people, the ceremony of marriage whereby the man and wife are legally united, is the most solemn occasion in any Christian life.

The Germanic people were brought up to respect this sacrament and its importance and sanctity. They regarded it as equal to the high feastdays of the church, hence, the old High German term, "Hogetidi," meaning "high feast," was used.

For some time before the wedding, there is a betrothal between the partners. If the couple are both from the same colony and had been in love for some time, the betrothal is quite simple. The fiance comes to the house of the betrothed one evening with some of his comrades, the girl in turn also inviting some of her girl friends. The fiance then asks the parents for permission to marry their daughter.

The daughter gives her consent and her hand to her fiance and the betrothal is consummated. The fiance gives the girl some money, usually 5 to 10 rubles, and sends for some wine or whisky to celebrate the happy occasion.

If the bride is from another village or community, the matter becomes somewhat more complicated. The fiance then selects a spokesman to ask the bride in marriage on his behalf, or, as it happens in recent times, he engages a 'broker' who solicits the selected bride for a price. If the solicitor succeeds in concluding the proposal and the agreement for the future is completed, the bride and groom proceed to the priest. Here arrangemetns are made for the publication of the banns and the couple receive an assignment for catechetical examination. Following this the preparations for the wedding begin.

Pigs are slaughtered, various kinds of cakes baked, and wine and whisky are ordered. Usually the betrothed couple come to the church the evening before the wedding for their catechismal examination and subsequently go to confession.

For approximately 50 years previous to the present time the bride and groom dressed as follows: the groom wore knitted trousers, a vest of brown silk with blue flowers, a dress-coat of blue cloth, a black silk cravat, a wide cap with a long visor, and leather shoes. The bride wore a brown cotton dress with blue flowers, white stockings, and patent leather shoes. On her head she wore a white cap-like coif on which rested a wreath of myrtle, and on both arms some colorful ribbons.

The bridesmaids usually wore white cotton dresses and a wreath on their head, but no coif.

The two best men wore Sunday clothes, but on their caps they wore a bouquet of flowers about 14 inches high and tied with ribbons.

As soon as they were all gathered together, the betrothed would kneel before their parents and asked to be blessed.

Following this there was the bridal procession to the church, the bride, bridesmaids and the best men leading the procession, followed by the bridegroom and "fathers-of-honor" who are usually the godparents of the betrothed. As soon as the procession emerged from the house the musicians began to play a march and accompanied the procession to the church, where they also usually played for the church service.

Immediately after the wedding ceremony, when the couple came out of the church, the bride is surrounded by her girl friends who tie ribbons around her arms. The musicians again play a march. The procession, this time with the bridegroom at the head, makes its way to the wedding house. Arriving at the house, they dance the "wedding dances." First the bride and groom made three turns. Then each "father-of-honor" and the best men dance three turns with the bride, after which everyone dances.

At two o'clock dinner is served. Following this the musicians play some favorite pieces, first for the bride and groom, and then for the other guests. At this time the bride's shoe is usually auctioned.

The wedding continues for 2 or 3 days.

Funeral Customs

As soon as someone becomes seriously ill, the priest must be called. The people of the Beresan do not wish to die without the comfort of the last sacraments.

If the sick person should continue to deteriorate, someone in attendance will lead the people in the prayers for the dying. When death has occurred, the body is placed on a bier, a lighted wax candle is placed at the head, and some holy water is placed near the body.

As soon as the relatives are notified of the sad news, they come to pay their respects, kneel down and pray for the repose of the soul of the deceased. Usually there is a mass said for his soul. The relatives also have a mass or service said on the third, seventh, and thirteenth day, for the repose of the soul of the dead person.

After the interment, the relatives and grave diggers gather at the home of the deceased for the funeral repast and to give their condolence to the surviving next of kin.

The grave is usually identified by a wooden or iron cross.

WEIGHTS AND MEASURES

Used by the Germans in Russia that occur in this book:

1 verst = 0.66 mile

1 dessiatine = 2.7 acres

1 pood = 40 pounds Russian

= 36 pounds Can. or U.S.

1 tchetvert = 10.0 pood

= 8.0 tchetverik

1 arshin = 28.0 inches

1 faden = 6.0 feet